Digital Democracy and the Digital Public Sphere

This sixth volume in Christian Fuchs' *Media, Communication and Society* series draws on radical Humanist theory to address questions around the digital public sphere and the challenges and opportunities for digital democracy today.

The book discusses topics such as digital democracy, the digital public sphere, digital alienation, sustainability in digital democracy, journalism and democracy, public service media, the public service Internet, and democratic communications. Fuchs argues for the creation of a public service Internet run by public service media that consists of platforms such as a public service YouTube and Club 2.0, a renewed digital democracy and digital public sphere version of the legendary debate programme formats Club 2 and After Dark.

Overall, the book presents foundations and analyses of digital democracy that are interesting for both students and researchers in media studies, cultural studies, communication studies, political science, sociology, Internet research, information science, as well as related disciplines.

Christian Fuchs is a critical theorist of communication and society. He is Chair Professor of Media Systems and Media Organisation at Paderborn University's Department of Media Studies. He is co-editor of the journal *tripleC: Communication, Capitalism & Critique*. He is the author of many publications, including the books *Digital Capitalism* (2022), *Foundations of Critical Theory* (2022), *Communicating COVID-19: Everyday Life, Digital Capitalism, and Conspiracy Theories in Pandemic Times* (2021), *Marxist Humanism and Communication Theory* (2021), *Social Media: A Critical Introduction* (3rd edition, 2021), *Communication and Capitalism: A Critical Theory* (2020), *Marxism: Karl Marx's Fifteen Key Concepts for Cultural and Communication Studies* (2020), *Nationalism on the Internet: Critical Theory and Ideology in the Age of Social Media and Fake News* (2020), *Rereading Marx in the Age of Digital Capitalism* (2019), *Digital Demagogue: Authoritarian Capitalism in the Age of Trump and Twitter* (2016), *Digital Labour and Karl Marx* (2014), and *Internet and Society* (2008).

Digital Democracy and the Digital Public Sphere

Media, Communication and Society
Volume Six

Christian Fuchs

Routledge
Taylor & Francis Group

LONDON AND NEW YORK

Designed cover image: John M Lund Photography Inc

First published 2023
by Routledge
4 Park Square, Milton Park, Abingdon, Oxon OX14 4RN

and by Routledge
605 Third Avenue, New York, NY 10158

Routledge is an imprint of the Taylor & Francis Group, an informa business

British Library Cataloguing-in-Publication Data
A catalogue record for this book is available from the British Library

ISBN: 9781032362731 (hbk)
ISBN: 9781032362724 (pbk)
ISBN: 9781003331087 (ebk)

DOI: 10.4324/9781003331087

Typeset in Univers
by codeMantra

Contents

Figures

Tables

Acknowledgements

Chapter 2 was first published as a journal article. Reprinted with permission of the journal *tripleC*: Christian Fuchs. 2014. The Dialectic: Not Just the Absolute Recoil, but the World's Living Fire that Extinguishes and Kindles Itself. Reflections on Slavoj Žižek's Version of Dialectical Philosophy in "Absolute Recoil. Towards a New Foundation of Dialectical Materialism". *tripleC: Communication, Capitalism & Critique* 12 (2): 848–875. DOI: https://doi.org/10.31269/triplec.v12i2.640

Chapter 3 was first published in German as a journal article using a Creative Commons CC-BY licence that allows the creation and publication of derivatives, which includes translations: Christian Fuchs. 2017. Die Kritik der Politischen Ökonomie der Medien/ Kommunikation: ein hochaktueller Ansatz. *Publizistik* 62 (3): 255–272. DOI: https://doi. org/10.1007/ s11616-017-0341-9

Chapter 4 was first published as a journal article. The author has retained the copyright, which allows republication. Christian Fuchs. 2015. Power in the Age of Social Media. *Heathwood Journal of Critical Theory* 1 (1): 1–29.

Chapter 5 was first published as a journal article. Reprinted with permission of Taylor & Francis: Fuchs, Christian. 2017. The Praxis School's Marxist Humanism and Mihailo Marković's Theory of Communication. *Critique* 45 (1–2): 159–182. DOI: https://doi. org/10.1080/ 03017605.2016.1268456

Chapter 6 was first published as a journal article. Reprinted based on the author agreement between the author and Elsevier that allows reprint of the accepted manuscript and the published journal article in a compilation of the author's works. Christian Fuchs. 2017. Sustainability and Community Networks. *Telematics and Informatics* 34 (2): 628–639. DOI: https://doi.org/10.1016/j.tele.2016.10.003

Chapter 8 was first published as a journal article using a Creative Commons CC-BY licence that allows reproduction: Fuchs, Christian Fuchs. 2020. Towards a Critical Theory of Communication as Renewal and Update of Marxist Humanism in the Age of Digital Capitalism. *Journal for the Theory of Social Behaviour* 50 (3): 335–356. DOI: https://doi. org/10.1111/jtsb.12247

Part I

Introduction

Chapter One
Democracy, Communicative Democracy, Digital Democracy

1.1 Foundations of Digital Democracy

The book *Digital Democracy and the Digital Public Sphere* asks: What is digital democracy? What are the democratic dimensions of communications and digital communications? What is the digital public sphere?

The book at hand is the sixth volume of a series of books titled *Media, Communication & Society*. The overall aim of *Media, Communication & Society* is to outline the foundations of a critical theory of communication and digital communication in society. It is a multi-volume book series situated on the intersection of communication theory, sociology, and philosophy. The overall questions that *Media, Communication & Society* deals with are: What is the role of communication in society? What is the role of communication in capitalism? What is the role of communication in digital capitalism?

This book presents theoretical and philosophical foundations of digital democracy and the digital public sphere. It engages with the dialectic as philosophical foundation of digital democracy, the Critique of the Political Economy of the Media and Communication as analytical foundation of digital democracy the concepts of alienation, power, praxis communication, the public sphere, and sustainability as dimensions and aspects of the analysis of digital democracy; journalism and democracy; public service media and the public service Internet as important aspects of democracy, democratic communications, digital democracy, and the digital public sphere.

DOI: 10.4324/9781003331087-2

Digital Democracy and the Digital Public Sphere is organised in three parts. Part I (Chapter 1) is an introduction to digital democracy. Part II (Chapters 2–9) discuss various dimensions of the foundations of digital democracy and the digital public sphere. Part III (Chapter 10) draws conclusions. Each chapter is focused on specific questions:

- Chapter 1: What is democracy? What is digital democracy?
- Chapter 2: What is the dialectic?
- Chapter 3: What is the Critique of the Political Economy of the Media and Communication?
- Chapter 4: What is power? How does power look like in the age of digital and social media?
- Chapter 5: How can we make sense of the notion of praxis as part of a critical theory of communication? How did the Yugoslav philosopher Mihailo Marković, a leading member of the Praxis School, conceive of communication?
- Chapter 6: What do sustainability and unsustainability mean in the context of community networks? What advantages do such networks have over conventional forms of Internet access and infrastructure provided by large telecommunications corporations? In addition, what disadvantages do they face at the same time?
- Chapter 7: How did Karl Marx see the role of journalism in the public sphere and democracy?
- Chapter 8: What is the role of communication in a Marxist-Humanist theory of communication that aims at advancing participatory democracy?
- Chapter 9: What are digital democracy and the digital public sphere? What are the main trends in the development of digital media today, what are digital media's democratic possibilities and deficits, and what role can public service media play in strengthening digital democracy and digital public sphere? What legal framework is needed so that public service media can strengthen digital democracy?
- Chapter 10: How can Marx' theory of alienation and Habermas' theory of the structural transformation of the public sphere be combined for advancing the understanding of democracy today?

1.2 What Is Democracy? What Is Communicative Democracy? What Is Digital Democracy?

In order to understand what digital democracy is all about, we need an understanding of what democracy is.

1.2.1 Definitions of Democracy

Let us have a look at some definitions of democracy from academic works.

a) "While the word 'democracy' came into English in the sixteenth century from the French démocratie, its origins are Greek. 'Democracy' is derived from demokratia, the root meanings of which are demos (people) and kratos (rule). Democracy means a form of government in which, in contradistinction to monarchies and aristocracies, the people rule. Democracy entails a political community in which there is some form of political equality among the people. 'Rule by the people' may appear an unambiguous concept, but appearances are deceptive. The history of the idea of democracy is complex and is marked by conflicting conceptions. There is plenty of scope for disagreement" (Held 2006, 1).

b) Democracy "is better thought of as a means of managing power relations so as to minimize domination [...] a central task for democracy is to enable people to manage power relations so as to minimize domination [...] democracy is about structuring power relations so as to limit domination" (Shapiro 2003, 3, 52).

c) "democracy understood as self-government in a social setting is not a terminus for individually held rights and values; it is their starting place. Autonomy is not the condition of democracy, democracy is the condition of autonomy. Without participating in the common life that defines them and in the decision-making that shapes their social habitat, women and men cannot become individuals. Freedom, justice, equality, and autonomy are all products of common thinking and common living; democracy creates them. [...] The key to politics as its own epistemology is, then, the idea of public seeing and public doing. Action in common is the unique province of citizens. Democracy is neither government by the majority nor representative rule: it is citizen self-government" (Barber 2003, xxxv, 211).

d) "for a democratic polity to exist it is necessary for a participatory society to exist, i.e. a society where all political systems have been democratised and socialisation through participation can take place in all areas. The most important area is industry; most individuals spend a great deal of their lifetime at work and the business of the workplace provides an education in the management of collective affairs that it is difficult to parallel elsewhere. The second aspect of the theory of participatory democracy is that spheres such as industry should be seen as political systems in their own right, offering areas of participation additional to the national level. If individuals are to exercise the maximum amount of control over

What Is Democracy? What Is Communicative Democracy? What Is Digital Democracy?

their own lives and environment then authority structures in these areas must be so organised that they can participate in decision making" (Pateman 1970, 43).

e) "What is essential in a modern democratic theory? As soon as democracy is seen as a kind of society, not merely a mechanism of choosing and authorising governments, the egalitarian principle inherent in democracy requites not only 'one man, one vote' but also 'one man, one equal effective right to live as fully humanly as he may wish'. Democracy is now seen, by those who want it and by those who have it (or are said to have it) and want more of it, as a kind of society – a whole complex of relations between individuals – rather than simply a system of government. So any theory which is to explicate, justify, or prescribe for the maintenance or improvement of, democracy in our time must take the basic criterion of democracy to be that equal effective right of individuals to live as fully as they may wish. This is simply the principle that everyone ought to be able to make the most of himself, or make the best of himself [...] democracy as a claim to maximize men's powers in the sense of power as ability to use and develop human capacities" (Macpherson 1973, 51–52).

f) "In monarchy the whole, the people, is subsumed under one of its particular modes of being, the political constitution. In democracy the constitution itself appears only as one determination, that is, the self-determination of the people. In monarchy we have the people of the constitution; in democracy the constitution of the people. Democracy is the solved riddle of all constitutions. Here, not merely implicitly and in essence but existing in reality, the constitution is constantly brought back to its actual basis, the actual human being, the actual people, and established as the people's own work. The constitution appears as what it is, a free product of man. [...] Just as it is not religion which creates man but man who creates religion, so it is not the constitution which creates the people but the people which creates the constitution. [...] Man does not exist for the law but the law for man – it is a human manifestation; whereas in the other forms of state man is a legal manifestation. That is the fundamental distinction of democracy. [...] In democracy the constitution, the law, the state itself, insofar as it is a political constitution, is only the self-determination of the people, and a particular content of the people. Incidentally, it goes without saying that all forms of state have democracy for their truth and that they are therefore untrue insofar as they are not democracy" (Marx 1843, 29, 30, 31).

g) "(a) Processes of [democratic] deliberation take place in argumentative form, that is, through the regulated exchange of information and reasons among parties who introduce and critically test proposals. (b) Deliberations are inclusive and public. No one may be excluded in principle; all of those who are possibly affected by the decisions have equal chances to enter and take part. (c) Deliberations are free of any external coercion. The participants are sovereign insofar as they are bound only by the presuppositions of communication and rules of argumentation. (d) Deliberations are free of any internal coercion that could detract from the equality of the participants. Each has an equal opportunity to be heard, to introduce topics, to make contributions, to suggest and criticise proposals. The taking of yes/no positions is motivated solely by the unforced force of the better argument. [...] (e) Deliberations aim in general at rationally motivated agreement and can in principle be indefinitely continued or resumed at any time. [...] (f) Political deliberations extend to any matter that can be regulated in the equal interest of all. This does not imply, however, that topics and subject matters traditionally considered to be 'private' in nature could be a fortiori withdrawn from discussion. In particular, those questions are publicly relevant that concern the unequal distribution of resources on which the actual exercise of rights of communication and participation depends. (g) Political deliberations also include the interpretation of needs and wants and the change of prepolitical attitudes and preferences. Here the consensus-generating force of arguments is by no means based only on a value consensus previously developed in shared traditions and forms of life" (Habermas 1996, 305–306).

h) "At the heart of strong democracy is talk. [...] strong democratic talk entails listening no less than speaking; [...] The participatory process of self-legislation that characterizes strong democracy attempts to balance adversary politics by nourishing the mutualistic art of listening. [...] talk appears as a mediator of affection and affiliation as well as of interest and identity [...] It can build community as well as maintain rights and seek consensus as well as resolve conflict. It offers, along with meanings and significations, silences, rituals, symbols, myths, expressions and solicitations, and a hundred other quiet and noisy manifestations of our common humanity. Strong democracy seeks institutions that can give these things a voice – and an ear. [...] The functions of talk in the democratic process fall into at least nine major categories. [...]

1) The articulation of interests; bargaining and exchange
2) Persuasion
3) Agenda-setting
4) Exploring mutuality

5) Affiliation and affection

6) Maintaining autonomy

7) Witness and self-expression

8) Reformulation and reconceptualisation

9) Community-building as the creation of public interests, common goods, and active citizens"

(Barber 2003, 173–179)

1.2.2 Democracy in General

Understandings of democracy have in common that they conceive of democracy as the self-government of human beings. Democracy is opposed to monarchies (rule of one emperor), oligopolies and aristocracies (rule of the few), and to dictatorships and tyrannies (rule by violence and terror). Democracy is not just a means for minimising domination but also the attempt of minimising the rule by violence.

There is no general agreement on what self-government means and what form it should best take, which is why there is a variety of models of democracy. David Held (2006) discusses nine models of democracy (see also Chapter 9 in this book): classical Athenian democracy, liberal democracy, direct democracy or plebiscitary democracy, competitive elitist democracy, pluralist democracy, legal democracy, participatory democracy, deliberative democracy, democratic autonomy. Democratic autonomy involves constitutional guarantees of fundamental rights, parliamentary election of representatives combined with direct democratic elements, citizens' forums and other deliberative mechanisms, extension of democracy to municipal services and self-managed companies, and transnational democratic institutions (cosmopolitan democracy).

1.2.3 Participatory Democracy

Liberal, pluralist, and competitive models of democracy often limit the very notion of democracy to the process of elections and the political system in a narrow sense. It is much more desirable that decisions in society are enforced by elections than by violence and terror. But democracy does not end at the voting booth. Liberal democracy is a still too limited concept of democracy. My own understanding of democracy combines participatory democracy (see definitions [c], [d], [e], [f]) and deliberative democracy (see definitions [g], [h]). Participatory democracy means that democracy is expanded beyond voting and beyond the narrow understanding of the political system into other realms of society such as the economy. One of liberal capitalist society's antagonisms is that as citizens humans live in a democracy, but as workers they live in a dictatorship. Participatory democracy argues and struggles for a society where the economy is democratically organised, i.e. worker-controlled, which means democratic management of economic organisations (worker self-management). Participatory democracy also means that there are economic foundations of democracy. Democracy requires space, time, and skills. In a society, where resources are unequally distributed and many lack time and opportunities to engage in politics, an impoverished form of politics where the few rule over the many is the likely outcome. A participatory democracy is a post-scarcity society where necessary labour is minimised by the use of highly productive technology so that all humans have the time and opportunities needed for practicing politics, political debate, and political decision-making.

One implication of a participatory understanding of democracy is that if we want to understand democracy, we need to look at political economy, i.e. the interaction of politics and economy. If we therefore want to understand the communicative and digital dimensions of democracy, we need to understand the Political Economy of Communication and digital technologies. This is the reason why we in this book also have a look at foundational political economy aspects of communicative and digital democracy such as the dialectic (Chapter 2) and the Critique of the Political Economy of Communication (Chapter 3).

1.2.4 Karl Marx: The Paris Commune as Participatory Democracy

For Marx (see definition [f]), democracy is opposed to the monarchy. For him, the first is the self-government and self-determination of humans and the latter a dictatorship that alienates humans politically. For Marx, democracy is the essence and truth of politics. For Marx, only a polity that is democratic is a true state. And socialism, the workers' collective ownership and self-managed governance of the means of production is the essence and truth of the economy. Given that politics and economy are interrelated, socialist democracy and democratic socialism are for Marx society's and political economy's essence and truth.

Marx's understanding of the Paris Commune (which existed from March until May 1871) as the "reabsorption of the State power by society, as its own living forces instead of as forces controlling and subduing it, by the popular masses themselves, forming their own force instead of the organized force of their suppression" (Marx 1871b, 487) is a reflection of the insight formulated in definition [b] that democracy as such works against and is opposed to violence, tyranny, and terror as means of governance.

What form of democracy did Marx favour? This question is answered in his analysis of the Paris Commune that he analyses in *The Civil War in France* (Marx 1871a, 1871b, 1871c). The Paris Commune was the democratic governance of Paris in the period from 18 March to 28 May 1871 after the end of the Franco-Prussian War. For Marx, the Paris Commune was both self-determination of workers who abolished the private property of the means of production and the democratic governance of the political system via elections.

In line with his earlier writings on democracy and politics, Marx stresses the opposition of the Paris Commune to the monarchy and oligarchy. "It [the Paris Commune] is not political self-government of the country through the means of an oligarchic club and the reading of *The Times* newspaper. It is the people acting for itself by itself" (1871b, 464). Political councillors were elected and politicians and officials were no longer serving a central force such as the emperor, "[p]ublic functions ceased to be the private property of the tools of the Central Government" (1871a, 331). They were appointed by the Commune to which they were responsible and by which they could be recalled (1871a, 331).

> In its most simple conception the Commune meant the preliminary destruction of the old governmental machinery at its central seats, Paris and the other great cities of France, and its superseding by real self-government which, in Paris and the great cities, the social strongholds of the working class, was the government of the working class.
>
> (1871c, 536)

The Commune consisted of elected councillors who together formed an assembly and took political decisions:

> The Commune was formed of the municipal councillors, chosen by universal suffrage in the various wards of the town, responsible and revocable at short terms. The majority of its members were naturally working men, of acknowledged representatives of the working class. The Commune was to be a working, not a parliamentary, body, executive and legislative at the same time. [...] Public functions ceased to be the private property of the tools of the Central Government. Not only municipal administration, but the whole initiative hitherto exercised by the State was laid into the hands of the Commune
>
> (Marx 1871a, 331)

The idea was to create many local communes that have their local democratic assemblies that are federated in a translocal assembly where decisions are taken on matters of general concern that go beyond the local community and are guided by a constitution:

> The rural communes of every district were to administer their common affairs by an assembly of delegates in the central town, and these district assemblies were again to send deputies to the National Delegation in Paris, each delegate to be at any time revocable and bound by the *mandat impératif* (formal instructions) of his constituents.
>
> (Marx 1871a, 332)

The Commune was a working-class government that served workers' interests and realised democratic ownership and control of the economy:

> Its true secret was this. It was essentially a working-class government the produce of the struggle of the producing against the appropriating class, the political form at last discovered under which to work out the economical emancipation of Labour. [...] It wanted to make individual property a truth by transforming the means of production, land and capital, now chiefly the means of enslaving and exploiting labour, into mere instruments of free and associated labour.
>
> (Marx 1871a, 334, 335)

For Marx, the Commune was a socialist democracy and democratic socialism. The monarchy was abolished and replaced by a democracy with universal franchise, a constitution, elected and translocal assemblies. The Commune was a socialist democracy because the Commune democratically enforced workers' interests. It was democracy in the interest of socialism. It combined elements of representative, participatory, and deliberative democracy. And the Commune was a democratic socialism because it abolished the private ownership of the means of production, extended democracy to the workplace, and put workers in collective control of the means of production. The Paris Commune's element of democratic socialism was a manifestation of participatory democracy, the extension of democracy from politics to the economy.

1.2.5 Deliberative Democracy: Democracy's Communicative Dimension

I am interested in deliberative democracy because deliberation inevitably is a communicative process where humans come together publicly to debate issues that concern them together and to try to reach a collective decision in a communicative manner. Without discussing the issues that matter and what solutions there might be, democracy cannot exist. This is why the existence of a public sphere is key to any democracy.

Deliberative democracy involves, as we can learn from Barber (definition [h]) and Habermas (definition [g]), everyone's right to speak and to be listened to, rational arguments, the equal access to resources that enable participation in deliberation, the power of speaking and listening. Deliberative democracy requires institutions such as high-quality journalism, public service media, and a public service Internet. These are institutions of the public sphere that support democratic information, democratic communication, and democratic decision-making by publishing information about matters of general concern in society, enabling debate of key political topics, and fostering learning, understanding by participation, social production, community, and creativity (see especially Chapter 9 in this book). *Digital Democracy* gives attention to institutions of the public sphere, especially in Chapters 7, 9, and 10. The public sphere is an important communicative aspect of democracy.

Communicative democracy has to do with communication in the public sphere that advances democracy and the democratic organisation of communication(s). Communicative democracy involves both democratic communication and democratic communications. Digital democracy has to do with digital communication in the public sphere that advances democracy and the democratic organisation of digital communication(s). Democracy requires both democratic processes and democratic institutions. Communication operates both at the level of democratic processes and democratic institutions. Democracy is organised as processes of communication where humans inform themselves, debate, and take collectively binding decisions. And democracy requires institutions of the public sphere that advance democratic information, communication, and co-operation. Digital democracy means on the one hand the practices and processes of democracy that are mediated by digital technologies. And on the other hand, it means a democratic society where democratic information, communication, and participation are supported by digital technologies. The theories of the public sphere, participatory democracy, and deliberative democracy help us to understand democracy, communicative democracy, and digital democracy. The approach taken by the present author is informed by critical theories of society and the Marxist-Humanist approach, which means to stress the political economy of the communicative and digital dimensions of democracy. The political economy of democracy, communicative democracy, and digital democracy requires us to think about and analyse how ownership, class, power, domination, capitalism, social struggles, and normative questions frame and shape democracy and its digital and communicative aspects. The political and moral quest of Marxist Humanism is the insight that socialist democracy and democratic socialism constitute a society that is adequate to the human being and realises Humanism. Democracy is socialist when it advances the common economic, political and cultural good of all humans. And socialism is democratic when the economy is together with society organised in a democratic manner. The implication for the realm of (digital) communication(s) is that communication as a public process should be organised in manners that advance socialism and democracy and that systems of (digital) communication should not be organised as dictatorships that are controlled and owned by the few but as democratic public systems that are publicly owned and governed by communications workers and citizens in a participatory manner. The public sphere, high-quality journalism, true public service media (that are autonomous from capital and the state), and a public service Internet are important aspects of democracy.

1.3 The Chapters in This Book

Chapter 1: Democracy, Communicative Democracy, Digital Democracy

This chapter gives an overview of the book *Digital Democracy and the Digital Public Sphere*. It also deals with the questions: What is democracy? What is communicative democracy? What is digital democracy?

The chapter stresses the importance of the notions and theories of the public sphere, participatory democracy, and deliberative democracy for a critical and Humanist understanding of democracy, communicative democracy, and digital democracy. The chapter stresses that advancing and understanding democracy requires the connection of politics/economy (political economy), democracy/socialism (socialist democracy, democratic socialism), democracy/communication (democratic communication(s), communicative democracy).

Chapter 2: The Dialectic: Not Just the Absolute Recoil, but the World's Living Fire that Extinguishes and Kindles Itself. Reflections on Slavoj Žižek's Version of Dialectical Philosophy in "Absolute Recoil. Towards a New Foundation of Dialectical Materialism".

Slavoj Žižek shows in *Absolute Recoil* (and previous Hegelian works such as *Less than Nothing*) the importance of repeating Hegel's dialectical philosophy in contemporary capitalism. Žižek contributes especially to a reconceptualisation of dialectical logic and based on it the dialectic of history. The reflections in this chapter stress that the dialectic is only the absolute recoil, a sublation that posits its own presuppositions, by working as a living fire that extinguishes and kindles itself. I point out that a new foundation of dialectical materialism needs a proper Heraclitusian foundation. I discuss Žižek's version of the dialectic that stresses the absolute recoil and the logic of retroactivity and point out its implications for the concept of history as well as Žižek's own theoretical ambiguities that oscillate between postmodern relativism and mechanical materialism. I argue that Žižek's version of the dialectic should be brought into a dialogue with the dialectical philosophies of the German Marxists Hans Heinz Holz and Herbert Hörz and that Žižek's achievement is that he helps keeping alive the fire of dialectical materialism in the 21st century that is needed for a proper revolutionary theory.

Chapter 3: The Critique of the Political Economy of the Media and Communication

This chapter asks: What is the Critique of the Political Economy of the Media and Communication? It discusses how topical the approach of the Critique of the Political Economy of Media/Communication is today. It analyses the status of this field. At the international level, there is a longer tradition in the Critical Political Economy of Media/Communication, especially in the United Kingdom and North America. Since the start of the new crisis of capitalism in 2008, the interest in Marx's works has generally increased. At the same time, communicative and ideological features of societal changes' unpredictable turbulences have become evident. This contribution introduces some specific approaches. It also discusses aspects of why the complex, multidimensional, open, and dynamic research approach of the critique of capitalism and society that goes back Marx's theory remains relevant today. It stresses that there are many elements in Marx's works that can help us to critically understand communication: critical journalism, limits on the freedom of the press, the analysis of the commodity form, the analysis of labour, exploitation, class, surplus-value, globalisation, crisis, modern technology, the General Intellect, communication, the means of communication, the contradiction between the productive forces and the relations of production, dialectics, ideologies, social struggles, and democratic alternatives.

Chapter 4: Power in the Age of Social Media

There are a lot of claims about social and other media's power today: Some say that we have experienced Twitter and Facebook revolutions. Others claim that social media democratise the economy or bring about a participatory culture. Other observers are more sceptical and stress social media's realities as tools of control. Understanding social media requires a critical theory of society that uses a dialectical concept of power. A critical theory of society can then act as framework for understanding power in the age of social media. This chapter is a contribution to critically theorising media power in the age of social media. It categorises different notions of power, introduces a dialectical notion of media power discusses the dialectics of social media power, and draws some conclusions about the need for a dialectical and critical theory of the media and society.

Chapter 5: The Praxis School's Marxist Humanism and Mihailo Marković's Theory of Communication

Mihailo Marković (1923–2010) was one of the leading members of the Yugoslav Praxis Group. Among other topics, he worked on the theory of communication and dialectical meaning, which makes his approach relevant for a contemporary critical theory of communication. This chapter asks: How can we make sense of the notion of praxis as part of a critical theory of communication? How did the Yugoslav philosopher Mihailo Marković, a leading member of the Praxis School, conceive of communication?

Marković turned towards Serbian nationalism and became the Vice-President of the Serbian Socialist Party. Given that nationalism is a particular form of ideological communication, an ideological anti-praxis that communicates the principle of nationhood, a critical theory of communication also needs to engage with aspects of ideology and nationalism. This chapter therefore also asks whether there is a nationalist potential in Marković's theory in particular or even in Marxist Humanism in general.

For providing answers to these questions, the chapter revisits Yugoslav praxis philosophy, the concepts of praxis, communication, ideology, and nationalism. It shows the importance of a full Humanism and the pitfalls of truncated Humanism in critical theory in general and the critical theory of communication in particular. Taking into account complete Humanism, the chapter introduces the concept of *praxis communication*.

Chapter 6: Sustainability and Community Networks

Community networks are IP-based computer networks that are operated by a community as a common good. In Europe, the most well-known community networks are Guifi in Catalonia, Freifunk in Berlin, Ninux in Italy, Funkfeuer in Vienna, and the Athens Wireless Metropolitan Network in Greece. This chapter deals with community networks as alternative forms of Internet access and alternative infrastructures and asks: What do sustainability and unsustainability mean in the context of community networks? What advantages do such networks have over conventional forms of Internet access and infrastructure provided by large telecommunications corporations? In addition, what disadvantages do they face at the same time? This chapter provides a framework for thinking dialectically about the un/sustainability of community networks. It provides a framework of practical questions that can be asked when assessing power structures in the context of Internet infrastructures and access. It presents an overview of environmental, economic, political, and cultural contradictions that community networks may face as well as a typology of questions that can be asked in order to identify such contradictions.

Chapter 7: Karl Marx, Journalism, and Democracy

This chapter asks: How did Karl Marx see the role of journalism in the public sphere and democracy? It examines Marx's significance for the theory of journalism. Marx was not only a critical journalist himself but also a defender of freedom of the press, which he justified theoretically. Marx anticipated Jürgen Habermas' critical theory of the public sphere. Marx's theoretical concepts of the critique of political economy are still of central importance for a critical theory of journalism today. The applicability of Marx's concepts of the commodity form, labour, and ideology to journalism theory are examined in this chapter.

Chapter 8: Towards a Critical Theory of Communication as Renewal and Update of Marxist Humanism in the Age of Digital Capitalism

This chapter asks: What is the role of communication in a Marxist-Humanist theory of communication that aims at advancing participatory democracy? The chapter's task is to outline some foundations of a critical, Marxist-Humanist theory of communication in the age of digital capitalism. It theorises the role of communication in society, communication and alienation, communication in social struggles, social struggles for democratic communication, the contradictions of digital capitalism, and struggles for Digital Socialist Humanism.

Marxist Humanism is a counter-narrative, counter-theory, and counter-politics to neoliberalism, new authoritarianism, and postmodernism. A critical theory of communication can draw on this intellectual tradition. Communication and work stand in a dialectical relationship. Communication mediates, organises, and is the process of the production of sociality and therefore of the reproduction of society. Society and communication are in class and capitalist societies shaped by the antagonism between instrumental and co-operative reason. Authoritarianism and Humanism are two basic, antagonistic modes of organisation of society and communication. Instrumental reason creates and universalises alienation.

Digital capitalism is a dimension of contemporary society where digital technologies such as the computer, the Internet, the mobile phone, tablets, robots, and AI-driven ("smart") technologies mediate the accumulation of capital, influence, and reputation. A Marxist-Humanist theory of communication aims to inform struggles for a good, commons-based, public Internet in a good, commons-based society that has a vivid, democratic public sphere.

Chapter 9: Digital Democracy, Public Service Media, and the Public Service Internet

This chapter deals with the relationship between digital democracy and public service media. It addresses three questions: What are digital democracy and the digital public sphere? What are the main trends in the development of digital media today, what are digital media's democratic possibilities and deficits, and what role can public service media play in strengthening digital democracy and digital public sphere? What legal framework is needed so that public service media can strengthen digital democracy?

Chapter 10: The Structural Transformation of the Public Sphere and Alienation: Challenges and Opportunities for the Advancement of Digital Democracy

This chapter asks: How can Marx' theory of alienation and Habermas' theory of the structural transformation of the public sphere be combined for advancing the understanding of democracy today?

The chapter builds on Habermas' concept of the public sphere. It relates Habermas' concept to Marx' notion of alienation. A fusion of these two concepts is used for showing that digital capitalism and capitalist social media do not form a public sphere but rather constitute a danger to democracy. In contrast, a public service Internet is a manifestation of the digital public sphere and digital democracy.

Internet platforms such as Facebook and Google, which dominate the social media sector, are among the largest corporations in the world. At the same time, social media have become an integral part of politics and public communication. World politicians like Donald Trump have a total of more than 100 million followers on various Internet platforms and spread propaganda and false reports about these media. The Arab Spring and the various Occupy movements have shown that social media like Facebook, Twitter, and YouTube are important in social movements. No politician, no party, no NGO, and no social movement can do without profiles on social media today. This raises the question of the connection between social media and the public. This article sheds light on this question.

The Chapters in This Book

Section 2 presents a concept of the public sphere as a concept of critique. Section 3 uses the concept of the public sphere to criticise capitalist Internet platforms. Section 4 deals with the potentials of a public service Internet.

References

Barber, Benjamin. 2003. *Strong Democracy. Participatory Politics for a New Age*. Berkeley: University of California Press. Twentieth Anniversary Edition.

Habermas, Jürgen. 1996. *Between Facts and Norms. Contributions to a Discourse Theory of Law and Democracy*. Cambridge, MA: The MIT Press.

Held, David. 2006. *Models of Democracy*. Cambridge: Polity.

Macpherson, Crawford B. 1973. *Democratic Theory: Essays in Retrieval*. Oxford: Clarendon Press.

Marx, Karl. 1871a. The Civil War in France. In *Marx & Engels Collected Works (MECW)*, Volume 22, 307–359. London: Lawrence & Wishart.

Marx, Karl. 1871b. First Draft of "The Civil War in France". In *Marx & Engels Collected Works (MECW)*, Volume 22, 437–514. London: Lawrence & Wishart.

Marx, Karl. 1871c. Second Draft of "The Civil War in France". In *Marx & Engels Collected Works (MECW)*, Volume 22, 515–551. London: Lawrence & Wishart.

Marx, Karl. 1843. Contribution to the Critique of Hegel's Philosophy of Law. In *Marx & Engels Collected Works (MECW)*, Volume 3, 3–129. London: Lawrence & Wishart.

Pateman, Carole. 1970. *Participation and Democratic Theory*. Cambridge: Cambridge University Press.

Shapiro, Ian. 2003. *The State of Democratic Theory*. Princeton, NJ: Princeton University Press.

Part II

Foundations of Digital Democracy

Chapter Two

The Dialectic

Not Just the Absolute Recoil, but the World's Living Fire that Extinguishes and Kindles Itself. Reflections on Slavoj Žižek's Version of Dialectical Philosophy in Absolute Recoil: Towards a New Foundation of Dialectical Materialism

2.1 Introduction

Hegel's dialectical philosophy has in the course of the 20th century lost influence in Marxist theory. Too many theorists repeated the bourgeois and postmodern reflex to dismiss Hegel as having a deterministic, closed, and totalitarian system of philosophy. The merit of Žižek's recent work, including *Absolute Recoil* (Žižek 2014), is that he has massively strived to bring back Hegel to the attention of critical theory. Recent discussions about how to use Hegel's *Logic* for reading Marx's Capital and critically understanding capitalism (for an overview, see: Moseley and Smith 2014) show how important Hegel's dialectic remains in 21st-century capitalism.

In this chapter, I reflect on Žižek's version of Hegelian dialectics and ask the question what kind of Hegelian dialectic is most appropriate today. This chapter consists of seven sections. Following the introduction, Section 2.2 discusses Žižek's logic of the dialectic as retroactivity (Section 2.2). Section 2.3 moves from Žižek's dialectical materialism to the discussion of his version of historical materialism. In Section 2.4, I suggest amendments to Žižek's dialectical logic and engages with the question of how dialectic works.

DOI: 10.4324/9781003331087-4

Sections 2.5 and 2.6 analyse the implications of Žižek's historical dialectic, first in general (Section 2.5) and second by asking how we should interpret Auschwitz and what the implications of Žižek's historical-dialectical materialism are in this respect (Section 2.6). Section 2.7 presents some conclusions.

2.2 Žižek on Retroactivity as Dialectical Logic

The title of Žižek's 2014 theory monograph *Absolute Recoil* refers to two passages in Hegel's *Science of Logic* that describe "the speculative coincidence of opposites in the movement by which a thing emerges out of its own loss" (Žižek 2014, 1).

> When positedness is self-sublated, an essence is no longer directly determined by an external Other, by its complex set of relations to its otherness, to the environment into which it emerged. Rather, it determines itself, it is 'within itself the absolute recoil upon itself' – the gap, or discord, that introduces dynamism into it is absolutely immanent.
>
> (Žižek 2014, 2)

The "action appears as its own counter-action, or, more precisely, [...] the negative move (loss, withdrawal) itself generates what it 'negates'" (Žižek 2014, 148). There is "a withdrawal that creates what it withdraws from", an "action appears as its own counter-action" (Žižek 2014, 148).

The proper dialectical process is for Žižek (2014, 149) that there is a starting point (positing reflection) that becomes negated so that the original situation is lost and the origin is experienced as inaccessible (external reflection) and the new situation is "transposed back into the Origin itself" (absolute reflection) (Žižek 2014, 149). Žižek conceptualises dialectical materialism as *retroactive dialectic*: The "event is prior to the unfolding of its consequences, but this can be asserted only once these consequences are here" (Žižek 2014, 73). The

> meaning of our acts is not an expression of our inner intention, it emerges alter, from their social impact, which means that there is a moment of contingency in every emergence of meaning. But there is another more subtle retroactivity involved here: an act is abyssal not in the sense that it is not grounded in reasons, but in the circular sense that it *retroactively posits its reasons*. A truly autonomous symbolic act or intervention never occurs as the result of strategic calculation, as I go through all possible reasons and then choose the most

appropriate course of action. An act is autonomous not when it applies a pre-existing norm but when it creates a norm in the very act of applying it.

(Žižek 2014, 21)

"An act proper is not just a strategic intervention into a situation, bound by its conditions – it retroactively creates its conditions" (Žižek 2008, 311).

Žižek discusses as an example that for Marx, capital is a self-moving automatic subject that acts on itself in the accumulation process, where invested monetary capital M is turned into an increased amount of money M' that forms the starting point M for a further cycle of accumulation. In "its self-movement, capital retroactively 'sublates' its own material conditions, turning them into subordinate moments of its own 'spontaneous expansion' – in pure Hegelese, it posits its own presuppositions" (Žižek 2014, 31; see also Žižek 2012, 250). Žižek concedes that capital is not really a subject-substance because it depends on "workers' exploitation" (Žižek 2012, 251).

One "should look for a non-dialecticizable moment of the dialectical process" that is the dialectic's "very motor" (Žižek 2014, 89). Žižek speaks of this non-dialecticisable moment also as "excessive element" (Žižek 2014, 363), the "chimneysweep element" (Žižek 2014, 363), an "intruder" (Žižek 2014, 363), "excesses which do not fit" (Žižek 2012, 455), sublation's "constitutive exception" (Žižek 2012, 471), or with Lacan as the objet a (Žižek 2014, 361, 392). For Žižek, retroactivity is a key concept in order to interpret "Hegel's thought" as harbouring "openness towards the future" (Žižek 2014, 221). "Den" is Democritus' term for less than nothing (see also Žižek 2012, Chapter 1). Žižek (2014, 396) says that the negation of one is zero and the negation of zero is den. For Žižek (2012, 38), the dialectic proceeds "from Nothing through Nothing to Nothing" so that there "is only Nothing". In his book *Less than Nothing*, Žižek (2012, 4) bases his analysis on the assumption that "reality is *less than nothing*".

Žižek (2014, 154) questions conceptions of the dialectical process as something, negation of the something, negation of the negation so that the origin of something is restored with new qualities at a higher level. He conceives the dialectic as beginning "with nothing", a "self-negation of nothing", so "that something appears" (Žižek 2014, 154). While "the negation of Something gives Nothing, the negated Nothing does not bring us back to Something but rather engenders a 'less than nothing'" (Žižek 2014, 331). Žižek distinguishes in this context between the standard Hegelian upward-Aufhebung (sublation) and a downward-Aufhebung (Žižek 2014, 332).[1] The latter results in less than nothing, it creates something without substance that cannot be sublated or negated, is undead, a ghost, and the lowest level (Žižek 2014, 331–333). In the downward-Aufhebung, there is "no positive synthetic result" (Žižek 2014, 336). First, "something is negated, we get nothing; then, in a second negation, we get less than nothing, not even nothing – not a Something mediated by nothing but a kind of pre-ontological inconsistency which lacks the principled purity of the Void" (Žižek 2014, 343). The dialectical triad for Žižek is: den (less than nothing) – nothing – something (Žižek 2014, 391).

2.3 Žižek and the Dialectic of History

For Žižek, retroactivity is one of the temporal dimensions of the dialectical logic. After a negation of the negation, the result becomes the starting point of a new dialectical process so that the dialectic is infinite, it is posited as a new precondition of another dialectical relation. The process of the positing of results as preconditions is a logical constituent of the dialectic that at the same time also enables the historical development of systems. "Something becomes an other; this other is itself somewhat; therefore it likewise becomes an other, and so on *ad infinitum*" (Hegel 1830, §93). Žižek however uses the notion of retroactivity for grounding an understanding of human history as developing in a specific sequence.

For Žižek, retroactivity means that the future is "a priori unpredictable" (Žižek 2012, 221). According to him, one can only look backwards in history to the past in order to make sense of what actually happened, what went wrong, etc. He argues that there is "the paradox of a contingent actual emergency which retroactively creates its own possibility: only when the thing takes place can we 'see' how it was possible" (Žižek 2008, 180).

Žižek says that the "future is open" (Žižek 2014, 36). He argues that although the concrete future is open, retroactively seen for Hegel history "will always go wrong, and the intended goal will turn into its opposite (as confirmed by the reversal of revolutionary emancipation into Stalinist nightmare)" (Žižek 2014, 36). A

> revolution also has to be repeated: for immanent conceptual reasons, its first strike has to end in fiasco, the outcome must turn out to be the opposite of what was intended, but this fiasco is necessary since it creates the conditions of its overcoming.
>
> (Žižek 2014, 37)

First, "a negation is enforced, but it fails, and the negation of negation draws the consequences of that failure, giving it, as it were, [in a second attempt] a positive spin" (Žižek

2014, 330). For Hegel, there are "unexpected reversals" (Žižek 2014, 23) in history: the October Revolution turned into Stalinism, consumerism into religious fundamentalism, etc. Only "the experience of catastrophe can make the revolutionary agent aware of the fateful limitation of the first attempt" (Žižek 2014, 38). Today we "find ourselves in a strictly homologous Hegelian moment: how to actualize the communist project after the failure of its first attempt at realization in the twentieth century" (Žižek 2014, 37). Žižek (2009a, 28) in *Living in the End Times* argues that the modern state would not have been possible "without having to pass through the 'superfluous' detour of the Terror".

Žižek refers to one of the messages of Richard Wagner's opera *Parsifal*: Die Wunde schließt der Speer nur der sie schlug – "The wound can be healed only by the spear that smote it" (Žižek 2014, 136). The "very disintegration of traditional forms opens up the space of liberation" (Žižek 2014, 136). Žižek gives the example that the proper answer to English colonialism in India is not a return to an alleged Indian origin that completely refuses everything that comes from the West as evil, but to appropriate English language and culture, to impurify them, turning them into something different in a specific Indian context so that the Indians "become more European than the Europeans themselves" (Žižek 2014, 150). Žižek sees history not as a process, in which domination negates and alienates society from an origin or essence – "there was nothing prior to the loss" (Žižek 2014, 136) – to which one has to return, something good may rather "come out of Evil" as "a contingent by-product" (Žižek 2014, 131). For Žižek, the solution to the problem can be found in the problem itself. The "wound as such is liberating – or rather, contains liberatory potential. [...] we should also fully endorse the liberating aspect of the wound" (Žižek 2014, 138). In "the course of the dialectical process, a shift of perspective occurs which makes the wound itself appear as its opposite – the wound itself is its own healing when seen from another standpoint" (Žižek 2014, 141). There "is no original unity preceding loss, what is lost is retroactively constituted through its loss, and the properly dialectical reconciliation resides in fully assuming the consequences of this retroactivity" (Žižek 2014, 347). The absolute recoil is "a thing emerging through its very loss" so that "the truth of every substantial thing is that it is the retroactive effect of its own loss" (Žižek 2014, 150).

2.4 The Dialectical Logic

In the *Science of Logic*, Hegel first mentions the absolute recoil in the discussion of reflection. Essence differentiates itself from something unessential; it shines into forms of being and is therefore also shine and reflection. Reflection is a threefold dialectic of positing reflection, external reflection, and determining reflection.

The positing reflection is an identity, "the movement of the nothing to the nothing", "self-referring negativity", "the negating of itself" (Hegel 2010, 346). It is the precondition of development, what Hegel calls "*Voraussetzen*" (Hegel 1813/1816, 26) – "*presupposing*" (Hegel 2010, 347). It is in this section on positing reflection, where the passage on the absolute recoil that Žižek (2014) refers to in the title of his book *Absolute Recoil* occurs:

> Die Reflexion also *findet* ein Unmittelbares *vor*, über das sie hinausgeht und aus dem sie die Rückkehr ist. Aber diese Rückkehr ist erst das Voraussetzen des Vorgefundenen. Dies Vorgefundene *wird* nur darin, dass es *verlassen* wird; seine Unmittelarkeit ist die aufgehobene Unmittelbarkeit. – Die aufgehobene Unmittelbarkeit umgekehrt ist die Rückkehr in sich, das *Ankommen* des Wesens bei sich, das einfache sich selbst gleiche Sein. Damit ist dieses Ankommen bei suchd as Aufheben seiner und die [sich] von sich selsbt abstoßende, voraussetzende Reflexion, und ihr Abstoßen von sich ist das Ankommen bei sich selbst. Die reflektierende Bewegung ist somit nach dem Betrachteten als *absoluter Gegenstoß* in sich selbst zu nehmen. Denn die Voraussetzung der Rückkehr in sich – das, woraus das Wessen *herkommt* und erst als dieses Zurückkommen *ist* –, ist nur in der Rückkehr selbst.
>
> (Hegel 1813/1816, 27)

Reflection thus *finds* an immediate *before it* which it transcends and from which it is the turning back. But this turning back is only the presupposing of what was antecedently found. This antecedent *comes to be* only by being *left behind*; its immediacy is sublated immediacy. – The sublated immediacy is, contrariwise, the turning back into itself, essence that *arrives* at itself, simple being equal to itself. This arriving at itself is thus the sublating of itself and self-repelling, pre- supposing reflection, and its repelling of itself from itself is the arriving at itself.

It follows from these considerations that the movement of reflection is to be taken as an *absolute* internal *counter-repelling*. For the presupposition of the turning back into itself – that from which essence *arises*, essence *being* only as this coming back – is only in the turning back itself.

> (Hegel 2010, 348)

"Absoluter Gegenstoß" has in the Cambridge translation of *Wissenschaft der Logik* been translated as absolute counter-repelling, whereas in the Humanities Press edition that Žižek the absolute recoil is used. Hegel argues that the posited reflection is the presupposition of the dialectic, but it always has a before, it is already the result of a previous sublation that has left something behind. Hegel here points out the cyclic form of the dialectic, where the end-point of a dialectical sublation is the starting point of a new contradiction.

Hegel brings up the notion of absolute counter-repelling or absolute recoil a second time in the *Science of Logic*, when he discusses the ground:

> Der Grund ist daher selbst eine der Reflexionsbestimmungen des Wesens, aber die letzte, vielmehr nur die Bestimmung, daß sie aufgehobene Bestimmung ist. Die Reflexionsbestimmung, indem sie zugrunde geht, erhält ihre wahrhafte Bedeutung, der absolute Gegenstoß ihrer in sich selbst zu sein, nämlich daß das Gesetztsein, das dem Wesen zukommt, nur als aufgehobenes Gesetztsein ist, und umgekehrt, daß nur das sich aufhebende Gesetztsein das Gesetztsein des Wesens ist. Das Wesen, indem es sich als Grund bestimmt, bestimmt sich als das Nichtbestimmte, und nur das Aufheben seines Bestimmtseins ist sein Bestimmen. – In diesem Bestimmtsein als dem sich selbst aufhebenden ist es nicht aus anderem herkommendes, sondern in seiner Negativität mit sich identisches Wesen.
>
> (Hegel 1813/1816, 80–81)

> Consequently, *ground* is itself *one of the reflected determinations* of essence, but it is the last, or rather, it is determination determined as sublated determination. In foundering to the ground, the determination of reflection receives its true meaning – that it is the absolute repelling of itself within itself; or again, that the positedness that accrues to essence is such only as sublated, and conversely that only the self-sublating positedness is the positedness of essence. In determining itself as ground, essence determines itself as the not-determined, and only the sublating of its being determined is its determining. – Essence, in thus being determined as self-sublating, does not proceed from an other but is, in its negativity, identical with itself.
>
> (Hegel 2010, 386)

The ground is not posited by something else, it is an essence that sublates any determination and positing and is "das Nichtbestimmte", "the not-determined", as Hegel says. We can say that the ground is the absolute recoil of the absolute recoil that posits essence. It is a kind of ultimate and therefore also first and substantial essence, a recoil of any recoil, a super-recoil, a substantial essence.

But the positing reflection that is an absolute recoil is only the starting point (that is at the same time an end point that forms a new starting point) of a dialectical process: The reflection-in-itself externalises itself into a negative other so that there is what Hegel calls external reflection: Reflection

> [a]t one time it is as what is presupposed, or the reflection into itself which is the immediate. At another time, it is as the reflection negatively referring to itself; it refers itself to itself as to that its non-being.
>
> (Hegel 2010, 348–349)

In external reflection, an immediate "becomes the negative or the determined". It is the negative of something other. This other is however also an immediate that is a negative and the determined of the external other. The external reflection connects two things that are both immediate beings and therefore also negatives that mutually negate each other's immediacy.

The determining reflection is "the unity of *positing* and *external* reflection" (Hegel 2010, 351). The sublation of the contradiction between one thing and another thing determines the emergence of what Hegel terms "*Gesetzsein*" (Hegel 1813/1816, 32) – the "*posited*" (Hegel 2010, 351).

> *Existence is only positedness*; this is the principle of the essence of existence. Positedness stands on the one side over against existence, and over against essence on the other: it is to be regarded as the means which conjoins exist-ence with essence and essence with existence. – If it is said, a determination is *only* a positedness, the claim can thus have a twofold meaning, according to whether the determination is such in opposition to existence or in opposition to essence. [...] In fact, however, positedness is the superior, because, as posited, existence is what it is in itself – some- thing negative, something that refers simply and solely to the turning back into itself. For this reason positedness is *only* a positedness with respect to essence: it is the negation of this turning back as achieved return into itself.
>
> (Hegel 2010, 347)

Positedness is a reflection-in-and-for-itself:

> It is *positedness* – negation which has however deflected the reference to an-other into itself, and negation which, equal to itself, is the unity of itself and its other, and only through this is an *essentiality*. It is, therefore, positedness,

negation, but as reflection into itself it is at the same time the sublatedness of this positedness, infinite reference to itself.

(Hegel 2010, 353)

Herbert Marcuse argues in his Hegel book *Reason and Revolution* that the "laws of reflection that Hegel elaborates are the fundamental laws of the dialectic" (Marcuse 1941/1955, 146):

> Essence denotes the unity of being, its identity throughout change. Precisely what is this unity or identity? It is not a permanent and fixed substratum, but a process wherein everything copes with its inherent contradictions and unfolds itself as a result. Conceived in this way, identity contains its opposite, difference, and involves self-differentiation and an ensuing unification. Every existence precipitates itself into negativity and remains what it is only by negating this negativity. It splits up into a diversity of states and relations to other things, which are originally foreign to it, but which become part of its proper self when they are brought under the working influence of its essence. Identity is thus the same as the 'negative totality', which was shown to be the structure of reality; it is 'the same as Essence.'

(Marcuse 1941/1955, 146)

The German Marxist philosopher Hans Heinz Holz analyses as part of his five volume history of dialectical philosophy (*Dialektik. Problemgeschichte von der Antike bis zur Gegenwart*) Hegel's works in detail. He also mentions Hegel's concept of the absolute recoil and argues that the absolute recoil connects the reflection-in-itself and the reflection-in-another: "In the positing of the other my reflection-in-myself becomes at the same time a reflection-of-myself-into-another ('external reflection')" (Holz 2011b, 158, translation from German[2]).

Holz also points out that determining reflection as the unity of posited reflection and external reflection is being-in-and-for-itself (Holz 2011b, 159). "*[B]eing-in-and-for-itself* only is by being equally *reflection* or *positedness*, and *positedness* only is by being equally *in-and-for-itself*" (Hegel 2010, 509). Holz from Hegel's dialectic of reflection draws the conclusion that "every substance is the (passive, posited) result of all substances' interaction and every substance is at the same time active (actively, positing) moment of this interaction" (Holz 2011b, 161, translation from German[3]).

Holz (2011b, 158) discusses the re-formulation of the *Science of Logic's* section on reflection in the *Encyclopaedia Logic's* section on the pure determinations of reflection

(Hegel 1830, §§115–122), where Hegel describes essence as a dialectic of the moments identity, difference, and ground, that are negatively opposed to existence (§§123–124), which constitutes a contradiction that is sublated in the thing (§§125–130). The notions of positing reflection and external reflection are in the *Encyclopaedia Logic* manifest in the dialectic of identity and distinction:

> Distinction in its own self is the essential [distinction], the positive and the negative: the positive is the identical relation to self in such a way that it is not the negative, while the negative is what is distinct on its own account in such a way that it is not the positive. Since each of them is on its own account only in virtue of not being the other one, each shines within the other, and is only insofar as the other is. Hence, the distinction of essence is opposition through which what is distinct does not have an other in general, but its own other facing it; that is to say, each has its own determination only in its relation to the other: it is only inwardly reflected insofar as it is reflected into the other, and the other likewise; thus each is the other's own other.
>
> (Hegel 1830, §119)

This contradiction of the one and the other also means that reflection-in-itself is "just as much reflection-into-another and vice versa" (Hegel 1830, §121). Something that exists is a unity of contradictory moments, a unity of one and another:

> Existence is the immediate unity of inward reflection and reflection-into-another. Therefore, it is the indeterminate multitude of existents as inwardly reflected, which are at the same time, and just as much, shining into-another, or relational; and they form a world of interdependence and of an infinite connectedness of grounds with what is grounded.
>
> (Hegel 1830, §123)

It should at this point be mentioned that the development of Hegel's works was dialectical itself. He posited a certain philosophical system and then negated it so that his own system re-posited, questioned, and re-constituted in a sublating manner its own preconditions. Hegel aimed at systematising his own philosophical system. The ultimate approach for this task was his *Encyclopaedia*. But the *Encyclopaedia* was itself a dialectical development constituted in a dialectical process in three steps: first, the 1808 Nürnberg version that was in a second step sublated by the 1817 Heidelberg version, which resulted in a negation of the negation by the 1827 and 1830 versions elaborated in Hegel's Berlin lectures. The 1830 edition, published one year before Hegel's death, is the ultimate and most systematic version of Hegel's dialectic. The *Encyclopaedia* is a "grounded systematic of knowledge as totality" (Holz 2011b, 176, translation from German). The *Science of Logic* is not the grand dialectical logic and the *Encyclopaedia Logic* is not the small logic. Saying the latter is small or short belittles its status, importance, and systematicity. The *Encyclopaedia Logic*'s third edition/version is rather Hegel's systematic dialectical logic.

Both Hans Heinz Holz and Herbert Marcuse in their discussion of Hegel point out that the part of reflection (positing reflection, including the absolute recoil) that Žižek makes the key foundation of his Hegel interpretation is only one moment of the whole dialectical process, namely identity or reflection-in-itself that is the starting point and simultaneous end point that becomes a new starting point of the dialectical process. And Žižek (2012, 200) indeed focuses predominantly on what he terms the "primacy of 'self-contradiction' over the external obstacle". If one looks at Hegel's system as a whole, as worked out in the *Encyclopaedia Logic* in systematic form, then it becomes evident that the dialectic does not need a non-dialectisisable moment, an excessive element, or intruder that is the motor of the dialectic and enables the retroactive positing of the dialectic's own preconditions so that something emerges out of nothing (or nothing from less than nothing).

In the dialectical process, there is always something emerging from something and at the same time something immersing into nothing. This is the precise threefold meaning of the German term "Aufhebung" (sublation) as (a) preservation, (b) elimination, and (c) uplifting. There is no pure nothing; otherwise, a spiritual being (God) would have had to create something out of nothing (creatio ex nihilo). In a dialectical-materialist worldview, there is a dynamic material substance of the world that is endless and has always existed. It is however a process substance that continuously develops from something into nothing and something new by negating negations that sublate (aufheben) parts of the world. In a dialectical process, something is sublated (aufgehoben): parts of it are eliminated, other parts preserved, and new parts emerge out of it. So something emerges from something, but this something is something different. But given that it is again something, the world and the something remain something, and is therefore one that returns into itself. But this return or what Hegel and Žižek call the absolute recoil is a sublating return that splits something off something and at the same time adds something to something so that a new something emerges. Sublation at the same time preserves, cancels out, and creates new qualities. That something emerges from something is one aspect of the dialectical process. But it is not the only one: The newly emerging something also has new qualities, so also nothing emerges out of something. Some older qualities may cease to exist so that parts of something turn into nothing, but the old continues to exist and shape the new. And finally, given that there are mere potentialities that have not been realised and constitute non-being (or not-yet being) in the old and the new, also and old nothing turns in a sublation into a new nothing: A new field of possibilities, of non-existing realities that are pure potentialities, emerges.

In the *Encyclopaedia*'s section on the logic of being, Hegel points out the double process of sublation (Aufhebung) as the creation of something out of something and turning something into nothing:

> Es ist hierbei an die gedoppelte Bedeutung unseres deutschen Ausdrucks aufheben zu erinnern. Unter aufheben verstehen wir einmal soviel als hinwegräumen, negieren, und sagen demgemäß z. B., ein Gesetz, eine Einrichtung usw. seien aufgehoben. Weiter heißt dann aber auch aufheben soviel als aufbewahren, und wir sprechen in diesem Sinn davon, daß etwas wohl aufgehoben sei.
>
> (Hegel 1830 [German], §96)

> At this point we should remember the double meaning of the German expression '*aufheben*'. On the one hand, we understand it to mean 'clear away' or 'cancel', and in that sense we say that a law or regulation is cancelled (*aufgehoben*). But the word also means 'to preserve', and we say in this sense that something is well taken care of (*wohl aufgehoben*)
>
> (Hegel 1830, §96)

Hegel explicates the relationship of being and nothingness:

> In becoming, being, as one with nothing, and nothing as one with being, are only vanishing [terms]; because of its contradiction becoming collapses inwardly, into the unity within which both are sublated; in this way its result is being-there.
>
> (§89)

The result of the dialectic is

> a determinate result, which here is not a pure nothing but a nothing which includes being within itself, and equally a being, which includes nothing. It follows that (1) being-there is the unity of being and nothing, in which the immediacy of these determinations, and therewith their contradiction, has disappeared in their relation – a unity in which they are only moments.
>
> (Hegel 1830, §89)

That is to say, becoming contains being and nothing within itself and it does this in such a way that they simply overturn into one another and reciprocally sublate one another as well as themselves. In that way becoming proves itself to be what is thoroughly restless, but unable to maintain itself in this abstract restlessness; for, insofar as being and nothing vanish in becoming – and just this is its concept – becoming is thereby itself something that vanishes, like a fire, that dies out within itself by consuming its material. But the result of this process is not empty nothing; instead it is being that is identical with negation, which we call being-there-and its significance proves to be, first of all, this: that it is what has become.

(Hegel 1830, addition to §89)

It is just one moment of the dialectic that becoming is "the *movement from nothing to nothing and thereby back to itself*" (Hegel 2010, 346). It is at the same time the interconnected movement from something to something, something to nothing, and nothing to something. The dialectic is a dialectic of coming-to-be and ceasing-to-be. It is a fire that dies out within itself by consuming its material that results in the moment of dying out in a new material that can and will itself catch fire or instigate a new fire. The dialectic is a fire that in the moment of dying out is born again.

Hegel's *Logic* was much influenced by Heraclitus' (535–475 BC) philosophy, in which the dialectic constitutes the world's objectivity, its being, and becoming. "There is no proposition of Heraclitus which I have not adopted in my Logic" (Hegel 1892, 279). For Heraclitus, being is nothing and nothing is being because they are two different and at the same time identical moments of the dialectic of becoming.

Heraclitus says: 'Everything is in a state of flux; nothing subsists nor does it ever remain the same'. [...] This universal principle is better characterized as Be coming, the truth of Being; since everything is and is not, Heraclitus expresses that everything is becoming. Not merely does origination belong to it, but passing away as well; both are not independent, but identical.

(Hegel 1892, 283)

Heraclitus

determined the real process in its abstract moments by separating two sides in it – 'the way upwards and the way downwards' – the one being division, in that it is the existence of opposites, and the other the unification of these existent opposites.

(Hegel 1892, 288)

Heraclitus draws from the dialectic the materialist conclusion that there is no God and the world has the capacity of a productive dialectic, i.e. to create itself like a living fire:

> With this in view, we find Heraclitus, according to Clement of Alexandria, saying: 'The universe was made neither by God nor man, but it ever was and is, and will be, a living fire, that which, in accordance with its laws, kindles and goes out'.
>
> (Hegel 1892, 289)

In a new translation of Heraclitus, this passage reads the following way: "That which always was, and is, and will be, everliving fire, the same for all, the cosmos, made neither by god nor man, replenishes in measure as it burns away" (Heraclitus 2001, §20). "As all things change to fire, [...] fire exhausted falls back into things" (Heraclitus 2001, §22).

The philosopher Hans Heinz Holz argues that Heraclitus "connected coming-to-be and ceasing-to-be in the cosmos [...] to the nature of the fire" (Holz 2011a, 212, translation from German). According to Holz, Heraclitus sees transition as the world's logos: The logos "retracts the many into the one and disassembles the one into the many" (Holz 2011a, 218, translation from German). Holz considers Heraclitus as a representative of a dialectic of the real understood as "the unity of the world and the manifoldness of things" (Holz 2011a, 222, translation from German). The fire would be a metaphor for the world's real dialectic (Holz 2011a, 222). Holz sees Heraclitus as the dialectic's "prime father in the Occident" (Holz 2011a, 223, translation from German). The German Marxist philosopher Herbert Hörz argues in his book *Materialistische Dialektik* (*Materialist Dialectic*) that Heraclitus formulated a "decisive foundational notion of the dialectic" when seeing "movement as matter's mode of existence. Nature, society and humans consist of contradictions, that are the driving forces of events" (Hörz 2009, 28, translation from German).

Matter is a causa sui, it has the capacity to organise itself and produce new forms and levels of organisation of matter. The self-organisation of matter is the ultimate absolute recoil: In every transition from one form of the organisation of matter to another (e.g. from inanimate to animate nature, from the animal to the human, from capitalism to communism, etc.), matter posits its own presuppositions as the ultimate absolute recoil, namely the capacity to produce forms of matter and to thereby reproduce itself. A specific quality of human matter is that it is matter that is conscious of its creation of active relationships: humans constitute the social world through their social work and social interconnection with others. Humans as a specific form of the organisation of matter, ask themselves: "What's the matter of matter in society?" They have the capacity to actively reflect on what society they want to live in and bring about. Such conscious planning capacity does not mean that human social actions are always successful (results corresponding to the original aims) or that plans do not fail, but rather that humans and society have the capacity for bringing about their own freedom and to create a society with freedom from scarcity. Matter as the ultimate absolute recoil is this recoil only in and through dialectical production, as the fire that extinguishes and kindles itself.

Marx describes the accumulation of capital and therefore the capitalist system as a dialectical process, in which first money turns into commodities and commodities turn back into money: $M - C.. P.. C' - M'$. The capitalist with a sum of capital M buys commodities C: labour power and means of production. In the first metamorphosis of capital, money turns into commodities. Labour uses the means of production to create a new product C' that has emergent qualities: C' contains surplus-value and a surplus-product. Labour transforms the commodity into something new that has a higher value than the sum of the value of the invested capital and labour power. This new commodity C' is offered for sale on the market and if the sale is successfully completed, the commodity C' is in another metamorphosis turned into an increased sum of money capital $M' = M + \Delta M$. The two basic transitions in the realm of circulation are $M - C$ and $C' - M'$. An additional transition is $C.. P.. C'$ in the realm of production. Marx (1867, 200) says: "The process of exchange is therefore accomplished through two metamorphoses of opposite yet mutually complementary character – the conversion of the commodity into money, and the re-conversion of the money into a commodity".

After this passage, Marx in a footnote cites a quote of Heraclitus that he took from Ferdinand Lassalle's book *Die Philosophie Herakleitos des Dunkeln von Ephesos* (*The Philosophy of Heraclitus the Dark Philosopher of Ephesus*): "all things exchange for fire, and fire for all things, just as gold does for goods and goods for gold" (Marx 1867, 200, footnote 16). Marx here uses Heraclitus' metaphor of the dialectic as self-transforming fire for analysing the metamorphoses of capital. The dialectic is a fire that extinguishes and kindles itself: Money capital is a substance that in the accumulation process is first immersing into commodities (the fire of money goes out through exchange, but in the going out of money in the hands of the capitalist a new fire kindles itself because labour power and means of production come into the capitalist's ownership as commodities). Labour then transforms commodities into a surplus product so that labour is a fire that extinguishes the physical and value form of the invested capital, but kindles at the same time a transition into a new commodity that has higher value and new qualities. This new commodity C′ is thrown onto the market, where exchange extinguishes the fire of the commodity in the hands of capitalists, but in doing so kindles a new fire – an increased sum of money M′ – that the capitalist controls. Already Heraclitus, as Marx and Lassalle show, understood the dialectic of the transition of money into goods and goods into money. Marx points out the importance of this Heraclitusian dialectic as a substance of the capital accumulation process in modern society.

Also in the *Grundrisse*, Marx uses the metaphor of fire for characterising transitions in the capital accumulation cycle. Capital and commodities are transformed like a self-transforming fire: The circulation of capital is a "revolution which capital must go through to fire itself up for new production, as a series of exchanges" (Marx 1857/ 1858, 663). "Commodities constantly have to be thrown into it anew from the outside, like fuel into a fire" (Marx 1857/1858, 255). Labour is a fire that gives form to commodities, it transforms purchased goods into surplus-value and a surplus product: "Labour is the living, form-giving fire; it is the transitoriness of things, their temporality, as their formation by living time" (Marx 1857/1858, 361). Fire is a metaphor for transition and change. Capital changes its form in the accumulation process like Heraclitus' self-transforming fire that constantly extinguishes and kindles itself. In this process, the crucial form-giving fire is labour that in its exploitation is compelled to produce value and surplus value and thereby drives the self-transformation of capital from M into M′.

The absolute recoil that Žižek stresses means in the case of capital accumulation that the end-point of accumulation M_1' turns into a starting point M_2 of a further cycle of accumulation. Accumulation has however not only a start and an end, but also a dialectical dynamic in between – the fire that extinguishes and kindles itself. The dialectical recoil and the dialectical fire are interconnected dialectical moments of the dialectical process.

Theodor W. Adorno was sceptical of Hegel's notion of the determinate negation, i.e. the idea that the dialectic always produces a "positive" result: The "thesis that the negation of the negation is positive, an affirmation, cannot be sustained" (Adorno 2008, 17). The problem would be that the positive has the linguistic meaning of both "something that exists" and "the good, the higher, the approvable" (Adorno 2008, 18), which could lead to the assumption that the result of the negation of the negation is "intrinsically positive *in itself*" (Adorno 2008, 18). Negative dialectics in contrast dissociates itself from the "fetishization of the positive" (Adorno 2008, 18). Adorno argues that Hegel's assumption that the "actual is the rational" is after Auschwitz no longer be tenable (Adorno 2008,

19). "After Auschwitz, our feelings resist any claim of the positivity of existence as sanc-
timonious, as wronging the victims" (Adorno 1973, 361). Žižek to a certain extent shares
Adorno's concern about the dialectic's positivity and therefore turns negative dialectics
into less-than-negativity dialectics. Negation

> is the negation of the determined fact which is resolved, and is therefore de-
> terminate negation; that in the result there is therefore contained in essence
> that from which the result derives – a tautology indeed, since the result would
> otherwise be something immediate and not a result. Because the result, the
> negation, is a determinate negation, it has a content.
>
> (Hegel 2010, 33)

The determinate negation is the result and content of the negation of the negation. The
dialectic of the positive and the negative enables the repetition of development, but says
nothing about the moral quality of development: "Something becomes an other; this
other is itself somewhat; therefore it likewise becomes an other, and so on *ad infinitum*"
(Hegel 1830, §93).

Sublation is a general process that creates a new positive, a something, out of an old
something, which means emergence and disappearance at the same time: coming-to-be
as the positive and ceasing-to-be as the negative pole of a positive/negative dialectic
constitute the new. But the new can have very different forms and qualities. New forms
can be very unlike each other. Roy Bhaskar (1993), in his book *Dialectic: The Pulse of
Freedom*, in my opinion, has correctly stressed that there are different kinds of sublations
and negations of the negation. He distinguishes three kinds of negation of the negation (Bhaskar 1993, 5–6): *Real negation* characterises absence, non-being, non-identity,
being other, and non-existence – it is distanciation without transformation (Bhaskar
1993, 5, 401). *Transformative negation* is the "transformation of some thing, property
or state of affairs" (Bhaskar 1993, 5). It "may be essential or inessential, total or partial, endogenously and/or exogenously effected" (Bhaskar 1993, 5–6). *Radical negation*
means "auto-subversion, transformation or overcoming of a being or condition" (Bhaskar
1993, 6). Bhaskar argues that confusions about Hegel emerge when one assumes the
three forms of negation are the same. Not all negations would be transformative or radical, frequently negations would only be connecting or separating. Real negation is for
Bhaskar the most general concept, a subset of real negations is also a form transformative negation, and a subset of transformative negations is also a form of radical negation:

real negation $\geq$ transformative negation $\geq$ radical negation (Bhaskar 1993, 6, 402).

The Dialectical Logic

Sublation as "species of determinate transformative negations, may be totally, essentially or partially preservative" (Bhaskar 1993, 12). Other dialectical results include "stand-offs, the mutual undoing of the contending parties, the preservation of the status quo ante, retrogression and many other outcomes besides sublation" (Bhaskar 1993, 12–13). Bhaskar has tried to differentiate dialectics so that it can account for various forms of transformations and invariability. Transformative negations result in the change of form and/or content of a system, parts, and relations between parts of a system change. Given a radical negation, a system changes fundamentally, its root parts, structures, and its condition are re-constituted, old systems vanish and new ones emerge. In society, radical negation is a revolutionary transformation.

So there are real negations, transformative negations, and radical negations (real negations ≥ transformative negations ≥ radical negations). All of these negations are forms of negating the negative and sublating contradictions. There are different kinds of sublations that produce different kinds of results. This means that in sublation there are varying degrees of preservation and elimination of qualities of the two poles of a dialectical relation. Not all negations of the negation produce radical novelty, only some of them are revolutionary sublations of the status quo. Other negations of the negation are only transformative, they do not create novelty at a fundamental level of social systems or society, but at a more superficial level (at a smaller level of granularity of social or societal reality) so that the overall existing system can reproduce itself.

Žižek distinguishes between upward- and downward-sublation, which is a differentiation of the concept of sublation into different forms. Bhaskar's differentiation is more differentiated. It is a surprise that Žižek in his two big Hegel books *Absolute Recoil* and *Less than Nothing* does not mention Bhaskar a single time and does not discuss this specific version of the dialectic (see Fuchs 2011, Chapter 2, for a detailed discussion of various form of the dialectic, including the ones by Bhaskar, Žižek, and others).

Think of claims that we live in a completely new society, a network, information, postmodern, risk, or X society. These claims are ideological because they assert a radical sublation of society, although capitalism and its inherent features such as exploitation, crisis, and inequality continue to exist. The same kinds of claims have been made about the WWW that is said to have become radically new, a web 2.0 or a form of social medium that was non-social before. Or about media studies that, according to the same claims, in the digital age radically turned into something completely different called media studies 2.0. Some critics point out that such claims are ideologies and that there is nothing new under the sun, but that rather the only thing we find is the continuity of capitalism. But wait a minute: Capitalism is dialectical in that it maintains exploitation and domination by its own contradictory dynamic, by changing its appearance it reproduces its basic structures and social forms. So we still have capitalism, but a capitalism that has entered a new stage, in which digital media play indeed an important role in the organisation of exploitation and domination, lift existing contradictions to a new level so that existing class relations are deepened, but at the same time the productive forces are further socialised so that potentials of a commons-based economy are advanced, etc. Capitalism in its own transformation undergoes sublations that in Bhaskar's terminology are not radical, but transformative at different levels so that a digital capitalism, a capitalist information society, a capitalist web 2.0, etc. emerge that to a certain degree have new qualities, but preserve and transform previous structures so that the most fundamental structures of class, exploitation, and domination can continue to exist and to reproduce themselves by continuity (of capitalism) and discontinuity (in technology, communications, etc.). The point is to transform the contradictions that these changes bring about in a political direction so that society and communications can be turned into a democratic-socialist society and democratic-socialist communications.

Žižek argues that the "refusal of a moment to become caught in a [dialectical] movement" is the rule (Žižek 2012, 294). There is no necessity or automatism of a negation of the negation. In society, crises and antagonisms condition radical changes, but do not call them forth. It depends on subjective factors such as ideology, collective action and organisation, contact networks, resource mobilisation, etc. if the oppressed and exploited attempt to overthrow the system or not. If they refuse to do so, then they do not stand outside the dialectic because there is no outside: They remain caught in social contradictions (such as class and domination) and embedded into these relations. There is no outside – something undialectical – of the dialectic because the world and its moment are not isolated, but relational. Everything exists in a negative relation to something else. If and when change occurs and the negative turns via a negation of the negation into something new depends on many factors and is not determined.

The assumption that the dialectic has a non-dialectisisable excessive element can also be found in Žižek's (2006) book *The Parallax View*. He defines the parallax view based on Kojin Karatani's work as a "constantly shifting perspective between two points between which no synthesis or mediation is possible" (Žižek 2006, 4). There is an "irreducible gap between the positions itself" (Žižek 2006, 20). Žižek sees the parallax view as the "first step in the rehabilitation of the philosophy of dialectical materialism" (Žižek 2006, 4), but also points out the proximity of this concept to Derrida's différance (Žižek 2006, 11).

The Dialectical Logic

Jacques Derrida, Kojin Karatani, Slavoj Žižek, and Alain Badiou not only share the criticism of Hegel's dialectic, of Hegelian-Marxist dialectics, and of the concept of the determinate negation, but they also have tried to overcome these perceived limits by introducing elements into the concept of the dialectical relationship that constitutes a difference gap between the two poles. This difference gap is for them irreducible, non-dialectisiable, and not integratable. Derrida, Karatani, Žižek, and Badiou's philosophies converge in what Frederic Jameson (2009) has characterised as postmodern "multiple dialectics" (Jameson 2009, 15) that stress incommensurable elements.

But what if the antagonism between exploiters and the exploited is overcome and a classless society emerges? Classes will vanish (destruction), non-owners will become collective owners (new quality), and the existing wealth and instruments of production will remain important material foundations of a society that take on new forms (preservation). In this Hegelian Aufhebung (sublation), difference does not vanish because in the dialectical process new qualities emerge. Incommensurability is built into the concept of the Hegelian dialectic itself. What is the irreducible, incommensurable, non-dialecticisable, non-overcomeable, subtractable parallax gap of the dialectical relation between exploiters and the exploited? There is none. The relationship all resolves around private property, the control, and non-control of private property. This relation can be overcome, private property is dialecticisable and does not constitute an "irreducible gap" (Žižek) that cannot be synthesised or mediated. The overcoming of the gap between control and non-control of private property is the process of revolutionary politics. To assume that there is a non-overcomeable gap between exploiters and the exploited so that we can only shift between the different positions of these two groups limits the revolutionary potential of dialectical philosophy.

By employing the logic of concepts such as différance, the parallax view, and subtraction, even a radical thinker such as Slavoj Žižek ends up with philosophical concepts that are close to postmodern theory. Žižek's works are in this respect inconsistent because he is also a radical critic of postmodernist opposition "to all foundationalism, [...] grand solutions and [...] global emancipatory projects" (Žižek 2008, 1). Against such relativism, Žižek brings back a focus on the totality that questions capitalism as such, tries to bring back the lost cause of communism and thereby big ideas. Given this laudable and important project, it is inconsistent that Žižek contends in his concept of the dialectic to the postmodernists that there is something non-dialectisisable, an assumption that philosophically questions the focus on the totality.

The alternative to postmodern dialectics is to assume that the determinate negation is not a deterministic, but a revolutionary concept, to assume with Bhaskar that there are different forms of negation (real negation ≥ transformative negation ≥ radical negation), and to see determinate negation not as a systemic or natural law, but as something that must be created by humans in social struggles against capitalism and other forms of domination. Determinate negation is a possibility, not an automatic necessity, it is transformed from possibility into actuality only by revolutionary politics. The parallax view might be able to explain that two elements in a dialectic cannot be reduced to each other (such as the economy and politics), but it cannot truly renew dialectical materialism and dialectical philosophy because it misses the elements of the determinate negation and the negation of the negation, which constitute the possibilities for change and radical change. If you apply the notion of the parallax gap as "new dialectical materialism" to the situation of the relation between exploiters and the exploited, then you end up oscillating between the positions of the two groups without being able to in a theoretically consistent manner consider the revolutionary sublation of this relation as a real possibility in the categorical universe.

For Žižek, the dialectic is not a triad of three steps, but a quadruple with four steps: There are

> four rather than only three stages of a dialectical process. [...] to these three steps another is added: the highest level which paradoxically coincides with the lowest – at this highest level, people do exactly the same as at the previous level, but with a subjective attitude which is the same as the attitude of those at the lowest level.
>
> (Žižek 2012, 314–315; see also 294, 501)

It "is negativity which can be counted two times, as a direct negation and as a self-relating negation" (Žižek 2012, 501).

Hegel's formulation at the end of the *Science of Logic* that Žižek refers to is that

> the term counted as *third* can also be counted as *fourth*, and instead of a *triplicity*, the abstract form may also be taken to be a *quadruplicity*; in this way the negative or the *difference* is counted as a *duality*. – The third or the fourth is in general the unity of the first and the second moment, of the immediate and the mediated.
>
> (Hegel 2010, 746, in German: Hegel 1813/1816, 564)

Identifying four steps in the dialectic is somewhat redundant and tautological because an identity at some level can never remain isolated, it automatically posits a new negativity and is so not just self-related, but also other-related. The negated negative is immediately negated in a dialectical relationship to an other. Given that sublation always means not just repetition, but repetition with a difference, the negation that is the second step following identity is repeated at a different level after the sublation so that we just need three steps in the dialectic. The fourth, fifth, and sixth steps emerge from the principle of the dialectic to repeat itself with a difference; the seventh, eighth, and ninth steps occur as the difference of a difference, as repetition with a difference of the fourth, fifth, and sixth step and as a repetition with a difference of the repetition with a difference (a double difference) of the first, second, and third step, etc. Heraclitus (2001, §59) expresses the dialectic of unity and diversity in the following way: "Two made one are never one. [...] We choose each other to be one, and from the one both soon diverge". A negation of the negation produces a new one, but this one repeats the divergence into two and thereby constitutes a difference that makes a difference to previous negations of unity.

The rectangle structure of the dialectical logic is over-specified because a rectangle can be dissolved into triangles. It is therefore no accident that Hegel's *Encyclopaedia*, his most systematic and consistent work, is made up of three books (the Logic, Nature, the Phenomenology) that consist each of three sections with three subsections, etc. In his conceptual system, this triangle structure necessarily reaches a top – the absolute spirit (the triple of art – religion – philosophy) – because books are necessarily finite, but the basic logic of the *Encyclopaedia* that Hegel repeats with a difference throughout all its three parts reflects the structure of the material world that is in itself endless: The world develops through sublations and the emerging new posits itself as self-related and at the same time other-related and thereby constitutes new potentials for sublations. The

> *third* is the immediate, but the immediate *through sublation of mediation*, the simple through the *sublating of difference*, the positive through the sublating of the negative; it is the concept that has realized itself through its otherness, and through the sublating of this reality has rejoined itself and has restored its absolute reality, its *simple* self-reference.
>
> (Hegel 2010, 747, in German: Hegel 1813/1816, 565)

Dialectical logic operates for Hegel (2010, 751; in German: Hegel 1813/1816, 571) as a "*circle* that winds around itself", "a *circle of circles*".

2.5 The Dialectic of History

In 2009, Žižek (2009b) named an entire book after a formulation that Marx made when commenting on a passage from Hegel, namely that "Hegel remarks somewhere that all facts and personages of great importance in world history occur, as it were, twice. He forgot to add: the first time as tragedy, the second as farce" (Marx 1869, 10). In the book *First as Tragedy, then as Farce*, Žižek (2009b) argues that the history of the first decade of the 21st century started with a tragedy and ended with a farce: "the attacks of September 11, 2001 and the financial meltdown of 2008" (Žižek 2009b, 1). Žižek calls for a re-invention of communism as the proper political response. "Today, our message should be the same: it is permitted to know and to dully engage in communism, to again act in full fidelity to the communist Idea" (Žižek 2009b, 7). Žižek here also points out the "series of reversals that characterize modern revolutions" (Žižek 2009b, 125): from Mao's cultural revolution to Chinese capitalism, from the October revolution to Stalin, etc. But Žižek in his 2009 book trusts the potential of revolutionary agency: the repetition of catastrophes in capitalism can be broken by the new proletariat's communist revolution.

In *Absolute Recoil*, Žižek (2014) says that history "will always [first] go wrong" (36), first it ends "in fiasco" (37), the opposite of what was intended, and only the second time can the wound that is thereby created be healed by the logic of the wound itself. A communist revolution, according to this logic, has to go wrong the first time, but the solution emerges through the experience of catastrophe, loss, and suffering. If one compares *Absolute Recoil* to *First as Tragedy, then as Farce*, then the logic of Žižek's argument is not consistent: If history developed in such a way that first there is a wound created by the smote, which then creates the conditions for the smote healing the wound, capitalism's history would also have to be self-healing. Capitalism and class societies can however develop from one catastrophe to the next, as Marx remarked. The economic crisis of 1929 did not result in a self-healing capacity of the socio-economic wounds created by it, but rather capitalism re-organised itself, created a new level of its own contradictions that exploded in the 1973–1975 crisis and recession that instigated the phase of neoliberal and post-Fordist capitalism that created its own set of contradictions that exploded in a series of crises, including the 2000 dot-com crisis and the 2008 financial crisis that developed into a new world economic crisis. Clearly, the wound that is healed by the smote that created it is not a universal pattern of history. In capitalism, one wound is rather created after another and the question is what the time lag is between one spear-wound and another. The point is that class societies are grounded in contradictions that have catastrophic potentials that can and eventually will erupt. The only potential that can overcome this immanent catastrophic potential of class societies is the working class' revolutionary potential actualised in collective action.

Žižek in *Absolute Recoil* grounds an ethics of suffering and a dialectic of failure and catastrophe: History and revolution *have* to go wrong and result in catastrophes, otherwise there *never can be* a free society. So although he says the "future is open" (Žižek 2014, 36) and that Hegel saw history as "open and contingent process" (Žižek 2012, 227), he does not draw the conclusion that this enables people to act as revolutionaries who have the potential to bring about a free society already at the first attempt, but rather says they can only do so if they have first gone through a revolution that failed, created suffering, catastrophes, inverted its own goals, etc. Such a logic is politically disabling, defeatist (if you fight a battle in the first instance, why should you fight it, if you are bound to fail?), and introduces a new theory of functionalist historical determinism that does not trust in humans' agency and power to bring about a free society without having first through the same logic created barbarism. Barbaric figures of history, such as Stalin, Pol Pot, Mao, Kim Il Sung, are then necessary figures of history, proofs that history goes wrong as the foundation for in a turn making history right. The point is that the people do not need despotic masters and have the power to make themselves a better history without any masters. We do not have to go through Stalin or any of his historical or contextual equivalents in order to create a truly free socialist society. The October Revolution did not with necessity have to end in the Gulag. It is the tragedy of history that it did, but this development was not a necessity, but rather one of several possibilities.

Žižek argues for materialist miracles – "the emergence of a phenomenon *ex nihilo,* not fully covered by the sufficient chain of reasons", "something radically new, outside the scope of the possibilities" (Žižek 2012, 230) – that are at work in history. Every "dialectical passage or reversal is a passage in which the new figure emerges *ex nihilo* and retroactively posits or creates its necessity" (Žižek 2012, 230). Every "dialectical passage or reversal is a passage in which the new figure emerges *ex nihilo* and retroactively posits or creates its necessity" (Žižek 2012, 231).

If something is not possible in a specific instance because of previously given structures, then it cannot emerge. Something new can only emerge out of previously existing conditions. "There are no structural miracles. Every structure is coagulated development" (Hörz 2009, 86, translation from German). It is not determined that something new will/ can emerge and what exactly the form and content of the new is, but not everything imaginable is possible. A tortoise cannot lay eggs out of which humans hatch. We can imagine a human/turtle-hybrid as the subject of a bad science fiction novel or of bad science-fiction-like science (the kind of popular academic books written by the likes of Hans Moravec and Raymond Kurzweil; it may indeed just be a matter of time until they move from the cyborg to the human turtle and argue that science and technology will turn us all into Teenage Mutant Ninja Turtles), but the very idea is nonetheless nonsensical because it is materially impossible. Human-hatching turtles will not exist at any time because they are structurally impossible (not even genetic engineering will help in this case). Hegel (1830, addition to §143) argues that "the most absurd and nonsensical suppositions" can be *thought* as being possible, but are just "empty possibilities". A proper materialist sees these empty possibilities not as truly possible, but as ideologies.

Given that there is a specific space of possibilities for the emergence of novelty, something new does not emerge ex nihilo without precondition, but from specific conditions. That actuality conditions possibility for the future does not mean that the future is determined, but rather that in a specific historical situation there is a number of possibilities for the future. Collective practices in complex causal networks of reality shape possibilities and add to or limit the space of possibilities. Practices and praxis can create new possibilities that did not exist before, but not everything is possible all of the time because existing structures of economic production, technology, politics, and culture enable and constrain possibilities and future possibilities. If agency opens up these levels for more freedom, then the space of possibilities is enhanced, which does however not mean that everything goes at any time in history.

For Žižek, history seems on the one hand in a way to be governed completely by chance so that reversals of history appear like miracles. Pure chance can however also be limiting for political agency because if we cannot do anything to increase the possibility of the realisation of certain possibilities, then we better not act at all politically. On the other hand, Žižek does not dismiss agency. He believes in the power of revolutionary action in the very moment we live in. But in this respect, his stress is not on revolutionary action in general (at any time), but *the very moment we live in*. It would be the second time that communism gets a chance, so now it could go right, whereas in the first instance it according to Žižek *had to fail*.

Immanuel Wallerstein has a different concept of history. He takes from the sciences of complexity the insight that complex systems have no certainty. Society as a historical system is therefore in the moment of structural crisis confronted with the uncertainty of the future. The system enters bifurcation points with multiple options for future development. "The system has at that point what we may think of as choice between possibilities" (Wallerstein 2011, 156). The only thing that is certain in such a point of change is that the future will be different from the present, but not how it will look like. History is shaped by

The Dialectic of History

a dialectic of chance and necessity. Wallerstein argues that capitalism's antagonisms are today culminating in a bifurcation point, a chaos that could last for up to 50 years. It is determined that some order will emerge out of this noise and chaos created by capitalism's contradiction, but it is uncertain and contingent how this order will look like and if it will be for the better or the worse. Some of the possible future development that Wallerstein (2011, 162–163) identifies are: neo-feudalism, democratic fascism (democracy within 20 per cent of the world that exerts fascist power over the rest), and a "highly egalitarian world order" (Wallerstein 2011, 163). The "choice will depend on our collective world behaviour over the next fifty years" (Wallerstein 2011, 163).

In a structural crisis, not only is the system unpredictable, but fluctuations can quickly intensify (the butterfly effect) so that a revolution's effects can be immense (Wallerstein 2013, 33). The point is that the world's uncertainty in the moment of crisis should not be seen as an occasion for despair ("It can all get worse! We may all die!"), but as possibilities for true socialism ("It may go wrong! But if not, then we may have democratic communism in the end!").

> History is on nobody's side. We all may misjudge how we should act. Since the outcome is inherently, and not extrinsically, unpredictable, we have at best a 50–50 chance of getting the kind of world-system we prefer. But 50-50 is a lot, not a little.
> (Wallerstein 2013, 35)

The German Marxist philosopher Herbert Hörz speaks of dialectical determinism and dialectical determination as principles that govern the relationship of chance and necessity.

> A certain causal relation impacts a system as the cause that through the given complex of conditions results in a field of possibilities, from which possibilities are realised. [...] A possibility that does not necessarily occur is random just like the individual scope that exists in the necessary event of a totality.
> (Hörz 2009, 69, translation from German)

The space of possibilities constitutes a space for different behaviours and futures. A dialectical negation of a negation that constitutes a contradiction results in "qualitative transitions" that lead "to new fields of possibilities" (Hörz 2009, 69, translation from German). An existing field of possibilities results in a specific new reality that creates a new phase and conditioned field of possibilities. Not every moment of a totality is connected to every other moment and not to the same degree. In a class society, some people for example have more power than others. As a result, possibilities are not equally likely, but have different likelihoods (Hörz 2009, 70).

It should be noted here that Hegel argued in this context that "possibility is mere chance itself" (Hegel 1830, §144). "The contingent is generally what has the ground of its being not within itself but elsewhere" (Hegel 1830, addition to §145). The chance present in the field of possibilities that Herbert Hörz talks about has its own necessity in the pre-conditions that constitute this field and the previous sublations that manifest themselves in this very field. For Hegel, the contingent dimension of the dialectic poses the possibility that actuality can be turned into something different: "Being actuality in its immediacy, the contingent is at the same time the possibility of an other. [...] But, in fact, any such immediate actuality contains within it the germ of something else altogether" (Hegel 1830, addition to §146).

A specific quality of the society is that humans can actively intervene in the objective dialectic through their subjective collective actions. They can act based on specific goals. There is no guarantee that their goals will become realised in actual changes in society, but collective action can increase or decrease the likelihood of specific possibilities. Dialectical determinism in society means that our future is always and necessarily conditioned and open at the same time. How the future looks like is not determined and depends on many complex interrelated contradictions and dialectics of dialectics, but it is also not completely accidental. If there were mere chance, then we would be just like under mere determination/necessity be left helpless, which would make the conscious goal-oriented shaping of society impossible. We cannot determine or steer the future because there is no finality and mechanical determination of history, but we can dialectically determine the existing fields of possibilities for the future, i.e. humans have the freedom to collectively act and struggle for changing what is possible and somewhat influence the likelihoods of possibilities. Given a specific field of possibilities, fluctuations, intensification, non-linearity, complexity, chaos, critical values, and bifurcations are aspects of chance (Fuchs 2003, 2008, Chapter 2). But chance can be somewhat organised, it is not completely undetermined (Hörz 2009, 187). Emergence of order from noise is a dialectic of chance and necessity, i.e. determined chance and open necessity. "Humans shape actuality and their social environment by active practice with specific objectives. They thereby change the fields of possibilities and the stochastic distribution of statistical laws" (Hörz 2009, 71).

Hegel in this context stresses the role of activity when discussing the dialectic of chance and necessity that constitutes actuality:

> The activity is (α) likewise existent on its own account, independently (a man, a character); and at the same time it has its possibility only in the conditions and in the matter [itself]; (β) it is the movement of translating the conditions into the

The Dialectic of History

matter, and the latter into the former as the side of existence; more precisely [it is the movement] to make the matter [itself] go forth from the conditions, in which it is implicitly present, and to give existence to the matter by sublating the existence that the conditions have.

(Hegel 1830, §148)

Hans Heinz Holz argues in his book *Weltentwurf und Reflexion* (2005) that a dialectical concept of history needs to take into account that a new status of the world after a negation of the negation not simply eliminates the old status, but that this old status affects and overgrasps into the new one: The "disappeared" is "irrevocably present and operates in the future – in whatever transformed and transported way" (Holz 2005, 484, translation from German).

Progress does not proceed in history along a time line of successive real conditions. It is mediated by the continuation of past contents and purposes' essence in the comprehension of the having-been and therefore it is progress of the consciousness of freedom.

(Holz 2005, 486–487, translation from German)

Historical progress in the consciousness of freedom is not necessarily and automatically a progress towards or of freedom itself. Humans look into past experiences and this past itself constitutes a new field of possibilities. Reflection about the past can allow doing something differently in the future. It is however open if catastrophes are repeated through human action or if humans do everything in order to avoid their repetition by acting as to make alternatives more likely. The point is that the historical dialectic works backwards in time when we reflect on how we have come to where we are. In the backward dialectic, we try to make sense of the past by reconstructing and causally interpreting what has happened. In the forward dialectic, we project the past and the present into the future in order to imagine how a different state of affairs could look like. So the dialectic is a collision and unity of a backward and a forward dialectic. The past and the presence do however not determine, but just condition the outcome of the forward dialectic.

Humans reflect the dialectical reflections (i.e. contradictions that drive development) of the world in objects that they produce. They produce their own thoughts, each other as social beings through communication and therefore society, as well as physical and non-physical use-values. They are active, conscious, social, producing beings that can reflect about how a desirable world should look like. What distinguishes the worst architect from the best of bees is that the architect builds the cell in his mind before he constructs it in wax. At the end of every labour process, a result emerges which had already been conceived by the worker at the beginning, hence already existed ideally. Man not only effects a change of form in the materials of nature; he also realizes *[verwirklicht]* his own purpose in those materials. And this is a purpose he is conscious of, it determines the mode of his activity with the rigidity of a law, and he must subordinate his will to it.

(Marx 1867, 284)

The architect has a specific taste and there are particular requirements for the building s/he designs, which are considerations that let him/her make specific choices and construct models before the actual construction begins. A writer anticipates what s/he wants to write about before starting, s/he for example decides if it is a novel, an art book, or a social science book, where the novel is set, what kind of art the book covers, or what part of society the social science study shall cover. A bee in contrast acts much more driven by instincts and immediate needs. Creativity, self-consciousness, empathy, and morality are crucial forms of the human constitution that also shape the work process. The conscious social shaping of the world is the activity that allows humans to increase the likelihood of specific alternatives in existing fields of possibilities. History can go wrong, but it can also go right.

History is not necessarily first a catastrophe, then as a result of a revolution a different catastrophe, and finally a better society emerging out of the same logic as the second catastrophe. It is also not with necessity a repetition of catastrophes, first as tragedy and then as farce. All of these (and other) developments are paths that history can take, but they are not determined. Moments of structural crisis are culmination points of a system's antagonism. The big crisis that started in 2008 is just like the one that started in 1929 (and that led to the Second World War) a point of bifurcation, in which we find a dialectic of chance and necessity: It is certain that there will be change, but how this change will look like is not determined, which should give us hope to attempt the communist revolution now and in every crisis. Fascism and the Second World War were the outcomes of the crisis in 1929. According to Žižek's logic of history, history in the 1929 moment that eventually led to modernity's biggest barbarity and catastrophe thus far, *had to* go wrong, socialism was no option, and the catastrophes of Auschwitz, Hiroshima, Nagasaki, etc. *had to* be the result and at the same time the precondition that another time – this time – history could work differently.

The point about history that Wallerstein, Hörz, and Holz make is in contrast that in 1929 just like in 2008 the capitalist system entered deep crises and that the outcomes are in such situations never determined. There can be a catastrophe just like there can be liberation. Barbarism, socialism, or something different are possibilities in such situations. And this is why people should collectively act in a revolutionary manner. The outcome of their action is uncertain, but if they don't act the likelihood that fascism or another form of barbarity is the outcome increases, whereas democratic-socialist action is no guarantee for freedom, but increases the likelihood of freedom. Revolution can go wrong, not just the first time, but any time. Capitalism or another class society can reconstitute itself, which will result in a new set or contradictions that result in crisis, catastrophes, etc. *But revolution can also go right, which is why it is worth to fight.* Intelligent revolutionary strategy learns from the history of revolution, from failures, successes, and their contradictions. Moishe Postone stresses that in today's deep crisis, just like in any deep crisis, "the old slogan of 'socialism or barbarism' acquires new urgency, even if our understanding of both terms has been fundamentally transformed" (Postone 2012, 249).

Tariq Ali argues that the transition from feudalism to capitalism that resulted in the present form of democracy took 500 years and was "the result of violent clashes" (Ali 2009, 112) and dictatorships by Cromwell, Robespierre, Napoleon, etc. The "second transition" from capitalism to socialism would also have

> produced a period of dictatorship: Lenin, Stalin and Mao. Why should the collapse of the old social dictatorships in Russia and China, and their replacement by capitalism, not be seen as part of a long transition whose ultimate destination is presently invisible?
>
> (Ali 2009, 113)

The point of history is that there is no ultimate destination or finality, just dialectical development resulting from the interaction of objective structural contradictions and the subjective contradictions created and acted out in human agency. That the idea of communism went through Stalin and Mao is in no way a guarantee that the second time it will and must go right. It could go wrong again. Or it could never happen. Or it could happen differently. I am not saying history is relative, but rather that humans certainly can learn from previous mistakes and try to avoid them, but history can eventually also repeat itself as the repetition of mistakes just like it can contain breaks that make a difference. Collective action based on the democratic communist idea is not a saviour, but can increase the likelihood that history takes a humane direction.

Žižek is sceptical of the idea that sublation is a return, re-appropriation, or de-alienation of a lost essence or origin because such assumptions imply that an origin or foundation must have already existed or unfolds automatically in history. Žižek rather assumes that the emergence of essence constitutes retroactively this very essence: "The Essence retroactively constitutes itself through its process of externalization" (Žižek 2012, 235). For Žižek (2012, 259), communism is not "the subjective (re)appropriation of the alienated substantial content". The problem would be to assume that the negation of the negation is "a magical mechanism which guarantees that the final outcome of a process will always be happy" (Žižek 2012, 300).

The Hegelian sublation of the antagonism between essence and existence need however not be understood as a reconciliation with or return to the origin, the reconstitution of a primordial state, and a historical foundation that once existed, but can be seen as the struggle for and establishment of the ethico-logical foundation of society. For Hegel, truth is the correspondence of essence and existence. The notion of essence is an inherently ethico-political one. It immediately brings up ethico-political questions like: What is a good society? What are the possibilities inherent in society itself? Does current society realise the best possible life for all or not? Any political project just like any form of ethics needs foundational principles for discerning what to struggle for respectively what to consider as appropriate status of society. But what is the foundation of society? What principles are constitutive for all societies?

Humans have in all societies to relate to each other positively in order to survive. They have to communicate, work collaboratively together, and form and maintain communities. There can be no society without co-operation and the social, but certainly a society without competition and egotism. Co-operation is more foundational and substantial than competition. It is part of the essence of all societies. Co-operation can certainly be used for negative means, such as warfare so that it becomes a principle alienated from itself that serves an alien purpose. Warfare just like class is no essential principle, but a historical form of domination. If a true society is one, in which the basic structures correspond to their own essence, then this means that a class society (a society grounded in exploitation and domination) violates the essence of all societies and is a false society. A democratic socialist society, a society where humans are in common control of their conditions of existence, in contrast fully realises human essence and is a fully social and societal human existence that overcomes class societies' crippling of society and the social. The ethico-political imperative can therefore only be: Act so as to increase the likelihood, degree, and reality of socialism. Socialist elements and seeds exist in most societies. The point is to make these elements grow ever more and to find possibilities to maximise socialism in order to reduce class and capital.

The disappearance of capitalism and a creation of a socialist society is neither a return to an origin that once existed in a primeval society nor a creatio ex nihilo (socialist potentials, degrees of reality and elements have exited before), but rather a realisation of the ethico-logical and ethico-political essence of society, the creation of a society that corresponds to the essence of humans and society. There is no historical necessity or determination that leads from that which exists to the realisation of society's substantial essence. Such a realisation is rather a potential and question of the complexities of class struggles. In class societies, the realisation of society's essence is a not-yet. The transformation of the not-yet into the now and yet is however possible through social struggles that are conditioned by that which exists. The essence constitutes potentialities and with the development of society that which is possible in terms of a good life and with it the maximum qualities of the essence can expand (or shrink). "The fact *is, before it exists concretely,* it is, first, as *essence* or as unconditioned; second, it has immediate existence or is determined" (Hegel 2010, 416). The transition from the unconditioned essence to the immediate existence is brought about by collective action. There is no guarantee that it happens. Essences are also somewhat relative because everything has its own essence. The essence of society is a foundational ground of humanity, whereas the essence of capitalism is not because capitalism is a specific existential manifestation of a society that has historical character as a particular form of class society.

Concrete history is an undetermined path of approximations and distantiations from the realisation of society's essence that takes place through social struggles. And even if the essence is once realised, history does not stop, but continues to develop and to bear potentials for regression from or for further extension of the realised essence's qualities.

> The negativity and its negation are two different phases of the same historical process, straddled by man's historical action. The 'new' state is the truth of the old, but that truth does not steadily and automatically grow out of the earlier state; it can be set free only by an autonomous act on the part of men, that will cancel the whole of the existing negative state
>
> (Marcuse 1941/1955, 315)

Essence in society is connected with what humans could be (Marcuse 1937):

Here the concept of what could be, of inherent possibilities, acquires a precise meaning. What man can be in a given historical situation is determinable with regard to the following factors: the measure of control of natural and social productive factors, the level of the organization of labor, the development of needs in relation to possibilities for their fulfilment (especially the relation of what is necessary for the reproduction of life to the 'free' needs for gratification and happiness, for the 'good and the beautiful'), the availability, as material to be appropriated, of a wealth of cultural values in all areas of life.

(Marcuse 1937, 71)

The ethico-political is connected to questions of what can and should be because society *can* based on the existing preconditions reduce pain, misery, and injustice (Marcuse 1964, 106), use existing resources and capacities in ways that satisfy human needs in the best possible way, and minimise hard labour (Marcuse 1964, 112). The conditions and tendencies of the present are in class societies structured by objective antagonisms (such as in capitalism the ones between use-value/exchange-value, labour/capital, productive forces/relations of production, necessary labour/surplus-labour, social needs/capitalist production, social production/private appropriation, real/virtual, etc.). These antagonisms form the space of conditions for action and social struggles. History is shaped by a meta-dialectic of objective dialectics and the subjective dialectic of collective action, between conditioning necessity and the possibility for freedom from necessity (or enslavement by it) through societal praxis.

Axel Honneth (2008, 32) argues that "reified social relations merely represent a false framework for interpretation, an ontological veil concealing the fact of an underlying genuine form of human existence". Honneth in contrast to other contemporary critical theorists does not give up the connection of the notions of alienation and de-alienation to human essence, but rather argues that there is an "elementary structure of the human form of life characterised by care and existential interestedness" that are "always already there" (Honneth 2008, 32).

Honneth takes up insights from Michael Tomasello's (1999, 2008) development psychology and socialisation research: Recognition precedes cognition because children learn to take over the perspective of another person, which enables thinking and interaction/communication. Tomasello (2008, 1999) stresses in this respect the "9 month revolution": The child in its development starts after about nine months of perceiving an attachment figure whose perspective it takes over. It develops an emotional relation to this person. The child starts relating to the world and objects by observing how the attachment figure relates to objects. Developmental psychology confirms for Honneth that recognition by and of others and empathetic engagement precedes cognition: "The acknowledgement of the other constitutes a non-epistemic prerequisite for linguistic understanding" (Honneth 2008, 50). Honneth shows that human essence lies in the social foundation of society, that human social relations constitute this essence, and that essence manifests itself in human subjectivity. Honneth asserts that the essence is not a historical primordial state of society that once existed and was lost, but that rather it is a foundational structure of human social relations.

Reification that occurs in instrumental reason, exploitation, and domination is for Honneth "forgetfulness of recognition" (Honneth 2008, 56): They can make us forget that our knowledge, being, and cognition are based on recognition and empathetic engagement. Judith Butler comments on Honneth's concept of reification that he has "an Arcadian myth" of a "'before'" (Butler, in: Honneth 2008, 108) and that both "love and aggression" would be coextensive with human being" (Butler, in: Honneth 2008, 109). Such relativism that assumes two human substances has problematic logical implications: Applying this form of argument to child development and recognition means that parents have to treat their kid both with love and aggression in order that the child develops. If thought to the end, then Judith Butler with her relativist anti-essentialism indirectly justifies violence against children. That there is an ethico-logical-political essence of society and the human is a crucial political foundation for a just world.

2.6 Auschwitz

Auschwitz is the negative symbol of the catastrophe of modernity, the absolute negativity of history. It is therefore well suited as a case for reflections on the dialectic of history. In one of his studies on Hegel, Adorno (1993) uses the dictum from *Parsifal* that "the wound can be healed only by the spear that smote it" that also Žižek employs:

> Using the language of epistemology and the language of speculative metaphysics extrapolated from it, Hegel expressed the idea that the reified and rationalized society of the bourgeois era, the society in which a nature-dominating reason had come to fruition, could become a society worthy of human beings — not by regressing to older, irrational stages prior to the division of labor but only by applying its rationality to itself, in other words, only through a healing awareness of the marks of unreason in its own reason, and the traces of the rational in the irrational as well. Since then the element of unreason has become

evident in the consequences of modern rationality, which threaten universal catastrophe. In Parsifal Richard Wagner, the Schopenhauerian, put Hegel's experience in terms of the ancient topos: only the spear that inflicted the wound can heal it. Hegel's philosophical consciousness suffered more from the estrangement between subject and object, between consciousness and reality, than had any previous philosophical consciousness. But his philosophy had the strength not to flee from this suffering back into the chimera of a world and a subject of pure immediacy. It did not let itself be distracted from its awareness that only through the realized truth of the whole would the unreason of a merely particular reason, that is, a reason that merely serves particular interests, disintegrate.

(Adorno 1993, 74)

Adorno expresses the same idea as Žižek, namely that change is mostly then progressive when it is not a return to a previous state of society, but a sublation of that which exists so that the best elements are taken from it, the bad ones shaken off, and new ones are developed based on that which exists. But we should here bear in mind Roy Bhaskar's insights that there are different forms of sublation. And each situation and contradiction may depend on the context and require a different, more or less substantial and radical form of the negation of the negation.

Marx's classical example of a constitutive negation that needs to be negated is the capitalist contradiction between productive forces and relations of production. Capitalist technology creates technological potentials that socialise labour and the means of production, but at the same time deepen the class antagonism. This means that a communism that emerges from capitalism should further develop preconditions that already exist in the capitalist means of production and communication. How such sublations of these means however look like depends very much on their specific forms.

There are use-values and technologies that are predominantly means of destruction. The atom bomb cannot be put to a positive use. Sublation of the atom bomb in a communist society must therefore mean a radical, substantial negation that gets rid of this technology of war. The same can be said of nuclear power plants: They are technologies of production, what Marx termed motor mechanisms that produce energy, but have destructive effects. So although in a socialist society, nuclear power plant workers may be paid well, a socialist nuclear power plant is just like a capitalist one not a good power plant because it threatens to extinct human life on Earth and destroys nature to a massive degree. It is not a common cause, but a common enemy of humanity. Given that not just human-produced use-values that we need in order to survive are commons, but also nature is a commons that all humans require in order to survive, we can infer that technologies that destroy nature cannot be socialist technologies at all because they do not foster common causes.

What about the Internet? It is certainly not a principal enemy of the people. In its current capitalist and state-controlled forms, it however is a means of domination and control. This becomes evident in corporate social media's exploitation of digital labour, the mass monitoring of online communication operated by the surveillance-industrial complex whose existence Edward Snowden revealed, etc. (Fuchs 2014a, 2014b, 2014c, 2015). Domination has been designed into a lot of online platforms. At the same time, the Internet fosters the knowledge commons that have socialist potentials. So a socialist transformation will not abolish the Internet in a radical sublation, but undertake sublations that abolish capitalist ownership of platforms, online commerce, state surveillance of users, etc. as well as the design patterns domination brings about, whereas it will further develop the online commons so that a commons-based and public service Internet can take full effect.

"The wound can be healed only by the spear that smote it". It is not the spear that smites, not the knife that kills, and not the gas chamber that causes mass extinction. Technologies are tools operated by human beings. It is humans and groups of humans having specific ideologies and installing specific systems who smite, kill, and attempt to extinct others. Wagner's theme is rather functionalist and reads agency in a techno-deterministic manner into technologies. If it is not the spear that creates the wound, but the human who with the help of the spear does so, then it is also not the Internet that does something (exploits us, monitors us, etc.), but there are human beings with specific interests shaping and designing the Internet in such ways that it is a means of control, exploitation, etc. Given that the Internet has no agency, it therefore will also not save us. Not technology will save us, only humans can. An alternatively designed and shaped Internet can however be a tool applied for the better in a free society.

According to Moishe Postone, the logic of capitalism resulted in Auschwitz. It was the specific agency of the Nazis that created and operated Auschwitz, but the Nazis operated in the context of capitalist modernity. Modern anti-Semitism emerged from the fetishistic structure of capitalism, it is "a particularly pernicious fetish form" (Postone 2003, 95). "The Jews were held responsible for economic crises and identified with the range of social restructuring and dislocation resulting from rapid capitalist industrialization" (Postone 2003, 89). The "specific characteristics of the power attributed to the Jews by modern anti-Semitism – abstractness, intangibility, universality, mobility – are all characteristics of the value dimension of the social forms fundamentally characterizing capitalism" (Postone 2003, 91).

Using Deleuze and Latour, Žižek writes:

> We can think of Auschwitz as an assemblage – in which the agents were not just the Nazi executioners but also the Jews, the complex network of trans, the gas ovens, the logistics of feeding the prisoners, separating and distributing clothes, extracting the gold teeth, collecting the hair and ashes and so on.
>
> (Žižek 2014, 8, footnote 8)

Applying Actor Network Theory (ANT) to Auschwitz not just bestows agency to inanimate things, but also creates the impression that all "actants", including the Jews, had the same influence and power in the very situation and event of Auschwitz. When asking the question of responsibility, such a relativist approach therefore implies that all involved human and non-human actants had the same kind of responsibility. It is then no longer possible to name and shame the beast – the Nazis, the SS, those who supported the Nazis, etc. – that actively planned and executed the Shoah. In the specific footnote just quoted, it is not clear if Žižek only outlines the application of ANT to Auschwitz or if he in this specific case shares this analysis.

Auschwitz was not an assemblage of humans and non-humans, but a negative factory:

> Auschwitz was a factory to 'destroy value', that is, to destroy the personifications of the abstract. Its organization was that of a fiendishly inverted industrial process, the aim of which was to 'liberate' the concrete from the abstract. The first step was to dehumanize and reveal the Jews for what they 'really are' – ciphers, numbered abstractions. The second step was to then eradicate that abstractness, trying in the process to wrest away the last remnants of the concrete material 'use-value': clothes, gold, hair.
>
> (Postone 2003, 95)

Adorno writes that after Auschwitz there is a new categorical imperative: "A new categorical imperative has been imposed by Hitler upon unfree mankind: to arrange their thoughts and actions so that Auschwitz will not repeat itself, so that nothing similar will happen" (Adorno 1973, 365). He argued that after 1945, there was a "continuing potential" for Auschwitz's "recurrence" because "barbarism continues as long as the fundamental conditions that favoured that relapse continue largely unchanged" (Adorno

2003, 19). Forces enabling a repetition would be authoritarian culture that creates and authoritarian personality and the "revival of nationalism" (Adorno 2003, 32). The one thing that could be done in order to reduce the danger of repeating Auschwitz would be anti-fascist education.

Adorno gave a lot of attention to how education in post-1945 Germany could be used for fostering anti-fascist engagement with the past in order to prevent a second Auschwitz from happening. He was not convinced that the danger of such a repetition was banned. Auschwitz haunts Germany like a ghost, a living dead that can re-awake its livelihood at any time:

> National Socialism lives on, and to this day we don't know whether it is only the ghost of what was so monstrous that it didn't even die off with its own death, or whether it never died in the first place – whether the readiness for unspeakable actions survives in people, as in the social conditions that hem them in.

> (Adorno 1986, 115)

Adorno does not assume that the catastrophe of modern history results in learning from the past, a conjuncture of barbarism and post-barbaric learning that avoids repetition. He is much more sceptical and argues that de-barbarising politics and education need to be fostered and attempted, but are no guarantee against the repetition of barbarism as long as the root causes that enable the possibility of barbarism continue to exist: "We will not have come to terms with the past until the causes of what happened then are no longer active. Only because these causes live on does the spell of the past remain, to this very day, unbroken" (Adorno 1986, 129).

If there is always a "liberating aspect of the wound" (Žižek 2014, 138) and the "wound itself is its own healing" (Žižek 2014, 141), then this can imply that there are liberating aspects of Auschwitz – the deepest wound of capitalism – and that Auschwitz is itself the solution that guarantees its own non-reoccurrence. This would mean that Auschwitz first has to occur in order to not occur a second time. If the Allied Forces had relatively quickly defeated Hitler and the Nazis, then Auschwitz, which started operating as a negative factory in late 1940, would not have happened at that time. So there could have been another solution that would have avoided going through Auschwitz in the first instance. One could then however argue: If it had not happened then, it would have happened at another place and at another time. This could certainly have been the case, but if we believe Adorno, then Auschwitz as a wound cannot heal itself and after 1945, the threat of repetition has remained. Authoritarian personalities implicated by authoritarian structures in society, anti-Semitism, and fascist potentials have not vanished.

Since the 2008 crisis started, far-right and fascist movements and parties have gained strength in many European countries. One can certainly learn from history, but this does not mean that all humans do or want to learn in such a way. Auschwitz does not guarantee its non-repetition. The only force that can guarantee Adorno's categorical imperative is anti-fascist agency and the political attempt to overcome the very causes of fascist potentials in society. Such agency can however not be idealistic and voluntaristic, but must be concretely related to the fascist potentials and dangers that exist at specific times in specific contexts in society. Auschwitz was no liberation, but hell on Earth. Non-repetition is not a logical-historical consequence of Auschwitz itself, but rather requires structural changes and agency that can break the continuity and re-creation of the conditions that created and can continue to create Auschwitz.

Žižek again and again analyses Nazi ideology and society, for example when writing that "Nazism displaces class struggle onto racial struggle" (Žižek 2008, 261). His own analysis makes sense in respect to the assumption that humans *can* learn from history:

> We can say that one result of Nazi Germany and its defeat was the institution of much higher ethical standards of human rights and international justice; but to claim that this result in any sense 'justifies' Nazism would be an obscenity.
> (Žižek 2014, 131)

There is, however, as Adorno stresses, no necessity and determination that humans learn from history and do not repeat the same catastrophes.

With formulations like the ones that the "wound itself is its own healing" (Žižek 2014, 141) and that history "will always [first] go wrong" (Žižek 2014, 36), Žižek contradicts parts of his own analysis and the assumption that history is a contingent process. There is a strange and unresolved ambivalence between absolute freedom and absolute necessity in Žižek's concept of history.

Žižek argues that Heidegger was neither "a fully fledged Nazi" nor "politically naïve", that there is neither a "direct link" nor a divisive gap between Heidegger's thought and Nazi ideology, but that "the space for Nazi engagement was opened up by the immanent failure or inconsistency of his thought" (Žižek 2012, 882). Žižek interprets Heidegger's thought as being constituted by a "missed potential" (Žižek 2012, 903) – the turn towards communism. Where "Heidegger erred most (his Nazi engagement), he came closest to the truth" (Žižek 2008, 148, see also 139). Heidegger was looking at Nazism for "a revolutionary Event" (Žižek 2008, 142), but it was, Žižek argues, the wrong revolutionary force that did not bring about a revolution at all, but a brutalisation of capitalism.

Žižek judges Heidegger based on a retroactive logic: looking backwards in history, he argues that Heidegger's theory had to make a choice if it sides with the Nazis or others, such as the socialists or communists. We do not know if Heidegger ever considered joining a left political movement, probably not. I don't see why we should judge intellectual thought and a theory based on what it could have (according to Žižek' assumptions) been. The point is that thought should rather be judged by how it actually developed.

That young radical thinkers such as Herbert Marcuse and Günther Anders saw a left potential in Heidegger does not imply that it was something that Heidegger himself ever considered as feasible. And even if so, then it is more important how his thought actually developed. Marcuse (1934) himself considered Heidegger after his turn against him as part of the anti-Hegelian Nazi philosophy. As Nazi philosopher, Heidegger's works engaged in "'existential' opportunism" (Marcuse 1934, 29) that justified Hitler's regime and tried to give a death blow to Hegel so that it envisaged a Fall of the Titans of German philosophy" (Marcuse 1934, 30). Hans Heinz Holz (2011b, 554) characterises Heidegger's work as a form of "romantic anti-Hegelianism".

The question how deeply influenced Heidegger's thought was by National Socialism remained disputed for a long time. On the one hand, there were apologists such as Hannah Arendt, Jean-Paul Sartre, Jacques Derrida, or Richard Rorty who felt inspired by Heidegger and defended and took up the content of his philosophical works. The impression that Heidegger's work made on their own thoughts blinded them for his politics. On the other hand, critical theorists, especially Theodor W. Adorno and Jürgen Habermas, argued that Heidegger was a fascist and that National Socialism also shaped his philosophy.

This controversy remains topical until today. New insights were gained by the 2014 publication of Heidegger's (2014a, 2014b, 2014c) *Black Notebooks*. Not just did he stay a member of the Nazi Party until the liberation from National Socialism in 1945, but the *Notebooks* show that Heidegger's thought was in these years also deeply entrenched in anti-Semitism, the ideological core of Nazism.

In these notebooks, Heidegger wrote that Jews are calculating profiteers, would have lived based on the principle of race, but resist that the Nazis apply this principle to them. He writes that the Nazis would only practice in an unlimited manner what the Jews would have practiced long before them. World Judaism would be uprooted and abstract and would not want to sacrifice the blood of Jews in wars, whereas the Germans would only have the choice to sacrifice what Heidegger describes as the best blood of all – German blood – in warfare. "The Jews have 'lived' the longest with their pronounced calculating aptitude according to the 'racial principle', which is why they most heavily contest its full application" (Heidegger 1936c, 56, translation from German[4]). Heidegger here basically blames the Jews for Auschwitz and says that they themselves have deeply advanced the instrumental logic on which it was based. Heidegger makes the typical Nazi move to blame the Jews for capitalism. He argues that they have an inherently *calculating, instrumental reason* and thereby identifies them with capitalism. He identifies the Jews "with the range of social restructuring and dislocation resulting from rapid capitalist industrialization" (Postone 2003, 89) and typically for "Nazism displaces class struggle onto racial struggle" (Žižek 2008, 261).

Many commentators have argued that the *Black Notebooks* show once and for all that Heidegger was a convinced Nazi, an anti-Semite, and a Nazi-apologiser. They criticise that Heidegger argues that the Jews are themselves to blame for the Shoah. Given Heidegger's anti-Semitism, it seems almost cynical that Žižek argues to see Heidegger not just in a negative light, but to consider retroactively that it could have been different. Heidegger did in the years 1934–1941 that are covered in the *Notebooks* not retroactively reflect on the ideological foundation of Nazism in order to make an ideological turn. He did not learn from his own history and stayed the same Nazi he was during his time as Rector at the University of Freiburg.

In a truly retroactive manner, the *Black Notebooks* allow us to posit Heidegger's thoughts own preconditions. The *Notebooks* give insights into the past that were thus far contested and not entirely clear because Heidegger tended to be silent on Auschwitz and the Nazis after 1945 (which is in itself problematic). Retroactively the *Notebooks* show and allow the judgement that Heidegger was a Nazi, that his thought was, is and remains deeply reactionary and fascist, and that critical theory can only be critical without Heidegger.

2.7 Conclusion

Žižek shows in *Absolute Recoil* (and previous Hegelian works such as *Less than Nothing*) the importance of repeating Hegel's dialectical philosophy in contemporary capitalism. In order to adequately and critically understand the world today, we need a materialist and dialectical theory that grasps society as a dialectical totality. Žižek keeps up the dialectical fire and gives the idea that Hegelian dialectics matters a broader publicity. Such Hegelian works are of high relevance for a critical theory of 21st century society and its constitution within the world in general.

Within a proper dialectical debate it is inevitable that questions about the dialectic of the dialectic arise: How shall the dialectic adequately be conceived today? Žižek contributes especially to reconceptualising the dialectical logic and based on it the dialectic of history. He uses both versions of the dialectic for critical interventions into specific questions of contemporary culture, politics, ideology, theory, and ethics.

The key aspects of Žižek's dialectical materialism are the Hegelian concept of the absolute recoil and the notion of retroactivity: In dialectical development, a sublation posits its own preconditions. It returns to itself and thereby constitutes itself. Žižek has in his books again and again stressed the importance of the logic of retroactivity and has in *Absolute Recoil* conceptualised the dialectic's positing of its own preconditions as retroactivity. This retroactivity is of logical nature, but at the same time the logical is historical and so retroactivity is for Žižek also an important principle of the dialectic of history.

I have argued in this chapter that the absolute recoil that in a retroactive manner constitutes its own preconditions and thereby makes a thing constitute itself, is an important, but incomplete dialectical principle. Marx uses this notion of the absolute recoil implicitly for describing the logic of the accumulation of capital: A specific capital M_1 must in order to survive increase itself into M_1' that again becomes the starting point of a new accumulation process M_2. But there is a dynamic in between that Žižek is aware of and that constitutes the starting and end point: the exploitation of labour and labour's production of commodities. Žižek is not unaware of the dialectical process, but the book title *Absolute Recoil* stresses as the main principle of the dialectic how the result of the dialectic turns into preconditions. This stress is incomplete because the dynamic in between starting and end point that becomes a new starting point is of crucial importance.

I have argued that we need to make a Heraclitusian move for properly conceptualising 21st-century dialectics: Yes, the dialectic is the absolute recoil that posits its own preconditions. But for this self-referencing and self-constitution, in which something returns into itself as something different that constitutes a new positive difference that makes a difference, to occur, the dialectic needs to burn: The dialectical fire extinguishes a contradiction and thereby itself, but this extinguishment is at the same time a self-kindling of the dialectic and the kindle of a new fire, in which the old is sublated as the new and constitutes a new contradiction. *The dialectic is the absolute recoil in and through being a fire that continuously extinguishes and kindles itself.*

For Žižek, the dialectic is a development from nothing to nothing and from less than nothing to nothing. This assumption is a specific Žižekian version of the negative dialectic. I have argued in this chapter that the dialectic develops from nothing to nothing and at the same time from something to something, nothing to something, something to nothing. It is this complex unity of dialectics of something and nothing that constitutes the world and its development potentialities.

In his conceptualisation of the dialectic of history, Žižek on the one hand uses the notions of the parallax, the absolute recoil, and retroactivity for stressing that there is a non-dialecticisable intruder/excess that keeps the dialectic open. I have argued that Žižek with this assumption gives too much into postmodern thought that he at the same time paradoxically detests as an enemy that does not want to question the capitalist totality. A proper dialectic of the totality sees the source of differentiation inside the dialectic itself as the dialectic is constituted within a complex field of possibilities that is based on a dialectic of chance and necessity. I have argued that whereas Žižek on the one hand concedes too much to postmodernism, he on the other hand also falls back into a version of a mechanical dialectic that sees the catastrophe as the absolute necessity for liberation so that history and revolutions *have to* fail the first time and through this failure can succeed later.

For conceptualising a dialectic for the 21st century world and the world's society, I have not just invoked Heraclitus, but also the works of the two German dialectical Marxist philosophers Herbert Hörz (born in 1933) and Hans Heinz Holz (1927–2011). Their major works, especially *Weltentwurf und Reflexion* (Holz 2005) and *Materialistische Dialektik* (Hörz 2009), are rather unknown internationally because they have thus far not been translated into English. I have stressed the importance of Hörz's concept of dialectical determinism for a proper dialectic of chance and necessity, openness and determinateness, freedom and constraint. Herbert Hörz grounds his dialectical heuristics in contemporary advances in science, such as the theories of complexity and self-organisation, and at the same time has worked out the specificity of the dialectic and the application of new theories to a society based on dialectical philosophy. Hans Heinz Holz is probably one of the most important dialectical philosophers of the totality of the 20th century. He shows how the totality is dialectical and thereby neither mechanically determined nor relativistic. And he grounded these insights in a detailed and profound study of the history of dialectical philosophy: His posthumous work *Dialektik: Problemgeschichte von der Antike bis*

Conclusion

zur Gegenwart presents in five volumes and almost 3,000 pages the history of dialectical philosophy. Also this major work is thus far not available in English. Holz's own dialectic connects Leibniz, Hegel, and Marx and takes a historical approach to the dialectical development of dialectical philosophy itself. Readers of this book who are in the structural position to bring about the publication of book translations, are well advised to have a look at the works of Hans Heinz Holz and Herbert Hörz if they care about the dialectic.

Wallerstein, Hörz, and Holz together allow us to see that history is constituted in a specific period as field of possibilities, in which humans can by collective praxis increase the possibility of certain alternatives. The future is contingent because society is inherently contradictory in complex manners. History is a dialectic of chance and necessity: The possible futures are constituted through the presence and the past, but the exact outcome is not determined and therefore open, which gives us hope that we can make a difference and that the future does not have to be catastrophic. The past lives on in the present, but it is not determined if humans adequately learn from it and can make a difference the next time. The next catastrophe always looms just democratic socialism looms.

Hans Heinz Holz has shown in impressive manner that the dialectic is itself subject to a historical dialectic. Slavoj Žižek's *Absolute Recoil* helps us keep the fire of the dialectic alive. The point is how to conceptualise the dialectic today so that it can be a proper revolutionary theory. The aspect I want to stress is twofold: (a) It is important that we further develop dialectical materialism by enabling engagement with major contributions (such as the ones by Holz and Hörz). (b) The dialectic manifests itself in specific realms of being. In the 21st century, one important (but of course not the only) dimension of society has to do with media, communication, culture, and the digital. This realm continues to be devalued in Marxist theory and belittled as a superstructure (not necessarily in Žižek's works itself). So we need to repeat Hegel's dialectic in general, but this repetition should at the same time be one that manifests itself in a critical dialectical theory of media, communication, culture, the digital, and the Internet (Fuchs 2008, 2011, 2014a, 2014c, 2015, Fuchs and Mosco 2012, Fuchs and Sandoval 2014, Sandoval et al. 2014).

Notes

1 In *Less than Nothing*, Žižek (2012, 315) distinguishes between total and partial sublations.
2 "Im Setzen des Anderen wird meine Reflexion-in-mich zugleich Reflexion-meiner-in-ein-Anderes ('äußere Reflexion')".

3 "Jede Substanz ist das (passive, gesetzte) Resultat der Wechselwirkung aller Substanzen und jede ist zugleich aktiv (aktives, setzendes) Moment dieser Wechselwirkung".

4 "Die Juden 'leben' bei ihrer betont rechnerischen Begabung am längsten schon nach dem Rasseprinzip, weshalb sie sich auch am heftigsten gegen die uneingeschränkte Anwendung zur Wehr setzen".

References

Adorno, Theodor W. 2008. *Lectures on Negative Dialectics*. Cambridge: Polity.

Adorno, Theodor W. 2003. *Can One Live after Auschwitz? A Philosophical Reader*. Stanford, CA: Stanford University Press.

Adorno, Theodor W. 1993. *Hegel: Three Studies*. Cambridge, MA: MIT Press.

Adorno, Theodor W. 1986. What Does Coming to Term with the Past Mean? In *Bitburg in Moral and Political Perspective*, ed. Geoffrey H. Hartmann, 114–129. Bloomington: Indiana University Press.

Adorno, Theodor W. 1973. *Negative Dialectics*. London: Routledge.

Ali, Tariq. 2009. *The Idea of Communism*. London: Seagull.

Bhaskar, Roy. 1993. *Dialectic: The Pulse of Freedom*. London: Verso.

Fuchs, Christian. 2015. *Culture and Economy in the Age of Social Media*. New York: Routledge

Fuchs, Christian. 2014a. *Digital Labour and Karl Marx*. New York: Routledge.

Fuchs, Christian. 2014b. *OccupyMedia! The Occupy Movement and Social Media in Crisis Capitalism*. Winchester: Zero Books.

Fuchs, Christian. 2014c. *Social Media: A Critical Introduction*. London: Sage.

Fuchs, Christian. 2011. *Foundations of Critical Media and Information Studies*. London: Routledge.

Fuchs, Christian. 2008. *Internet and Society. Social Theory in the Information Age*. New York: Routledge.

Fuchs, Christian. 2003. The Self-Organization of Matter. *Nature, Society, and Thought* 16 (3): 281–313.

Fuchs, Christian and Vincent Mosco, eds. 2012. Marx Is Back. The Importance of Marxist Theory and Research for Critical Communication Studies Today. *tripleC: Communication, Capitalism & Critique* 10 (2): 127–632.

Fuchs, Christian and Marisol Sandoval, eds. 2014. *Critique, Social Media and the Information Society*. New York: Routledge.

Hegel, Georg Wilhelm Friedrich. 2010. *The Science of Logic*. Cambridge: Cambridge University Press.

Hegel, Georg Wilhelm Friedrich. 1892. *Lectures on the History of Philosophy*. Volume 1. London: Kegan.

Hegel, Georg Wilhelm Friedrich. 1830. *The Encyclopaedia Logic (With the Zusätze)*. Indianapolis, IN: Hackett.

Hegel, Georg Wilhelm Friedrich. 1830 [German]. *Enzyklopädie der philosophischen Wissenschaften I: Die Wissenschaft der Logik. Werke 8.* Frankfurt am Main: Suhrkamp.

Hegel, Georg Wilhelm Friedrich. 1813/1816. *Wissenschaft der Logik II. Werke 6.* Frankfurt am Main: Suhrkamp.

Heidegger, Martin. 2014a. *Überlegungen II–IV (Schwarze Hefte 1931–1938). Gesamtausgabe 94.* Frankfurt am Main: Vittorio Klostermann.

Heidegger, Martin. 2014b. *Überlegungen VII–XI (Schwarze Hefte 1938–1939). Gesamtausgabe 95.* Frankfurt am Main: Vittorio Klostermann.

Heidegger, Martin. 2014c. *Überlegungen XII–XV (Schwarze Hefte 1939–1941). Gesamtausgabe 96.* Frankfurt am Main: Vittorio Klostermann.

Heraclitus. 2001. *Fragments.* New York: Penguin.

Holz, Hans Heinz. 2011a. *Dialektik. Problemgeschichte von der Antike bis zur Gegenwart. Band I: Antike. Die Ausbreitung der Dialektik.* Darmstadt: Wissenschaftliche Buchgesellschaft.

Holz, Hans Heinz. 2011b. *Dialektik. Problemgeschichte von der Antike bis zur Gegenwart. Band V: Neuzeit 3. Einheit und Widerspruch III. Die Ausbreitung der Dialektik.* Darmstadt: Wissenschaftliche Buchgesellschaft.

Holz, Hans Heinz. 2005. *Weltentwurf und Reflexion. Versuch einer Grundlegung der Dialektik.* Stuttgart: J.B. Metzler.

Honneth, Axel. 2008. *Reification. A New Look at an Old Idea. With Commentaries by Judith Butler, Raymond Geuss and Jonathan Lear.* Oxford: Oxford University Press.

Hörz, Hebert. 2009. *Materialistische Dialektik. Aktuelles Denkinstrument zur Zukunftsgestaltung.* Berlin: trafo.

Jameson, Frederic. 2009. *Valances of the Dialectic.* London: Verso.

Marcuse, Herbert. 1964. Ethik und Revolution. In *Schriften*, Volume 8, 100–114. Frankfurt am Main: Suhrkamp.

Marcuse, Herbert. 1941/1955. *Reason and Revolution. Hegel and the Rise of Social Theory.* London: Routledge. Second edition.

Marcuse, Herbert. 1937. The Concept of Essence. In *Negations: Essays in Critical Theory*, 43–87. London: Free Association.

Marcuse, Herbert. 1934. The Struggle against Liberalism in the Totalitarian View of the State. In *Negations. Essays in Critical Theory*, 1–30. London: MayFlyBooks.

Marx, Karl. 1869. *The Eighteenth Brumaire of Louis Bonaparte.* Moscow: Progress.

Marx, Karl. 1867. *Capital.* Volume 1. London: Penguin.

Marx, Karl. 1857/1858. *Grundrisse.* London: Penguin.

Moseley, Fred and Tony Smith, eds. 2014. *Marx's Capital and Hegel's Logic.* Leiden: Brill.

Postone, Moishe. 2012. Thinking the Global Crisis. *The South Atlantic Quarterly* 111 (2): 227–249.

Postone, Moishe. 2003. The Holocaust and the Trajectory of the Twentieth Century. In *Catastrophe and Meaning. The Holocaust and the Twentieth Century*, ed. Moishe Postone and Eric Santner, 81–114. Chicago, IL: University of Chicago Press.

Sandoval, Marisol, Christian Fuchs, Jernej A. Prodnik, Sebastian Sevignani and Thomas Allmer, eds. 2014. Philosophers of the World Inite! Theorising Digital Labour and Virtual Work – Definitions, Dimensions and Forms. *tripleC: Communication, Capitalism & Critique* 12 (2): 464–801.

Tomasello, Michael. 2008. *Origins of Human Communication.* Cambridge, MA: MIT Press.

Tomasello, Michael. 1999. *The Cultural Origins of Human Cognition.* Cambridge, MA: Harvard University Press.

Wallerstein, Immanuel. 2013. Structural Crisis, or Why Capitalists May No Longer Find Capitalism Rewarding. In *Does Capitalism Have a Future?* 9–35. Oxford: Oxford University Press.

Wallerstein, Immanuel. 2011. *Historical Capitalism.* London: Verso.

Žižek, Slavoj. 2014. *Absolute Recoil. Towards a New Foundation of Dialectical Materialism.* London: Verso.

Žižek, Slavoj. 2012. *Less than Nothing. Hegel and the Shadow of Dialectical Materialism.* London: Verso.

Žižek, Slavoj. 2009a. *Living in the End Times.* London: Verso.

Žižek, Slavoj. 2009b. *First as Tragedy, then as Farce.* London: Verso.

Žižek, Slavoj. 2008. *In Defense of Lost Causes.* London: Verso.

Žižek, Slavoj. 2006. *The Parallax View.* Cambridge, MA: MIT Press.

References

Chapter Three

The Critique of the Political Economy of the Media and Communication

3.1 Introduction

The Critique of the Political Economy of Media and Communication is an approach that applies theory, philosophy, and empirical research to analyse and critically reflect on the interrelation of communication, capitalism, domination, and power, thereby generating knowledge that can play a significant role in social praxis aimed at changing the world.

> The basic questions of media economics in communication studies as a critique of the political economy of the media include the analysis of the relationship between the media and capitalist society, i.e. the role of the media in all material, economic, social, political and cultural human life.[1]
>
> (Knoche 2002, 105)

The Critique of the Political Economy is one of the approaches within the Political Economy of the Media and Communication. Other forms of the Political Economy of the Media and Communication go back to neoclassical economics, neo-Keynesianism, institutionalism, feminist political economy, political ecology, and other approaches (see Hardy 2014, Mosco 2009, Winseck 2011). These approaches are partly overlapping and cannot be clearly distinguished from each other. Nevertheless, one can certainly distinguish

DOI: 10.4324/9781003331087-5

in general between orthodox approaches, which are neoclassical, neoliberal, and neo-conservative, and heterodox approaches.

This discussion piece deals with the relevance of the Critique of the Political Economy of the Media and Communication in today's society. Section 3.2 provides a brief introduction to the field of the Critique of the Political Economy of the Media and Communication. Section 3.3 explores the relevance of Marx's theory for media and communication studies. Section 3.4 presents an example of the application of the Critique of the Political economy of the Media and Communication, namely the analysis of the political economy of alternative media and social movements.

3.2 The Research Field of the Critique of the Political Economy of the Media and Communication

The approaches to the critique of capitalism, which go back to Marx and are summarised by the terms "critique of the political economy" and "critical political economy", have a long tradition and a relatively large number of manifestations (cf. Bidet and Kouvelakis 2008). These approaches differ in terms of their subject matter, the way in which theory is formed and oriented, the role of empirical and theoretical research, the relationship between structure and agency, and the relationship between economy and society. However, they also have in common that they always see the analysed subject area in the context of capitalist rule, power structures, classes, class struggles, forms of production and reproduction, and alternative societal formations. To speak of Marx therefore does not mean fixating on one person or one book, but orienting oneself towards a complex, multi-layered, open, and dynamically developing tradition of theory and research. If one wants to rediscover Marx, there are many starting points, possibilities, and theoretical versions.

The expression of interest in the Marx-inspired critique of capitalism and critical social analysis is related in a complex way to societal development and the results of social struggles and class struggles. In the wake and immediate aftermath of the 1968 student movement, this interest was relatively strong. With the rise of neoliberal capitalism combined with the collapse of "actually existing socialism" and the rise of postmodern approaches that have rejected Marx-influenced critical social analysis as a totalitarian "grand narrative", have devoted themselves to microanalysis and micropolitics, and have believed in an end to history, the interest in the critical political economy declined

TABLE 3.1 Average annual number of mentions of categories critical of capitalism in the titles of social science journal articles in specific time periods

Time period	Number of average mentions per year
1970–1979	535
1980–1989	821
1990–1999	506
2000–2009	434
2010–2019	799

Data source: Social Sciences Citation Index (accessed 13 April 2021; keyword search: Marx* OR capitalis* OR commodi*).

significantly. The new global economic crisis that started in 2008, the crises of national and transnational state power (including the European Union) as a result of austerity measures and short-sighted reactions to refugees and war, the political and ideological crisis of the neoliberal model of regulation, and the social crisis characterised by precarious living and working conditions that affect young people in particular in many parts of the world, have together led to a crisis of legitimacy of capitalism. In the course of this crisis, interest in the critique of capitalism and society influenced by Marx has increased significantly.

This theoretical analysis can be empirically substantiated for the social sciences. Table 3.1 shows the number of mentions of keywords critical of capitalism in the titles of social science journal articles indexed in the Social Sciences Citation Index for different time periods. In the 1970s and 1980s, the number was significantly higher than in the 1990s and the first decade of the new millennium. Since 2010, the annual average number has increased significantly again, almost to the level of the 1980s. The turbulent social times in which we live have obviously led to an increase in interest in and engagement with the critique of political economy in the social sciences.

The Critique of the Political Economy of the Media and Communication has become institutionalised to a certain degree, especially internationally and in Great Britain, the United States, Canada, and Latin America (see Mosco 2009, Wasko 2014). In the International Association for Media and Communication Research, there has been a very active Political Economy Section since 1978. Dedicated to the Political Economy of Communication are a number of academic journals such as *tripleC: Communication, Capitalism & Critique* or *The Political Economy of Communication*; conferences, textbooks and courses, anthologies, handbooks, research projects, young researchers in the form of doctoral students, etc.

Vincent Mosco (2009, 2) defines the approach of the Political Economy of the Media and Communication as "the study of the social relations, particularly the power relations, that mutually constitute the production, distribution, and consumption of resources, including communication resources". According to Mosco, an analysis of communication phenomena using the approach of the critique of the political economy is about relating the object of study to processes of commodification (of content, labour, and audience), globalisation and internationalisation, privatisation, liberalisation, commercialisation, concentration processes (horizontal and vertical integration, strategic alliances, joint ventures), structuration processes (class relations, racism, gender relations, etc.) and social praxis (social movements, social change, protest, etc.).

Graham Murdock and Peter Golding emphasise that capitalist media sell information as a commodity and/or are integrated into the overall economy as advertising platforms (-see Murdock and Golding 1974). The specificity of the media system, they argue, is that it publicly communicates ideas about the economy and politics, making ideology critique a central task of the Critique of the Political Economy of the Media and Communication, in addition to analysing the role of the media in capitalism. Murdock and Golding (2005, 61) argue that the Critique of the Political Economy of the Media and Communication differs from mainstream approaches in four ways:

> Firstly, it is holistic. Secondly, it is historical. Thirdly, it is centrally concerned with balance between capitalist enterprise and public intervention. Finally, and perhaps most importantly of all, it goes beyond technical issues of efficiency to engage with basic moral questions of justice, equity and the public good.

One can say that the Critique of the Political Economy of the Media and Communication is materialistic in that it avoids technology- and media-centricity, and has "sought to decenter the media of communication" (Mosco 2009, 66), which means to always view and analyse the media and communication in the context of society as a whole.

In the debate between Cultural Studies and Critical Political Economy, the question was what role structure/agency, macro/micro, social science/humanities, domination/resistance, production/consumption, economy/culture, exploitation/power, class/identity play in the analysis of communication phenomena and how the relationship between these categories is to be grasped. Today, the approach that both sides of these contradictions are to be treated dialectically and integratively has become more internationally accepted. This fact becomes clear, for example, in the last interview Stuart Hall gave before his death, in which he said:

> They would have to go back to the political function of cultural studies, the political dimension of cultural studies, and they would have to ask themselves, 'If the economy does not determine everything in the last instance, then what is the role of the economic in the reproduction of the material and symbolic life?' They would have to ask themselves economic questions. [...] There's a kind of return. [...] But as Gramsci always said, the economy can never be forgotten. It has to be taken into account. [...] You won't be surprised to know I think it's more like a return to what cultural studies should have been about and was during the early stages. It sort of lost its way.
>
> (Jhally 2016, 337–338)

Hall argues for Cultural Studies to be more concerned with the "Marxist tradition of critical thinking" (Jhally 2016, 338).

Horst Holzer (1994, 185, 2017) spoke of the fact that the Critique of the Political Economy of the Media and Communication is a "forgotten theory" in the German-speaking world. There have been representatives with excellent approaches throughout, such as Horst Holzer, Manfred Knoche, Dieter Prokop, Jörg Becker, Wulf Hund, Bärbel Kirchhoff-Hund, Franz Dröge, Jörg Aufermann, Rudi Schmiede, Lothar Bisky, Jürgen Alberts, etc. With exceptions, however, such as Manfred Knoche's professorship in Salzburg (1994–2009), the approach of the critique of the political economy has not become institutionalised in media and communication studies in the German-speaking world.

Horst Holzer combined critical social theory and empirical social research to analyse the media and communication. He thus advocated the approach of a Critique of the Political Economy of the Media and Communication based on a dialectic of theory and empiricism. For example, Holzer used the method of content analysis, the secondary analysis of empirical studies, and the analysis of macroeconomic data to analyse the connection between communication, economy, and democracy (see Holzer 1971). Like Habermas, Holzer emphasised that advertising, media concentration, the commercial orientation of the media, "the personalisation of societal facts" and the "emphasised mixing of individual life problems and public affairs"[2] (Holzer 1971, 151) undermine the democratic character of the public sphere. The difference between Habermas and Holzer is that the

The Research Field of the Critique of the Political Economy of the Media and Communication latter does not argue purely in terms of social theory, but interprets empirical results in a critical way and on the basis of a critical theory of communication and society.

Holzer's dialectical theory of society and communication emerged as a critique of action theory and systems theory. He criticised systems theory, which was decisively influenced by Talcott Parsons, for conceiving of social systems as subjects (cf. Holzer 1971, 255) and for "hypostatising an actual status quo of society as societal order as such"[3] (Holzer 1971, 250). According to Holzer, Luhmann's systems theory of communication is not capable of illuminating the connection between communication, body and psyche, and the "entanglement of mass communication's genesis, quality structure and functions"[4] (Holzer 1994, 182) with media production, media organisations, media content, media use, media reception, and human consciousness.

Holzer criticises that Habermas' theory does not conceive of the relation between work and interaction as a dialectic, but rather as a dualism (see Holzer 1987). Habermas is "not capable to discern the essential quality of societal production: In the process of production, we not just develop the productive forces, but also societal relations, including communication and interaction, that humans enter in this production process"[5] (Holzer 1987, 27).

In contrast to Habermas, Georg Lukács in his book *Zur Ontologie des gesellschaftlichen Seins* (*The Ontology of Society's Being*) characterised the social production process, which is based on a dialectic of work and communication (see Fuchs 2016a, Chapter 2).

Holzer worked on a materialist theory of communication based on Marx's theory of society (see Holzer 2017, 2018). There is a dialectic of work and communication. Holzer argues that "cognition and communication [...] are two sides of the process" that "regulates the societally organised metabolism with nature and society's internal social conflicts"[6] (Holzer 1973, 57).

What is decisive for such a theory is that it is a Critique of the Political Economy of the Media and Communication. Holzer analysed communication and the media in capitalism at the level of individual capitals and total capital (see Holzer 1973, 129–137, 1994, 202–204, 2017, 715–718). At the level of individual capital, the media and communication system has a capital economy in which information is directly a form of capital valorisation and surplus value production, and plays a role in the circulation of commodities as the creator of "a climate fostering consumption and the advertisement of specific products and services" (Holzer 2017, 715).

At the level of capitalism as a whole, the communication system has an ideological role "to secure and legitimise the rule of capital"[7] (Holzer 1973, 131) and "of society's organisational principle" (Holzer 2017, 715) as well as a reproductive role as Information and entertainment source that is used to "produce, preserve and reproduce"[8] (Holzer 1973, 131) labour power.

The Critique of the Political Economy of the Media and Communication has so far failed and has been institutionally prevented in the German-speaking world. The view that Critical Political Economy is an important theoretical and empirical contribution and approach to the study of media and communication has not prevailed. Although the Critique of the Political Economy of the Media and Communication is highly relevant today, it is forgotten and little established in the German-speaking world. One of the influencing factors is illustrated by the example of Horst Holzer, who was banned from holding a professorship in Bremen in 1971 because of his membership in the German Communist Party, which also prevented his tenure at Ludwig Maximilian University of Munich in 1974 and led to the end of his academic career (see Bönkost 2011, Scheu 2012).

More than 45 years after Holzer faced an occupational ban, the political hunt against Marxists has not yet come to an end. Media and communication studies scholars are still affected today: In autumn 2012, the Bavarian Office for the Protection of the Constitution initiated an investigation when Kerem Schamberger was offered a funded doctoral position in the field of media and communication studies at Ludwig Maximilian University of Munich. Schamberger is known in Bavaria as a left-wing activist. He describes what happened as follows:

> In July 2016, I applied to a position as research assistant supervised by Professor Meyen. When I got the job offer I had to complete the 'Questionnaire for Assessing Constitutional Loyalty' (*Bogen zur Prüfung der Verfassungstreue*) that lists organisations that are, according to the opinion of the Bavarian Office for the Protection of the Constitution, anti-constitutional. All applicants applying to public service positions in Bavaria have to complete this Orwellian questionnaire. It is a scandal that the list contains anti-fascist organisations such as the Union of Persecutees of the Nazi Regime (*Vereinigung der Verfolgten des Naziregimes*) right next to Nazi organisations such as National Democratic Party of Germany (NPD) or militant, fascist fraternities. The list also contains left-wing organisations critical of capitalism such as the DKP or Red Aid (*Rote Hilfe*). So if you check that you are the member of such an organisation, then the Office for the Protection of

The Research Field of the Critique of the Political Economy of the Media and Communication

the Constitution is asked for information on the background of the applicant. That is also what happened in my case. [...] I checked association with the German Communist Party (Deutsche Kommunistische Partei, DKP), the Union of Persecutees of the Nazi Regime – Association of Antifascists (Vereinigung der Verfolgten des Naziregimes – Bund der AntifaschistInnen, VVN), Red Help (Rote Hilfe), and the Socialist German Workers Youth (Sozialistische deutsche Arbeiterjugend, SDAJ), where I was a member until 2013.

(Schamberger 2017, 84 & 85)

Ludwig Maximilian University of Munich eventually hired Schamberger despite the Office for the Protection of the Constitution's negative review, as the university had no doubts about his loyalty to the constitution and his advocacy of the democratic form of socialism.

3.3 Karl Marx as a Critic of Capitalism and Communication Theorist

Marx was a historical and dialectical thinker. Since society changes, the categories with which it is analysed must therefore also change. Therefore, in terms of social theory, however, two extremes should be avoided. Namely, on the one hand, the assumption that we now live in a radically new postmodern, digital, or information society. And on the other hand, the premise is that society has not changed at all since the 19th century. Both approaches can be avoided through the dialectical approach to social analysis, which assumes a dialectic of continuity and discontinuity in society's development. A new phase of societal and capitalist development sublates older phases, i.e. to a certain degree, the existing is preserved, eliminated, and supplemented by new emergent qualities. This degree is determined by a dialectic of chance and necessity, structures and action, crises, and social struggles.

We live today in a capitalism that is based on the exploitation of labour, as it was in the 19th century. However, capitalist change has at the same time led to changes within capitalism, which is now organised as a multiplicity of interlocking capitalisms, for example, financial market capitalism, digital capitalism, knowledge and information capitalism, neoliberal capitalism, authoritarian capitalism, mobility capitalism, hyperindustrial capitalism, etc.

The study of the critique of political economy is in many ways relevant to the critical analysis of media and communication today (cf. Fuchs 2008, 2011, 2014a, 2015, 2016a,

2016b, 2017a, 2017b, 2020, 2021, Fuchs and Mosco 2012, 2017a, 2017b). It goes back to Marx's analysis of capitalism and society.

A *first* interesting aspect about the Critique of Political Economy is the fact that Marx was a *critical journalist* and intellectual who was comprehensively critical of the political developments of his time. In times of erosion of investigative journalism, Marx's journalistic practice reminds us of a time when the commercialisation and capitalisation of the media and thus the colonisation of the public sphere was less advanced. For Marx, journalism was a means of social critique.

Marx was an ardent advocate of democracy, freedom of the press, and freedom of expression. He saw the danger of restricting this freedom through state censorship and pointed to the danger of the restriction of freedom through capitalisation and media concentration: "The primary freedom of the press lies in not being a trade" (Marx 1842, 175). Today we live not only in a world where there is a strong concentration of capital in the traditional media sector, but also in the new digital media sector. Google has monopolised capital in the search engine sector, Facebook in the social networking sector, Amazon in online commerce, Microsoft in operating systems, etc. The mechanisms by which capital concentration and commodification operate and the forms in which they are expressed have changed with the shift to digital capitalism, but the phenomena of media concentration and media monopolies remain fundamental structural principles of capitalism. Google has a dominant position in the online advertising market. This is a global market because the Internet is a global means of information and communication. In October 2020, Google controlled 69.30 per cent of all desktop search engine queries, 92.9 per cent of all mobile search engine queries, and 88.3 per cent of search queries conducted on tablets.[9] Google search and Google advertising are algorithmic. They are based on constant surveillance, storage, and analysis of (almost) all online activities of all users, generating and commodifying Big Data. The online concentration of capital operates in a global market based on algorithms and Big Data.

The analysis of the *commodity form* as the elementary form of capitalism is a *second* interesting aspect of the critique of capitalism. Marx begins the first chapter in the first volume of *Das Kapital* with the words: "The wealth of societies in which the capitalist mode of production prevails appears as an 'immense collection of commodities'; the individual commodity appears as its elementary form" (Marx 1867, 125).

The political-economic strategy of capitalism is to subsume more and more realms of society under the commodity form. In the last few decades, this has not stopped at realms that were traditionally protected or spared from commodification, such as public services (including public media, education, health, and universities), the human body, the human mind, communication, nature, etc. In the field of digital media, commodification has affected labour (digital labour), digital content, digital technologies, access to platforms, online audiences, online prosumers (producing consumers), and Big Data.

The categories of the *exploitation* of labour, *surplus value* and *class* relations are a *third* current aspect of Critical Political Economy. In capitalism, the workers are considered as "merely a machine for the production of surplus-value" and capitalists as "a machine for the transformation of this surplus-value into surplus capital" (Marx 1867, 742). The historical differentiation of capitalism has made the class structure more complex (see Dalla Costa and James 1973, Federici 2012, Negri 1982/1988, 2017, Smythe 1977, Wright 1997). This can be seen in the emergence of managers, unpaid interns, the precariat, freelancers, knowledge workers, digital labour, etc. The relations of production of digital capitalism are based on an international division of digital labour in which different forms of exploitation (such as slave labour, digital housework, Taylorist industrial labour, precarious digital labour, the work of highly paid and overworked software engineers, unpaid digital shadow labour, low paid digital labour in developing countries) interact.

The *globalisation of capital* represents a *fourth* current aspect of the critique of political economy. Marx emphasised that capitalism has a fundamental tendency to expand spatially in order to create markets, spheres of production and consumption for commodities, labour, and capital. "The need of a constantly expanding market for its products chases the bourgeoisie over the whole surface of the globe. It must nestle everywhere, settle everywhere, establish connexions everywhere" (Marx and Engels 1848, 487). In recent decades, capitalism has transnationalised the production of goods and surplus value and strongly promoted the export of capital, similar to the beginning of the 20th century. One consequence of this has been that since the 1990s there has been a lot of talk about globalisation in public discussions and the social sciences.

This terminology is not wrong, but the social critique based on Marx has the advantage of having captured the specific form of capitalist globalisation as imperialism. In more recent discussions, David Harvey, for example, has coined the notion of the new imperialism (see Harvey 2005) to highlight the combination of financialisation and neoliberalism as a characteristic of contemporary capitalist globalisation. The economic sector of media, information, communication, culture, and digital capital is subject to such a capitalist globalisation tendency. In 2020, the world's 30 largest transnational corporations included 9 such companies: Apple (#9), AT&T (11), Alphabet/Google (#13), Microsoft (#13), Samsung Electronics (#16), Verizon Communications (#20), Amazon (#22), Comcast (#27), and China Mobile (#28).[10] Among these 30 companies were 11 financial corporations (banks, insurance companies) and five energy and mobility corporations (oil, gas, energy supply, car production). This fact indicates that capitalism today is a combination of financial capitalism, mobility capitalism, hyperindustrial capitalism, and information/-digital capitalism.

And these dimensions of capitalism are intertwined and overlapping. Digital companies are a good example of this: many of these corporations are financed by venture capital companies, which makes the Internet economy vulnerable to crises of financial markets, as these financial investments are often very risky. Digital media cannot exist without energy supply. The global Internet consumes about 10 per cent of the energy consumed globally (cf. De Decker 2015). In times of Big Data and server farms, this share is increasing. Digitalisation has supported and mediated a flexibilisation and global mobilisation of goods, people, and information.

The *crisis-proneness of capitalism* is a *fifth important aspect* of the critique of political economy. Capitalism is an inherently crisis-prone system.

> The fact that the movement of capitalist society is full of contradictions impresses itself most strikingly on the practical bourgeois in the changes of the periodic cycle through which modern industry passes, the summit of which is the general crisis.
>
> (Marx 1867, 103)

The new world economic crisis and its consequences highlight the importance of the objective dialectics of capitalism, i.e. its susceptibility to crisis. A complex combination of wage stagnation, class struggle from above, financialisation, precarisation, and the increase in the technical and organic composition of capital through computerisation, informatisation, and automation had ripened contradictions over the decades that were then sublated in the crisis. Due to its financialisation, the capitalist Internet economy is a highly crisis-prone realm of capitalism. The dot-com crisis in 2000 made this clear. The social media economy is also subject to similar financialisation tendencies.

The dialectic of technology and society is a sixth significant aspect of the critique of political economy. Marx presented this dimension in the so-called "Fragment of Machines"

Karl Marx as a Critic of Capitalism and Communication Theorist in the *Grundrisse* as well as in the fifteenth chapter of the first volume of *Capital* ("Machinery and Large-Scale Industry"). For example, he argues:

> machinery in itself shortens the hours of labour, but when employed by capital it lengthens them; since in itself it lightens labour, but when employed by capital it heightens its intensity; since in itself it is a victory of man over the forces of nature but in the hands of capital it makes man the slave of those forces; since in itself it increases the wealth of the producers, but in the hands of capital it makes them into paupers.
>
> (Marx 1867, 568–569)

The dialectic of technology is understood to mean that technology develops contradictorily in a class society under the influence of existing and developing social contradictions. At the same time, technology is not only socially produced, but also has unpredictable internal contradictions and development dynamics. This applies especially to highly complex systems that involve a risk of catastrophe. Communication technologies and other technologies do not develop in a certain way by necessity, nor is their development completely random. Rather, a dialectic of chance and necessity plays a role. Raymond Williams, who was a Marx-influenced theorist throughout his life, has emphasised in his critique of Marshall McLuhan's technological determinism that technology is not a "self-acting force which provides materials for new ways of life" (Williams 2003/1974, 6). Rather, human intentions and actions influenced by certain societal conditions play a significant role.

The seventh important aspect of the critique of political economy is the examination of the knowledge-based nature of society and capitalism. Marx introduced the concept of the General Intellect in the *Grundrisse*, a draft of *Das Kapital*, in a section also known as the "Fragment of Machines". Marx (1857/1858, 706) describes a condition where "general social knowledge has become a direct force of production" and "the conditions of the process of social life itself have come under the control of the general intellect and been transformed in accordance with it". On the one hand, Marx emphasised with the concept of the general intellect that knowledge, technology, and science represent general conditions of the modern economy, which flow into many production processes at the same time and are created and used cooperatively by many people. On the other hand, with this category, he anticipated the computerisation of the economy.

Related to the general intellect is also the fact that Marx was concerned with the new media of his time (especially the telegraph) and their role in society. The *eighth aspect* is therefore that the study of Marx offers historical, theoretical, and methodological insights for the *sociology of technology* and media and the analysis of the *means of communication* and *human communication*. For example, Marx described information and communication systems "whereby the individual can acquire information about the activity of all others and attempt to adjust his own accordingly" and whereby "relations and connections are introduced" (Marx 1857/1858, 161). This formulation bears a striking resemblance to the communicative properties of the Internet, but was written in the 1850s, more than 100 years before the technical creation of the Internet.

The *ninth aspect* of the critique of political economy that is relevant today is the *contradiction between productive forces and relations of production* (see Marx 1894, 373–374).

Capitalist development gives rise to new forms of cooperation and cooperative technologies that are the foundations for new commons, but at the same time, as capitalist private property, are means of exercising domination. This contradiction is clearly visible today in networked digital technologies, which at the same time produce new ways of commodification and exploitation and can resist commodification and create spheres of non-capitalist communication. The contradiction of productive forces and class relations is expressed in digital capitalism as a contradiction between digital commons and digital commodities. In this context, Toni Negri (2017, 25) writes that digitalisation is shaped by an "antagonism between the social cooperation of the proletariat and the (economic and political) command of capital".

The *tenth important aspect* of the critique of political economy is the contribution to *communication theory*. "Peter only relates to himself as a man through his relation to another man, Paul, in whom he recognizes his likeness" (Marx 1867, 144, footnote 19). Through the process of communication, people mutually relate their mental reflections to each other in a complex way, which leads to cognitive changes and produces and reproduces human sociality and societality. Important contributions to communication theory have been made in the Marx-based tradition by Georg Lukács' Ontology of Society's Being and the works of Raymond Williams, Ferruccio Rossi-Landi, Theodor W. Adorno, Herbert Marcuse, Lev Vygotsky, Valentin Vološinov, among others (see Fuchs 2016a). If these theoretical approaches are thought together, this results in a communicative materialism that is an alternative to the dualistic critical communication theory of Jürgen Habermas and Niklas Luhmann's instrumental systems theory of communication.

The *11th topical aspect* has to do with the fact that in the base/superstructure problem Marx poses the *question of the connection* between economy and society, labour activity and communication, labour and ideology, body and mind, physical and mental labour, production and reproduction, nature, and society. Raymond Williams, in his approach of cultural materialism, emphasises Marx's insight that society is a context of social production of human sociality (see Williams 1977). Social production mediated by communication is an identical moment of all realms of society. Social production is the economic moment of the social. At the same time, however, all social systems and realms have emergent qualities that distinguish and set them apart from other systems and spheres and the purely economic aspect.

The *12th reason* why the critique of political economy has relevance today is the role that *ideologies and the fetish character of commodities* play in contemporary society. By commodity fetishism, Marx understands that "the definite social relation" between humans assumes "the fantastic form of a relation between things" (Marx 1867, 165). Ideology naturalises and normalises naturalisation. Characteristic of ideology in capitalism today is the spread of new nationalisms combined with new racism and xenophobia, directed mainly against migrant workers and refugees. Nationalism is an ideology that constructs a fictitve ethnicity (see Balibar and Wallerstein 1991) and proclaims a fictitious unity of the interest of capital and labour in a national interest. This proclaimed national interest distracts from the complex causes and interrelations of social problems. Nationalism is a political form of fetishism in which the nation and a national and *völkisch* collective are fetishised. Nationalism "professed to unite all classes by reviving for all the chimera of national glory" (Marx 1871, 330).

The thirteenth aspect of the critique of political economy that is important today is the role of social struggles and class struggles in societal and social change. Marx sees here a historical dialectic of chance and necessity, praxis and structural conditions. When he writes that humans "make their own history, but they do not make it just as they please; they do not make it under circumstances chosen by themselves, but under circumstances directly encountered, given and transmitted from the past" (Marx 1852, 103), this insight has practical relevance today. Today, in the context of discussing social change, there are discussions about the role social media play in rebellions, protests, revolutions, and social movements. This raises the question of whether people, crises, or media technologies make history. To answer this question, one needs a theoretical model of social change that takes into account the dialectic of structures and practice and the influence of communication technologies. The orientation of the critique of the political economy towards social struggles is based on a practical humanism that questions relations in which the human being is "a debased, enslaved, forsaken, despicable being" (Marx 1844, 182).

The *14th* aspect emphasised by the Marx-based critique of capitalism is the necessity and importance of *democratic alternatives* to capitalism and capital accumulation. Marx focuses on the extension of democracy from politics to the economy. In the field of the media, this refers to non-commercial, non-profit alternative media that are oriented towards the communicative commons. In the field of academic publishing, for example, non-profit open access journals and books have gained greater importance, challenging the capital accumulation strategies of commercial publishers (see Fuchs and Sandoval 2013, Knoche 2014).

The discussion of the relevance of the critique of political economy could go on for a long time, as the number of its representatives with important ideas in this theoretical tradition is very large.

3.4 An Example Application of the Critique of the Political Economy of the Media and Communication: Social Movements and Alternative Media in Capitalism

The critique of political economy has a humanities tradition in the form of dialectical social philosophy and a social sciences tradition in the form of critical social analysis. Practically speaking, these two dimensions cannot be strictly separated; they often appear in combined form as theory-led empirical critiques of capitalism and society.

The field of social movement communication studies has established itself internationally as a sub-aspect of media and communication studies. In the context of the Arab Spring and the Occupy movements, there has been much discussion about the role of social media in protests and revolutions (cf. Fuchs 2014b, 2017b, 2021). Most of the work published on such questions deals purely micro-sociologically with the question of how social movements communicate, without taking into account the broader macro-sociological context in which these movements operate, namely the capitalist world system. The study *OccupyMedia! The Occupy Movement and Social Media in Crisis Capitalism* (see Fuchs 2014b), on the other hand, was designed as a work that used the critique of political economy as an empirical approach. Methodologically, an online survey was conducted in which 418 Occupy activists participated.

One of the findings was that neither online communication nor face-to-face communication alone is the decisive form of communication for activists occupying public spaces, but that there is a dialectic: the more active an activist is in the movement, the larger their social protest network is and the more they tend to use online and offline communication, which are mutually reinforcing, for internal movement communication and external, public mobilisation communication. However, internal and external movement communication are now in the context of capitalist and state power, which such movements usually oppose. This raises the question of how capitalist and state control of communication influences social movements. The survey highlighted a contradiction between public communication and communication control on capitalist social media: activists see it as a great advantage that these online platforms have large user numbers, as this enables them to reach a wide public. Since the companies (such as Facebook and Twitter) that run these platforms are part of "the 1%" and some of them, as Edward Snowden's revelations have shown, are involved in the surveillance industrial Internet complex, the problem for protest movements is that the use of these platforms can be associated with deliberate or algorithmic censorship as well as state surveillance of their communications.

A contradiction also emerged with regard to the use of alternative, non-commercial social media: on the one hand, they offer more autonomy and protection from the state and capital, but on the other hand, they are relatively unknown to the public and activists, thus reaching few people, and are additionally confronted with the resource inequality typical of capitalism, which means that alternative media often have little visibility, money, staff, reputation, influence, etc., are based on voluntary self-exploitation and precarious work, or disappear or become capitalist due to a lack of resources.

When asked how the contradiction of alternative media in capitalism should be dealt with, 54.7 per cent supported the model of voluntary donations, 9.4 per cent user fees on a non-profit basis, 8.0 per cent personalised advertising and 7.0 per cent state subsidies (see Fuchs 2014b). However, the donation and crowdfunding models popular among activists are again confronted with the contradiction that the donations for alternative projects largely come from activists who are usually not millionaires but often precariously employed, which can easily make such models financially unstable. The fundamental capitalist contradiction in this context is between digital corporations like Google and Facebook, which make billions and pay hardly any taxes, and the permanent crisis of critical alternative media. This contradiction cannot be resolved under capitalism. What is needed are radical reforms that tax capital, profit, and advertising and use the revenues thus generated (e.g. in the form of a basic income, participatory budgeting for non-commercial alternative media and non-commercial projects, etc.) for public and critical purposes. The basic problem is the structural restriction and limitation of communicative democracy in capitalism.

Currently, the greatest challenge for the study of political communication is the massive rise in nationalism and right-wing populism. In this context, social media, reality TV, and other popular media play an important role. Traditions of political economy criticism, such as the theory of the authoritarian personality of the Frankfurt School (Franz L. Neumann, Erich Fromm, Theodor W. Adorno, Leo Löwenthal, Herbert Marcuse, etc.), represent an important starting point in this context.

3.5 Conclusions

The critique of political economy is a fruitful approach to the empirical and theoretical analysis of and elucidation of contemporary communication that has a true practical relevance.

In this chapter, I have tried to show that in media and communication studies, scholars' "fear of Marx [...] is unjustified"[11] (Knoche 2005, 411). On the contrary, today we are in a social situation in which the crisis of capitalism is linked to a general crisis of legitimacy and authoritarian movements and authoritarian capitalism are attacking the foundations of democracy. Neoliberal capitalism today tends to turn into authoritarian capitalism in a negative dialectic. Communication platforms, strategies, and ideologies play an important role in this turbulent social situation. The intellectual legacy of Karl Marx, Max Horkheimer, Theodor W. Adorno, Georg Lukács, Raymond Williams, and other scholars in this critical tradition enables a truly practice-relevant, socially critical communication science that offers theoretical and analytical research approaches to better understand crises and authoritarianism in today's situation, as well as starting points for a critical, public social science (see Aulenbacher et al. 2017, Buraway 2005) that is truly relevant to practice and intervenes in public discourses.

The case of Schamberger illustrates that representatives of the Critique of the Political Economy of the Media and Communication in the German-speaking world still have to have a "justified fear"[12] of "being considered Marxist"[13] (Knoche 2005, 411).

Theories of capitalism, the authoritarian personality, crises, ideology, critical communication, etc., as found in the critique of political economy, are now central to the study of society and communication studies. The founding of the Critical Communication Studies Network (KriKoWi: Netzwerke Kritische Kommunikationswissenschaft) in spring 2017 (see https://dimbb. de/wp-content/uploads/2017/03/Netzwerk-KriKoWi_Aufruf-zur-Gr%C3% BCndung.pdf) and the establishment of an associated mailing list (https://lists.riseup. net/www/info/krikowi) is a welcome development in this context. To what extent it will or will not make a real difference remains to be seen.

Notes

1 Übersetzung aus dem Deutschen:

  Zu den Grundfragen einer kommunikationswissenschaftlichen Medienökonomie als Kritik der Politischen Ökonomie der Medien gehört die Analyse des Verhältnisses von Medien und kapitalistischer Gesellschaft, also die Rolle der Medien für das gesamte materielle, wirtschaftliche, gesellschaftliche, soziale, politische und kulturelle menschliche Leben.

2 Translation from German: "die Personalisierung gesellschaftlicher Tatbestände"; "betonte Vermischung von individuellen Lebensproblemen und öffentlichen Angelegenheiten" (Holzer 1971, 151).

3 Translation from German: "die Hypostasierung eines realgesellschaftlichen Status quo zur Ordnung von Gesellschaft schlechthin".

4 Translation from German: "die Verschränkung von Genese, Beschaffenheit und Funktion der Massenkommunikation".

5 Translation from German: Habermas ist "nicht imstande, die wesentliche Bestimmung der gesellschaftlichen Produktion zu erkennen: daß im Prozeß der Produktion eben nicht nur die Produktivkräfte entwickelt werden, sondern auch die gesellschaftlichen Beziehungen – eingeschlossen: ‚Kommunikation', ‚Interaktion' –, die die Menschen in diesem Produktionsprozeß miteinander eingehen".

6 Translation from German: "Erkenntnis und Kommunikation […] zwei Seiten des Prozesses" sind, "der den gesellschaftlich organisierten Stoffwechsel mit der Natur und die innergesellschaftlichen Auseinandersetzungen regelt".

7 Translation from German: "zur Sicherung und Legitimation der Kapitalherrschaft".

8 Translation from German: "Herstellung, Erhaltung und Wiederherstellung".

9 http://www.netmarketshare.com, accessed on 13 April 2021.

10 Data source: Forbes 2000 List for the Year 2020, https://www.forbes.com/global2000/list/, accessed on 13 April 2021.

11 Translation from German: "Angst der WissenschaftlerInnen vor Marx […] unberechtigt".

12 Translation from German: "berechtigte Angst".

13 Translation from German: "als Marxist zu gelten".

References

Aulenbacher, Brigitte, Michael Burawoy, Klaus Dörre, and Johanna Sittel, eds. 2017. *Öffentliche Soziologie: Wissenschaft im Dialog mit der Gesellschaft*. Frankfurt: Campus.

Balibar, Étienne and Immanel Wallerstein. 1991. *Race, Nation, Class*. London: Verso.

Bidet, Jacques and Stavis Kouvelakis, eds. 2008. *Critical Companion to Contemporary Marxism*. Leiden: Brill.

Bönkost, Jan. 2011. Im Schatten des Aufbruchs. Das erste Berufsverbot für Horst Holzer und die Uni Bremen. *Grundrisse* 39: 29–37.

Buraway, Michael. 2005. For Public Sociology. *American Sociological Review* 70 (1): 4–28.

Dalla Costa, Mariarosa and Selma James.1973. *The Power of Women and the Subversion of Community.* Bristol: Falling Wall Press. Second edition.

De Decker, Kris. 2015. Why We Need a Speed Limit for the Internet. *Low-Tech Magazine*, October 19, 2015, 9, http://www.lowtechmagazine.com/2015/10/can-the-internet-run-on-renewable-energy.html

Federici, Silvia. 2012. *Revolution at Point Zero. Housework, Reproduction and Feminist Struggle.* Oakland, CA: PM Press.

Fuchs, Christian. 2021. *Social Media: A Critical Introduction.* London: Sage. Third edition.

Fuchs, Christian. 2020. *Communication and Capitalism: A Critical Theory.* London: University of Westminster Press. DOI: https://doi.org/10.16997/book45

Fuchs, Christian. 2017a. *Marx lesen im Informationszeitalter: Eine medien- und kommunikation-swissenschaftliche Perspektive auf "Das Kapital. Band 1".* Münster: Unrast.

Fuchs, Christian. 2017b. *Social Media: A Critical Introduction.* London: Sage. Second edition.

Fuchs, Christian. 2016a. *Critical Theory of Communication. New Readings of Lukács, Adorno, Marcuse, Honneth and Habermas in the Age of the Internet.* London: University of Westminster Press.

Fuchs, Christian. 2016b. *Reading Marx in the Information Age: A Media and Communication Studies Perspective on Capital*, Volume 1. New York: Routledge.

Fuchs, Christian. 2015. *Culture and Economy in the Age of Social Media.* New York: Routledge.

Fuchs, Christian. 2014a. *Digital Labour and Karl Marx.* New York: Routledge.

Fuchs, Christian. 2014b. *OccupyMedia! The Occupy Movement and Social Media in Crisis Capitalism.* Winchester: Zero Books.

Fuchs, Christian. 2011. *Foundations of Critical Media and Information Studies.* London: Routledge.

Fuchs, Christian. 2008. *Internet and Society: Social Theory in the Information Age.* New York: Routledge.

Fuchs, Christian and Vincent Mosco, eds. 2017a. *Marx and the Political Economy of the Media.* Chicago, IL: Haymarket Books.

Fuchs, Christian and Vincent Mosco, eds. 2017b. *Marx in the Age of Digital Capitalism.* Chicago, IL: Haymarket Books.

Fuchs, Christian and Vincent Mosco, eds. 2012. Marx Is Back – The Importance of Marxist Theory and Research for Critical Communication Studies Today. *tripleC: Communication, Capitalism & Critique* 10 (2): 127–632. DOI: https://doi.org/10.31269/triplec.v10i2.427

Fuchs, Christian and Marisol Sandoval. 2013. The Diamond Model of Open Access Publishing: Why Policy Makers, Scholars, Universities, Libraries, Labour Unions and the Publishing World Need to Take Non-Commercial, Non-Profit Open Access Serious. *tripleC: Communication, Capitalism & Critique* 11 (2): 428–443. DOI: https://doi.org/10.31269/triplec.v11i2.502

References

Hardy, Jonathan. 2014. *Critical Political Economy of the Media. An Introduction*. Abingdon: Routledge.

Harvey, David. 2005. *The New Imperialism*. Oxford: Oxford University Press.

Holzer, Horst. 2018. Communication & Society: A Critical Political Economy Perspective. *tripleC: Communication, Capitalism & Critique* 16 (1): 357–405. DOI: https://doi.org/10.31269/triplec.v16i1.1029

Holzer, Horst. 2017. The Forgotten Marxist Theory of Communication & Society. *tripleC: Communication, Capitalism & Critique* 15 (2): 686–725. DOI: https://doi.org/10.31269/triplec.v15i2.908

Holzer, Horst. 1994. *Medienkommunikation*. Opladen: Westdeutscher Verlag.

Holzer, Horst. 1987. *Kommunikation oder gesellschaftliche Arbeit? Zur Theorie des kommunikativen Handelns von Jürgen Habermas*. Berlin: Akademie.

Holzer, Horst. 1973. *Kommunikationssoziologie*. Reinbek bei Hamburg: Rowohlt.

Holzer, Horst. 1971. *Gescheiterte Aufklärung? Politik, Ökonomie und Kommunikation in der Bundesrepublik Deutschland*. München: Piper.

Jhally, Sut. 2016. Stuart Hall: The Last Interview. *Cultural Studies* 30 (2): 332–345.

Knoche, Manfred. 2014. Emanzipatorische Transformation der Wissenschaftskommunikation statt Irrweg Verlags-TOLL OPEN ACCESS. *Medien Journal* 38 (4): 76–78.

Knoche, Manfred. 2005. Medienökonomische Theorie und Ideologie im Kapitalismus. In *Bausteine einer Theorie des öffentlich-rechtlichen Rundfunks*, ed. Christa-Maria, Wolfgang R. Langenbucher, Ulrich Saxer, and Christian Steininger, 406–435. Wiesbaden: VS.

Knoche, Manfred. 2002. Kommunikationswissenschaftliche Medienökonomie als Kritik der Politischen Ökonomie der Medien. In *Medienökonomie in der Kommunikationswissenschaft. Bedeutung, Grundfragen und Entwicklungsperspektiven. Manfred Knoche zum 60. Geburtstag*, ed. Gabriele Siegert, 101–109. Münster: Lit.

Marx, Karl. 1894. *Capital*, Volume 3. London: Penguin.

Marx, Karl. 1871. The Civil War in France. In *Marx & Engels Collected Works (MECW)*, Volume 22, 307–359. London: Lawrence & Wishart.

Marx, Karl. 1867. *Capital*, Volume 2. London: Penguin.

Marx, Karl. 1857/1858. *Grundrisse: Foundations of the Critique of Political Economy*. London: Penguin.

Marx, Karl 1852. The Eighteenth Brumaire of Louis Bonaparte. In *Marx & Engels Collected Works (MECW)*, Volume 11, 99–197. London: Lawrence & Wishart.

Marx, Karl. 1844. Contribution to the Critique of Hegel's Philosophy of Law: Introduction. In *Marx & Engels Collected Works (MECW)*, Volume 3, 175–187. London: Lawrence & Wishart.

Marx, Karl. 1842. Proceedings of the Sixth Rhine Province Assembly. First Article. Debates on Freedom of the Press and Publication of the Proceedings of the Assembly of the Estates. In *Marx & Engels Collected Works (MECW)*, Volume 1, 133–181. London: Lawrence & Wishart.

Marx, Karl and Friedrich Engels. 1848. The Manifesto of the Communist Party. In *Marx & Engels Collected Works (MECW)*, Volume 6, 477–519. London: Lawrence & Wishart.

Mosco, Vincent. 2009. *The Political Economy of Communication*. London: Sage. Second edition.

Murdock, Graham and Peter Golding. 2005. Culture, Communications and Political Economy. In *Mass Media and Society*, ed. James Curran and Michael Gurevitch, 60–83. London: Hodder Arnold. Fourth edition.

Murdock, Graham and Peter Golding. 1974. For a Political Economy of Mass Communications. In *The Political Economy of the Media*, ed. Peter Golding and Graham Murdock, Volume I, 3–32. Cheltenham: Edward Elgar.

Negri, Antonio. 2017. *Marx and Foucault*. Cambridge: Polity.

Negri, Antonio. 1982/1988. Archaeology and Project: The Mass Worker and the Social Worker. In *Revolution Retrieved: Selected Writings on Marx, Keynes, Capitalist Crisis & New Social Subjects*, 199–228. London: Red Notes.

Schamberger, Kerem. 2017. tripleC-Interview with Kerem Schamberger about Occupational Bans, Left-Wing Communication Studies and Critique of German Academia. *tripleC: Communication, Captialism & Critique* 15 (1): 82–90.

Scheu, Andreas M. 2012. *Adornos Erben in der Kommunikationswissenschaft. Eine Verdrängungsgeschichte?* Köln: Herbert von Halem.

Smythe, Dallas W. 1977. Communications: Blindspot of Western Marxism. *Canadian Journal of Political and Social Theory* 1 (3): 1–27.

Wasko, Janet. 2014. The Study of the Political Economy of the Media in the Twenty-First Century. *International Journal of Media & Cultural Politics* 10 (3): 259–271.

Williams, Raymond. 2003/1974. *Television*. London: Routledge.

Williams, Raymond. 1977. *Marxism and Literature*. Oxford: Oxford University Press.

Winseck, Dwayne. 2011. The Political Economies of Media and the Transformation of the Global Media Industries. In *The Political Economies of Media. The Transformation of the Global Media Industries*, ed. Dwayne Winseck and Dal Yong Jin, 3–48. London: Bloomsbury Academic.

Wright, Erik Olin. 1997. *Class Counts: Comparative Studies in Class Analysis*. Cambridge: Cambridge University Press.

Chapter Four
Power in the Age of Social Media

4.1 Introduction

2011 was also the year, in which various Occupy movements emerged in North America, Greece, Spain, the United Kingdom, and other countries. One of their protest tactics is to build protest camps on public squares that are centres of gravity for discussions, events, and protest activities. Being asked about the advantages of Occupy's use of social media, respondents in the OccupyMedia! Survey[1] said that they allow them to reach a broad public and to protect themselves from the police:

- "As much as I wish that occupy would keep away from a media such as Facebook it got the advantage that it can reach out to lots of people that [...] [are] otherwise hard to reach out to" (#20).
- "All of these social media [...] Facebook, Twitter etc. helps spread the word but I think the biggest achievement is Livestream: those of us who watch or participate in change can inform other streamers of actions, police or protest moving from one place [...] to another. That saved many streamers from getting hurt or less arrests" (#36).

At the same time, the respondents identified risks of the use of commercial social media:

- "Facebook is generally exploitative, and controls the output of Facebook posts, the frequency they are seen by other people. It's a disaster and we shouldn't use it at all. But we still do" (#28).

DOI: 10.4324/9781003331087-6

- "There have been occasions where the police seemed to have knowledge that was only shared in a private group and/or text messages and face-to-face" (#55).
- "Events for protests that were created on Facebook, but not organised IRL [in real life]. Many 'participants' in calls for protests on Facebook, but at least 70% of them [don't] [...] show up at the actual demonstration" (#74).
- "Twitter has been willing to turn over protestors tweets to authorities which is a big concern" (#84)
- "Censorship of content by YouTube and email deletions on Gmail" (#103)
- "Yes, my Twitter account was subpoena'd, for tweeting a hashtag. The supboena was dropped in court" (#238)
- "Facebook = Tracebook" (#203)

This example indicates that social media seems to be embedded into asymmetric power structures (for a detailed discussion see also Fuchs 2014a, 2014b): It has the potential to support protest mobilisation and protest communication. At the same time using social media generates data traces of activists' communications and movements, which makes it easier for corporate Internet platforms and the police to monitor, control, censor, and infiltrate political movements. This contradictory character of media power can only be understood by using critical theory for conceptualising and analysing power relations, its realities, asymmetries, potentials, and struggles.

This chapter is a contribution to critically theorising media power in the age of social media. It first categorises different notions of power (Section 4.2), introduces a dialectical notion of media power (Section 4.3), discusses the dialectics of social media power (Section 4.4), and draws some conclusions about the need for a dialectical and critical theory of the media and society (Section 4.5).

4.2 Three Theoretical Concepts of Power

There are objective, subjective, and dialectical concepts of power and consider the latter approaches as integrating and synthesising the former two (Table 4.1).

4.2.1 Objective Concepts of Power

The power to take and influence collective decisions is a central aspect of politics. There are on the one hand objective concepts of power that consider it as being localised in institutions and structures such as nation states, parliaments, ministries,

TABLE 4.1 Three concepts of power

	Human subjects	Objects
Objectivism		Power is located in coercive institutions that realise the particular will of a group by commanding and sanctioning other groups and individuals.
Subjectivism	Power is a productive, transformative human capacity that is immanent in the human body and all social relationships.	
Subject-Object-Dialectic	Power is a dialectical process, in which human actors enter social relationships that are to certain degrees competitive and co-operative in order to reach decisions so that decision-oriented structures emerge and are reproduced that enable and constrain further decision-oriented social practices. Power is conceived as a dynamic process that connects power structures and power practices, objects, and subjects of power.	

public administration bodies, coercive state apparatuses such as police, military, law, the judicial system, the prison system, and secret services that coercively assert the will of certain groups against the will of others. A classical definition of power that stands in this objectivist tradition is the one of Max Weber who sees it as the "chance of a man or a number of men to realize their own will in a social action even against the resistance of others who are participating in the action" (Weber 1978, 926). He defines domination as "probability that certain specific commands (or all commands) will be obeyed by a given group of people" (Weber 1978, 212). Weber's definition implies that power is something that is necessarily coercively defended by one group against other groups. This also means an unbridgeable gap and relationship of domination between the powerful and the powerless. The difference between power and domination in Weber's theory is vague; both seem to be related to sanctions, struggle, disciplines, commands, and coercion. For Weber power is something that is exerted on someone against his own will.

Jürgen Habermas (1986)[2] has given a definition of power that is similar to the one of Weber. For Habermas power has to do with the realisation of collective goals, means of coercion, symbols of power and status, decision-making authorities, disadvantages, power of definition, counter-power, organisation, and legitimation (Habermas 1987, 267–272).

For Niklas, Luhmann power is a symbolically generalised medium of communication that regulates and overcomes contingency and increases the possibility of selections in communication processes (Luhmann 1975, 2000). In a first general sense, Luhmann's

Three Theoretical Concepts of Power

definition of power as the ability to act effectively reminds one of Gidden's definition and as an action that affects other actions it seems close to Foucault (Luhmann 2000, 39). But Luhmann continues that such a definition is too broad because it would imply that all simple activities like brushing one's teeth would have to do with power. Hence in a narrower definition, he sees power as the achievement of inducing someone to act in a certain way that he wouldn't act normally and only does so due to the announcement of possible sanctions (ibid.). Power would always be connected to influence that is generated by communicating possible (positive or negative) sanctions. Political power would be based on negative sanctions, threats, and coercion. Physical violence would be the best means of threatening someone and for generating power; it would be closely connected to the state system (55). Power would never include consensus, the life-world wouldn't as assumed by Habermas be a pool of consensus (53–54, 76). Consensus would make the use of power superfluous.

Luhmann analyses power as something necessarily coercive and hence his concept is closer to Weber than to Foucault and Giddens. His assumptions imply that organisations that are largely based on consensus and co-operation are powerless organisations. Collective modes of organisation are an expression of a certain degree of power that can be employed in order to achieve goals. If there is a low level of conflict in an organisation and all actors can achieve their goals by co-operating and achieving consensus by dialogue, neither they nor their organisation are powerless, but can be considered as an expression of co-operative modes of power. Tooth brushing and other activities don't have much to do with power not because conflict and coercion are missing, but because they are simple individual activities, whereas power occurs only in social relationships and situations that require collective decisions.

4.2.2 Subjective Concepts of Power

Opposed to such objective concepts of power that stress repressive institutions, Foucault has asked: "If power were never anything but repressive if it never did anything but say no, do you really think we should manage to obey it?" (Foucault 1980, 119). He stressed a productive, creative aspect of power: Power

> runs through, and it produces things, it induces pleasure, it forms knowledge, it produces discourse; it must be considered as a productive network which runs through the entire social body much more than a negative instance whose function is repression.

> (Foucault 1980, 119)

We must cease once and for all to describe the effects of power in negative terms: it 'excludes,' it 'represses,' it 'censors,' it 'abstracts,' it 'masks,' it 'conceals.' In fact, power produces, it produces reality, it produces domains of objects and rituals of truth. The individual and the knowledge that may be gained of him belong to this production.

(Foucault 1977, 250)

Foucault (1977, 1980, 1982) pointed out that power is not an abstract entity "out there", it is not something that one cannot know or pinpoint. His work made clear that power doesn't exist outside of the human being, but operates in and through the human body and within daily routines and actions. Foucault opposed the idea that power is only located in dominating classes and the state and that it is something that others don't have and is withheld from them. Power would have a networked character that affects all social relationships. Foucault never gave a definition of power, only one of the power relations:

The exercise of power is not simply a relationship between partners, individual or collective; it is a way in which certain actions modify others. [...] Power exists only when it is put into action, even if, of course, it is integrated into a disparate field of possibilities brought to bear upon permanent structures. What defines a relationship of power is that it is a mode of action which does not act directly and immediately on others. Instead it acts upon their actions: an action upon an action, on existing actions or on those which may arise in the present or future.

(Foucault 1982, 219–220)

For Foucault power is productive and produces knowledge. The exercise of power may need violence, but violence for Foucault is not inherent in a power relation.[3] A power relation would be an action that influences another action and determines a field of possibility for it. In this field, ways of resistance and counteraction would always be present – "there are no relations of power without resistance" (Foucault 1980, 142).

With Foucault the concept of power took a subjective turn, he pointed out that power is related to people's bodies, sexuality, consciousness, and everyday life. Foucault in no way was optimistic that oppressed individuals and groups can produce counter-power and resistance. He thought that modern society is so oppressive that it even reaches the drives and sentiments of humans. But one can interpret Foucault's assumptions that power is productive and that it is immanent in all social relationships in a way that means that all

Three Theoretical Concepts of Power

oppressed groups and individuals have power potentials as social groups that they can make use of in order to change their situation in society. Power doesn't exist outside of social relationships and isn't a thing that is simply controlled by some groups that try to withhold it from others; it is produced and reproduced in and through agency.

Also Anthony Giddens has elaborated a rather subjective concept related to the notion of human agency. Giddens defines power as "'transformative capacity', the capability to intervene in a given set of events so as in some way to alter them" (Giddens 1985, 7), as the "capability to effectively decide about courses of events, even where others might contest such decisions" (Giddens 1985, 9). For Giddens power is related to (allocative and authoritative) resources, to material facilities and means of control. Power is characteristic for all social relationships, it "is routinely involved in the instantiation of social practices" and is "operating in and through human action" (Giddens 1981, 49–50). For Giddens power is related to the command over economic resources and humans: "Allocative resources refer to capabilities – or, more accurately, to forms of transformative capacity – generating command over objects, goods or material phenomena. Authorities resources refer to types of transformative capacity generating command over persons or actors" (Giddens 1984, 33).

Foucault argues that power is not necessarily something repressive and coercive. Both Foucault and Giddens point out that it operates in and through social relationships and on the foundation of daily routines. Power stems from the creative political relationships of human beings. They are both subjects and objects of power. The problem of Foucault's work is that his concept of power is very diffuse. He doesn't give a clear definition. Giddens defines power in a more concrete way in relationship to collective decisions and resources. For him, the political realm of society has to do with the "capability of marshalling authoritative resources or what I shall call administrative power" (Giddens 1985, 19). This would always include control, surveillance, domination, sanctions, physical violence, and threats of the use of violence. Giddens thereby naturalises relationships of domination, coercion, and heteronomy as fundamental aspects of all social systems and societies. But historical and archaeological studies show that there were cultures such as the Minoan one that was remarkably peaceful. One can imagine social systems and societies that are largely based on co-operation instead of domination, violence, and coercion. It is therefore an unrealistically defeatist position when Giddens (1984) argues that the end of domination is an unrealistic goal and vision. Suggesting that political power is always repressive and dominative results in an unclear differentiation between power and domination (as it also can be found in the works of Max Weber).

4.2.3 A Dialectical Concept of Power

Synthesising objective and subjective approaches allows conceiving power as a dynamic process that includes power practices and power structures. Power is the disposition over means required to influence processes and decisions in one's own interest. Domination refers to the disposition over means of coercion that are employed for influencing others, processes, and decisions. Means of power are economic resources (money, means of production, commodities), social relationships, human activities, capabilities, and knowledge. This means that what Pierre Bourdieu (1986a, 1986b) has termed economic, political, and cultural capital are structures that allow those individuals and groups who control a certain share of these capital types to influence decisions to certain degrees (see Fuchs 2003a).

Power structures are not confined to politics, there are economic, political, and cultural power: property, collective decision-making power, and definition power. Economic power is a disposition over property, political power the capacity to influence decisions that are binding for all, and cultural power the capacity to shape definitions, meanings, interpretations, norms, and values. Table 4.2 provides an overview of the three dimensions of power structures. Power is relational. It is a social relation, in which individuals or groups control specific shares of a specific structure.

Objective power structures enable and constrain further (actual or potential) power struggles and practices that aim at changing the distribution of power in social systems and society. Power has both a subjective and an objective level that produces each other mutually. It is a permanent dynamic production process in which actors enter relations, conflicts, and

TABLE 4.2 Three forms of power structures

Dimension of society	Definition of power	Structures of power in modern society
Economy	Control of use-values and resources that are produced, distributed, and consumed.	Control of money and capital.
Politics	Influence on collective decisions that determine aspects of the lives of humans in certain communities and social systems.	Control of governments, bureaucratic state institutions, parliament, military, police, parties, lobby groups, civil society groups, etc.
Culture	Definition of moral values and meaning that shape what is considered as important, reputable and worthy in society.	Control of structures that define meaning and moral values in society (e.g. universities, religious groups, intellectual circles, opinion-making groups, etc).

Three Theoretical Concepts of Power

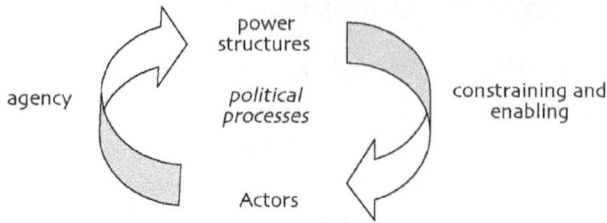

FIGURE 4.1   Power as dynamic process

discourse in order to constitute, change, and reproduce collective structures that enable and constrain further social practices, etc. Power structures emerge or are reproduced dynamically from social power practices that influence further practices and relations so that existing power structures are reproduced, there is the potential for the emergence of new ones emerge, etc. (cf. Figure 4.1, for a more detailed discussion cf. Fuchs 2003b). There are different enabling and constraining degrees of power structures ranging from very open structures that allow a maximum of freedom and rights (including the right to welfare and social security, the right to participation, leisure, and self-expression, the guarantee of the realisation of human rights for all, freedom of speech, press, assembly, association, and belief, etc.) to very closed coercive structures that minimise freedom and rights.

Power structures take on a specific form in modern society – the capital form. Modern society is a capitalist society. For Marx, capital is self-expanding value and accumulation is its inherent feature. Capital needs to permanently increase; otherwise companies, branches, industries, or entire economies enter phases of crisis. Capitalism is therefore a dynamic and inherently expansive system, which has implications for the exploitation of nature, centralisation, concentration, uneven development, imperialism, military conflicts, the creation of milieus of unpaid and highly exploited labour, the destruction of nature and the depletion of natural resources, etc. "The employment of surplus-value as capital, or its reconversion into capital, is called accumulation of capital" (Marx 1867, 725). The capitalist

> shares with the miser an absolute drive towards self-enrichment. But what appears in the miser as the mania of an individual is in the capitalist the effect of a social mechanism in which he is merely a cog. Moreover, the development of capitalist production makes it necessary constantly to increase the amount of capital laid out in a given industrial undertaking, and competition subordinates every individual capitalist to the immanent laws of capitalist production, as external

and coercive laws. It compels him to keep extending his capital, so as to preserve it, and he can only extend it by means of progressive accumulation.

(Marx 1867, 739)

Capitalism is a society that is grounded in and driven by the accumulation of capital.

The drive to accumulate is in contemporary society not limited to money capital. We also find the accumulation imperative in the accumulation of political decision power and the accumulation of cultural distinction, reputation, and definition power. Capitalism is not a purely economic system, but rather a society, in which the subsystems are driven by the accumulation imperative. Accumulation logic is multidimensional and shapes the modern economy, politics, culture, private life, everyday life, and the modern humans' relationship to nature. The subsystems of modern society have their own specific forms of the accumulation logic, which means that they all have their own specific economies of production, circulation, and distribution of power. Power takes on economic, political, and cultural forms. Pierre Bourdieu (1986a, 1986b) has generalised the concepts of capital and accumulation and describes capitalism as a class system based on the accumulation of economic, political, and cultural capital.

Human actors and groups in modern society have a certain share of the total available capital. These structures are in modern society organised in such a way that humans compete for accumulating capital shares at the expense of others. This results in social and symbolic power struggles that are an expression of asymmetrical distributions of power. Power struggles organised in the form of, e.g. elections, wars, industrial conflict, or everyday disputes produce and reproduce objective power structures and institutions such as laws, decision-making bodies, the state system, nation states, parliaments, ministries, bureaucracies, courts, public offices, departments, public administration bodies, coercive state apparatuses such as police, military, law, the judicial system, the prison system, secret services, etc. These structures are influenced and controlled by different social groups to certain degrees according to the outcome of power struggles.

Power and politics do not necessarily involve leadership as suggested by Max Weber.[4] Power can be distributed in different forms in social systems. Domination always includes sanctions, repression, threats of violence, and an asymmetric distribution of power. In political relationships, it is determined how power is constituted, distributed, allocated, and disposed. Highly co-operative and inclusive social systems that are characterised by solidarity and altruism are not systems without power, but systems with a rather symmetrical distribution of power and a minimisation of domination. Power can be distributed in different manners: In more symmetrical distributions actors can influence the decisions which affect them to a large degree, in an asymmetrical distribution of power certain actors control resources in such a way that they can influence decisions in their own sense and circumvent the possibility that others can also influence these decisions. Domination is based on asymmetrical distributions of power, but it means more than that, it also includes means of coercion that are employed in order to influence others, processes, and decisions in one's own sense. Domination always includes sanctions, repression, threats of violence, and an asymmetric distribution of power. It is a coercive, institutionalised social relationship of power. Domination cannot be distributed in a symmetrical manner. It always involves an asymmetrical distribution of resources and possibilities. It necessarily is exerted on someone against his will. Coercive means are an expression of the possibility of disciplines, sanctions, and repression. Domination means that these coercive means exist along with the threat of being used against someone or certain groups. Domination can also be found where these means are not directly employed, but only exist as a means of threat.

Power does not necessarily imply violence, whereas domination often is violent and repressive. Power is potentially a violent social relation, but not necessarily. Domination in contrast implies the existence of an asymmetrical power relation and the use of repression or even violence in this relation. But what is violence? Johan Galtung (1990, 292) defines violence as "avoidable insults to basic human needs, and more generally to life, lowering the real level of needs satisfaction below what is potentially possible" (Galtung 1990, 292). Violence can according to Galtung (1990) be divided into three principal forms: direct violence (through physical intervention; an event), structural violence (through state or organisational mandate; a process), and cultural violence (dehumanising or otherwise exclusionary representations; an invariance). According to Galtung, in exerting violence one can physically coerce somebody (physical violence), exclude him/her from access to vital resources (structural violence) or manipulate his/her mind or ruin his/her reputation (ideological violence). Violence not only exists if it is actually exerted, but also if it is only a threat: "Threats of violence are also violence" (Galtung 1990, 292). The three forms of Galtung's understanding of violence are forms of how people or groups try to accumulate different forms of power.

Sylvia Walby argues against broad forms of violence. She argues that physical assault is more dangerous and often a more severe and more direct threat to life than what Galtung terms cultural/ideological violence. Violence is the intentionally caused physical harm to a human being (Walby 2022). Violence is turning of the human being "into a thing in the most literal sense: it makes a corpse out of him" (Weil 2005, 183). Violence is not the same as power. It is a dimension of coercive societies and a social relation, where humans try to intentionally cause physical harms to other humans who don't agree to the cause of that harm (see Walby 2022 for a detailed discussion). The harm caused is usually "a physical injury" (Walby et al. 2017, 33), but can also in addition involve mental or psychological harm. Physically injuring others can take on a variety of forms such as assault, torture, rape, killing, murder, war, genocide, enslavement, etc. Violence is a means towards an end such as gaining control of resources (e.g. land, humans), exterminating certain humans, i.e. the absolute exclusion from society through death, gaining pleasure or reputation, etc. Violence is a means for creating alienation, but it is not in itself an alienated system or condition. Repression is a more general category than violence. Violence is a specific form of repression.

Different forms of repression can be exerted in order to accumulate different forms of power. In modern society, economic, political, and cultural power can be accumulated and tend to be asymmetrically distributed. The logic of accumulation (getting more and more of something) is vital for modern society. It has its origins in the capitalist economy. But it also shapes the logic of modern politics and culture that are focused on the accumulation of political and cultural power. Capitalism is therefore not just an economic system, but also a form of society. Physical, structural, and ideological repression can be used in any of the three dimensions/fields of modern society for trying to accumulate power at the expense of others. Many structures of modern society are based on specific forms of repression that help accumulating power. For example, a corporation makes use of the structural repression of the market and private property in order to accumulate capital. Or the state uses of the monopoly of physical violence and the institutional power of government institutions in order to make collective decisions.

Power exists in all situations where humans enter social relationships and have to act in order to transform structures by taking decisions of how to act. In this sense, it can be considered as decision-oriented capacity to act that produces structures that in a recursive and self-referential loop enable and constrain further practices. For transforming structures and taking decisions humans depend on each other and on resources, depending on how these relationships are organised (symmetrically vs. asymmetrically, i.e. all control resources and humans together in self-managed processes or an elite controls resources and humans) different distributions of power are possible. Asymmetrical distributions of power are characteristic of coercive systems, but coercive power is not

Three Theoretical Concepts of Power

something fixed. Oppressed groups can challenge coercion by realising the power potential that they as collective actor comprised of human capacities possess.

Counter-action and counter-power are not always realistic and achievable, but it is at least always a possibility of action that under certain circumstances can result in liberation from domination. Anthony Giddens speaks in this context of the dialectic of control:

> All strategies of control employed by superordinate individuals or groups call forth counter-strategies on the part of the subordinates. [...] To be an agent is to be able to make a difference to the world, and to be able to make a difference is to have power (where power means transformative capacity).
>
> (Giddens 1985, 10–11)

For Giddens, counter-power is however not a potential, but an automatism ("calls forth"). He does not see that specific interests, violence, and ideology can forestall change and cement the existence of domination. There is no guarantee that humans who are oppressed see the need for change and engage in building counter-power. Counter-power is always a potential, but never a necessity. Counter-power does not automatically result from domination. It is a potential for changing the social world.

Power is institutionalised and objectified in structures. At the same time, structures need to be reproduced in order to exist continuously. Any system of power, be it a fascist state, a slave system, a company that highly exploits its workers or a patriarchal family structure, is upheld by the practices that are organised within it. Those oppressed by asymmetric power structures must engage in practices that reproduce these structures in order for them to continue to exist: the citizens obey the laws of the fascist state, the slave and the worker in the company produce profits for the slave-master and the capitalist day-in day-out, the wife continues to have sex with the husband who beats her up, etc. These practices are what Gramsci calls hegemony. Hegemony means "an active and voluntary (free) consent" (Gramsci 1971, 271). But why do oppressed people not always resist their oppressor? It is partly out of fear of violence or getting killed, fear that others may be harmed to, or the ideological belief that the system is good the way it is, that it could be worse, or that there is no alternative. Even if there is hegemony, there is always the potential for people to resist, build counter-power and try to overthrow the dominant structures of power. Often this is however difficult and they are confronted with a lack of resources, motivation, courage, and organisation. Resistance is therefore a structurally difficult, but morally important form of work.

Marx stresses the object-subject dialectic of power in his analyses of French politics. He stresses on the one hand the objective power dimension of dominative systems: He Marx points out how the French bourgeoisie ruled over the working class with the help of violence, censorship, surveillance, military rule, and ideological education. Marx says that the bourgeoisie rules by the sword:

> It apotheosised the sword; the sword rules it. It destroyed the revolutionary press; its own press has been destroyed. It placed popular meetings under police supervision; its salons are under the super- vision of the police. It disbanded the democratic National Guards; its own National Guard is disbanded. It imposed a state of siege; a state of siege is imposed upon it. It sup- planted the juries by military commissions; its juries are supplanted by military commissions. It subjected public education to the sway of the priests; the priests subject it to their own education. It transported people without trial; it is being transported without trial.
>
> (Marx 1852, 101–102)

So power has for Marx an objective-structural dimension. Those in power "repressed every stirring in society by means of the state power; every stirring in its society is suppressed by means of the state power" (Marx 1852, 102).

A revolutionary or protest movement challenges existing power structures. Its constitution and practices are a form of power of the people in itself. Therefore Marx describes social struggles as "struggle between the two powers" (Marx 1852, 62) and a "[w]ar between the two powers" (Marx 1852, 75). Power for Marx is something that is exerted by ruling groups, individuals, and classes, but is not merely located in institutions, but also something that can be built and conquered in social struggles. Marx (1852, 81) therefore also speaks of oppressed people conquering the control of power. Power is distributed in different ways and this distribution can be changed by social struggles. Marx described that in France under Louis Philippe (French King from 1830–1848) the "commercial bourgeoisie" held "the lion's share of power" (Marx 1852, 88). This formulation implies that power is distributed and redistributable.

In his analysis of the Paris Commune (1871), Marx argues that a revolutionary movement that takes over state power has to transform this power. He sees revolution as a transformation of power structures and a change in the distribution of power: "But the working class cannot simply lay hold on the ready-made state machinery and wield it for their own purpose. The political instrument of their enslavement cannot serve as the

Three Theoretical Concepts of Power

political instrument of their emancipation" (Marx 1871, 533). In the Paris Commune, the revolutionaries' appropriation of power – its "break[s] with the modern state power" (Marx 1871, 333) – resulted in the transformation of administrative, educational, judicial, repressive and other state institutions:

> Not only municipal administration, but the whole initiative hitherto exercised by the state was laid into the hands of the Commune. Having once got rid of the standing army and the police – the physical force elements of the old government – the Commune was anxious to break the spiritual force of repression, the 'parson-power', by the disestablishment and disendowment of all churches as proprietary bodies. The priests were sent back to the recesses of private life, there to feed upon the alms of the faithful in imitation of their predecessors, the apostles. The whole of the educational institutions were opened to the people gratuitously, and at the same time cleared of all interference of church and state. Thus, not only was education made accessible to all, but science itself freed from the fetters which class prejudice and governmental force had imposed upon it. The judicial functionaries were to be divested of that sham independence which had but served to mask their abject subserviency to all succeeding governments to which, in turn, they had taken, and broken, the oaths of allegiance. Like the rest of public servants, magistrates and judges were to be elective, responsible, and revocable.
>
> (Marx 1871, 331–332)

Marx describes that a revolutionary movement not just has the power to transform political structures, but also economic ones:

> Yes, gentlemen, the Commune intended to abolish that class property which makes the labor of the many the wealth of the few. It aimed at the expropriation of the expropriators. It wanted to make individual property a truth by transforming the means of production, land, and capital, now chiefly the means of enslaving and exploiting labor, into mere instruments of free and associated labor. But this is communism, "impossible" communism!
>
> (Marx 1871, 335)

Marx describes power as a dialectic of structures and practices: The French regime used state power to oppress citizens and workers economically and politically. The revolutionary movement broke in 1871 with the hegemonic reproduction of these power structures and seized power. It then started to transform the existing power structures by making them democratic.

In modern society, the two most important dimensions of institutionalised power are capital and the state. Framed more generally, this is the question of how the economy and the state are related. Marx says in this context that "state power assumed more and more the character of the national power of capital over labor, of a public force organized for social enslavement, of an engine of class despotism" (Marx 1871, 329). And: "And yet the state power is not suspended in midair. Bonaparte represents a class, and the most numerous class of French society at that, the small-holding peasants" (Marx 1852, 105). The question is what it means that state power represents class. It does not mean that capitalists directly rule, run, and control the state. But how can we best think about this relationship of capital and the state?

The state is not a homogenous apparatus or machine of the ruling class for dominating the ruled class, but a field of power forces. First, there are factions of the capitalist class (e.g. transnational corporations, small and medium enterprises, finance capital, commercial capital, manufacturing capital, cultural capital, etc.) that compete for shares of capital and power and therefore have to a certain degree conflicting interests. Second, although there are overlaps of the capitalist class and the political elite (e.g. when managers become politicians or bureaucrats become consultants for companies or when private–public partnerships are established as part of neoliberal governance systems), their activities, personnel, and interests are not co-extensive. The differentiation of the state and the capitalist economy in modern society has also brought about a division of labour between capitalists and politicians.

Third, the state's class power can be challenged by left-wing political movements that want to establish a transitory state that drives back capitalist interests and advances welfare and social benefits for all. It is of course doubtful in this context that a socialist state can exist in a capitalist society and that state power is necessary in all forms of society, but at the same time, progressive movements' goal to conquer state power is not necessarily a social democratic-reformist strategy, but can be based on politics of radical reformism that are politically immanent and transcendental at the same time. The state is however not just challenged and reproduced by political parties, but also by social movements organised in civil society.

Given these complexities and contradictions of the state, it can only be conceived as a contradictory force field with temporal unity – a power bloc – between conflicting

Three Theoretical Concepts of Power

interests that form political alliances. The state is an "institutional crystallization", "the material condensation of a relationship of forces", "a strategic field and process of intersecting power networks, which both articulate and exhibit mutual contradictions and displacements" (Poulantzas 1980, 136). The state does not directly map or mirror the interests of the capitalist class, but rather crystallises the complexities of the class structure in contradictory ways. It is precisely by the articulation of complex factions and oppositions through which dominant interests are transposed from economic power into state power and in a dialectical reversal back from state power to economic power. The

> state crystallizes the relations of production and class relations. The modern political state does not translate the 'interests' of the dominant classes at the political level, but the relationship between those interests and the interests of the dominated classes – which means that it precisely constitutes the 'political' expression of the interests of the dominant classes.
>
> (Poulantzas 2008, 80)

4.3 Media, Communication, and Power

When discussing media and communication power, Manuel Castells' approach has in recent years received the most attention.

The task that Manuel Castells has set himself for his book *Communication Power* is to suggest answers to the question: "where does power lie in the global network society?" (Castells 2009, 42). Castells defines communication power as a fourfold form of power characteristic for the network society: networking power, network power, networked power, network-making power (Castells 2009, 42–47, 418–420). Network-making power is for Castells the "paramount form of power in the network society" (Castells 2009, 47). It is held and exercised by programmers and switchers. Programmers have the power "to constitute network(s), and to program/reprogram the network(s) in terms of the goals assigned to the network". Switchers have the power "to connect and ensure the cooperation of different networks by sharing common goals and combining resources while fending off competition from other networks by setting up strategic cooperation" (Castells 2009, 45). Communication power is for Castells the power to create, maintain and shape networks by communication. He reduces the power of the media and communication thereby to the cultural level – the production, and distribution and interpretation of information in social relations.

Castells (2009, 10) defines power in a Weber-inspired way as "the relational capacity that enables a social actor to influence asymmetrically the decisions of other social actor(s) in ways that favor the empowered actor's will, interests, and values" (10). Power is associated with coercion, domination, violence or potential violence, and asymmetry. He refers to the power concepts of Foucault, Weber, and Habermas and argues that he builds on Giddens' structuration theory. However, as Section 4.2 showed, Giddens conceives power in a completely different way, a way that is neither mentioned nor discussed by Castells. For Giddens, power is s transformative capacity in all social relationships.

In Giddens structuration theory, power is not necessarily coercive, violent, and asymmetrically distributed. Therefore it becomes possible to conceive of and analyse situations and social systems, in which power is more symmetrically distributed, for example situations and systems of participatory democracy. Power as transformative capacity seems indeed to be a fundamental aspect of all societies. This also means that there is a huge difference between Castells' approach and Giddens' structuration theory, which as such is not problematic, but should also be explicated, especially because Castells (2009, 14) says that he builds on Giddens' structuration theory (14), which he in fact does not. The problem with Castells' notion of power is that he sees coercive, violent, dominative power relationships as "the foundational relations of society throughout history, geography, and cultures" (Castells 2009, 9). Such power is for him "the most fundamental process in society" (Castells 2009, 10). Furthermore, Castells (2009, 13) dismisses the "naïve image of a reconciled human community, a normative utopia that is belied by historical observation".

Is it really likely that all history of humankind and that all social situations and systems, in which we live, are always and necessarily shaped by power struggles, coercion, violence, and domination? Relationships of love, intimacy, and affection are in modern society unfortunately often characterised by violence and coercion and are therefore frequently (in Castells' terms) power relationships. But isn't love a prototypical phenomenon, where many people experience feelings and actions that negate violence, domination, and coercion? Isn't the phenomenon of altruism in love the practical falsification of the claim that coercive power is the most fundamental process in society? Not coercive power, but co-operation is the most fundamental process in society (Fuchs 2008, 31–34, 40–58). It is possible to create social systems without coercive power (in Castells' terms) or with a symmetric distribution of power (in Giddens' terminology). Conceiving power as violent coercion poses the danger of naturalising and fetishising coercion and violent struggles as necessary and therefore not historical qualities of society. The problematic ideological-theoretical implication is that in the final instance war must exist in all societies and a state of peace is dismissed and considered as being categorically impossible. Castells surely does not share this implication, as his analysis of communication power in the Iraq war shows.

The task of Castells' book *Communication Power* is to "advance the construction of a grounded theory of power in the network society" (Castells 2009, 5). Castells does not want to place himself in theoretical debates, he bases his approach on "a selective reading of power theories" (Castells 2009, 6), does not want to write books about books (Castells 2009, 6, 2010, 25), and thinks that social theory books are contributing to the deforestation of the planet (Castells 2009, 6), which is just another expression for saying that they are unimportant and not worth the paper they are printed on. Lacking grounding in social theory, Castells cannot explain why he uses a certain definition of power and not another one. His lack of engagement with social theory results in a fetishisation of domination as an endless and natural social phenomenon.

John B. Thompson (1995) distinguishes four forms of power (see Table 4.3). The problem with Thompson's approach is that the media's power is reduced to the symbolic

TABLE 4.3 John B. Thompson's four forms of power (based on Thompson 1995, 12–18)

Type of power	Definition	Resources	Institutions
Economic power	"Economic power stems from human productive activity, that is, activity concerned with the provision of the means of subsistence through the extraction of raw materials and their transformation into goods which can be consumed or exchanged in a market" (14).	Material and financial resources	Economic institutions
Political power	Political power "stems from the activity of coordinating individuals and regulating the patterns of their interaction" (14).	Authority	Political institutions (e.g. states)
Coercive power	"Coercive power involves the use, or threatened use, of physical force to subdue or conquer an opponent" (15).	Physical and armed force	Coercive institutions (military, police, carceral institutions, etc)
Symbolic power	Symbolic power is the "capacity to intervene in the course of events, to influence the actions of others and indeed to create events, by means of the production and transmission of symbolic forms" (17)	Means of information and communication	Cultural institutions (church, schools, universities, media, etc).

dimension and that the relationship of violence and power is unclear. Symbolic power is an important dimension of the media: the media not only have form but also communicate content to the public, which allows attempts to influence the minds of the members of the public. But ideology is not the only aspect of the media, the media are rather a terrain where different forms of power and power struggles manifest themselves: the media have specific structures of private or public ownership that tend to be concentrated. There are attempts to politically control and influence the media and the media often have political roles in elections, social movement struggles, etc. Violence is a frequent topic in media content. The media are not just a realm of symbolic power, but rather material and symbolic spaces, where structures and contradictions of economic, political, coercive, and symbolic power manifest themselves. It is unclear why Thompson defines violence as a separate form of power. Nick Couldry (2002, 4) defines media power as "the concentration in media institutions of the symbolic power of 'constructing reality'". Like Thompson's definition of power, also the one given by Couldry focuses on the symbolic and cultural dimension of the media.

Media power is not cultural, superstructural, or ideational. It is a multidimensional form of economic, political, and cultural power. The media are not just cultural, they also have a political economy that frames the production, diffusion, and interpretation of information. James Curran (2002, Chapter 5) has identified 11 dimensions of media power and seven dimensions of media counter-power. I have classified these dimensions according to the three dimensions of media power (see Table 4.4): economic media power, political media power, and cultural media power. Curran stresses that media power is not just symbolic, but multidimensional. The distinction of three realms of society (economy, politics, and culture) allows us to classify forms of media power (Table 4.4). Curran stresses the contradictory character of contemporary media: There are "eleven main factors that encourage the media to support dominant power interests" (Curran 2002, 148), but "the media are also subject to countervailing pressures which can pull potentially in the other direction" (Curran 2002, 151).

The systematic typology of media power that is based on Curran's approach shows that modern media can best be viewed dialectically: they are subject to elite control, but have potentials for acting as and being influenced by counter-powers that question elite control. This form of struggle is a potential, which means that it does not automatically arise. The power of dominant and alternative media tends to be distributed unequally (see: Fuchs 2010; Sandoval and Fuchs 2010): alternative media are often facing resource inequalities and have to exist based on precarious labour and resource precariousness.

Media, Communication, and Power

TABLE 4.4 Power and counter-power in the media (based on: Curran 2002, Chapter 5)

Dimension of media power	Forms of media power	Forms of media counter-power
Economic media power	High entry and operation costs; media concentration; private media ownership; influence of companies on the media via advertising; market pressure to produce homogenous (often uncritical) content with wide appeal; content that appeals to wealthy consumers; the unequal distribution of economic resources (money) allows economic elites more influence on and control of the media	Public media, alternative grassroots media, public funding for alternative media; staff power (e.g. critical journalism, investigative reporting); consumer power (e.g. by support of alternative media in the form of donations)
Political media power	State censorship of the media; public relations of large (political and economic organisations) results in bureaucratic lobbying apparatus that aims to influence the media; the unequal distribution of political resources (influence, decision power, political relations) allows economic elites more influence on and control of the media	Media regulation that secures quality, fair reporting, diversity, freedom of expression, assembly and opinion; alternative news sources state redistribution of resources from the more powerful to the less powerful
Cultural media power	Focus on content covering prestige institutions, celebrities, and others who have high reputation; dominant ideologies influence dominant media to a certain degree; the unequal distribution of cultural resources (reputation, prestige) allows economic elites more influence on and control of the media	creation of counter-organisations that develop counter-discourses and operate their own media

4.4 Social Media and Power

Discussions about "social media" such as Facebook, YouTube, Twitter, or Weibo have in recent years often been discussions about power. The question in such debates is often: What's the power of social media? This question is wrongly posed and tends to imply that technological system in a linear and deterministic manner have specific one-dimensional implications for society. The major claim of management gurus, the tabloid press, certain politicians, observers, and one-dimensional scholars has been that social media empowers citizens, consumers, has resulted in political revolutions, and makes society, the economy, and culture more democratic. Conservative blogger Andrew

Sullivan's (2009) claimed that the "revolution will be twittered" in the context of the 2009 Iran protests. In light of the Arab Spring, there was talk about a "revolution 2.0" (Ghonim 2012). *Foreign Policy Magazine* titled an article "The revolution will be tweeted"[5] and the *New York Times* wrote that the "Egyptian revolution began on Twitter".[6] In the scholarly world academics such as Manuel Castells (2012, 229) claimed that the "networked movements of our time are largely based on the Internet". Clay Shirky argues that social media "will result in a net improvement for democracy" (Gladwell and Shirky 2011, 154). Concerning the economic realm, management gurus Tapscott and Williams (2007, 15) argue that social media result in "a new economic democracy [...] in which we all have a lead role". Henry Jenkins sees social media in the context of the development that "the Web has become a site of consumer participation" (Jenkins 2008, 137).

Authors sceptical of such claims have stressed that social media are in contemporary society embedded into structures of control and domination. Malcolm Gladwell writes that Facebook and Twitter activism only succeeds in situations that do not require "to make a real sacrifice" (Gladwell 2010, 47), such as registering in a bone-marrow database or getting back a stolen phone. "The evangelists of social media", such as Clay Shirky,

> seem to believe that a Facebook friend is the same as a real friend and that signing up for a donor registry in Silicon Valley today is activism in the same sense as sitting at a segregated lunch counter in Greensboro in 1960.
>
> (Gladwell 2010, 46)

Social media would "make it easier for activists to express themselves, and harder for that expression to have any impact" (Gladwell 2010, 49). Social media "are not a natural enemy of the status quo" and "are well suited to making the existing social order more efficient" (Gladwell 2010, 49).

Evgeny Morozov (2010) argues that the notion of "Twitter revolution" is based on a belief in cyber-utopianism – "a naive belief in the emancipatory nature of online communication that rests on a stubborn refusal to acknowledge its downside" (Morozov 2010, xiii) that combined with Internet centrism forms a techno-deterministic ideology. Technological solutionism is recasting "all complex social situations either as neatly defined problems with definite, computable solutions or as transparent and self-evident processes that can be easily optimised – if only the right algorithms are in place". The consequence of solutionism would be the risk to create "unexpected consequences that could eventually cause more damage than the problems they seek to address". Morozov shows that solutionism is a typical ideology of Silicon Valley entrepreneurs and intellectuals who glorify the Internet as being the solution to societal problems or what is seen as societal problems and may in fact not be problems at all. Thinkers that Morozov criticises for being Internet centrists are on the one hand the likes of Eric Schmidt (Google) and Mark Zuckerberg (Facebook) and on the other hand intellectuals such as Yochai Benkler, Nicholas Carr, Jeff Jarvis, Kevin Kelly, Lawrence Lessig, Clay Shirky, Don Tapscott, and Jonathan Zittrain. Internet centrism and technological solutionism "impoverish and infantilize our public debate" (Morozov 2013, 43).

Social or other media neither result in positive or negative consequences. They do not act. They do not make society. They do not have one-dimensional impacts. Media are systems that are in a complex manner embedded into antagonistic economic, political and cultural power structures that are antagonistic.

Social media in contemporary society are shaped by structures of economic, political, and cultural power:

- Social media have specific ownership structures. If social media's economic power is asymmetrically distributed, then a private class owns social media. If it is more symmetrically distributed, then a collective of users or all people own social media.

- Social media have specific decision-making structures. If social media's political power is asymmetrically distributed, then a specific group controls decision-making. If it is more symmetrically distributed, then all users or all people in the society can influence decision-making.

- Social media have specific mechanisms for the generation of reputation and popularity. If social media's cultural power is asymmetrically distributed, then the reputation and visibility of certain actors are in contrast to the attention and visibility given to others large. Social media can also act as conveyors of ideologies that misrepresent reality. If highly visible actors communicate such ideologies, then it is likely that they have some effect. If cultural power is more symmetrically distributed, then all users have a significant degree of visibility and attention.

Social media are spaces, where media power and counter-power are played out. Dominant platforms such as Facebook, Google/YouTube, and Twitter are privately owned and there are economic, political, and ideological forms of media power at play: private ownership, concentration, advertising, the logic of consumption and entertainment, the high visibility of and attention given to elites and celebrities shape and filter communication on dominant social media platforms. At the same time, dominant structures are questioned by phenomena such as file sharing, commons-based social media that are non-profit and non-commercial (e.g. Wikipedia, Diaspora*), social movements' use of social media for political purposes, the development of alternative social media, protests against the dominance of platforms like Google, protests and legal disputes over privacy violations, etc. Contemporary social media is a field of power struggles, in which dominant actors command a large share of economic, political, and ideological media power that can be challenged by alternative actors that have fewer resources, visibility, and attention, but try to make the best use of the unequal share of media power they are confronted with in order to fight against the dominant powers.

Social media optimism and pessimism assume that the Internet is the solution to society's problem and can perfect society and get rid of the existence of problems. Karl Marx (1867) used the term "fetishism" for the logic of assuming that things are more important than social relations between humans: Techno-optimism and techno-pessimism are forms of technological fetishism that sees an artefact as a solution to human-made problems. Max Horkheimer (1947) spoke in this context of instrumental reason and Herbert Marcuse (1941/1998) of technological rationality: instrumental/technological rationality assumes that society function like machines, are fully controllable and programmable like an algorithm. Internet fetishism assumes that society is a machine and functions like the Internet and that the Internet is therefore the solution for everything in society. Technological rationality wants to implement "dictates of the apparatus" that use a "framework of standardized performances" (Marcuse 1941/1998, 44): Google's standardized algorithms tell people what they should like, define as reality, where they should go, what they should consider important, etc. A tool like Google Maps can indeed be helpful for finding the way around, but it also allows Google (and as a consequence potentially also other companies and the police) to track your movements and to subject movements in space to the logic of advertising: targeted advertisements follow you wherever you take your mobile phone and present reality and what you should eat, drink, watch and like according to the logic of advertisers: "Expediency in terms of technological reason is, at the same time, expediency in terms of profitable efficiency" (Marcuse 1941/1998, 47). Marcuse (1941/1988, 41) warned that organising society according to technological rationality can result in fascism and said that Nazi Germany was ruled by "technical considerations of imperialistic efficiency and rationality".

It is no accident that Internet centrism and technological solutionism have become so predominant in the early stage of the 3rd millennium. After 9/11, policing has increasingly looked for security by algorithms in a world of high insecurity. It advances a fetishism of technology — the belief that crime and terrorism can be controlled by technology. Technology promises an easy fix to complex societal problems. 9/11 has resulted in "the misguided and socially disruptive attempts to identify terrorists and then predict their attacks" (Gandy 2009, 5). The world economic crisis that started in 2008 has added additional uncertainties and created a situation of high insecurity. 9/11 was indicative of a crisis of the hegemony of Western thought that was questioned by people and groups in Arab countries that put religious ideology against Western liberal and capitalist ideology. The "war against terror", the security discourse, and the intensification of surveillance resulted in a political crisis, in which war and terrorism tend to reinforce each other mutually, which results in a vicious cycle that intensifies hatred and conflict. Financialization and neoliberalism made capitalism more unjust (which constitutes a social crisis) and also crisis-prone, which resulted in a new world economic crisis that started in 2008.

Capitalism faced a multidimensional crisis in and beyond the first decade of the 21st century. This crisis has further advanced ideologies of control and technological fixes that advance the ideology of the solvability of societal problems by technologies. Unemployment and lack of jobs? Social media will create them! Economic crisis? Invest in new Internet platforms and everything will be fine! Uprisings, revolutions, and riots? All created by social media! It is no accident that ideological discourses like these proliferate in times of crisis: The Internet promises easy solutions to complex societal phenomena and contradictions intrinsic to capitalism, bureaucratic control, and resulting inequalities.

Stuart Hall et al. (1978) describe how a moral panic about street robbery ("mugging") developed in the United Kingdom in the 1970s. They argue that this panic must be seen in the context of the crisis of the mid-1970s. This crisis would have been a global crisis of capitalism (recession), a crisis of political apparatuses (such as ruling-class and working-class parties), a crisis of the state, and a crisis of hegemony and political legitimacy (Hall et al. 1978, 317–319). In crises, people look for causes and answers. Ideology that wants to maintain the system does not engage with the systemic causes of crises, but rather displaces the causes ideologically. There is a "displacement effect": "the connection between the crisis and the way it is appropriated in the social experience of the majority – social anxiety – passes through a series of false 'resolutions'" (Hall et al. 1978, 322). Technological solutionism and Internet centrism are contemporary ideological false resolutions in situations of global crisis.

Technological solutionism and Internet/social media fetishism constitute a permanent form of what Hall et al. (1978) called signification spirals: In a signification spiral, a threat is identified and it is argued that "more troubling times" will come "if no action is taken", which results in the "call for 'firm steps'" (Hall et al. 1978, 223). If we do not act and use the latest Internet platform or app, the contemporary ideologues tell us, society cannot be saved and we will become the victims of criminals, terrorists, paedophiles, deviants, extremists, and our own non-knowledge that can only be, as they want to tell us, technologically controlled. Today, there are many Internet signification spirals, where the Internet is seen as the cause of and/or solution to evils in the world.

In a moral panic, a "control culture" (such as police discourses about crime or terrorism) and a "signification culture" (like criminal hyperbole created by tabloid media) often act together (Hall et al. 1978, 76). The media, just like the police, then act as "an apparatus of the control process itself — an 'ideological state apparatus'" (Hall et al. 1978, 76). The Internet as a relatively new medium of information, communication, and collaboration (Fuchs 2008) is inserted into contemporary moral panics in a different way than the mainstream media that simply tend to act as ideological control institutions. The Internet and social media act as arena of ideological projections of fears and hopes that are associated with moral panics — some argue that they are dangerous spaces that are used by terrorists, rioters, vandals, and criminals and therefore needs to be policed with the help of Internet surveillance, whereas others argue that the Internet is a new space of political hope that is at the heart of demonstrations, rebellions, protests and revolutions that struggle for more democracy. What both discourses share is a strong belief in the power of technology independently of society, they mistake societal phenomena (crime, terror, crises, political transformations) to be caused and controllable by technology. But societal phenomena merely express themselves in communicative and technological spaces; technologies do not cause them. Technological determinism inscribes power into technology; it reduces power to a technologically manageable phenomenon and thereby neglects the interaction of technology and society. The Internet is not like the mainstream mass media an ideological actor, but rather an object of ideological signification in moral panics and moral euphoria.

4.5 Conclusion: The Need for a Dialectic and Critical Theory of Media and Society

A critical theory of media and technology is based on dialectical reasoning (see Figure 4.2). This allows us to see the causal relationship of media/technology and society as multidimensional and complex: a specific media/technology has multiple, at least two, potential effects on society and social systems that can co-exist or stand

Technological/Media determinism:

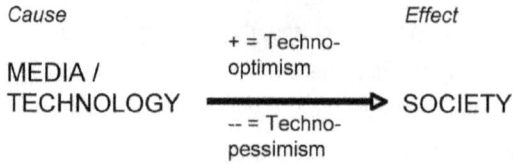

Cause   *Effect*

+ = Techno-
optimism

MEDIA /
TECHNOLOGY ────────────▷ SOCIETY

-- = Techno-
pessimism

Dialectic of technology/media & society:

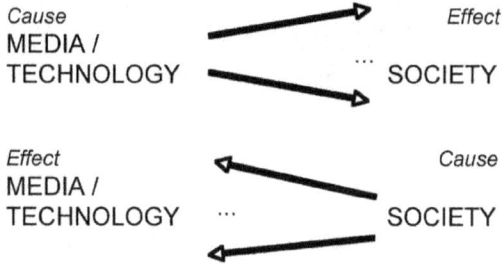

Cause
MEDIA /   *Effect*
TECHNOLOGY   ··· SOCIETY

Effect
MEDIA /   *Cause*
TECHNOLOGY   ···   SOCIETY

FIGURE 4.2   Two logics of the relationship between media technology and society

in contradiction to each other. Which potentials are realised is based on how society, interests, power structures, and struggles shape the design and usage of technology in multiple ways that are also potentially contradictory. Andrew Feenberg says in this context that Critical Theory "argues that technology is not a thing in the ordinary sense of the term, but an 'ambivalent' process of development suspended between different possibilities" (Feenberg 2002, 15).

The revolution in Egypt was not a Twitter revolution, but related to the context of a highly stratified society. Real wages have been decreasing over 20 years, strikes were forbidden, there was repression against the political left and unions, the gap between the rich and the poor has been large, poverty constantly increased, wages in industry have been low, the global economic crisis has resulted in mass lay-offs and a food crisis, Mubarak controlled together with the army Egyptian politics and bureaucracy since 1981, the illiteracy rate has been high, and there has been a contradiction between Islamic traditions and the values of modernisation (Björklund 2011).

Pierre Bourdieu (1986b) distinguished between economic capital (money), political capital (power), and cultural capital (status, skills, and educational attainments). Egypt was under Mubarak a society with a highly stratified class structure: there was a class that controlled the political-economic-military complex and accumulated economic, political, and cultural capital at the expense of the masses of Egyptian people. The Egyptian revolution was a revolution against capitalism's multidimensional injustices, in which social media were used as a tool of information and organisation, but were not the cause of the revolution.

The UK riots were not a Twitter mob, but related to the societal structure of the United Kingdom. The latter has a high level of income inequality, its Gini level was 32.4 in 2009 (0 means absolute equality, 100 absolute inequality), a level that is only topped by a few countries in Europe and that is comparable to the level of Greece (33.1) (data source: Eurostat). 17.3 per cent of the UK population had a risk of living in poverty in 2009 (data source: Eurostat). In early 2011, the youth unemployment rate in the UK rose to 20.3 per cent, the highest level since these statistics started being recorded in 1992.[7] The United Kingdom is not only one of the most advanced developed countries today, it is at the same time a developing country with a lot of structurally deprived areas. Is it a surprise that riots erupted especially in East London, the West Midlands, and Greater Manchester? The UK Department of Communities and Local Government reported in its analysis *The English Indices of Deprivation 2010*[8]:

> Liverpool, Middlesbrough, Manchester, Knowsley, the City of Kingston-upon Hull, Hackney and Tower Hamlets are the local authorities with the highest proportion of LSOAs amongst the most deprived in England. [...] The north east quarter of London, particularly Newham, Hackney and Tower Hamlets continue to exhibit very high levels of deprivation.
>
> (1–3)

Decades of UK capitalist development shaped by deindustrialisation and neoliberalism have had effects on the creation, intensification, and extension of precariousness and deprivation. Capitalism, crisis, and class are the main contexts of unrests, uproar, and social media today.

Social media are embedded into contradictions and the power structures of contemporary society. This also means that in society, in which these media are prevalent, they are not completely unimportant in situations of social struggles. Social media have contradictory characteristics in contradictory societies: they do not necessarily and automatically support/amplify or dampen/limit rebellions, but rather pose contradictory potentials that stand in contradictions with influences by the state, ideology, capitalism, and other media. Social media are not the causes of societal phenomena. They are rather a mirror of the power structures and structures of exploitation and oppression that we find in

Conclusion: The Need for a Dialectic and Critical Theory of Media and Society contemporary society. They are tools of communication embedded in power structures. They can both play a role for exerting control, exploitation, and domination as well as for challenging asymmetric power structures of domination and exploitation. And in actual reality, they do both at the same time.

One can however not assume that the economic, political, and cultural power structures that frame media use are equally accessible and available for both sides. Economic, political, and cultural elites tend to enjoy advantages in access to media and mediated visibility. The political task is to find ways how less powerful groups can be empowered so that their voices can be heard in the media and can have transformative influences on society. How social and other media can empower citizens, workers, consumers, and pro-sumers is not a given. It is not an automatism or a necessity. It is a difficult and complex political challenge that has thus far not been adequately approached.

Notes

1 The data collection for the OccupyMedia Survey! took place from November 6th, 2012, until February 20th, 2013. I conducted the research as online survey. Its aim was to find out more about how Occupy activists use social media and what opportunities and risks of social media they see. The survey resulted in a dataset with $N=429$ respondents.

2 "Power means every chance within a social relationship to assert one's will even against opposition" (Habermas 1986, 74).

3 "In itself the exercise of power is not violence; nor is it a consent which, implicitly, is renewable. It is a total structure of actions brought to bear upon possible actions: it incites, it induces, it seduces, it makes easier or more difficult; in the extreme it constrains or forbids absolutely; it is nevertheless always a way of acting upon an acting subject or acting subjects by virtue of their acting or being capable of action" (Foucault 1982, 220).

4 Politics is for Weber (2008, 155–156) "leadership, or the influence exerted on the leadership, of a political association".

5 The Revolution will be tweeted. *Foreign Policy Online.* June 20, 2011.http://www.foreignpolicy.com/articles/2011/06/20/the_revolution_will_be_tweeted#sthash.fzgJPMdN.dpbs.

6 Spring awakening. How an Egyptian revolution began on Facebook. *New York Times Online.* February 17, 2012. http://www.nytimes.com/2012/02/19/books/review/how-an-egyptian-revolution-began-on-facebook.html?pagewanted=all&_r=0.

7 http://www.guardian.co.uk/business/2011/jan/19/youth-unemployment-heads-towards-1-million.

8 http://www.communities.gov.uk/documents/statistics/pdf/1871538.pdf.

References

Björklund, Per. 2011. *Arvet efter Mubarak. Egyptens kamp för frihet.* Stockholm: Verbal.

Bourdieu, Pierre. 1986a. *Distinction: A Social Critique of the Judgement of Taste.* New York: Routledge.

Bourdieu, Pierre. 1986b. The (Three) Forms of Capital. In *Handbook of Theory and Research in the Sociology of Education,* ed. John G. Richardson, 241–258. New York: Greenwood Press.

Castells, Manuel. 2012. *Networks of Outrage and Hope: Social Movements in the Internet Age.* Cambridge: Polity Press.

Castells, Manuel. 2010. *The Rise of the Network Society. The Information Age: Economy, Society and Culture,* Volume 1. Malden, MA: Wiley-Blackwell. Second edition with a new preface.

Castells, Manuel. 2009. *Communication Power.* Oxford: Oxford University Press.

Couldry, Nick. 2002. *The Place of Media Power.* London: Routledge.

Curran, James. 2002. *Media and Power.* London: Routledge.

Feenberg, Andrew. 2002. *Transforming Technology: A Critical Theory Revisited.* Oxford: Oxford University Press.

Foucault, Michel. 1982. *The Subject and Power. Afterword.* In *Michel Foucault: Beyond Structuralism and Hermeneutics,* ed. Hubert Dreyfus and Paul Rabinow, 207–226. Brighton: Harvester Press.

Foucault, Michel. 1980. *Power/Knowledge: Selected Interviews and Other Writings, 1972–77.* Brighton: Harvester.

Foucault, Michel. 1977. *Discipline and Punish.* New York: Vintage.

Fuchs, Christian. 2014a. *OccupyMedia! The Occupy Movement and Social Media in Crisis Capitalism.* Winchester: Zero Books.

Fuchs, Christian. 2014b. *Social Media: A Critical Introduction.* London: Sage.

Fuchs, Christian. 2010. Alternative Media as Critical Media. *European Journal of Social Theory* 13 (2): 173–192.

Fuchs, Christian. 2008. *Internet and Society. Social Theory in the Information Age.* New York: Routledge.

Fuchs, Christian. 2003a. Some Implications of Pierre Bourdieu's Works for a Theory of Social Self-Organization. *European Journal of Social Theory* 6 (4): 387–408.

Fuchs, Christian. 2003b. *Structuration Theory and Social Self-Organisation. Systemic Practice and Action Research* 16 (2): 133–167.

Galtung, Johan. 1990. Cultural Violence. *Journal of Peace Research* 27 (3): 291–305.

Gandy, Oscar H. 2009. *Coming to Terms with Chance. Engaging Rational Discrimination and Cumulative Disadvantage.* Farnham: Ashgate.

Ghonim, Wael. 2012. *Revolution 2.0. The Power of the People Is Greater than the People in Power. A Memoir.* New York: Houghton Mifflin Harcourt.

Giddens, Anthony. 1985. *A Contemporary Critique of Historical Materialism. The Nation-State and Violence,* Volume 2. Cambridge: Polity Press.

Giddens, Anthony. 1984. *The Constitution of Society*. Berkeley: University of California Press.

Giddens, Anthony. 1981. *A Contemporary Critique of Historical Materialism. Power, Property and the State*, Volume 1. London/Basingstoke: Macmillan.

Gladwell, Malcolm. 2010. Small Change. Why the Revolution Will Not Be Tweeted. *The New Yorker*, October 2010: 42–49.

Gladwell, Malcolm and Clay Shirky. 2011. From Innovation to Revolution. Do Social Media Make Protests Possible? *Foreign Affairs* 90 (2): 153–154.

Gramsci, Antonio. 1971. *Selections from the Prison Notebooks*. New York: International Publishers.

Habermas, Jürgen. 1987. *The Theory of Communicative Action. Lifeworld and System: A Critique of Functionalist Reason*, Volume 2. Boston, MA: Beacon Press.

Habermas, Jürgen. 1986. *Hannah Arendt's Communications Concept of Power*. In *Power*, ed. Steven Lukes, 75–93. New York: New York University Press.

Hall, Stuart, Chas Critcher, Tony Jefferson, John Clarke and Brian Roberts. 1978. *Policing the Crisis. Mugging, the State and Law and Order*. London: Macmillan.

Horkheimer, Max. 1947. *Eclipse of Reason*. New York: Continuum.

Jenkins, Henry. 2008. *Convergence Culture*. New York: New York University Press.

Luhmann, Niklas. 2000. *Die Politik der Gesellschaft*. Frankfurt am Main: Suhrkamp.

Luhmann, Niklas. 1975. *Macht*. Stuttgart: Enke.

Marcuse, Herbert. 1941/1998. Some Social Implications of Modern Technology. In *Technology, War and Fascism*, ed. Douglas Kellner, 39–65. London: Routledge.

Marx, Karl. 1871. The Civil War in France. In *Marx & Engels Collected Works*, Volume 22, 307–355. London: Lawrence & Wishart.

Marx, Karl. 1867. *Capital*. Volume 1. London: Penguin.

Marx, Karl. 1852. *The Eighteenth Brumaire of Louis Bonaparte*. Moscow: Progress

Morozov, Evgeny. 2013. *To Save Everything, Click Here. Technology, Solutionism and the Urge to Fix Problems that Don't Exist*. London: Allen Lane.

Morozov, Evgeny. 2010. *The Net Delusion. How Not to Liberate the World*. London: Allen Lane.

Poulantzas, Nicos. 2008. *The Poulantzas Reader*. London: Verso.

Poulantzas, Nicos. 1980. *State, Power, Socialism*. London: Verso.

Sandoval, Marisol and Christian Fuchs. 2010. Towards a Critical Theory of Alternative Media. *Telematics and Informatics* 27 (2): 141–150.

Sullivan, Andrew. 2009. The Revolution Will be Twittered. http://www.theatlantic.com/daily-dish/archive/2009/06/the-revolution-will-be-twittered/200478/

Tapscott, Don and Anthony D. Williams. 2007. *Wikinomics. How Mass Collaboration Changes Everything*. New York: Penguin.

Thompson, John B. 1995. *The Media and Modernity. A Social Theory of the Media*. Cambridge: Polity.

Walby, Sylvia. 2022. *Theorizing Violence*. Cambridge: Polity.

Walby, Sylvia et al. 2017. *The Concept and Measurement of Violence against Women and Men.* Bristol: Policy Press.

Weber, Max. 2008. *Max Weber's Complete Writings on Academic and Political Vocations.* New York: Algora.

Weber, Max. 1978. *Economy and Society.* Berkeley: University of California Press.

Weil, Simone. 2005. *An Anthology.* London: Penguin.

References

Chapter Five
The Praxis School's Marxist Humanism and Mihailo Marković's Theory of Communication

5.1 Introduction

5.2 Praxis

5.3 Communication

5.4 Ideology

5.5 Nationalism

5.6 Conclusion

References

5.1 Introduction

The Praxis Group was a community of scholars in Yugoslavia. It was predominantly based at the University of Zagreb and the University of Belgrade. The founders included Gajo Petrović, Milan Kangrga (both based in Zagreb) and Mihailo Marković (based in Belgrade). The Group edited the *Praxis* journal from 1964 until 1974. The international edition was published from 1965 until 1973. Between 1963 and 1974, the group also organised the annual Korčula Summer School. Having supported student protests in 1968, members of the group came under increased criticism and were expelled from the Communist Party (Bogdanović 2015). In 1975, eight of them (the Belgrade Eight) were suspended from their jobs at the University of Belgrade's Faculty of Philosophy (ibid.). It became impossible to continue organising the journal and the summer school. In 1981, the group founded the journal *Praxis International* that existed until 1993.

Mihailo Marković (1923–2010) was the Group's internationally most active and visible member. This for example becomes evident when one looks at the biographies and bibliographies of group members published in the 1979 volume *Praxis: Yugoslav Essays in the Philosophy and Methodology of the Social Sciences* (Marković and Petrović 1979, 389–398) that collected English translations of the *Praxis* journal's key articles. The bibliographies indicate that Marković was the only member who had in 1979 published two monographs in English: *From Affluence to Praxis* (Marković 1974a) and *The*

DOI: 10.4324/9781003331087-7

Contemporary Marx (Marković 1974b). The only other Praxis Group-monographs that had at that time been published in English were Svetozar Stojanović's (1973) *Between Ideals and Reality: Critique of Socialism and its Future* and Gajo Petrović's (1967) *Marx in the Mid-Twentieth Century*. Marković's (1984) book *Dialectical Theory of Meaning* (first published in Serbo-Croatian in 1961) is explicitly dedicated to the analysis of the mental, symbolic, linguistic, communicative realm, which makes his work particularly interesting for engagement when one is interested in foundations of a critical theory of communication. This chapter therefore asks: How did Mihailo Marković conceive of communication?

Ideology is a particular type of communication. Marković became in the 1980s a spokesperson for Serbian nationalism. From 1990 to 1992, he was the Vice President of Slobodan Milošević's Serbian Socialist Party (SPS). So one can observe a peculiar contradiction of internationalism and nationalism. When dealing with communication in Marković's works, we therefore have to inevitably also ask questions about ideology and nationalism. This chapter proceeds by engaging with the concepts of praxis (Section 5.2), communication (Section 5.3), ideology (Section 5.4), and nationalism (Section 5.5). Section 5.6 draws general conclusions.

5.2 Praxis

Marković (1974a, 63) discerns between three types of activity: work, alienated labour and praxis. Work is general production, whereas labour is an alienated form of work, in which humans do not control the conditions and results of their activities. In another work, he adds the term practice: Practice is "any Subject's activity of changing and object" (Marković 1979, xxviii). Practice can be alienated. Praxis in contrast is "a specifically human activity" that is "characterized by self-determination, i.e., by a conscious purposeful commitment to practically realize one specific, freely chosen possibility among a set of alternatives" (Marković 1979, xxxi). Praxis is "free creative activity" that realises "specific potential faculties and satisfies the needs of other human individuals" (xxviii). "Work becomes praxis only when it is freely chosen and provides an opportunity for individual self-expression and self-fulfillment" (xxix). Praxis is "a free human activity with definite esthetic qualities, in which man objectifies all his potential powers, affirms himself as a personality, and satisfies the needs of another person" (1974a, 53). It "enriches the lives of others and indirectly becomes part of them" and shows "direct concern for another person's needs" (65). Praxis "establishes valuable and warm links with other human beings" (65).

Marković's concept of praxis is not consistent. In *Dialectical Theory of Meaning* (Marković 1984), he uses praxis and practice synonymously, i.e. he does not give any political meaning to the praxis concept. "Praxis is *subjective-objective*" (xiv). Practice is "activity by means of which people transform their nature and social environment in order to improve their living conditions" (38), it is human subjects' "purposeful creation of inorganic and organic objects and the social conditions of human life" (39). Praxis, or what he also calls practice or practical interaction, has for Marković two dimensions: the interaction with nature, i.e. the "utilization of natural resources for human purposes, growing production", and social interaction, in which "we become aware of 'other minds'" (xvi). It here already becomes evident that there is a certain dualism inherent in Marković's approach that separates the physical and natural world from the mental and communicative world. Praxis is a uniting concept, but the two forms of praxis are left separate.

Are there advantages of discerning between practice and praxis? In Marxist theory, the distinction goes back to Marx's *Theses on Feuerbach*:

> #3 [...] The coincidence of the changing of circumstances and of human activity or self-change can be conceived and rationally understood only as revolutionary praxis. [...] #8 All social life is essentially practical. All mysteries which lead theory to mysticism find their rational solution in human praxis and in the comprehension of this praxis.
>
> (Marx 1845, 3, 5)[1]

It becomes clear that Marx sees human life as practical in the sense that humans change the world in and through their practices. When he speaks of praxis, he means a particular form of practice, namely political practice that aims at creating a humane society, understands the needs of such a society, and deconstructs ideologies that mystify domination. For Gramsci (1971), the philosophy of praxis is critical because it criticises common sense (330). Praxis aims at "absolute humanism" (417). Both Marx and Gramsci show that *praxis* is the critical and political dimension of theory and human activity. By using praxis in parts of his works as synonymous with practice, Marković depoliticises social theory.

In contrast to Marković, Gajo Petrović, who was another important member of the Praxis Group, argues in his book *Marx in the Mid-Twentieth Century* for an axiological-political concept of praxis: "'Man is praxis means' man in society, freedom, history and future" (23). "There is no praxis without freedom, and there is no free Being that is not praxis" (118). Praxis aims at a "free community of free personalities" (133). Praxis is the "authentic 'mode' of Being that reveals the true meaning of Being", it is the "developed Essence of Being" (189).

Most of Yugoslav praxis philosophy took the Marxian understanding of praxis serious and focused on the political goal of a self-managed society and economy. In Yugoslavia, Tito's 1948 break with Stalin created foundations for such a form of democratic socialism. "Yugoslavia today is the only country in the world that is attempting to create and apply an integrated system of workers' self-management" (Supek 1975, 3). Workers' self-management in Yugoslavia was "the first successful implementation of an integrated system of workers' self-management" (Horvat 1975a, 36–37). The Praxis Group analysed Yugoslav self-management and showed its potentials, problems and limits. On the ethico-political level, human praxis demands self-management. According to Rudi Supek (1971/1979, 253), self-management means that

> man as the producer has the right to make decisions about the results of his work, that the state is not entitled to appropriate and dispose of the work surplus, that the right to manage an enterprise is shared by all workers and employees who work in it.
>
> (Supek 1971/1979, 253)

Yugoslav self-management's basic idea was that all workers formed a general assembly and elected a workers' council that in turn elected a management committee:

> All workers and employees of a firm constitute the work collective *[radni kolektiv]*. The collective elects a workers' council *[radnički savet]* by secret ballot. The council has 15 to 120 members elected originally for one year and recently for a two-year period. The council is a policy-making body and meets at intervals of one to two months. The council elects a managing board *[upravni odbor]* as its executive organ; the board has 3 to 11 members, three-quarters of whom must be production workers. The director is the chief executive and is an ex officio member of the managing board.
>
> (Horvat 1975b, 165)

The Praxis Group argues that self-management as a form of participatory democracy needs to be used at multiple levels of society.

> Socialist self-government should he constructed as an *integral* social system. This means, first, that it must embrace *all parts* of society, and second, that in addition to the sell government of individual elements, it must be seen as the

self-government of society *as a whole*. This assumes the governance of self-governing elements into a complete self-governing society.

(Stojanovič 1975, 467)

One of the Group's criticisms was that Yugoslavia was not a self-governing, self-managing society, but limited self-managing to the level of economic organisations: A "vivid dualism exists in practice – self-managing groups in the base and a rather strong statist structure above them" (Stojanovič 1975, 469). Another problem was that banks and trade organisations took on a monopolistic role that they used in order to control self-managed companies and "to illegally draw off profits from the producing organizations" (Supek 1971/1979, 258). There was also a "middle class liberalism" (257) that tried to foster entrepreneurialism and that atomised society into competing individuals. The results were "uneven compensation for the same work" and that unions "were forbidden to fight for a uniform standard by which laborers were compensated" (259). The workers' council elected the company-director from candidates nominated in public competition by a selection committee that to a majority consisted of representatives of the commune (Horvat 1975b, 166). Workers often considered the director as "a representative of 'alien' interests in the firm" (166).

Yugoslav self-management certainly created its own contradictions that had to do with the contradictory relation between state power and workers' power in transitional society, but it is clear that it was a very important attempt to foster democracy in the economy.

Marxist Humanism is based on Marx's insight that in approaching a problem, humans need to "grasp the root of the matter. But for man the root is man himself", "man is the highest being for man" (Marx 1844a, 182). So it is convinced that all humans deserve a good life and the good life for all is an important political goal worth struggling for. Therefore Marx formulated the "*categorical imperative to overthrow all relations* in which man is a debased, enslaved, forsaken, despicable being" (182). The Praxis Group was guided by Marx's Humanism and so assumed that "all relationships in which man is a humbled, oppressed, abandoned and despised being should be destroyed" (Vranicki 1972/1979, 234). For Stalin, humans and their practices, praxis and knowledge were in contrast mere reflections of the objective world (ibid.).

The Praxis Group was an important representative of Marxist Humanism. But what are the most important assumptions of Marxist and socialist Humanism in general? Erich Fromm (1965) edited a collection on *Socialist Humanism* that presented 36 chapters written by Marxist Humanist scholars. Taken together, the volume outlines Marxist Humanism's basic assumptions:

Ontology:

- Society is grounded in human practice and social production.
- Only humans themselves can achieve a humane society by their practical self-activity in social struggles. Praxis is a key aspect of achieving a humane society.
- Capitalism, class and domination constitute a form of human alienation that constitutes a difference between how social life is and how it could potentially be.

Epistemology:

- Marx's early writings, especially the *Economic-Philosophic Manuscripts*, are important intellectual foundations of Marxist Humanism.
- There is no epistemological break in Marx's works that led him away from Humanism. Marx's later works are guided by the general principles formulated in his early works.
- Humanism requires an open form of theory, dialectic, and praxis. Orthodoxies such as Stalinism turn socialism into a dogmatic, deterministic, mechanistic, reductionist, and quasi-religious practice.

Axiology:

- Given society's grounding in human praxis and social production, humans should be collectively in control of the conditions and results of human activity.
- Democratic socialism is the society adequate for humans. It is not limited to politics, but the collective self-management of the economy and society.
- Democratic socialism is the foundation for the full realisation of humans' and society's potentials.

Based on the analysis of practice and praxis, we can next have a look at the concept of communication.

5.3 Communication

Communication is for Marković besides sense development, reason, imagination, creativity, harmonisation of interests and aspirations, evaluative choice among alternative possibilities, and self-consciousness a fundamental human capacity (1974a, 13–14). Communication involves language and the "ability to understand the thoughts, feelings, desires, and motives of other persons from other social groups, nations, classes, races, religions, and cultures" (13). Language plays a key role in communication: Language "is an activity (*energeia*) which is a medium used by people to communicate and coordinate their praxis" (1984, 262), it is the "*activity* of speaking and writing, i.e. a system of operations with signs" (320). Language is one of the human means of communication that are used as means for the production of meanings and social relations. Raymond Williams (2005, 50–63) therefore speaks of means of communication as means of production.

Marković in his analysis of communication again mixes up praxis and practice. Communication is certainly a human practice that in ethical and political action can turn into praxis communication. All *praxis communication* is *communicative practice*, but not all *communicative practices* are *praxis communication*. The problem of Habermas' (1984) theory of communication is as in Marković's terminology the mix-up of the ethico-political and the ontological level of communication (for a critique of Habermas, see Chapter 6 in Fuchs 2016). For Habermas (1984, 285), communicative aims at transcending "egocentric calculations of success", but at "reaching understanding". Communication is not naturally fair and does not naturally and automatically stand above or outside of structures of domination. Communication is the basic human practice of creating and reproducing social relations through symbol use, which implies that it is used both in domination and emancipation from domination. That humans make meaning of each other in communication does not include and automatically imply that they understand and agree with each other. The transformation of communicative practices into praxis communication is a political task of social struggles that is not automatically given. Praxis communication is communication that acts within democratic-socialist structures or aims at establishing such structures and a society built on them.

In *Dialectical Theory of Meaning*, Marković (1984, 39) defines communication as one of six forms or elements of practice. The others are work/material production, co-operation, experience, evaluation, and thought/intellectual activity. "*Communication* is that specific form of practice, which consist in operations *with* signs, by means of which people come to mutual understanding and stimulate one another to engage in a particular type of action" (39). This distinction's problem is that it separates work and communication. Work is seen as material production and "purposeful creation" (39). The implication is that communication is neither material nor purposeful. But communication's purpose is that humans make meaning of each other and the world. It is a purposeful activity. And in

TABLE 5.1 Marković's (1984, 72) typology of objects

Objects			
Material objects		Mental objects	
Physical objects	Material social objects	Social mental objects	Individual mental objects

cultural and communicative work, which is a form of work that has become widespread, humans create use-values that offer opportunities for making meanings to others. Ferruccio Rossi-Landi (1983) and Raymond Williams (1977) therefore stress that communication and work should not be separated, but be seen as material practices (see Fuchs 2016, Chapter 6).

Marković (1984) draws a strict separation between the material and the mental world (see Table 5.1). He sees the realm of the material as the world of physical objects that are either created by nature or by humans in society. Individual ideas or collective mental phenomena, "including common experiences, feelings, ideas, value judgements, interpretations of symbols, [...] 'class consciousness', [...] public opinion" (70) are in contrast for him mental and "nonmaterial" (71). Matter "consists of all objects that exist in space and time" (70). Mental is a "synonym of 'psychic'" (73). The problem of such an approach is that it draws a crude distinction between base and superstructure that renders the realm of culture and communication secondary and of minor importance. The problem is not just that one thereby cannot explain the importance of communicative and cultural work, but also that the result is a philosophical idealism that postulates two substances of the world (matter and mind) and cannot answer the question of how the world is at the foundational level grounded. Mental processes are not, as Marković argues, non-spatial and non-temporal: Individual ideas and values are stored in the human brain for a particular period of time (until an individual dies, forgets them or gives them up). And collective ideas have space-time because a particular community shares them during specific time periods. A community of humans has certain structures of feeling, it shares particular collective "meanings and values which are lived in works and relationships" (Williams 1961/2011, 337).

Now you can ask: What about dreams, the characters in a novel, fantasies, ideologies, lies, myths, or the idea of God? Are these not ideas that do not have a material correlate and are therefore "immaterial"? No, like all ideas, these ideas are material because particular humans or groups of humans live and express them. But we can say that certain ideas are material, but not real. They are unreal. Any idea has a relation to an object. In the case discussed here, the object is imagined and does not exist in the world.

For Hegel (1830), reality is being-there (*Dasein*), "being with a *determinacy*" that is im-mediate and is something with quality (§90). Reality is not just "inner and subjective", but has "moved out into being-there" (addition to §90). So reality is an aspect of qualita-tive being (*Sein*). Reality that does not have a referent in reality external to the human is an unreal being. For Hegel, actuality (*Wirklichkeit*) is the unity of essence and existence (§142). Actuality is reasonable being.

A house that I build is real just like the thoughts I have about it. Thoughts about how a house I want to build should look like are unreal being that is however potential reality. A dream about a house built out of chocolate on the imaginary chocolate planet Choco-late Moon is a material being, but it is unreal and impossible and therefore no potential reality. It is an imaginary being. What are the implications of these distinctions for the notion of communication? Communication is a material and real process that creates and maintains social reality by offering in symbolic forms interpretations about real and unreal being, potential and imaginary being to other humans, who based on it produce particular meanings of the (real, unreal, potential, imaginary) world. Communicative practices turn into *praxis communication* when they are oriented not just on how society is or can be, but on how it can be made an actual society.

A form of communication that invents imaginary existence and proclaims that the im-aginary is actuality in order to defend and legitimate domination is termed ideology. Ideology is an important dimension of critical communication theory.

5.4 Ideology

Ideology is one of the most difficult concepts in cultural theory because there are multi-ple understandings and uses of it.

Marković writes that ideology can on the one hand be understood as

> any conceptualization of values, needs and interests, any theory about an ac-cepted ideal, any choice of a general value orientation, any project of a future for which we are ready to engage, and consequently, a critical attitude toward existing social realities.
>
> (1974a, 53)

He on the other hand contrasts this understanding with the definition of ideology as the expression and disguise of "*particular* group interests [...] in the form of indicative statements, creating the impression that they refer to obvious facts, and thus demand acceptance as indubitable truths" (1974a, 54). In the book *From Affluence to Praxis*, Marković (1974a) says Marx's theory is an ideology in the first sense and anti-ideological in the second sense, but he leaves open his own understanding of ideology.

In the article *Science and Ideology*, Marković (1974b, 42–80) argues that both understandings of ideology can be found in Marx's works: Marx and Engels in the German Ideology understand ideology as "inadequate, twisted, mystified" consciousness (44), whereas Marx in the *Preface to A Contribution to the Critique of Political Economy* speaks of the legal, political, philosophical, religious, aesthetic and philosophic realms as ideological forms that constitute "the superstructure of a historical epoch" (61). Marković clarifies that he prefers the general definition because the other one does not allow speaking of the "*revolutionary* ideology of the proletariat" (73). He therefore defines ideology as "the ensemble of ideas and theories with which a class expresses its interests, its aims and the norms of its activity" (74).

Marković's justification for the superiority of the general ideology concept is confused. The proletariat's consciousness is neither automatically unitary nor progressive, as the contemporary tendency of blue-collar workers' support for far-right parties shows. It is possible that we simply speak of a "revolutionary worldview", which does not require the notion of ideology. Also not all revolutions are politically progressive, so there can be revolutionary worldviews that are ideological, in which case we can speak of a "revolutionary ideology". The problem is that the general concept of ideology is ethically and politically relativist. If praxis is progressive social action, then situating the consciousness associated with it on the same level as fascist consciousness ("socialist ideology", "fascist ideology") denigrates the first and trivialises the second. One can now interpose that Stalinism is certainly an ideology in the negative sense of the term. The critical concept of ideology, however, allows us in such cases to argue that Stalinism is an ideology and opposed to socialist worldviews. General concepts of ideology, such as the ones by Marković, Louis Althusser, Antonio Gramsci, or Karl Mannheim, "thoroughly purge from the ideology concept the remains of its accusatory meaning"[2] (Horkheimer 1972, 28).

Nationalism is a particular form of ideology, an ideological anti-praxis. We will next focus on this concept.

5.5 Nationalism

According to Bogdanović (2015, 461), the Serbian part of the Praxis Group in the context of the breakdown of Yugoslavia "practically overnight turned coats" and "turned into nationalists and/or liberals". Marković from the mid-1980s onwards propagated Serbian nationalism. We will in this chapter analyse this development, which however requires that we first take a look at the context of the Yugoslav wars (Section 5.5.1) and discuss left-wing positions on it (Section 5.5.2) before we then more closely engage with Marković's perspective (Section 5.5.3).

5.5.1 The Crisis and Break-Up of Yugoslavia

After Tito's death in 1980, Yugoslavia entered a phase of permanent economic and political crisis, featuring high unemployment, high inflation, high inequality, high national debt, strongly falling average income, etc. It started disintegrating. Yugoslavia had to take on IMF loans that brought along structural adjustment programmes. Over decades there had been an uneven development, in which Slovenia and Croatia developed and Kosovo, Bosnia-Hercegovina, Serbia, Montenegro, and Macedonia were lagging behind. Economic problems are a frequent trigger and context of the rise of ideologies, including nationalism that invents scapegoats that are blamed for social problems. Nationalism and independence movements were on the rise in the 1980s and 1990s in all parts of Yugoslavia. According to the documentary film *Yugoslavia: The Avoidable War*, Germany armed Croatian separatists.[3] In 1990, Serbia limited the autonomy of Kosovo and Vojvodina.

In June 1991, Slovenia and Croatia declared their independence from Yugoslavia. War broke out between Yugoslavia, Slovenia, and Croatia. In late 1991, the Serbs of Croatia proclaimed the Republic of Serbian Krajina that was not internationally recognised. Also Macedonia proclaimed independence. In 1992, the EU, the USA, and the UN recognised Slovenia and Croatia, which further spurred nationalism in the Balkans. Especially Germany's foreign minister Hans-Dietrich Genscher and his Austrian equivalent Alois Mock played important roles in recognising the two newly formed states. In 1992, Bosnia-Herzegovina declared independence and the Bosnian Serbs declared the independence of the Republika Srpska. The Bosnian war started. The USA, the EU and the UN recognised Bosnia-Herzegovina. Serbia and Montenegro formed the Federal Republic of Yugoslavia (FRY) that was not internationally recognised. In 1993, Croatia got involved in the war in Bosnia. Macedonia was internationally recognised in the same year. NATO bombed the Republika Srpska in August and September 1995. In December 1995, Bosnia-Herzegovina, Croatia, and the FRY signed the Dayton Peace Agreement. In 1998, war broke out between the Kosovo Liberation Army and the FRY. From March until June 1999, NATO intervened militarily and bombed the FYR and Kosovo. The FYR forces withdrew

Nationalism

from Kosovo. The NATO intervention in Kosovo set a precedent that was later repeated in the 2003 Western intervention in Iraq: It was a war without a UN Security Council decision that was undertaken although no NATO country had been attacked or threatened and that NATO justified on humanitarian grounds (Chandler 2000).

5.5.2 The Left-Wing Discourse on the Yugoslav Wars

There are at least two characteristic positions in the left-wing debate on the Yugoslav wars. Noam Chomsky represents the *first position*. He focuses in his analysis on NATO's bombing of Serbia and Kosovo in 1999. Chomsky argues that the US chose to "escalate the violence" (2000, 44), which would have resulted in an escalation of Serbian attacks on Kosovo-Albanian civilians in Kosovo, hundred thousands of refugees fleeing the bombings in Kosovo, and in unpredictable long-term consequences. Chomsky says that in the situation of humanitarian crisis, it would always be possible to act according to the principle "First, do no harm" (2000, 48) and to do nothing if that elementary principle cannot be upheld. But the situation of having to do nothing would never arise because "[d]iplomacy and negotiations are never at an end" (2000, 48). The NATO bombings of the Balkans in 1999 are for Chomsky characteristic of international politics that do not rely on a universal framework such as the UN Charter or the International Court of Justice, but are based on the principle that the "powerful do as they wish" (Chomsky 1999, 154). Whereas the US would tolerate the ethnic cleansing of Kurds in Turkey, it would intervene in ethnic cleansings in Kosovo. "Serbia is one of those disorderly miscreants that impede the institution of the U.S.-dominated global system, while Turkey is a loyal client state that contributes substantially to this project" (1999, 13).

Herman and Peterson (2007) in a detailed analysis whose content is comparable to the one by Chomsky argue that internal and external factors played a role in the breakdown of Yugoslavia and that the external factors have often been denied. These factors would include finding a justification for NATO's existence after the fall of the Soviet bloc, the global assertion of the "Washington consensus", the role of the Arbitration Commission of the Peace Conference on Yugoslavia, and liberals and leftists' support of Western military intervention. Herman and Peterson also argue that the wars and bombings in the Balkans stimulated al-Qaeda and Islamic fundamentalism and resulted in a massive wave of displacement and refugees.

Slavoj Žižek (1999) is a representative of the *second position*. He argues that Yugoslavia did not disintegrate when Slovenia declared independence, but already when Milošević deprived "Kosovo and Vojvodina of their limited autonomy" (40) so that Yugoslavia was already dead and could only I have lived on under Serbian domination. Žižek's assessment is comparable to Chomsky in respect to the critique of NATO's selective interventions in the name of the defence of human rights based on its "strategic interests" (41) and the "the end of any serious role of [the] UN and [the] Security Council" (50) in international relations. However, Žižek much more than Chomsky also focuses his critique on Serbian nationalism, arguing that the NATO interventions and the Milošević-regime are not opposites, but symptoms of the New World Order that should be opposed (44). "When the West fights Milošević, it is NOT fighting its enemy [...]; it is rather fighting its own creature, a monster that grew as a result of the compromises and inconsistencies of the Western politics itself" (46) that over years mistook Milošević as a factor of stability in the region, not seeing his "anti-Albanian nationalist agenda" (49).

> The way to fight the capitalist New World Order is not by supporting local proto-Fascist resistances to it, but to focus on the only serious question today: how to build TRANSNATIONAL political movements and institutions strong enough to seriously constrain the unlimited rule of [...] capital, and to render visible and politically relevant the fact that the local fundamentalist resistances against the New World Order, from Milošević to Le Pen and the extreme Right in Europe, are part of it?
>
> (50)

Jürgen Habermas (1999) took a comparable position, arguing that NATO acted without a UN Security Council mandate, that "[n]ationalistic dreams of a Greater Albania [...] are not the slightest bit superior to the nationalistic fantasies of a Greater Serbia which the intervention is supposed to contain" (266). He also stresses that NATO intervenes in the case of Kosovo, but not in favour "of the Kurds, Chechians, or Tibetians" (269), which shows the selectivity of the politics of military intervention. Habermas concludes that the only adequate answer in such situations is to establish "a global democratic legal order" based on "UN institutions" (270) and "strengthened diplomatic efforts" (271).

The analytical difference between the first and the second left-wing position on the Yugoslav wars is that the first is based on an analysis of empirical facts and data, whereas the second on uses political-theoretical reasoning. They reflect a certain difference between Anglo-Saxon empiricism and European continental philosophy. The political difference is that the first position takes an anti-imperialist position that opposes US interventions and seems to have some sympathies with Serbia, whereas the second rejects the logic "the enemy of my enemy is my friend" and argues that there should be no sympathies with any side because they are all barbaric and classical anti-imperialism is mistaken here.

Nationalism

Given that war always involves psychological war waged via the media and in public, it is always difficult to trust any sources that report on the causes and consequences of war. Often there are very different stories about the extent and perpetrators of war crimes. So it is best that one encounters reports about war with scepticism and critically and compares different sources. In respect to the war in Bosnia, there were several investigations. Human Rights Watch (1992, 5) found that "all sides have committed serious abuses, Helsinki Watch found that the most egregious and overwhelming number of violations of the rules of war have been committed by Serbian forces" (Human Rights Watch 1992, 5). A United Nations expert commission concluded that "[a]ll of the combatant forces, in significantly different degrees, have committed grave breaches of the Geneva Conventions" (UN Security Council 1994, §127). The International Committee of the Red Cross (1999, v) reported:

> The war enveloped all the communities of Bosnia-Herzegovina. A third of both Serbs and Bosniacs (31 per cent and 30 per cent, respectively) say a close family member was killed. The Serbs report the highest incidence of being forced to leave their homes (54 per cent). A near majority (45 per cent) of Croats lost contact with a close relative; more than a third (36 per cent) were forced to leave home; and 18 per cent report the death of a close family member. The Bosniac community experienced the highest level of injuries related directly to the war: 18 per cent of the total Bosniac population were wounded in the fighting, 10 per cent were imprisoned, 7 per cent were tortured and 5 per cent know somebody who was raped. In each instance, the percentage was two or three times that for the other communities.

No matter to which extent one trusts these sources or not, they taken together suggest that in the Yugoslav wars, all sides committed war crimes. Nationalism was a driving force on the Croatian, Slovenian, Serbian, Bosnian, Kosovo-Albanian, Macedonian and Montenegrin sides. The Yugoslav war reminds us first and foremost of the violent dangers of any form of nationalism.

Given this context, we can now turn to the discussion of Marković and Serbian Nationalism.

5.5.3 Mihailo Marković and Nationalism

Marković co-authored the Memorandum of the Serbian Academy of Sciences and Arts (SANU Memorandum) that was published in 1986 and that according to observers incited

Serbian nationalism (Magaš 1993, 4, 123, 199–200, Naimark 2002, 149). Marković was from 1990 to 1992 the Vice President of Slobodan Milošević's SPS. In 1995, Milošević dismissed Markovic from the SPS's executive committee (Djukic and Dubinsky 2001, 86).

The SANU Memorandum argues that in the 1960s, Yugoslav self-management was "pushed into a backseat" and remained limited to the microeconomic realm of the enterprise, lacking an expression at the macro-economic and political realms. "Consequently, self-management is mere window dressing and not the pillar of society" (Serbian Academy of Sciences and Arts 1995, 103). "Sovereignty of the people" and "[s]elf-determination of nations" (117) would (besides human rights and efficiency) have to be part of the solution of Yugoslavia's crisis. Yugoslavia would have unevenly developed national autonomies at the expense of the Serbs, who would suffer from "persecution and expulsion [...] from Kosovo" (118) and political discrimination. Because of discrimination, Serbia would also have an underdeveloped economy (120). The Memorandum speaks of the "physical, political, legal, and cultural genocide of the Serbian population in Kosovo and Metohija" (128) via the "Albanianization of Kosovo" (128). Serbs would also have been suppressed in other parts of Yugoslavia. "Prominent Serbian writers are the only ones featuring on the black lists of all the Yugoslav mass media" (135). "The establishment of the Serbian people's complete national and cultural integrity, regardless of which republic or province they might be living in, is their historical and democratic right" (138)

Also in 1986, Marković and other *Praxis* intellectuals such as Ljubomir Tadić and Zagorka Golubović signed a petition that argued that there was a continuous Albanian takeover of Kosovo and that called for the abolition of the autonomy of Kosovo (Magaš 1993, 4, 51, 52). It spoke of the need for the "defence of the foundations of Serb national culture" and the right "to the physical survival of our nation on its land" (51). Golubović, Marković and Tadić wrote in 1987,

> In Kosovo the pursuit of a project of an ethnically pure Kosovo has resulted in a flat refusal of any policy of family planning. [...] In 1940 there were 55 per cent Albanians in Kosovo, in 1985 it is already 80 per cent [...] something can be done and must be done about the forceful assimilation and expulsion of the non-Albanian population from Kosovo.
>
> (59–60)

In a *New York Times*-report, Markovič argued in 1992 that the EU's recognition of Slovenia, Croatia, and Bosnia as states, which was led by Germany, led to war. The

United States and European countries suddenly decided to recognize Bosnia without any guarantees for the Serbian or Croatian community. That made war inevitable. [...] We Serbs don't understand why our three traditional allies – Britain, France and the United States – don't recognize that Germany is return-ing to its old role, this time using economic and political means rather than military invasion.

(Kinzer 1992)

The alternative is creation of a Muslim state in the heart of Europe. Perhaps the Americans want to support this in order to be doing something for the Muslims, hoping they could exercise influence here through their Turkish allies. [...] But we find this very disturbing [...] and we don't like the idea that Turkey, which invaded our land and ruled us for 400 years, would consider this territory as part of the Muslim world.

(Kinzer 1992)

Markovič in such statements completely forgets his Marxist roots. Strong population growth has social causes. Kosovo was in the late 1980s Yugoslavia's poorest region, with an income of only 27 per cent of the Yugoslavian average (Herman and Peterson 2007, 4). In 1993, Marković contributed a chapter to a book on the democracy-theorist C. B. Macpherson's intellectual legacy. The editor Joseph Carens had, given Marković's role in Milošević's SPS, doubts about including the chapter and prefaced it with a cautionary note, to which Marković responded. Marković argued that there was widespread media manipulation in reports about Serbia's role in the war and that "Serbia has not committed any aggression against its neighbors" (2003, 240).

So it is evident that at least between 1986 and 1993, Markovič, a key figure of Yugo-slav democratic and Marxist Humanism, resorted argued for Serbian nationalism. Mira Bogdanović (2015, 464), who studied Markovič's intellectual and political life, ar-gues that his turn towards nationalism is for her "inconceivable". How can one explain such an intellectual development from Marxist Humanism towards nationalism? Was it a radical rupture and break? Or was there an element in Markovićs' interpretation of Humanist Marxism that was prone to nationalism? According to Magaš (1993), the *Praxis* editors' alignment with Serb nationalism "delineates a complete break with the political and philosophical tradition represented by the journal" (52). So her argument is that Marković betrayed Marxist Humanism. Keith Doubt (2006) takes a different position and in contrast argues that "there is something in Marković's writing that allows us not to be surprised by his ignoble conduct supporting and planning Milošević's genocidal campaign of terror throughout former-Yugoslavia" (45–46). Doubt says that Marković's identified six aspects of praxis: Intentionality, freedom as self-determination, creativity, sociality, rationality, and individual self-realisation. These dimensions would for Marković be independent and detachable.

> In Marković's reasoning, one's practice can exemplify intentionality but not creativity, sociality but not rationality, individual self-realization but not freedom as self-realization. [...] Unless the six optimal dispositions that constitute Marković's concept of *praxis* are seen as coinciding within a whole, 'a higher order of normative principle', it is difficult to see how Marković's notion of what good practice is is anything except chaos. Marković's understanding of *praxis* is nihilistic. Marković's theorizing within the tradition of critical theory foreshadows, indeed predicts, his bad faith with which he cynically supported and promoted evil in Bosnia. [...] Although Marković is not a philosopher of Heidegger's stature, the issues that Marković and Heidegger's biographies raise are comparable. [...] The argument here is the opposite: it is the deficiency of metaphysical thinking in Marković's work that explains his ignoble promotion of genocide in Bosnia.
>
> (Doubt 2006, 49–50)

In order to analyse whether there is a nationalist potential in Marković's theoretical thought, we need to have a deeper look at his works. One can in his writings find antinationalist proclamations, as is typical for Marxist-Humanist thought. Marković (1974a) for examples argues that "nationalism and racialism" are "disintegrative and regressive processes" (Marković 1974a, 79). Explaining the causes of nationalism, Marković (1974b, 90) argues that "scarcity, weakness, lack of freedom, social and national insecurity, a feeling of inferiority, emptiness and poverty [...] give rise to [...] nationalism and class hatred, egoism, escape from responsibility, aggressive and destructive behaviour, etc.". Fascism is distinct from capitalism and socialism in that "the nation or the race" is "the aim of politics" (1974a, 147). Fascism "tries to mobilize all social classes for the promotion of national and racial interests" (1974a, 152). Fascists aim at "grabbing the possessions of other nations and races" (1974a, 156).

The latter quote is on the one hand critical of racism and nationalism, but seems to assume that different human races exist. We saw in Section 5.3 that Marković sees language as a way of how social groups, "including nations, classes, races" (1974a, 13) communicate. In this general definition, Marković assumes that different human races exist. The assumption that nations exist is ambivalent because the term is often used either as actually existing nation-states or as an ideological construct that proclaims the existence of a community based on biological or cultural ties.

Markovićs was always critical of Marx's concept of essence. He says Marx "smuggled values into 'essences'" (Marković 1993, 242). For Marx, "selfishness, greed, envy, and aggressiveness" are not part of human essence, but of alienation (Markovićs 1974a, 218). The 20th century was

> an age of incredible eruptions of human irrationality and bestiality. The scope and character of bloodshed and mass madness [...] can no longer be explained by the romantic, dualistic picture of a latent positive essence and a transient bad appearance. Evil as a human disposition must lie very deep. Obviously it is also a latent pattern of human behaviour, which is the produce of the whole previous history of the human race, always ready to unroll as soon as favorable conditions arise.
>
> (Markovićs 1974a, 219)

Markovićs (1974b, 156–157) argues that Machiavelli's *Prince* sees humans as inherently egoistic, whereas Marx's *Economic and Philosophic Manuscripts* advance "an over-optimistic utopian conception of man as essentially free, peace-loving social, creative being" (156). Both would have a "reified conception of human nature" (158). "Human nature is constituted by contradictory latent predispositions" (1974b, 151). Human history would show the existence of such essential contradictions, for example "a striving for inter-group and international collaboration and solidarity but also class, national, and racial egoism" (159).

The question arises whether there is a contradiction between human essence and human existence in class society or whether a fundamental contradiction between solidarity and egoism forms human essence. The problem is that the transferal of nationalism and racism onto the level of human nature (although in a contradictory manner) does not allow us to provide an ethical grounding of the argument that nationalism and racism and all other forms of domination are harmful. The consequence is a certain naturalisation of domination.

We know from studies in development psychology that in the "9-month revolution", babies because of the recognition and care they receive start perceiving attachment figures whose perspectives they take over, which contributes to their social development (Tomasello 2008). Care for others is absolutely essential for human development. In contrast, violence towards babies harms their development. This example shows that care, co-operation, solidarity, altruism, and recognition are more fundamental than neglect, competition, separation, egoism, and hatred. Society and human development are not possible without the first, but without the second.

The theoretical implication is, as Marx (1844b, 299) says in the *Economic and Philosophic Manuscripts*, that the "individual is *the social being*" and that structures of domination harm the development of humans and society. Marković in contrast wants to make his readers believe that the social and the anti-social are two equally essential features of humans. It is surprising that Marković rejects the *Economic and Philosophic Manuscripts'* notion of the human, but operates within the theoretical and political universe of Marxist Humanism. It is not an understatement to say that the *Manuscripts* are one of Marxist Humanism's foundational texts. As a consequence, Marković's approach does provide an adequate foundation for the critique of ideologies such as nationalism and racism.

Marković not only assumed that nations and races have a real existence, but also that they have a right to self-determination and state-formation. This becomes for example evident in the SANU Memorandum's demand for the "[s]elf-determination of nations" (Serbian Academy of Sciences and Arts 1995, 117), or when the 1986 petition that Marković signed talks about the "defence of the foundations of Serb national culture" (Magaš 1993, 51), or when Marković (1989, 408) writes that in Kosovo, "[t]wo nations [Serbs and Albanians] claim the same territory" (Marković 1989, 408). Such assumptions naturalise and essentialise the existence of nations. They disregard the basic insights of Marxist critiques of nationalism. Rosa Luxemburg (1976) applied Marx's fetishism critique to the nation and nationalism. She argues that nationalism and the assumption that biologically, historically, or culturally determined nations exist ignore "completely the fundamental theory of modern socialism – the theory of social classes" (135). "In a class society, 'the nation' as a homogeneous socio-political entity does not exist" (136).

Marxist critiques of nationalism commonly assume that nation-states are the results of wars, domination, violence and political conflict and that the nation is an invented, ideological, fabricated, and illusionary product (Balibar and Wallerstein 1991, Hobsbawm and Ranger 1983, Özkirimli 2010). Nationalism is an ideology that veils the class and dominative character of society. That I speak the same language, hold the same passport, live in the same region or nation-state, am ruled by the same elites as others do not constitute a real bond that defines a particular group as superior to another. National bonds are illusionary, unreal, imaginary, ideological bonds that always constitute an out-side and a potential for the violent defence of the imaginary border between the inside and the outside of the nation. A worker has much less common interests with the owner of the company that employs him than he has with the worker in a distant country, who works in the local branch of the same company or the same industry.

Humans are different. When humans live together or next to each other, one needs to take into account both their diversity (different ways of life) and what unites (basic hu-man needs). Living together will fail when either diversity or unity is fetishised. Such fetishisms can lead to the eruption of violence and sectarianism. Living together requires human unity in diversity, a dialectic of the common and plurality. Unity in diversity re-quires also that the basic needs of all can be fulfilled. It is therefore not compatible with the principle of class.

There is also a nationalist potential in Marković's (1975) peculiar interpretation of self-management. He argues that self-management means self-determination (329). A subject creates new conditions in order to achieve "self-realization, [...] the actu-alization of basic human capacities, [...] the satisfaction of genuine human needs" (330). Self-management requires a federation of councils made up of representatives from different economic levels, critical information sources, and a "powerful, demo-cratic public opinion" based on free expression, open communication, and dialogue (331) "The fourth condition of self-determination is the discovery of the true *self* of the community, the development of consciousness about real general needs of the people" (331). The individual, nation, and class would need "a full sense of self-identity" (331).

The theoretical problem of what the "self" in self-management is becomes in Marković's interpretation a question of nationality. For Marxist Humanism, the self is the community of humanity that produces society in common and whose interest as a common humanity is therefore undermined by divisions such as class, nation, and racism that play off one group against another. Rosa Luxemburg (1970, 391) warned that nationalism resulted in the First World War, in which "working men kill[ed] and destroy[ed] each other". The right to national self-determination was for Luxemburg (1976) a "metaphysical cliché" (110). There would only be a right of the working class to self-determination (108).

The right of the working class to self-determination is a universal demand for human-ity without the class principle, the demand for a classless society without domina-tion. Marx's argument that humans are social beings that should jointly control the products of their common production implies a universal moral right to democratic socialism. Although humans have different individual realities, preferences, and choices, they all share the status of being human and as such deserving a good life. Marković's assumption that there is a right to national self-determination is based on the acceptance of the ideological constructs of nations and nationality, which undermines Humanism's universality. Marković can only make such an assumption because the principle of division, including national division, is for him part of human essence.

Praxis International in 1989 published Marković's (1989) paper *Tragedy of National Conflicts in "Real Socialism". The Case of Kosovo.* It says that "race, blood or biology" (409) have nothing to do with the conflict between Kosovo-Albanians and Serbs and argues that the conflict has national, political, socio-economic, religious and ideological causes. Marković's formulation that "[t]wo nations claim the same territory – one, Albania, on ethnic grounds, the other, Serbian on historical and cultural ones" (408) implies however that nations are not ideological constructs resulting from class and political conflicts, but are unitary historical, cultural and "ethnical" realities. Such an assumption reifies nations. Whereas he criticises Albanian nationalism that aims to establish Greater Albania, he rather lauds Milošević for having "invited people everywhere to an 'anti-bureaucratic' revolution" directed against the discrimination of Serbs and focused on "Serbia's having state functions on its entire territory as did other republics" (411). Marković complains that the "Kosovo has the highest birth rate in Europe" (414) and calls for population policies directed at Kosovo-Albanians in order "to prevent overcrowding of Kosovo" (424). Here Marković is actually, other than initially indicated, resorting to biological logic, indicating the view that procreation is a political threat to Serbs.

Seyla Benhabib was co-editor of *Praxis International* from 1986 until 1992. She says that Marković at the time of the publication of the above-mentioned paper had become a "theorist of the 'great Serbia' dream" (Benhabib 1995, 676). She argues that the article is "racist-nationalist propaganda" (676). It "exhibits the tragic mixture of forward-looking social engineering (use of monetary incentives to control birth rates) with paternalistic racism (if the Moslem Albanians do not stop reproducing at this rate, they will never be able to advance themselves economically)" (680, footnote 1). "Many of us felt that the wool was being pulled over our eyes by our colleagues in former Yugoslavia in what they were or were not publishing in the pages of the journal" (675), which contributed to *Praxis International's* termination.

For Marković, selfishness, greed, envy, and aggressiveness are part of the human essence. He thereby downplays the role of solidarity as an essential feature of humans and society, which opens up a potential for the reification of nationalism in his theoretical approach. It is therefore theoretical consequent that Marković uncritically accepts the demand for the right to self-determination of a "nation" that is based on a reification of nations. The foundational problem of Marković's approach is that he rejects Marx's concept of the human in the *Economic and Philosophic Manuscripts*, which makes his approach prone to theoretical nationalism. There are therefore certain potentials for anti-Humanism and nationalism in Marković's theoretical approach.

5.6 Conclusion

Marković has an ambivalent use of the *praxis* concept and tends to depoliticise it by using it synonymously with the notion of *practice*.

He sees the realm of communication and ideas as immaterial and standing outside of material production, which results in an idealist and dualist approach. His unclear distinction between practice and praxis lacks an ethico-political dimension and therefore fails in being able to discern between the ontological concept of communicative practice and the ethico-political notion of praxis communication. Both Habermas and Marković collapse communication's ontology and axiology into one and thereby rob communication theory of an adequate critical potential. Whereas Habermas interprets the ontological as axiological ("All communication is morally good"), Marković reduces axiology to ontology ("The concept of communication praxis is ontological"). Marković propagates a general notion of ideology that is purely analytical and robs it of its potential as an intellectual weapon of critique.

Marković rejects Marx's insight that there is a positive social essence of humans. Marx's assumption has however been confirmed by contemporary development psychology. Marković opposes Marx's positive notion of the human as the social being. As a consequence, he introduces division and separation into the concept of human essence, which poses a potential for theoretical and political nationalism. The divisionary and dualist character of Marković's approach also manifests itself in his theory of meaning and communication that separates the material realm from the mental realm.

There is a latent nationalist potential in Marković's theory that derives from his ambivalent equalisation of the concepts of practice and praxis, his general concept of ideology that depoliticise critical theory, and the filling of this depoliticised vacuum by the political assumption that diversion, separation, egoism, selfishness, nationalism, greed and envy are just like sociality, co-operation, altruism, and solidarity part of human essence. Development psychology has shown that such an assumption is mistaken. It is, however, not just mistaken, but also politically dangerous because it opens up a divisive potential in social theory that can undermine Humanism's universality. The problem of Marković's theoretical approach is that it is not Humanist enough. It is a truncated form of Humanism that at the political level turned into anti-universalism, anti-Humanism, and nationalism.

This analysis does however under no circumstances imply that Marxist Humanism has in general a latent nationalist potential. On the contrary, the positive, universal concept of the human

Truncated Humanism is no Humanism at all because it is anti-universalist and makes division and separation part of human essence. Rudi Supek (1971/1979), who was another key member of the Praxis Group, points out the democratic character of Marxist Humanism's universalism. He stresses that Humanism is opposed to "ethno-centrism, every stressing of one's own social group or nation at someone else's cost" (270). Nationalists "are not capable of solving the problem of equality among peoples" (270). Equality would only be achievable "from an international standpoint, from the standpoint of a huge communion of peoples from whom should be expelled every ethno-centrism, international hatred and prejudice" (270).

There is positive and constructive legacy for a contemporary critical theory communication of that part of the Praxis School that advocated a complete Humanism as it can be found in Marx's *Economic and Philosophic Manuscripts*. Gajo Petrović (1967, 42–43) summarises the Humanism that can be found in the *Manuscripts*:

> A fundamental idea of Marx's *Economic and Philosophical Manuscripts* is that man is a free creative being of praxis who in the contemporary world is alienated from his human essence, but that the radical form man's self-alienation assumes in the contemporary society creates real conditions for a struggle against self-alienation, for realizing socialism as a de-alienated, free community of free men.
>
> (42–43)

The ethico-political concept of praxis allows us to discern between communicative practice and *praxis communication* and to thereby situate communication as *praxis communication* in the context of the struggle for a complete humanity and democratic socialism.

Notes

1 In the English translation of the third and eighth Feuerbach-theses, the term "practice" instead of the term "praxis" was used. I have in the quotation changed in all three cases the occurrence of *practice* by the term *praxis* because Marx in the German original used the term *Praxis*.
2 Translation from German.
3 https://www.youtube.com/watch?v=u04IL4Od8Qo.

References

Balibar, Étienne and Immanuel Wallerstein.1991. *Race, Nation, Class*. London: Verso.

Benhabib, Seyla. 1995. The Strange Silence of Political Theory: Response. *Political Theory* 23 (4): 674–681.

Bogdanović, Mira. 2015. The Rift in the Praxis Group: Between Nationalism and Liberalism. *Critique* 43 (3–4): 461–483.

Chandler, David. 2000. International Justice. *New Left Review* 2 (6): 55–66.

Chomsky, Noam. 2000. Crisis in the Balkans. In *Rogue States: The Rule of Force in World Affairs*, 34–50. London: Pluto Press.

Chomsky, Noam. 1999. *The New Military Humanism: Lessons from Kosovo*. Monroe, ME: Common Courage.

Djukic, Slavoljub and Alex Dubinsky. 2001. *Milosevic and Markovic: A Lust for Power*. Montreal: McGill-Queen's University Press.

Doubt, Keith. 2006. *Understanding Evil. Lessons from Bosnia*. New York: Fordham University Press.

Fromm, Erich, ed. 1965. *Socialist Humanism: An International Symposium*. Garden City, NY: Anchor.

Fuchs, Christian. 2016. *Critical Theory of Communication: New Readings of Lukács, Adorno, Marcuse, Honneth and Habermas in the Age of the Internet*. London: University of Westminster Press. DOI: https://doi.org/10.16997/book1

Gramsci, Antonio. 1971. *Selections from the Prison Notebooks*. New York: International Publishers.

Habermas, Jürgen. 1999. Bestiality and Humanity: A War on the Border between Legality and Morality. *Constellations* 6 (3): 263–272.

Habermas, Jürgen. 1984. *The Theory of Communicative Action*. Volume 1. Boston, MA: Beacon Press.

Hegel, Georg and Wilhelm Friedrich. 1830. *The Encyclopaedia Logic (With the Zusätze)*. Indianapolis, IN: Hackett.

Herman, Edward and David Peterson. 2007. The Dismantling of Yugoslavia. *Monthly Review* 59 (5): 1–60.

Hobsbawm, Eric and Terence Ranger, eds. 1983. *The Invention of Tradition*. Cambridge: Cambridge University Press.

Horkheimer, Max. 1972. *Sozialphilosophische Studien*. Frankfurt am Main: Fischer.

Horvat, Branko. 1975a. A New Social System in the Making: Historical Origins and Development of Self-Governing Socialism. In *Self-Governing Socialism. Volume One: Historical Development. Social and Political Philosophy*, ed. Branko Horvat, Mihailo Marković and Rudi Supek, 3–66. White Plains, NY: International Arts and Sciences Press.

Horvat, Branko. 1975b. The Labor-Managed Enterprise. In *Self-Governing Socialism. Volume One: Historical Development. Social and Political Philosophy*, ed. Branko Horvat, Mihailo Marković and Rudi Supek, 164–176. White Plains, NY: International Arts and Sciences Press.

Human Rights Watch. 1992. *War Crimes in Bosnia-Hercegovina*. Washington, DC: HRW.

International Committee of the Red Cross. 1999. *People on War: Country Report Bosnia-Hercegovina*. https://www.icrc.org/eng/assets/files/other/bosnia.pdf

Kinzer, Stephen. 1992. A Sort of 'Super Serb' Defends Serbian Policy. *New York Times*. August 26, 1992.

Luxemburg, Rosa. 1976. *The National Question: Selected Writings*. New York: Monthly Review Press.

Luxemburg, Rosa. 1970. *Rosa Luxemburg Speaks*. New York: Pathfinder.

Magaš, Branka. 1993. *The Destruction of Yugoslavia: Tracking the Break-Up of 1980–92*. London: Verso.

Marković, Mihailo. 1993. Property and Democracy. In *Democracy and Possessive Individualism, the Intellectual Legacy of C.B. Macpherson*, ed. Joseph H. Carens, 235–261. Albany: State University of New York Press.

Marković, Mihailo, 1989. Tragedy of National Conflicts in "Real Socialism". The Case of Kosovo. *Praxis International* 9 (4): 408–424.

Marković, Mihailo. 1986. Self-Governing Political System and De-Alienation in Yugoslavia. *Praxis International* 6 (2): 159–174.

Marković, Mihailo. 1984. *Dialectical Theory of Meaning*. Dordrecht: Reidel.

Marković, Mihailo. 1979. Introduction: Praxis: Critical Social Philosophy in Yugoslavia. In *Praxis*, ed. Mihailo Marković and Gajo Petrović, xi–xxxvi. Dordrecht: Reidel.

Marković, Mihailo. 1975. In *Self-Governing Socialism. Volume One: Historical Development. Social and Political Philosophy*, ed. Branko Horvat, Mihailo Marković and Rudi Supek, 327–350. White Plains, NY: International Arts and Sciences Press.

Marković, Mihailo. 1974a. *From Affluence to Praxis: Philosophy and Social Criticism*. Ann Arbor: University of Michigan Press.

Marković, Mihailo. 1974b. *The Contemporary Marx*. Nottingham: Spokesman.

Markovic, Mihalo and Gajo Petrović, eds. 1979. *Praxis: Yugoslav Essays in the Philosophy and Methodology of the Social Sciences.* Dordrecht: D. Reidel Publishing.

Marković, Mihailo. 1965. Humanism and Dialectic. In *Socialist Humanism: An International Symposium*, ed. Erich Fromm, 84–97. Garden City, NY: Anchor.

Marx, Karl. 1845. Theses on Feuerbach. In *Marx & Engels Collected Works, Volume 5*, 3–5. London: Lawrence & Wishart.

Marx, Karl. 1844a. Contribution to the Critique of Hegel's Philosophy of Law. Introduction. In *Marx & Engels Collected Works*, Volume 3, 175–187. London: Lawrence & Wishart.

Marx, Karl. 1844b. Economic and Philosophic Manuscripts of 1844. In *Marx & Engels Collected Works, Volume 3*, 229–346. London: Lawrence & Wishart.

Naimark, Norman. 2002. *Fires of Hatred: Ethnic Cleansing in Twentieth-Century Europe.* Cambridge, MA: Harvard University Press.

Özkirimli, Umut. 2010. *Theories of Nationalism: A Critical Introduction.* Basingstoke: Palgrave Macmillan. Second edition.

Petrović, Gajo. 1967. *Marx in the Mid-Twentieth Century.* Garden City, NY: Anchor.

Rossi-Landi, Ferruccio. 1983. *Language as Work and Trade. A Semiotic Homology for Linguistics & Economics.* South Hadley, MA: Bergin & Garvey.

Serbian Academy of Sciences and Arts. 1995. *Memorandum of the Serbian Academy of Sciences and Arts. Answers to Criticisms.* Belgrade: Serbian Academy of Sciences and Arts.

Stojanovič, Svetozar. 1975. Between Ideals and Reality. In *Self Ggoverning Socialism. Volume One: Historical Development. Social and Political Philosophy*, ed. Branko Horvat, Mihailo Marković and Rudi Supek, 467-–478. White Plains, NY: International Arts and Sciences Press.

Stojanovič, Svetozar. 1973. *Between Ideals and Reality: Critique of Socialism and its Future.* Oxford: Oxford University Press.

Supek, Rudi. 1975. The Sociology of Workers' Self-Management. In *Self-Governing Socialism. Volume Two: Sociology and Politics. Economics*, ed. Branko Horvat, Mihailo Marković and Rudi Supek, 3–13. White Plains, NY: International Arts and Sciences Press.

Supek, Rudi. 1971/1979. Some Contradictions and Insufficiencies of Yugoslav Self-Managing Socialism. In *Praxis*, ed. Mihailo Marković and Gajo Petrović, 249–271. Dordrecht: Reidel.

Tomasello, Michael. 2008. *Origins of Human Communication.* Cambridge, MA: MIT Press.

UN Security Council 1994. *Final Report of the Commission of Experts Established Pursuant to Security Council Resolution 780 (1992).* http://www.icty.org/x/file/About/OTP/un_commission_of_experts_report1994_en.pdf

Vranicki, Predrag. 1972/1979. Theoretical Foundations for the Idea of Self-Management. In *Praxis*, ed. Mihailo Marković and Gajo Petrović, 229–247. Dordrecht: Reidel.

Williams, Raymond. 2005. *Culture and Materialism.* London: Verso.

Williams, Raymond. 1977. *Marxism and Literature.* Oxford: Oxford University Press.

Williams, Raymond. 1961/2011. *The Long Revolution.* Cardigan: Parthian.

Žižek, Slavoj. 1999. Against the Double Blackmail. *Third Text* 13 (1): 39–50.

Chapter Six
Sustainability and Community Networks

6.1 Introduction

The sustainability concept has originated and developed in the context of policy. It has first taken on a purely environmental meaning that has later been extended to include economic, institutional, and social dimensions. In the context of information technologies, sustainability has played a role in the World Summit on the Information Society. This chapter deals with community networks as alternative forms of Internet access and alternative infrastructures and asks: What do sustainability and unsustainability mean in the context of community networks?

In Europe, the most well-known community networks are Guifi in Catalonia, Freifunk in Berlin, Ninux in Italy, Funkfeuer in Vienna, and the Athens Wireless Metropolitan Network in Greece. The minimal definition of a community network that we can give is that it is an IP-based computer network that is operated by a community as a common good (see Baig, Freitag and Navarro 2015, Baig et al. 2015, Maccari 2013, Maccari and Lo Cigno 2014). Community networks can be closed or open: they are either only accessible to a specific community and then form a closed commons or provide "bandwidth resources free of charge to the general public" as an open commons (Damsgaard, Parikh and Rao 2006, 106).

The chapter starts with a section that focuses on theoretical foundations and methodology (Section 6.2). There are environmental (Section 6.3), economic (Section 6.4), political (Section 6.5), and cultural (Section 6.6) aspects of the sustainability and unsustainability of Internet access and community networks. These aspects are subsequently discussed in this chapter's sections. The analysis is drawn together in the conclusion (Section 6.7).

6.2 Theoretical Framework and Methodology

The methodology chosen is that the contradictions are analysed with the help of a literature review of works explicitly focused on community networks. The method chosen for identifying these contradictions is a synthesis of expert literature on community networks. These works were identified by a search for they keyword "community networks" in Google Scholar, Scopus, and Web of Science. So expert literature should be understood as works located in such databases. Such works tend to be highly specialised. This chapter presents such works' core findings and abstracts from them in order to analyse how society's macro-power structures shape community networks' opportunities and risks.

This chapter employs dialectical thought as a method of inquiry: Dialectics examines reality as relational, dynamic, and contradictory (for a detailed discussion, see: Fuchs 2011; Fuchs 2014; Fuchs 2016, Chapter 2.4). As a methodological approach for studying society, this means to study the dialectics of technology/society, opportunities/risks, and the powerful/the less powerful. Society is therefore analysed based on a critical theory of power. Identifying, understanding and critically acquiring power structures is the key task of a dialectical analysis of society. This chapter provides a typology of contradictions and a practical checklist with questions relating to such contradictions that alternative Internet projects can use for critically reflecting on the opportunities and risks they face.

So the aim of this chapter is to identify the contradictions that community networks face in contemporary society that is shaped by power structures and power inequalities. Many social theories share a distinction between economy, politics, and culture as the three main domains of society (Fuchs 2008, 2011): The economy is the realm of society, where humans enter a metabolism with nature so that work organises nature and culture in such a way that use-values that satisfy human needs emerge. Given that it is the economy, where the man–nature relationship is established and that the ecological system is closely linked to the economy, one could treat the ecological system as part of the economy. The political system is the realm of society, where humans deliberate on or struggle about the distribution of decision power in society. Culture is the realm of the recreation of the human body and mind in such ways that meanings, identities, and values emerge and are renegotiated in everyday life. It includes aspects of society such as the mass media, science, education, the arts, ethics, health care and medicine, sports, entertainment, and personal relations.

Definitions of power used in the social sciences often are based on Max Weber's (1978, 926) understanding as life chances exerted over the will of others. The problem with such a definition is that it cannot account for processes of empowerment and cannot discern between power and domination (Fuchs 2015). In the theoretical approach underlying this chapter, power therefore is a process and social relation, through which humans influence change in society.

Based on these foundations, we can now subsequently address each of society's dimensions and have a look at how it relates to questions of community network's un/sustainability.

6.3 Environmental Aspects of Internet Access and Community Networks

According to estimations, around 50 million tonnes of e-waste are generated per year and predictions are that within four years there will be further growth of 33 per cent.[1] This amount of e-waste is around 7 kg per person in the world. Data on electronic waste in Europe is incomplete. The recycling rate of e-waste has ranged in 2010 between 11.0 per cent in Malta and 64.9 per cent in Sweden (data source: Eurostat). The total waste from electrical and electronic equipment has increased in the EU28 countries from 14 million tonnes in 2004 to 18 million tonnes in 2010 (ibid.). In 2012, the amount was 16 million tonnes. Given the recycling rates, it becomes evident that millions of tonnes of non-recyclable electronic waste are discarded every year in the European Union. The total hazardous waste generated in 2012 in the EU28 countries in the manufacture of computer, electronic and optical products, electrical equipment, motor vehicles, and other transport equipment amounted to 2.0 million tonnes in 2010 and 2.4 million tonnes in 2012 (ibid.).

It is estimated that the total amount of e-waste generated in 2014 was 41.8 million metric tonnes (Mt). It is forecasted to increase to 50 Mt of e-waste in

> 2018. This e-waste is comprised of 1.0 Mt of lamps, 6.3 Mt of screens, 3.0 Mt of small IT (such as mobile phones, pocket calculators, personal computers, printers, etc.).
>
> (Baldé et al. 2015, 8)

The worldwide e-waste generated per capita is forecast to increase from a figure of 5.0 kg in 2010 to 6.7 kg in 2018 (Baldé et al. 2015, 24).

Up to 45 per cent of the total e-waste is treated informally and illegally (Rucevska et al. 2015, 4, 7).

> Key destinations for large-scale shipments of hazardous wastes, such as electrical and electronic equipment, include Africa and Asia. In West Africa, a significant recipient is Ghana and Nigeria, but high volumes also go to, but not limited to Cote D'Ivoire, and the Republic of the Congo. South Asia and Southeast Asia also appear to be major regional destinations, including, but not limited to, China, Hong Kong, Pakistan, India, Bangladesh, and Vietnam.
>
> (Rucevska et al. 2015, 8)

E-waste recycling is a profitable business. The goal is to extract precious metals such as gold, silver, etc. The problem, however, is that electronic goods contain hazardous materials such as arsenic, mercury, cadmium, bromides, etc., which can easily poison e-waste workers and the soil.

> E-waste recycling is flourishing in many parts of the world. South Asia and Southeast Asia appear to be major regional destinations, including, but not limited to, China, Hong Kong, India, Pakistan and Vietnam. In West Africa, common, but not limited destinations are Ghana, Nigeria, and Benin among others.
>
> (Rucevska et al. 2015, 38)

The average lifespan of a mobile phone is just 18 months[2] and of a laptop two years.[3] Planned obsolescence and lifestyle branding are part of the way in which computers, tablets, and mobile phones are presented as a way of life that enforces the generation of even more e-waste (Lewis 2013, Maxwell and Miller 2012). ICT companies such as Apple are at the heart of the computer age's ecological problems. The large-scale production and use of green ICTs that are re-useable and have flexibly exchangeable components are not in sight. The vast amount of e-waste and its negative impacts on the environment makes the information society ecologically unsustainable.

The production and consumption of energy can be measured in tonnes of oil equivalent (toe). One toe is the "energy released by burning one tonne of crude oil. It is approximately 42 gigajoules".[4] In 2014, the worldwide production of energy was 13.8 billion toe and worldwide consumption 13.7 billion toe.[5] In 2000, these values were 10.0 billion toe for both production and consumption. So the increase in world energy production and consumption was almost 40 per cent in 15 years. Energy production and consumption as such is not a problem as long as it does not harm the environment. One problem is that at the same time, the emission of carbon dioxide increased from 22.8 Mega tonnes in 2000 to 31.2 Mega tonnes in 2014. The world's main energy and electricity sources are oil, gas, and coal. Wind and solar energy made up 4.0 per cent of electricity production in 2014.

In 2012, the world energy generation was 21.53 trillion kilowatt hours (kWh) and the world energy consumption 19.71 trillion kWh.[6] Table 6.1 shows the share of various energy sources in world energy production for the year 2012. Nuclear energy tends to be considered as a renewable energy source. However, the nuclear power plant disasters in Chernobyl and Fukushima have shown how dangerous this energy form is for humans and nature. The share of relatively clean, renewable energy types (hydroelectric, geothermal, wind, solar, tidal, wave, biomass, and waste energy) in world energy production was therefore 21.7 per cent in 2012.

It is essential to consider how much energy the Internet consumes. Running the global Internet "consumed 1,815 TWh of electricity in 2012. This corresponds to 8 per cent of global electricity production in the same year (22,740 TWh)" (De Decker 2015b). By 2017,

TABLE 6.1 Share of energy sources in world energy generation, year 2012

Energy type	Share
Nuclear energy	10.9%
Hydroelectric energy	16.8%
Geothermal energy	0.3%
Wind energy	2.4%
Solar, Tidal and wave power	0.4%
Biomass and waste energy	1.8%
Fossil fuels	67.3%

Data source: International Energy Statistics, https://www.eia.gov, accessed on March 6, 2015.

Environmental Aspects of Internet Access and Community Networks

"the electricity use of the internet will rise to between 2,547 TWh (expected growth scenario) and 3,422 TWh (worst case scenario)" (De Decker 2015b). Given the fact that the majority of the world's energy consumption is based on fossil fuels and nuclear energy, the Internet's growing energy consumption certainly contributes to environmental risks.

De Decker (2015a) argues that long-distance Wi-Fi that uses point-to-point antennas for establishing connections of up to several hundred kilometres consumes relatively low amounts of energy.

> Long range WiFi also has low operational costs due to low power requirements. A typical mast installation consisting of two long distance links and one or two wireless cards for local distribution consumes around 30 watts. In several low-tech networks, nodes are entirely powered by solar panels and batteries.

Baliga et al. (2011) analysed the energy consumption of seven different wired (DSL, PON, FTTN, PtP, HFC) and wireless (WiMAX, UMTS) Internet access network types.

> At access rates greater than 10 Mb/s, wired access technologies are significantly more energy-efficient than wireless access technologies. [...] Wireless technologies will continue to consume at least 10 times more power than wired technologies when providing comparable access rates and traffic volumes. PON will continue to be the most energy-efficient access technology. [...] Passive optical networks and point-to-point optical networks are the most energy-efficient access solutions at high access rates.
>
> (Baliga et al. 2011, 75–76)

If wireless networks consume much more energy than wired ones, then a world of wireless community networks promises to be more energy-intensive than one of wired Internet access. Community networks do, however, not have to be predominantly wireless, but can to a certain degree also rely on optical fibre cables. Energy production and consumption as such is not necessarily an environmental problem. Nuclear power and fossil fuels are the dominant unclean electricity sources. If community networks want to be environmentally sustainable, then they should strive to base their electricity consumption on wind, solar, tidal, wave, and geothermal power.

Wireless communications are part of the rise of mobile communication. The typical user nowadays has not just one computer or laptop, but accesses the Internet from different places for a significant time per day with various devices such as a computer, a laptop, a tablet, and a mobile phone. All of these devices consume energy and given the short average lifespan of the devices also contributes to the production of e-waste and its toxic effects on humans and nature.

The nodes of the Guifi community network use cheap wireless routing devices such as Ubiquity or MikroTik (Vega et al. 2012). The community networks FunkFeuer and Ninux tend to use devices such as the TP-Link TL-wr841nd or Ubiquiti nanostations (Maccari and Lo Cigno 2014). Freifunk in Germany recommends the use of routers like TP-Link TL-WR842ND, TP-Link TL-WDR3600, TP-Link TL-WDR4300, Ubiquiti NanoStation M2 & Loco, Ubiquiti NanoStation M5 & Loco, Ubiquiti NanoBridge M5, TP-Link CPE210/510.[7] Such routers consume energy and it is a technical task to try and minimise their energy efficiency. Another question is, however, how long such routers are used and if they are re-useable and updateable. If not, then there is a risk that they will end up as e-waste in developing countries, polluting the environment and poisoning e-waste workers.

There is no comprehensive and reliable data available on the average lifespan of wireless routers. We also do not have data on how many routers end up as e-waste per year. Routers are classified as small IT e-waste together with other devices such as mice, keyboards, external drives, printers, mobile phones, desktop PCs, and game consoles (Baldé et al. 2015, 71–72). We know that in 2014, 3.0 Million tonnes of small IT e-waste was generated globally and that in 2016 35 per cent more e-waste was produced than in 2010 (Baldé et al. 2015, 24). It is therefore likely that also the volume of routers cast away as e-waste has increased.

6.4 Economic Aspects of Internet Access and Community Networks

Yochai Benkler defines commons the following way:

> Commons are an alternative form of institutional space, where human agents can act free of the particular constraints required for markets, and where they have some degree of confidence that the resources they need for their plans will be available to them. Both freedom of action and security of resource availability are achieved in very different patterns than they are in property-based markets.
>
> (Benkler 2006, 144)

Vasilis Kostakis and Michel Bauwens (2014) provide an understanding of the commons that is related to the one by Benkler. They argue that the Commons are a "social process"

(39) that involves resources, a community that creates use-values, and rules so that they constitute "a paradigm of a pragmatic new societal vision beyond the dominant capitalist system" (38).

Open Wi-Fi systems, such as wireless community networks, would form an "open-access-spectrum commons" (Benkler 2013, 1510). For Benkler (2006, 395), both open wireless community networks and municipal broadband initiatives are opposed to the enclosure of the spectrum and the Internet by private property. Benkler (2002) compares wireless communications based on a spectrum property market to open wireless networks that use a spectrum commons. Open wireless networks are based on end-use devices, and are an ad hoc infrastructure, scalable, both mobile and fixed (Benkler 2002, 37). Benkler argues that open wireless networks, in which nobody owns parts of the spectrum, tend to more rapidly increase the capacity of users to communicate information wirelessly, are more cost-effective, more advanced technological innovations, adapt better to changing consumer preferences, and tend to be more robust and technically secure. These are technological and economic advantages.

Vincent Mosco (2014, 6) argues that in the contemporary world of the Internet and cloud computing, we should think back to the 1950s, when there were discussions about whether computing is a utility. We can say that the Internet as communications networks is just like transportation, water supply, power supply, the education system, the sewage system, the health care system, a clean and healthy natural environment, cultural institutions, housing, food, and the political system. Like these the Internet is a public interest infrastructure that is in the common interest of all: All humans need these infrastructures in order to lead a decent life. Turning infrastructures into a commodity operated by for-profit companies increases inequality in society. Those with lower incomes and with little wealth will tend to find it more difficult to access infrastructures or will only get access to second-class infrastructures than the class of the wealthy. It is therefore a matter of justice and equality that infrastructures are treated as public or common goods and not as commodities controlled by for-profit companies.

Internet backbones are long-distance data routes. The world's largest Internet backbone owners include companies such as Telefonica (Spain), AT&T (USA), Hurricane Electric (USA), Telecom Italia (Italy), Zayo Group (USA), Tata Communications (India), Orange (France), Level 3 Communications (USA), Deutsche Telekom (Germany), Global Telecom & Technology (USA, Italy), NTT (Japan), XO Communication s (USA), TeliaSonera (Sweden, Finland), Verizon (USA), CenturyLink (USA), Cogent Communications (USA),[8] and Sprint Corporation (USA).[9] These are so-called tier 1 networks: They own so much Internet backbone infrastructure that they do not have to make peering agreements with other networks. They rather rent out their own backbone to smaller ISPs.[10] Large for-profit corporations control the Internet's infrastructure.

PSINet and UUNET created the Commercial Internet eXchange (CIX) in 1991. CIX was an interconnection service funded by all participating firms. "Each member of CIX paid a flat fee to support the cost of the equipment and maintenance, and each agreed *not* to charge each other on the basis of the volume of traffic they delivered" (Greenstein 2015, 80). Today, the data exchange between networks is established by Internet Exchange Points (IXPs). Measured in average data throughput, the world's largest IXPs are the DE-CIX (Deutscher Commercial Internet Exchange) in Frankfurt, the AMS-IX (Amsterdam Internet Exchange), and the LINX (London Internet Exchange).[11] IXPs are typically non-profit organisations with commercial Internet Service Providers (ISPs) as their members. Their principle goes back to the CIX: All ISPs want to benefit from network effects: The more users one can reach, the better the network. They therefore have a commercial incentive to be connected to other networks. The larger the Internet's reach, the more users they are likely to attract and the larger their profits promise to be. One can say that Internet Exchanges are a commons for capital: It is a commonly owned infrastructure that serves the interests of capital. It is an example of the "communism of capital": The commons are subsumed under capitalist interests.

The Internet's domain name system (DNS) was privatised in 1992. The private company Network Solutions controlled the DNS. In 1995, it started to charge for the registration of domain names. In 1998, the Internet Corporation for Assigned Names and Numbers (ICANN) was created. It is responsible for the Internet's global DNS and top-level domains. Also, the domain name service is a capitalist business.

A problem with the argument that community networks benefit areas in which commercial providers cannot make a profit so that the market fails is that market failure not only occurs in serving communications services to remote and sparsely populated regions. The market principle is a failure in itself. In communications markets this becomes evident by the fact that they tend to be highly concentrated, i.e. capitalist competition leads to oligopoly or monopoly. Community networks can therefore be a general mechanism to challenge the economic concentration of communications markets.

Sadowski (2014) studied Dutch broadband co-operatives, in which large numbers of local community members joined and paid membership fees in order to set up fibre networks. In a survey of such members of broadband co-operative (*N*=481), Sadowski found that the motivation to support the co-operative was not just the lack of other providers, but also the associated individual technical support, the idea to pluralise the communications market, the hope for the availability of specific advanced services via the co-operative, the creation of local identity, and the promotion of the co-operative idea. These results provide indications that alternatives to capitalist communications providers have the potential to be accepted for a variety of reasons. Also in situations when they compete against capitalist providers because citizens tend to appreciate co-operatives not simply for obtaining economic advantages, but also for political and cultural reasons.

The question is how one should understand sustainability with respect to community networks. A neoliberal, economic reductionist understanding would be to think about how to make an economic profit by creating such networks. Such a position, however, would neglect that the for-profit logic can easily come into contradiction with social issues that concern justice, fairness, equality, and democracy. There are indications that community networks tend to be receptive to a different understanding of sustainability. It is certainly important to think about the economic issue of how the necessary resources can be guaranteed and maintained in a community network. But this does imply the necessity of for-profit logic. Klaus Stoll (2005) studied the introduction of Wi-Fi in a remote, poor village in the Ecuadorian rainforest El Chaco. He shows that the people in El Chaco asked:

> How can the Internet help us in our schools, in our local government, in the small and medium enterprises, in the ecology, the health services and tourism? How can we make it sustainable not only in a financial but also in a technical, social, cultural and political sense?
>
> (Stoll 2005, 192)

The question is do community networks have the potential to "sustain entirely novel communication paradigms that not only break the Telco and Internet Service Providers (ISP) oligopoly in communications" (Lo Cigno and Maccari 2014, 49).

Non-commercial community networks committed to the idea of providing gratis or cheap access as a matter of freedom and democracy, face the problem of how to sustain the service and how to survive if there is competition with commercial providers, who may be able to provide faster and more stable access. Alison Powell and Leslie Shade (2006) discuss this problem in the Canadian context with the example of the Montreal-based community network Île Sans Fil (ISF):

Like all volunteer-based groups, ISF must worry about long-term sustainability. The organization is worried that over time their core volunteers will eventually be unable to take on the responsibilities of deploying and servicing a larger number of hotspots. This issue is even more pronounced for a group which aims to provide a specific telecommunications service like free public wireless Internet when technological developments make it likely that cities like Montreal will soon be covered with ubiquitous wireless Internet signals.

(Powell and Shade 2006, 399).

The problem such projects can face is that under neoliberal conditions, municipalities and governments tend to use taxpayers' money for attracting for-profit businesses or for-profit private/public partnerships and that co-operation of non-profits with for-profits may require the first one to either commodify access or usage, i.e. to introduce access fees or advertising. In all of these cases, the autonomy and freedom of non-commercial projects are undermined. Alternative, non-commercial, non-profit media and technology projects in general face existential threats in a capitalist environment (Fuchs 2010a, Sandoval and Fuchs 2010). They often lack labour-power, resources, money, influence, attention, and broad participation. Nico Carpentier (2008, 250) argues in this context that like "most alternative media", many "community Wi-Fi organizations remain vulnerable, dependent on a limited number of volunteers". One community Wi-Fi activist remarked in this context: "If I disappear, the network will disappear" (Carpentier 2008, 250). The danger is that resource precarity renders community networks a "secondary Internet" (Sandvig 2004, 596) that always remains marginal and cannot challenge the power of capitalist incumbents.

Douglas Schuler (1996) in his study of early computer-mediated community networks devotes a chapter (Chapter 10) to the question of how community networks can survive. He explicitly uses the term sustainability in this context. He however does not just mean economic survival, but also survival of what he considers to be community networks' six core values of conviviality, co-operative education, strong democracy, health and well-being, economic equity, information, and communication. He argues that for-profit organisations are ill-suited to sustain community networks because the profit motive contradicts "social, ethical or environmental concerns" and because corporations do not like to be criticised and therefore tend to censor free speech and alternative voices (355). Schuler stresses the potentials of non-profit communities and community/public co-operation.

Schuler discusses as funding options support by direct users or indirect users. The first includes donations, payment for certain services, membership fees, and support by

Economic Aspects of Internet Access and Community Networks

participating organisations. The second entails support by foundations and public funding. Schuler (1996, 370–371) also mentions advertising, but at the same time sees the problem that it is likely to change or even destroy the community character. It results in what Howard Rheingold (2000, 389) called the "commodification of community".

Tapia, Powell, and Ortiz (2009) argue that ISF managed to survive in a capitalist communications environment because it was able to create a hybrid public/community model, in which a municipality and civil society co-operate and so provide a "better alternative" (368) to privately owned for-profit networks. The authors suggest that public/commons hybrid networks can be economically sustainable and require that we "think of broadband as a utility and a public service" (369). They stress that grants are needed for funding "broadband deployment for both municipal and citizen groups" (370).

Municipal and community networks have good potentials to help overcoming digital divides. Forlano et al. (2011, 22–23) argue that "[d]igital inclusion has been the impetus behind many municipal and community wireless projects". A survey conducted among 22 community networks shows that overcoming the material access digital divide by providing affordable gratis Internet connectivity is an important motivation for running such projects (Dimogerontakis et al. 2016, Maccari and Lo Cigno 2014). One can, however, not always assume that poor local communities in developing countries consider Internet access as a primary need and in some cases they may, for various reasons, be sceptical including the suspicion of imperialism: that technology is offered to them in order to create economic dependence on the West.

A frequently heard argument is that an advantage of community networks is that this model can provide Internet access in rural and other areas, in which deploying infrastructure is not viable for commercial providers. Community networks certainly have a potential for lowering the digital divide by providing access to underserved areas. If community networks are, however, significantly slower than commercial networks, then a new digital bandwidth divide is created and poor regions then only have a second-class Internet. Another problem is that in urban areas there is a tendency that wireless community networks are predominantly used by young, educated, and affluent citizens and do not appeal to the poor (Oliver, Zuidweg and Batikas 2010). Oliver, Zuidweg, and Batikas (2010) show that the Guifi community network in Catalonia has helped to reduce the geographical digital divide in Catalonia by increasing the Internet access rate in Osona-county.

Whereas free software, as all knowledge, only needs to be developed once in order for one version to exist that can be shared with others, hardware infrastructure has considerable maintenance and renewal costs (Medosch 2015), which makes it more difficult to provide gratis access. Nonetheless creating access to wireless Internet networks tends to be relatively inexpensive (Apostol, Antoniadis and Banerjee 2008; Bar and Galperin 2004): Wi-Fi uses an industry-wide standard (IEEE 802.11), unlicensed spectrum, and relatively cheap equipment. In a wireless mesh network, not all, but only some nodes need to be connected to a fixed-lined Internet connection. Problems may arise when this architecture is significantly slower and much more unreliable than competing commercial Wi-Fi networks. In many countries, there are legal limits on the unlicensed use of the channels in the 5 GHz band-spectrum that tends to be less congested than the 2.4 GHz spectrum. This circumstance puts additional pressure on non-commercial community networks in areas where they have to compete with commercial providers.

Free software guru Richard Stallmann (2001) argues that the freedom of free software is that

> the users have the freedom to run, copy, distribute, study, change and improve the software. Thus, 'free software' is a matter of liberty, not price. To understand the concept, you should think of 'free' as in 'free speech', not as in 'free beer'. We sometimes call it 'libre software' to show we do not mean it is gratis.

Such an understanding of freedom also underlies, in the realm of community networks, the Guifi Network's licence (FONN Compact: Compact for a Free, Open & Neutral Network):

> You have the freedom to use the network for any purpose as long as you don't harm the operation of the network itself, the rights of other users, or the principles of neutrality that allow contents and services to flow without deliberate interference.[12]

Armin Medosch (2015) takes a different position and argues for understanding freedom as gratis use. He says that the economic crisis and the precarity it has created should make us see that "[f]ree or at least cheap telecommunications is an important issue of our times". Freedom should also be an issue of being "cheaper and fairer" (Medosch 2015). We can add that providing gratis access to a common resource is a matter of equality that guarantees that certain basic goods and services are available to all.

In 2013, there were reports that the Federal Communications Commission under, its then Chairman, Julius Genachowski planned to free up frequencies that enable free public

Wi-Fi (Super Wi-Fi) that uses lower frequencies located between the ones that television channels use (so-called white spaces). Jeremy Rifkin (2015, 180–181) interprets this development very optimistically and sees the future of the Internet as one of gratis access for anyone everywhere:

> In the near future, everyone will be able to share Earth's abundant free air waves, communicating with each other for nearly free, just as we'll will share the abundant free energy of the sun, wind, and geothermal heat. [...] The use of open wireless connections over a free Wi-Fi network is likely going to become the norm in the years to come, not only in America, but virtually everywhere.

But there are strong capitalist interests that may well be able to impede such future developments because communications corporations fear their profits could be reduced: In the United States, Republicans and companies such as AT&T, Intel, Qualcomm, T-Mobile, and Verizon criticised the free Wi-Fi model with the argument that licensing the airwaves to corporations who then rent it out to customers would be a better approach and warned that free Wi-Fi could harm Internet businesses.[13] In August 2015, the FCC adopted rules that allow the unlicensed use of certain channels in the 600 MHz band for Wi-Fi communication.[14] But it also planned a Broadcast Incentive Auction for 2016, in which TV stations are offered to sell the use rights of channels in the 600 MHz band-spectrum so that wireless operators can bid for the use.[15] So the decision that the FCC actually took is to free up parts of the 600 MHz band for unlicensed use and to auction other parts to corporations.

6.5 Political Aspects of Internet Access and Community Networks

Armin Medosch (2015) argues that "free networks contribute to the democratisation of technology" because users are involved in the establishment and maintenance of technology. Antoniadis and Apostol (2014) write that community networks can make a contribution to fostering participatory democracy by advancing the right to the ownership of the urban commons, by which they mean "commonly held property, and use, stewardship and management in common of the available and produced resources". The urban commons also include the communications commons. A survey conducted among 22 community networks shows that decision-making tends to be participatory and transparent in such community networks (Dimogerontakis et al. 2016).

Edward Snowden has revealed the existence of global Internet surveillance programmes that have been driven by the collaboration of the US security agency NSA and American communications companies: In June 2013, Edward Snowden revealed with the help of the *Guardian* the existence of large-scale Internet and communications surveillance systems such as Prism, XKeyscore, and Tempora. According to the leaked documents, the National Security Agency (NSA), a US secret service, in the PRISM programme obtained direct access to user data from seven online/ICT companies: AOL, Apple, Facebook, Google, Microsoft, Paltalk, Skype, and Yahoo![16]

The Snowden leaks show that Internet surveillance concerns both the hardware infrastructure of both wired and wireless networks as well as the levels of data storage and applications. Community networks provide a wired and wireless infrastructure, based on which general and network-specific applications operate. Surveillance is therefore for a community network both an issue at the physical layer as well as at layers up to the application level.

It has become evident that Internet surveillance, privacy violations, and lack of adequate data protection have resulted in major threats to democracy. Internet surveillance is a threat to political-democratic sustainability. Thus far no adequate responses on how to effectively tackle Internet surveillance's threats and strengthen the Internet's democratic sustainability have been undertaken.

Surveillance after Snowden has on the one hand increased the interest in wireless community networks (Antoniadis and Apostol 2014, Lo Cigno and Maccari 2014, Medosch 2015) because decentralised networks promise more security against the surveillance-industrial complex. At the same time, there have been countries such as Germany, where complex legal battles have occurred about the question whether a wireless community network can be made legally liable for the illegal use of a network for terrorism, crime, copyright infringement, child pornography, etc. (Medosch 2015). Wireless community networks face a contradiction between privacy-enhanced openness and surveillance. Empirical research shows that privacy may not automatically be larger in wireless community networks than in other networks if the majority of the traffic is transported over some key nodes (Maccari and Lo Cigno 2014). The network architecture and routing method therefore play a key role in the question of privacy and security in community networks.

A survey among 22 community networks showed that such projects tend to be concerned about protecting users' privacy (Dimogerontakis et al. 2016). Depending on national legislation concerning user identification, data retention and surveillance, there can be more or less complications for community networks because implementing such measures is

Political Aspects of Internet Access and Community Networks

expensive (ibid.) and may violate privacy. Wireless community networks tend to use the frequency bands of 2.4 GHz and 5 GHz that are mostly seen as open spectrum, for whose use one does not need a licence. The regulation of spectrum use and the right to build and use outdoor antennas can, however, create legal, administrative, and financial problems for community networks (ibid.).

In respect to the political shutdown of the Internet in authoritarian regimes, community networks are

> means to communicate independently from the central command of governments and traditional operators. They enable citizen to organize (politically or otherwise) even in the eventuality that the established powers activate the so-called 'kill-switch' and shut down communications networks in a given area.
> (De Filippi and Tréguer 2015)

The potential that community networks and decentralised peer-to-peer systems for network access and the storage, production, communication, distribution, and consumption of information have for guaranteeing anonymity, privacy, security, and data, poses at the same time also a problem in a political system that is obsessed with the idea that surveillance can prevent terrorism and crime. There is the danger that given such circumstances, decentralised IT systems that allow anonymity will be outlawed. If access, storage, and processing are distributed, then it is legally difficult to argue that the participating peers are liable for certain infringements because one cannot assign intention and awareness to them (Dulong de Rosnay 2015, Giovanella 2015, Musiani 2014).

Melanie Dulong de Rosnay (2015) argues that the problem is that the Western legal system is based on liberal individualism. She identifies the "need for cultural change away from the neoliberal paradigm" so that the law is distributed and recognises "community rights and duties and collective persons as opposed to individual persons" (Dulong de Rosnay 2015). The question is if in the case of illegal use, the individual user, the ISP, or the community network should and could be held accountable (Giovanella 2015). Federica Giovanella (2015) argues that it is unlikely that community networks can be held accountable by European law, except if they are organised as associations. She acknowledges the problem of applying "old legal schemes to [...] new technology" (Giovanella 2015, 67) and argues that potential solutions are to hold the networks liable and/or to introduce user identification systems. Some community networks, such as Guifi, are already organised as non-profit foundations. The difficulty is that the question arises if a foundation should legally be held accountable for network use that is beyond their control. It could limit liability by prohibiting illegal use of the network by issuing terms of use.

Let us, however, assume that Daesh terrorists use such a community network for organising terrorist attacks. If the individual user cannot be identified, then the legal authorities and the police may either try to shut the network down or hold it legally accountable. This can then bias the network towards introducing a surveillance system that may infringe users' privacy and freedom of speech. Another possibility is that the network introduces a user identification system. But of course, fake names and addresses could be used. Only identification by an ID or a credit card could guarantee personal identification. The first option, however, can be quite inconvenient because verification can be time and resource intensive. Using credit cards for user identification can bias a network towards charging for access, which may undermine the idea of free and open network access. In a society that is obsessed with monitoring users, it is difficult to run free and open communications networks.

In the ideal case, we could overcome the idea that communications surveillance is a solution to crime and terrorism and instead focus on fighting the social causes of these phenomena. As long as such politics is not in place, community networks are confronted with the danger that the surveillance ideology may lead legal and policing authorities to consider outlawing or criminalising them. They therefore have to think about how to position themselves towards the political contradiction between privacy-enhancing, free, open community networks and the surveillance ideology. The antagonism between privacy and the surveillance ideology also shows that community networks must, by necessity, be political if they care about freedom and democracy.

The Internet is today predominantly a communication system under commercial, authoritarian, and paternal control (see Williams 1976). Community networks promise a democratic communications system in Raymond Williams's (1976) understanding, but at the same time face the problems of an environment governed by the political-economic control of communications.

6.6 Cultural Aspects of Network Access

A survey conducted among 22 community networks shows that providing local education and training in technical skills is an important activity of such projects (Dimogerontakis et al. 2016). Wireless communities have opportunities for users to engage in participatory learning about "the structure and the functioning of the Internet" (Medosch 2015).

Community networks are not just technical networks, but allow creating neighbourhood communities (Apostol, Antoniadis, and Banerjee 2008). Alison Powell (2008) distinguishes between geek publics and community publics in community networks. The first is a community that is brought together through creating and discussing community networks, whereas the second is brought together through local discussions using a community network. Powell found in a study of community networks in Canada that they tended to primarily create geek publics – "social club[s] for geeks" (1078). Everyday users were "not necessarily interested in using technology as a means of creating social links" (1081), but in gratis Wi-Fi access.

Christian Sandvig (2004) concludes in a case study of Wi-Fi co-operatives that the studied cases were communities of technical experts (geek communities) that were difficult to join for outsiders. These communities therefore remained marginal.

> Overall, the Wi-Fi co-ops examined here are inward-looking: they emulate Douglas's 'cult of the boy operator' in radio before 1920 more than they provide an outward-looking CN that builds its own internal community through an explicit mission of helping those outside the group that are disadvantaged. [...] Indeed, co-ops are in some cases so expert that this makes it impossible to imagine their success as a populist movement.
>
> (Sandvig 2004, 596)

In Alison Powell's research, the geek publics were strong communities organised around joint activities and communication, and the community publics were weak communities organised around sharing access to the same network as a gratis resource. One may be disappointed that in her studied case no strong social user communities developed, but one should not downplay the importance of the fact that users are interested in gratis Internet access, which means that they consider Internet infrastructure as a common good that should be available to everyone everywhere cheap or free of charge. The public these users envision is one of public or common ownership of the Internet infrastructure. That they all use a specific network is a potential for the creation of cultural communities, but it is no automatism and not an absolute necessity.

Tapia, Powell, and Ortiz (2009) discuss the example of the community network ISF in Montreal that managed via a public/community partnership to develop from a geek public into a more outward-looking community. The example shows that it is also not an automatism and a necessity that community networks are "alternative ghettos" of tech-savvy experts, from which everyday citizens feel excluded. In the end, it is an organisational question to which degree community networks are able to reach out to and engage the general public.

6.7 Conclusion: A Framework for Understanding (Un-)Sustainability and Community Networks

We have discussed four dimensions of sustainable and unsustainable development of Internet access and how they affect community networks. Section 6.3 showed that community networks face environmental issues in respect to the generation of e-waste and energy consumption. Section 6.4 indicated that with respect to the economy, community networks operate in a capitalist environment, which poses the question of how their existence is confronted and threatened by corporate monopolies, how they deal with this threat, and the question of how to obtain the resources necessary for paying their workers and providing the necessary technology without having to use the same logic. Section 6.5 discussed that community networks have the potential to provide more privacy-friendly communications and at the same time exist in the context of contemporary surveillance societies that are based on the ideology of categorical suspicion and the technological-determinist assumption that surveillance can solve political problems such as crime and terrorism. In September 2016, the European Court of Justice made a decision on a legal dispute between Sony Entertainment and a supporter of the German Pirate Party.[17] Its decision was that open Wi-Fi hotspots are no longer allowed to be anonymous, but need to implement user identification and individual password-based logins. This rule provides a drawback for community networks' quest for privacy in Europe. Section 6.6 showed that the culture associated with community networks faces questions about being exclusive and limited to geeks or being open to and oriented on a broad public. The discussion showed overall that there are environmental, economic, political, and cultural questions that community networks face.

Table 6.2 provides a checklist that based on the previous discussion identifies key issues that should be considered when thinking about how sustainable development of a community network can best be achieved. It identifies ecological, economic, political, and cultural sustainability issues.

At the **environmental** level, community networks face a **contradiction between network effects and environmental problems**: The more users a network has, the better

TABLE 6.2 Checklist for sustainability issues in community networks

Dimension	(Un-)sustainability issue	Sustainability questions
Nature	Energy use	To what extent does the community network rely on relatively environmental-friendly energy sources (wind energy, solar power, tidal power, wave power, geothermal energy, biomass, and waste energy)?
		To what extent does the network rely on suppliers of such energy forms?
		What is the share of the total energy consumed per year by the network that is based on relatively clean power sources?
Nature	e-waste	What is the average lifespan of different hardware types used in the community network?
		Can measures be taken for ensuring the long-term re-use and update of hardware?
		If hardware devices have to be replaced, is it possible to recycle the old ones? How?
		If hardware devices have to be trashed, is it possible to do so in a way that does not threaten humans and nature? How?
		If hardware devices have to be trashed, is it possible to do so in a way that avoids the creation of e-waste that is shipped to developing countries where it poses threats to e-waste workers, humans, and nature? How?
		If old hardware devices that a network no longer uses are donated to other networks, can it be ensured that this does not result in a two-tier Internet access structure, in which poorer communities have slower Internet access than others?
Economy	Monopoly power and corporate concentration	How strongly concentrated is the Internet access market in a specific region, country, and the world? What share of users and financial resources (revenue, capital assets, profits) does the incumbent Internet service provider have in a specific region, country and the world?
		Does the operation of the community network help to challenge the financial and market power of dominant Internet service providers? How?
		What are the dangers and what happens when a community network suddenly faces competition by a private for-profit Internet service provider?
Economy	Survival and resources	Will the community network manage to survive economically, i.e. to afford the necessary hardware and labour-power necessary for running the network? How does it do that? What are its financial sources?
		Can the community network ensure that it has enough resources, supporters, workers, volunteers, and users? Can the risk be avoided that the community network is a "secondary Internet" that is marginal, slower, and less attractive than other services? How? What strategies can be used for avoiding marginalisation and resource precarity?
		Are there possibilities for the community network to obtain public or municipal funding or to co-operate with municipalities, public institutions or the state in providing access?

Dimension	(Un-)sustainability issue	Sustainability questions
Economy	Economic democracy	Is the community network collectively owned and controlled by its members as a common good? How can the community network best ensure that it is a not-for-profit project that is democratically owned and controlled?
		Are those who work professionally for the maintenance of the network, fairly remunerated for their labour so that they can lead decent lives?
		To what extent does the network rely on community control, municipal control, or private corporate control?
		What are the potential dangers of collaboration with or inclusion of private for-profit companies? How can they be avoided?
Economy	Tragedy and comedy of the commons	Is the network large enough to attract significant numbers of users so that this community can have mutual benefits from network effects?
		How can possible congestion and slowdown of the network best be avoided if it is very popular?
Economy	Network wealth for all	How can the community network provide gratis/cheap/affordable network and Internet access for all? Can it help to lower the digital divide? How? How can the community network help to avoid a two-tier Internet with slower Internet access for some and faster for others?
		How can the community network avoid the commodification of a) access (i.e. using access fees) and b) users (i.e. using advertisements) that bring about a) inequality of access and b) the exploitation of users' digital labour?
Politics	Participation	How is the community network governed? How does it decide which rules, standards, licences, etc. are adopted?
		Does the community network allow and encourage the participation of community members in governance processes? How?
		Are there clear mechanisms for conflict resolution and proceedings in the case of the violation of community rules?
Politics	Privacy-enhancement and protection from surveillance	How can a community network best be designed and governed so that the privacy of users is guaranteed, is technically secure, and protects users from corporate and state surveillance?
		How can privacy-enhancing and privacy-friendly community networks best face the threat that, in a culture of law-and-order politics and a surveillance society in which governments believe that surveillance is a way of preventing crime and terrorism, they are outlawed? How can they best challenge the argument that they provide a safe harbour for the communication of criminals and terrorists?
		How does the community network deal with actual crime occurring in its network? How can it best minimise the occurrence of crime?

(Continued)

Conclusion: A Framework for Understanding (Un-)Sustainability and Community Networks

Dimension	(Un-)sustainability issue	Sustainability questions
Culture	Conviviality, learning, and community engagement	Does the community network provide mechanisms for learning, education, training, communication, conversations, community engagement, strong democracy, participation, co-operation, and well-being? How?
		To which degree is the community network able to foster a culture of togetherness and conviviality that brings together people? How?
Culture	Unity in diversity	To which degree is the community network a "geek public" that has an elitist, exclusionary culture or a "community public" that is based on a culture of unity in diversity? How can a culture of unity in diversity best be achieved?

and more attractive it is (network effect). But more Internet use today also tends to mean more energy consumption, more deployed hardware, and more use of digital media devices, which can increase the consumption of unclean energy sources and thereby the depletion and pollution of nature and the generation of e-waste that can harm humans and society. Community networks' environmental challenge is therefore how to attract a large user community, keep the network up-to-date with technological progress and at the same time rely on clean, renewable energy sources and avoid e-waste.

At the **economic** level, community networks face a **contradiction between the monopoly power of large communications companies and the resources required for managing the network as a non-profit, commonly owned and commonly governed, democratic, gratis good, and service**: The communications sector is a highly concentrated industry. Large communications corporations own large parts of the Internet's infrastructure. Communications in capitalism are shaped by monopoly power. Communication is a process that is necessary for human survival. In contemporary society, the access to communications networks and the Internet is therefore of importance for organising everyday communication. If means of communication are privately owned, then inequalities in access and use tend to emerge. Non-profit community networks can challenge the power of corporate communications corporations. They can be foundations of an alternative organisation of the Internet. But they also require resources such as hardware, labour-power, money, users, attention, reputation, influence, support, and volunteers, etc. The history of alternative media has not just been a history of spaces for alternative, democratic communications, but also a history of resource precarity and unpaid, highly self-exploitative volunteer labour. The danger for alternative media is that they cannot economically survive or that they develop into privately owned for-profit companies that turn access, content, or users into commodities and thereby foster inequality and exploitation. Community networks' economic challenge is to run community networks as democratic, non-profit, gratis commons that challenge the power of corporate monopolies and the economic concentration of communications, but can at the same time economically survive and do not exist as second-class Internet that is marginalised.

At the **political** level, community networks face a **contradiction between open, privacy-friendly participation and political control**: Community networks have the potential to be inclusive, allow open participation, to be democratic, and to enhance privacy and the protection from corporate and state surveillance. At the same time, given the prevalence of surveillance ideologies ("surveillance helps to fight and prevent crime and terrorism"), they face the threat of being shut down or criminalised by the state. They also face the problem of how to avoid openness and being misused by criminals. Community networks' political challenge is how to be open, participatory, and privacy-friendly and at the same time challenge the surveillance ideology and respond to actual criminal abuse.

At **the cultural** level, community networks face a **contradiction between geek publics and community publics**: Community networks have the potential to be open public networks for learning, training, community engagement, togetherness, and communication. But studies have shown that there is the danger that they develop a self-centred, closed geek culture dominated by techies that is unattractive to others and has an exclusionary and elitist character. There is also the danger that tech-experts develop into a power elite inside of such networks. Community networks' cultural challenge is how to foster a culture of unity in diversity and to be a community public.

Community networks in a society, in which power is asymmetrically distributed, face environmental, economic, political, and cultural contradictions. They have potentials to foster sustainability in the information society, but at the same time face the problem of how to survive and not become part of powerful mechanisms that advance unsustainable development. Establishing a sustainable information society is not just a question of introducing new technological networks and organisation forms, it is also a question of changing the existing distribution of communication power and to foster struggles that question this power's asymmetrical distribution.

Acknowledgement

The research presented in this chapter was conducted with funding provided by the EU Horizon 2020 project netCommons: Network Infrastructure as Commons, http://netcommons.eu/, grant agreement number: 688768.

Notes

1 Toxic "e-waste" dumped in poor nations, says United Nations. *The Guardian Online*, December 14, 2013.
2 http://www.thesecretlifeofthings.com/#!phone-facts/c611.
3 What is the lifespan of a laptop? *The Guardian Online*, January 13, 2013.
4 Wikipedia: Tonne of oil equivalent, https://en.wikipedia.org/wiki/Tonne_of_oil_equivalent, accessed on March 6, 2015.
5 Data source for all data in this paragraph: Global Energy Statistical Yearbook 2015, https://yearbook.enerdata.net, accessed on March 6, 2015.
6 Data source: International Energy Statistics, https://www.eia.gov, accessed on March 6, 2015.
7 https://wiki.freifunk.net/FAQ_Technik, accessed on March 7, 2016.
8 See: https://en.wikipedia.org/wiki/Tier_1_network.
9 https://en.wikipedia.org/wiki/Sprint_Corporation.
10 See https://en.wikipedia.org/wiki/Tier_2_network for an overview of important tier 2 networks that buy transit from tier 1 networks.
11 See: https://en.wikipedia.org/wiki/List_of_Internet_exchange_points_by_size.
12 http://guifi.net/en/FONNC, accessed on February 8, 2016.
13 Tech, telecom giants take sides as FCC proposes large public WiFi networks. *The Washington Post Online*, February 3, 2013.
14 https://apps.fcc.gov/edocs_public/attachmatch/DOC-334757A1.pdf.
15 FAQ: The FCC's upcoming broadcast-TV spectrum auction. *Computerworld Online*, October 15, 2015.
16 NSA Prism program taps in to user data of Apple, Google and others. *The Guardian Online*. June 7, 2013.
17 Wi-Fiprovidersnotliableforcopyrightinfringements,rulestopEUcourt.Butjudgementspellstroublefor anonymityonwirelessnetworks,warnMEPs.ArsTechnica,September15,2016.http://arstechnica.co.uk/tech-policy/2016/09/wi-fi-providers-not-liable-for-copyright-infringements-cjeu/.

References

Antoniadis, Panayotis and Ileana Apostol. 2014. The Right(s) to the Hybrid City and the Role of DIY Networking. *Journal of Community Informatics* 10 (3).

Apostol, Ileana, Panayotis Antoniadis and Tridib Banerjee. 2008. From Face-Block to Facebook of the Other Way Around? Presentation at the International Meeting. *"Sustainable City and Creativity: Promoting Creative Urban Initiatives"* in Naples. http://citeseerx.ist.psu.edu/viewdoc/download?doi=10.1.1.218.6904&rep=rep1&type=pdf

Baig, Roger, Felix Freitag and Leandro Navarro. 2015. On the Sustainability of Community Clouds in guifi.net. In *12th International Conference on Economics of Grids, Clouds, Systems and Services (GECON 2015)*. New York: IEEE.

Baig, Roger, Ramon Roca, Felix Freitag and Leandro Navarro. 2015. guifi.net, a Crowdsourced Network Infrastructure Held in Common. *Computer Networks* 90: 150–165.

Baldé, Kees, Feng Wang, Ruediger Kuehr and Jaco Huisman. 2015. *The Global e-Waste Monitor – 2014*. Bonn: United Nations University, IAS – SCYCLE.

Baliga, Jayant, Robert Ayre, Kerry Hinton and Rodney S. Tucker. 2011. Energy Consumption in Wired and Wireless Access Networks. *IEEE Communications Magazine* 49 (6): 70–77.

Bar, François and Hernan Galperin. 2004. Building the Wireless Internet Infrastructure: From Cordless Ethernet Archipelagos to Wireless Grids. *Communications & Strategies* 54 (2): 45–68.

Benkler, Yochai. 2013. Commons and Growth: The Essential Role of Open Commons in Market Economies. *University of Chicago Law Review* 80: 1499–1555.

Benkler, Yochai. 2006. *The Wealth of Networks: How Social Production Transforms Markets and Freedom*. New Haven, CT: Yale University Press.

Benkler, Yochai. 2002. Some Economics of Wireless Communications. *Harvard Journal of Law & Technology* 16 (1): 25–83.

Carpentier, Nico. 2008. The Belly of the City: Alternative Communicative City Networks. *The International Communication Gazette* 70 (3–4): 237–255.

Damsgaard, Jan, Mihir A. Parikh and Bharat Rao. 2006. Wireless Commons: Perils in the Common Good. *Communications of the ACM* 49 (2): 105–109.

De Decker, Kris. 2015a. How to Build a Low-Tech Internet. *Low-Tech Magazine*, October 26, 2015.

De Decker, Kris. 2015b. Why We Need a Speed Limit for the Internet. *Low-Tech Magazine*, October 19, 2015.

De Filippi, Primavera, and Félix Tréguer. 2015. Expanding the Internet Commons: The Subversive Potential of Wireless Community Networks. *Journal of Peer Production* 6

Dimogerontakis, Emmanouil, Leandro Navaro, Bart Braem and Roc Meseguer. 2016. Socio-Economic Experiences, Challenges and Lessons in Community Networks around the World. *Draft manuscript.*

Dulong de Rosnay, Melanie. 2015. Peer-to-Peer as a Design Principle for Law: Distribute the Law. *Journal of Peer Production* 6

Forlano, Laura, Alison Powell, Gwen Shaffer, and Benjamin Lennett. 2011. *From the Digital Divide to Digital Excellence: Global Best Practices for Municipal and Community Wireless Networks*. Washington, DC: New America Foundation.

Fuchs, Christian. 2016. *Critical Theory of Communication: New Readings of Lukács, Adorno, Marcuse, Honneth and Habermas in the Age of the Internet*. London: University of Westminster Press.

Fuchs, Christian. 2015. Power in the Age of Social Media. *Heathwood Journal of Critical Theory* 1 (1): 1–29.

Fuchs, Christian. 2014. The Dialectic: Not Just the Absolute Recoil, but the World's Living Fire That Extinguishes and Kindles Itself. Reflections on Slavoj Žižek's Version of Dialectical Philosophy in "Absolute Recoil: Towards a New Foundation of Dialectical Materialism". *tripleC:*

References

Communication, Capitalism & Critique. Open Access Journal for a Global Sustainable Informa-tion Society 12 (2): 848–875.

Fuchs, Christian. 2011. *Foundations of Critical Media and Information Studies*. London: Routledge.

Fuchs, Christian. 2010. Alternative Media as Critical Media. *European Journal of Social Theory* 13 (2): 173–192.

Fuchs, Christian. 2008. *Internet and Society: Social Theory in the Information Age*. New York: Routledge.

Giovanella, Federica. 2015. Liability Issues in Wireless Community Networks. *Journal of European Tort Law* 6 (1): 49–68.

Greenstein, Shane. 2015. *How the Internet Became Commercial*. Princeton, NJ: Princeton Univer-sity Press.

Kostakis, Vasilis and Michel Bauwens. 2014. *Network Society and Future Scenarios for a Collab-orative Economy*. Basingstoke: Palgrave Macmillan.

Lewis, Justin. 2013. *Beyond Consumer Capitalism. Media and the Limits to Imagination*. Cam-bridge: Polity Press.

Lo Cigno, Renato and Leonardo Maccari. 2014. Urban Wireless Networks: Challenges and Solu-tions for Smart City Communications. In *WiMobCity '14: Proceedings of the 2014 ACM Inter-national Workshop on Wireless and Mobile Technologies for Smart Cities*, 49–54. New York: ACM.

Maccari, Leonardo. 2013. An Analysis of the Ninux Wireless Community Network. In *Wireless and Mobile Computing, Networking and Communications (WiMob), 2013 IEEE 9th International Conference on*, 1–7. New York: IEEE.

Maccari, Leonardo and Renato Lo Cigno. 2014. A Week in the Life of Three Large Wireless Com-munity Networks. *Ad Hoc Networks* 24 (B): 175–190.

Maxwell, Richard and Toby Miller. 2012. *Greening the Media*. Oxford: Oxford University Press.

Medosch, Armin. 2015. *The Rise of the Network Commons*. Book draft (accessed on February 8, 2016). http://www.thenextlayer.org/NetworkCommons

Mosco, Vincent. 2014. *To the Cloud: Big Data in a Turbulent World*. Boulder, CO: Paradigm.

Musiani, Francesca. 2014. Decentralised Internet Governance: The Case of A "Peer-to-Peer Cloud". *Internet Policy Review* 3 (1).

Oliver, Miquel, Johan Zuidweg and Michail Batikas. 2010. Wireless Commons against the Digital Divide. In *2010 IEEE International Symposium on Technology and Society (ISTAS)*, 457–465. New York: IEEE.

Powell, Alison. 2008. Wifi Publics: Producing Community and Technology. *Information, Communi-cation & Society* 11 (8): 1068–1088.

Powell, Alison and Leslie Regan Shade. 2006. Going Wi-Fi in Canada: Municipal and Community Initiatives. *Government Information Quarterly* 23 (3–4): 381–403.

Rheingold, Howard. 2000. *The Virtual Community: Homesteading on the Electronic Frontier*. Cam-bridge, MA: MIT Press. Revised edition.

Rifkin, Jeremy. 2015. *The Zero Marginal Cost Society*. New York: Palgrave Macmillan.

Rucevska, leva et al. 2015. *Waste Crime – Waste Risks: Gaps in Meeting the Global Waste Challenge. A UNEP Rapid Response Assessment*. Arendal: United Nations Environment Programme and GRID.

Sadowski, Bert M. 2014. *Consumer Cooperatives as a New Governance Form: The Case of the Cooperatives in the Broadband Industry*. Eindhoven Centre for Innovation Studies Working Paper 14.03. Eindoven: Eindhoven University of Technology.

Sandoval, Marisol and Christian Fuchs. 2010. Towards a Critical Theory of Alternative Media. *Telematics and Informatics* 27 (2): 141–150.

Sandvig, Christian. 2004. An Initial Assessment of Cooperative Action in Wi-Fi Networking. *Telecommunications Policy* 28 (7–8): 579–602.

Schuler, Douglas. 1996. *New Community Networks: Wired for Change*. New York: ACM Press.

Stallmann, Richard. 2001. What is Free Software? https://www.gnu.org/philosophy/free-sw.en.html

Stoll, Klaus. 2005. How Wi-Fi Came to El Chaco. *Journal of Community Informatics* 1 (2): 190–196.

Tapia, Andrea H., Alison Powell and Julio Angel Ortiz. 2009. Reforming Policy to Promote Local Broadband Networks. *Journal of Communication Inquiry* 33 (4): 354–375.

Vega, Davide, Llorenç Cerdà-Alabern, Leandro Navarro and Roc Meseguer. 2012. Topology Patterns of a Community Network: Guifi.net. In *Wireless and Mobile Computing, Networking and Communications (WiMob), 2012 IEEE 8th International Conference on*, 612–619. New York: IEEE.

Weber, Max. 1978. *Economy and Society*. Berkeley: University of California Press.

Williams, Raymond. 1976. *Communications*. Harmondsworth: Penguin. Third edition.

References

Chapter Seven
Karl Marx, Journalism, and Democracy

7.1 Introduction

"Marxism and communism mean state control, censorship and surveillance of the press. They are incompatible with free journalism". This is a common assumption about journalism and Marxism.

The task of this chapter is to clarify the significance of Karl Marx's theory, the critique of political economy, for the theory of journalism. To this end, Marx's relationship to journalism is first examined. Then, some of Marx's important theoretical concepts are introduced and their relevance for the critical theory of journalism is discussed.

The assumption mentioned in the first paragraph has partly to do with the real lack of freedom of journalism in the Soviet Union, where the press was controlled and directed by the state.

Immediately after the October Revolution, the Council of People's Commissars decided in the Decree on the Press to ban the bourgeois press. The Left Socialist-Revolutionaries objected to this decision. The question was then discussed in the All-Russian Central Executive Committee. Lenin said at this meeting: "Earlier on we said that if we took power, we intended to close down the bourgeois newspapers. To tolerate the existence of these papers is to cease being a socialist" (Lenin 1917, 286). The Bolsheviks moved to support the decree, which was adopted by the Central Committee with 34 "yes" votes, 24 no votes, and one abstention. This sealed state control of the press in the Soviet Union. In November 1917, the Socialist Revolutionaries became the strongest party in

DOI: 10.4324/9781003331087-9

the election to the Constituent Assembly, where they then had an absolute majority. The Bolsheviks dissolved the Assembly by force of arms on 6 January 1918, whereupon the Socialist Revolutionaries went underground and fought the Bolsheviks' power.

Stalin implemented the destruction of all opposition by means of terror. On the freedom of the press, he said:

QUESTION. Why is there no freedom of the press in the U.S.S.R.?

ANSWER: What freedom of the press do you mean? Freedom of the press for which class – the bourgeoisie or the proletariat? If you mean freedom of the press for the bourgeoisie, then it does not and will not exist here while the proletarian dictatorship exists. But if you mean freedom for the proletariat, then I must say that you will not find another country in the world where freedom of the press for the proletariat is as wide and complete as it is in the U.S.S.R. [...] We have no freedom of the press for the bourgeoisie. We have no freedom of the press for the Mensheviks and Socialist-Revolutionaries, who in our country stand for the interests of the defeated and overthrown bourgeoisie. But is that surprising? We never pledged ourselves to grant freedom of the press to all classes, to make all classes happy. When taking power in October 1917, the Bolsheviks openly declared that this meant the power of one class, the power of the proletariat, which would suppress the bourgeoisie in the interests of the labouring masses of town and country, who form the overwhelming majority of the population of the U.S.S.R. How, after this, can the proletarian dictatorship be required to grant freedom of the press to the bourgeoisie?

(Stalin 1927, 215–217)

Lenin and Stalin thus implemented state control of the press. This can give the false impression that Marx and Engels held the same view, which can lead to the rejection of engagement with their theoretical works on the basis of the argument that Marxism and communism hold an authoritarian and ideological view of journalism.

Historian Tristam Hunt (2009, 361) gives a clear answer to the question of whether Marx and Engels are responsible for the crimes committed under the banner of Marxism in the 20th century:

In no intelligible sense can Engels or Marx bear culpability for the crimes of historical actors carried out generations later, even if the policies were offered up in their honor. Just as Adam Smith is not to blame for the inequalities of the free market West, nor Martin Luther for the nature of modern Protestant evangelicalism, nor the Prophet Muhammad for the atrocities of Osama bin Laden, so the millions of souls dispatched by Stalinism (or by Mao's China, Pol Pot's Cambodia, and Mengistu's Ethiopia) did not go to their graves on account of two nineteenth-century London philosophers.

Rosa Luxemburg was an anti-Stalinist and Lenin-critical Marxist who criticised the abolition of the opposition and freedom of the press as a deficit of the October Revolution:

> Freedom only for the supporters of the government, only for the members of one party – however numerous they may be – is no freedom at all. Freedom is always and exclusively freedom for the one who thinks differently. Not because of any fanatical concept of 'justice' but because all that is instructive, wholesome and purifying in political freedom depends on this essential characteristic, and its effectiveness vanishes when 'freedom' becomes a special privilege.
> (Luxemburg 1922, 169)

Luxemburg advocated the overthrow of the tsarist regime in Russia and a socialist society but, unlike the Bolsheviks, stressed that socialism must be democratic. She characterises the constituent assembly, the suffrage law, freedom of the press, and the rights of association and assembly as "the whole apparatus of the basic democratic liberties" (Luxemburg 1922, 48) and as "the most important democratic guarantees of a healthy public life and of the political activity of the laboring masses" (Luxemburg 1922, 66). It "is a well-known and indisputable fact that without a free and untrammelled press, without the unlimited right of association and assemblage, the rule of the broad mass of the people is entirely unthinkable" (Luxemburg 1922, 66–67).

Marx's theory must therefore not be equated with the Soviet Union. It is worthwhile even today to take a look at Marx's contributions to the understanding of journalism.

7.2 Marx and Journalism

Marx was himself active as a journalist (see Herres 2005): in 1842 and 1843 he was editor-in-chief of the *Rheinische Zeitung* until it was banned by the Prussian regime. After the newspaper was banned, Marx went to Paris. There he first published the *Deutsch-Französische Jahrbücher* together with Arnold Ruge and from 1844 to 1845 the weekly newspaper *Vorwärts. Pariser Deutsche Zeitschrift*. Through an intervention of the Prussian government, which found the criticism of absolutism in the Vorwärts a thorn in the flesh, Marx was expelled from France. Marx and Engels went to Belgium. In Brussels, they collaborated on the *Deutsche-Brüsseler Zeitung*. The French February Revolution of 1848 triggered a revolutionary phase throughout Europe. Marx was expelled from Belgium, whereupon he went to Paris. In the course of the German March Revolution, he went to Cologne, where he published the *Neue Rheinische Zeitung* in 1848 and 1849, on which Engels also worked as editor. After the suppression of the revolution, Marx was expelled from the country. He went to London, where he lived until his death in 1883. From 1852 to 1862, Marx was the European correspondent of the *New York Tribune*, the world's largest-circulation newspaper at the time. Marx was considered by the *Tribune* to be one of its most important contributors. Marx wrote about 500 articles for this daily newspaper, many of which were editorials. The *New York Tribune* continued to exist until 1966, from 1924 under the name *New York Herald Tribune*. In the late 19th and 20th centuries, it was a quality daily newspaper of a conservative character, for which Walter Lippmann, among others, worked as a columnist. From the 1860s onwards, Marx spent a lot of time working on his main work *Das Kapital*, but continued to be active as a journalist, including as a correspondent for the Vienna-based *Die Presse*. Marx also wrote for *Der Volksstaat* and *Der Social-Demokrat*. *Der Volksstaat* was the organ of the Social Democratic Workers' Party (Sozialdemokratische Arbeiterpartei, SDAP) of Wilhelm Liebknecht and August Bebel. *Der Social-Demokrat* was the organ of the General German Workers' Association (Allgemeiner Deutscher Arbeiterverein, ADAV) founded by Ferdinand Lassalle. In 1875, the ADAV and the SDAP merged to form the Socialist Workers' Party of Germany (SAP). *Der Social-Demokrat* became the SAP-published *Vorwärts* in 1876, which still exists today as the organ of the Social Democratic Party of Germany (SPD).

Marx's journalism is characterised by the fact that he asked critical questions about the powerful and power structures. Marx's journalistic works are documented in the *Marx & Engels Collected Works* (MECW) and are still worth reading in the 21st century as an example of critical journalism.

The political economist of the media and communication Vincent Mosco (2012, 575, 576) characterises Marx's journalism as follows:

> his approach was to take an event in the news such as the second Opium War in China or the American Civil War and, using the most up-to-date material, address its political economic significance. [...] Whereas the *Grundrisse* suggested ways to theorize knowledge and communication labour, his journalism demonstrated how to practice it with passion and intelligence. These are

lessons that communication students, and not just Marxist scholars, would do well to learn.

Marx scholar and biographer David McLellan (1973, 288) argues that Marx linked his articles to the statistics and reports he used for his own research and that his journalistic works are "remarkably detached and objective". In an anthology edited by Jakobs and Langenbucher (2004), whose contributions were printed as a series in the Süddeutsche Zeitung, Marx is listed as one of the 50 "role models of journalism".[1] "Especially as a journalist, he adopted an investigative approach that analysed interactions and attempted to take into account a wide variety of factors"[2] (Herres 2005, 26).

Marx was not only a critical journalist but also a vehement advocate of the freedom of the press. Marx' "practice of journalism was his relentless effort to fight back all attacks on free speech" (Shaw 2012, 620). Journalism theorist Hanno Hardt (2001) emphasises the freedom-loving character of Marx's journalism and theory. Marx

> sees freedom as a prerequisite for the success of socialism [...] [and] comes down on the side of press freedom in ways that produce a sharp contrast to later 'Marxist-Leninist' interpretations of the role and function of the press in socialist societies.
>
> (39)

Marx's opposition to press censorship was linked to his own journalistic practice, in which he was confronted with censorship. The *Rheinische Zeitung für Politik, Handel und Gewerbe* was a daily newspaper. The newspaper was created in 1842, opposed Prussian absolutism, and was pro-democracy. The main issue of political struggle at the time was over the alternatives of absolutism and democracy. Marx began working for the *Rheinische Zeitung* in 1842, rising to the position of editor in October 1842. In Prussia, there was strict press censorship based on a law from 1819, the Carlsbad Resolutions, which included a press law. Paragraph 6 stipulated that the Prussian state could dissolve publications such as newspapers for the purpose of "maintaining peace and tranquillity in Germany".[3] Clause 7 imposed a five-year ban on the editor of a newspaper or magazine banned by the state: "If a newspaper or magazine has been suppressed by a decision of the Federal Assembly, the editor of the same shall not be admitted to the editorship of a similar publication in any state within five years".[4] This also explains why Marx left Germany after the banning of the *Rheinische Zeitung* on 31 March 1843. In his early writings, Marx (1844) formulated the concept of the human being as a social being (cf. Fuchs 2020a, Chapters 3 & 4). Thus he argues that language and thought are "social

Marx and Journalism

activity" (Marx 1844, 298). For Marx, the human being also includes the abilities to write and read. He argues that censorship seeks to restrict human essence:

> The press is the most general way by which individuals can communicate their intellectual being. It knows no respect for persons, but only respect for intelligence. Do you want ability for intellectual communication to be determined officially by special external signs? What I cannot be for others, I am not and cannot be for myself. If I am not allowed to be a spiritual force for others, then I have no right to be a spiritual force for myself; and do you want to give certain individuals the privilege of being spiritual forces? Just as everyone learns to read and write, so everyone must *have the right* to read and write.
>
> (Marx 1842, 177)

Marx uses the logic of essence from Hegel's dialectic for the theoretical justification of the freedom of the press. For Hegel, something is authentic if it corresponds to its essence. For Marx, freedom of the press is a human right that follows from the essence of man as a social, speaking, and reading being. This implies for Marx that censorship is an expression of social conditions that are domineering and politically-ethically wrong. Censorship does not guarantee equality of people before the law and must therefore be abolished:

> The law against a frame of mind is *not a law of the state* promulgated for its *citizens,* but the *law of one party against another party.* The law which punishes tendency abolishes the equality of the citizens before the law. It is a law which divides, not one which unites, and all laws which divide are reactionary. [...] The real, *radical cure for the censorship* would be its *abolition;* for the institution itself is a bad one, and institutions are more powerful than people. Our view may be right or not, but in any case the Prussian writers stand to *gain through the new instruction,* either in *real freedom,* or in freedom of *ideas,* in *consciousness.*
>
> (Marx 1843, 120 & 131)

Marx argues against the view that the poor-quality press must be censored. Such a logic that Marx opposed allows the state arbitrariness. For Marx, the question of whether the press is good or bad is not one of content, but of the social form of the press. He argues that a press that glorifies the repressive state contradicts its own essence and argues for a critical press:

A free press that is bad does not correspond to its essence. The censored press with its hypocrisy, its lack of character, its eunuch's language, its dog-like tail-wagging, merely realises the inner conditions of its essential nature.

The censored press remains bad even when it turns out good products, for these products are good only insofar as they represent the free press within the censored press, and insofar as it is not in their character to be products of the censored press. The free press remains good even when it produces bad products, for the latter are deviations from the essential nature of the free press. A eunuch remains a bad human being even when he has a good voice. Nature remains good even when she produces monstrosities.

The essence of the free press is the characterful, rational, moral essence of freedom. The character of the censored press is the characterless monster of unfreedom; it is a civilised monster, a perfumed abortion.

(Marx 1842, 158)

Marx was not simply a political theorist or economist, but a political economist. He sees politics and economics as dialectically connected. Therefore, Marx does not conceive of press censorship as either a purely political or an economic phenomenon, but as both political and economic. For Marx, not only does state censorship and control threaten the freedom of the press, but he also considers the capitalist form of the press to be one that is vulnerable to censorship. Marx was very critical of the idea that the press should be commercially organised and profit-oriented: "*The primary freedom of the press lies in not being a trade*" (Marx 1842, 175). In this context, Marx criticises the tendency of press capital to concentrate and form monopolies. He considers the monopoly capital tendency as an economic censorship mechanism:

Press freedom in England up to now has been the exclusive privilege of capital. The few weekly journals which represent the interests of the working class – daily papers were, of course, out of the question – manage to survive thanks to the weekly contributions of the workers, who in England are making very different sacrifices for public purposes than those on the Continent. The tragicomic, blustering rhetoric with which the Leviathan of the English press – *The Times* – fights *pro aris et focis*, i.e., for the newspaper monopoly, now modestly comparing itself with the Delphic oracle, now affirming that England possesses only one single institution worth preserving, namely *The Times;*

now claiming absolute rule over world journalism, and, without any Treaty of Kuchuk-Kainardji, a protectorate over all European journalists.

(Marx 1855, 121–122)

Since the middle of the 19th century, the structural transformation of the public sphere has gradually led to the commercialisation of the media and thus also to the rise of advertising and media concentration. This was accompanied by the rise of media moguls. These included, for example, in Great Britain, Lord Beaverbrook, Lord Camrose, Lord Kemsley, Lord Northcliffe, and Lord Rothermere; in the United States, James Gordon Bennett junior, William Randolph Hearst, Frank A. Munsey and Joseph Pulitzer; and in Germany, Alfred Hugenberg, Rudolf Mosse, Leopold Ullstein, and August Scherl.

The 20th century saw the rise of a differentiated culture industry. The concentration tendencies in the media sector then also took place more vertically and through the formation of corporate conglomerates. The media moguls of the 20th and 21st centuries are the owners of multimedia conglomerates that are organised and operate internationally. Well-known examples of rich owners of 20th- and 21st-century media conglomerates include Andrej Babiš, David and Frederick Barclay, Silvio Berlusconi, Jeff Bezos, Michael Bloomberg, Robert Chapek, Richard Desmond, Hans Dichand, Jack Dorsey, Robert Maxwell, Rupert Murdoch, Brian L. Roberts, Axel Springer, Ted Turner, Mark Zuckerberg, etc.

Marx wrote against censorship and was involved in struggles for freedom of the press. State, economic and ideological control are forms of censorship for Marx. In this way, he anticipated Habermas' critique of the public sphere.

In the book *Structural Transformation of the Public Sphere*, Jürgen Habermas (1991), drawing on Marx, argues that money capital and state power colonise the public sphere, feudalise it and thus prevent or destroy democracy. If people lack education and resources, there are restrictions on freedom of opinion and speech (227–228). When economic (corporations, economic interest groups) or political organisations (parties, states, state institutions, lobby groups, etc.) "enjoy an oligopoly of the publicistically effective and politically relevant formation of assemblies and associations" (Habermas 1991, 228), When economic (corporations, economic interest groups) or political organisations (parties, states, state institutions, lobby groups, etc.) "enjoy an oligopoly of the publicistically effective and politically relevant formation of assemblies and associations" (Habermas 1991, 228), the result is the limitation of the freedom of assembly and the freedom of association. Habermas argues that advertising, commerce and capital turn the public sphere into the public sphere into "a sphere of culture consumption" that is only a "pseudo-public sphere" (Habermas 1991, 162) and a "manufactured public sphere" (Habermas 1991, 217). Habermas argues that the public sphere is autonomous from capital and state power. In the public sphere, the "[l]aws of the market [...] [are] suspended as were laws of the state" (Habermas 1991, 36). Habermas has redeveloped the concept of the "refeudalisation" of the public sphere (Habermas 1991, 142, 158, 195, 200, 231) that he formulated in *The Structural Transformation of the Public Sphere* into the concept of the colonisation of the lifeworld through "monetarisation and bureaucratisation" (Habermas 1987, 321, 323, 325, 386, 403), which he formulated in *The Theory of Communicative Action*. One aspect that Habermas underestimates, but which, along with capital and the state, plays an important role in Marx's works, is the colonisation of the public sphere through ideologisation (Fuchs 2020b, 2020c, Chapter 9).

Marx saw the Paris Commune of 1871 as a model of a democratic public sphere that sought to implement the democratic organisation of politics and the economy:

> The Commune was formed of the municipal councillors, chosen by universal suffrage in the various wards of the town, responsible and revocable at short terms. The majority of its members were naturally working men, of acknowledged representatives of the working class. The Commune was to be a working, not a parliamentary, body, executive and legislative at the same time. [...] Public functions ceased to be the private property of the tools of the Central Government. Not only municipal administration, but the whole initiative hitherto exercised by the State was laid into the hands of the Commune.
>
> (Marx 1871, 331)

Marx's (1842, 175) reference above to the connection between freedom and non-commerciality of the media is an indication of the importance of non-profit media enterprises for a Marxist theory of journalism, communication and the media in the form of public service broadcasting and citizen media. Table 7.1 illustrates the difference between four political economies of the media in Marxist theory (see also Williams 1976, 130–137; Jarren and Meier 2002, 103). In the Marxist theory of communication, journalism, and the media, a distinction is made between capitalist media, public service media, citizen media, and authoritarian state media (Fuchs 2020a, Chapter 8). In the age of the Internet, this distinction is highly topical. The four political economies of the Internet are (a) the hegemonic model of the capitalist Internet platform, where personalised

TABLE 7.1 Four political economies of the media (see Fuchs 2020a, Chapters 8 & 12 & 14)

	Capitalist media	Public service media	Citizen media	Authoritarian state media
Organisation	Capitalist company	Public organisation	Civil society organisation	State control and censorship of media organisations
Goal	Surplus-value, profit, capital accumulation	Public service remit, Public Value: information, education, entertainment; advancement of democratic understanding, arts, culture, science, diversity	Participation	Dissemination of state ideology and propaganda
Main actors	Professional journalists	Professional journalists	Citizen journalists, prosumers (consumers as producers)	State-controlled journalists
Main funding source	Advertising, subscriptions, sale of single copies	Licence and media fee	Donations, membership fees, public subsidies	State funding or state funding combined with another funding source
Property	Private property	Public property	Non-profit association/ organisation, co-operatives/- self-managed companies	State ownership or private ownership under state control or mixed ownership forms where the state plays a key role

advertising is the dominant capital accumulation model; (b) public service Internet platforms; (c) platform co-operatives; and (d) authoritarian, state-controlled Internet platforms (Fuchs 2021a, 2021b).

Public service media and citizen media are alternatives to the capitalist, profit-oriented organisation of the media as well as to authoritarian state media. Citizen media often have the problem that although they are independent, they are based on unpaid or low-paid labour, have few resources, and only a small audience (Sandoval and Fuchs 2010). Marx was aware of such possible limitations of the non-commercial alternative press, which explains why he wrote not only for the socialist press but also for mainstream media like the *New York Tribune* and bourgeois newspapers like *Die Presse*.

In addition to Marx's importance for critical journalism practice and a critical understanding of press freedom and the public sphere, his theory also offers a number of general concepts that are relevant to journalism theory. The next section explores this topic.

7.3 Marx's Concepts for Critical Journalism, Communication, and Media Theory

There are a number of concepts in Marx's theory that are important for the critical exploration and theorisation of communication, journalism, and media (Fuchs 2020b, 2020c). These include dialectics, materialism, the commodity form, capital, capitalism, labour, surplus value, the working class, alienation, the means of communication, the general intellect, ideology, socialism, communism, and class struggles. In the present chapter, for reasons of space, we shall confine ourselves to discussing the relevance of three of these concepts: the commodity form, labour, and Ideology.

7.3.1 The Commodity Form

The first volume of Karl Marx's main work *Das Kapital* begins with a sentence that has become famous: "The wealth of societies in which the capitalist mode of production prevails appears as an 'immense collection of commodities'; the individual commodity appears as its elementary form" (Marx 1867, 125). The capitalist economic form is generalised commodity production. The production and sale of commodities predates capitalism, but under capitalism commodity production is the generalised form of production through which monetary profit is made. On the one hand, labour power is s commodity, which has given rise to wage labour and the modern working class. On the other hand, the everyday life of people under capitalism is shaped by the commodity form. In capitalism, many activities are mediated through the commodity form. In the 20th century, advertising has become a ubiquitous phenomenon in everyday life. According to Marx, a commodity has a use-value and an exchange value. The use-value is the qualitative aspect through which people satisfy needs in the consumption of commodities. "The usefulness of a thing makes it a use-value" (Marx 1867, 126). Exchange value is the quantitative aspect of the commodity. A commodity is sold on a market. It exchanges itself for other commodities in a certain proportion. In capitalism, money is the general equivalent of exchange. Marx characterises exchange value as x commodity A = y commodity B (Marx 1867, 139). One commodity is exchanged for another commodity in a quantitative proportion. In the money form, commodity exchange takes on the form x commodity A = y commodity B = z money units. The implication of the commodity and money form is that without money one has no access to certain goods and services. Class relations and distributive injustice go hand in hand with commodity exchange. Marx understands the value of a commodity to be the average number of hours of labour required to produce the commodity.

Table 7.2 gives an overview of different commodity forms that we find in the media, culture, communication and digital industries. Horkheimer and Adorno (2002) called the transformation of the organisation of cultural use-values into exchange-values the culture industry. The culture industry is the process where the

> use value in the reception of cultural assets is being replaced by exchange value; enjoyment is giving way to being there and being in the know, connoisseurship by enhanced prestige. The consumer becomes the ideology of the amusement industry whose institutions he or she cannot escape.
>
> (Horkheimer and Adorno 2002, 128)

In the news media, two commodity forms are particularly important: advertising and the sale of access to content in the form of subscriptions and single copies. Both capital accumulation models (advertising, access to content) take digital forms (digital advertising, access to digital content) as well as physical forms (print advertising, printed newspaper copies).

Table 7.3 illustrates some data on the development of global newspaper revenues from 2013 to 2019.

Global newspaper revenue decreased from $126.2 billion in 2013 to $97.5 billion in 2021. In 2021, about 45 per cent of global news revenue was sold through advertising and about 55 per cent was sold through access to content. The share of revenue generated digitally has been steadily increasing. The revenue share of advertising in printed newspapers has fallen by 12 per cent in seven years. Newspapers are therefore trying to compensate for this through the models of digital advertising, print, and digital subscriptions. Overall, however, this does not succeed to a sufficient degree, which is why total revenues and thus total profits in the newspaper industry are falling.

Table 7.4 illustrates the structural change in the political economy of advertising: While 64.1 per cent of global advertising turnover was generated in print media in 1980, this figure was only 7.8 per cent in 2020. Digital advertising has become the dominant form of advertising, accounting for 53.1 per cent of global advertising revenue in 2020. The absolute majority of digital advertising is controlled by Facebook and Google,[5] which has

TABLE 7.2 A typology of cultural goods in the culture industry

Cultural commodity type	Exchange value	Use-value	Value	Examples
Cultural labour power	Wage labour: Cultural workers sell their labour power to cultural corporations in order to earn a living. In exchange for achieving a wage, they help creating cultural products that the companies sell as commodities	Creation and distribution of meanings and ideas	The average value of cultural labour power is the average number of hours of reproductive labour that it takes to create its means of subsistence	Artists, musicians, journalists, designers, software engineers, actors, dancers, presenters, technicians, printers, etc.
Access to cultural events	Audience members pay a one-time fee for access to a live event, where they are either present in the space where the event is performed or watch via cultural consumption technologies over a distance. Consumption is limited to a single occasion	Entertainment, education, information, distraction, enjoyment	The value of a cultural event is the average amount of labour-time that it takes to organise and perform the event	Theatre performances, exhibitions, talks, lectures, readings, discussions, concerts, live performances, movie screening in the cinema, pay-per-view access to live television events, etc.
Cultural content	Audience members pay for having access to a copy of cultural content that they can consume repeatedly	Entertainment, education, information, distraction, enjoyment	The value of a certain cultural content is the average amount of hours that its production, organisation, and distribution take. The value of a single copy is the total amount of utilised labour divided by the number of created copies	Books, newspapers, magazines, audio recordings (e.g. vinyl records), recorded audio-visual content (e.g. movies distributed on DVDs, Blu-ray discs, computer hard disks, or downloaded on the Internet) purchased artworks, posters, or prints

(*Continued*)

Marx's Concepts for Critical Journalism, Communication, and Media Theory

Cultural commodity type	Exchange value	Use-value	Value	Examples
Advertising space	Advertisers sell advertising space and audiences' attention to ad clients, who in return reach audiences with their product propaganda	Companies advertise their commodities	The more regular audience members there are, the higher the ad price can be set	Outdoor and transit ads, direct mail, newspaper and magazine ads, radio ads, television ads, digital, and online ads
Subscriptions for regular access to cultural content	Regular payment of money for securing the access to content for a particular subscription period	Entertainment, education, information, distraction, enjoyment	The value of a subscription service is the average amount of hours it takes to organise and maintain this service	Newspaper and magazine subscriptions, theatre subscription, museum subscription, cinema subscription, pay television
Technologies for the production, distribution, and consumption of information	Audiences purchase technologies that enable the production, distribution, or consumption of information	Humans are enabled to produce, distribute or consume information	The value of a communication technology is the average amount of hours that it takes to plan, produce, market, and sell the technology	Record player, stereo, television set, computer, mobile phone, laptop, camera, and audio recorder
Access to communication networks	The public pays a fee for access to information and communication networks	Access to information and communication networks	The value of the access to a network is the number of labour hours spent per year to maintain the network divided by the number of client contracts	Mobile phone contracts, contracts with Internet service providers
Mixed models of cultural commodities	Cultural corporations make use of capital accumulation strategies, where they combine the sale of several types of cultural commodities	Entertainment, education, information, distraction, enjoyment	Mixed models combine different cultural commodities and therefore involve multiple forms of value	Newspaper and magazine models that combine the sale of advertising, printed copies and subscriptions, one-time digital access, and digital subscriptions; cultural corporations that sell technologies and access to content

Source: Fuchs (2020b, 2020c, Chapter 4).

TABLE 7.3 The evolution of global newspaper sales, 2015–2021

	2015	2016	2017	2018	2019	2020	2021
Digital ad revenue (bn US$)	9,115	9,680	10,201	10,710	11,206	12,192	12,804
Revenue from digital content (bn US$)	2,745	3,351	3,967	4,499	4,963	6,105	6,697
Revenue from print advertising (bn US$)	55,535	51,530	47,924	44,760	41,959	33,777	31,595
Revenue from print content (bn US$)	58,841	58,107	57,138	56,101	54,987	47,949	46,448
Total revenues (bn US$)	126,236	122,668	119,230	116,070	113,115	100,023	97,544
Advertising (%)	51.2	49.9	48.8	47.8	47.0	46.0	45.5
Content (%)	48.8	50.1	51.2	52.2	53.0	54.0	54.5
Digital (%)	9.4	10.6	11.9	13.1	14.3	18.3	20.0
Print (%)	90.6	89.4	88.1	86.9	85.7	81.7	80.0
Revenue share of digital advertising (%)	7.2	7.9	8.6	9.2	9.9	12.2	13.1
Revenue share of digital content (%)	2.2	2.7	3.3	3.9	4.4	6.1	6.9
Revenue share of print advertising (%)	44.0	42.0	40.2	38.6	37.1	33.8	32.4
Revenue share from the sale of printed content (%)	46.6	47.4	47.9	48.3	48.6	47.9	47.6

Data source: World Press Trends Database (World Press Trends 2020–2021 Outlook).

TABLE 7.4 The development of the share of certain forms of advertising in global advertising sales, in percent (%)

	1980	1990	2000	2010	2020
Advertising in magazines and newspapers	64.1	57.2	47.7	29.7	7.8
Television advertising	24.2	28.4	34.1	41.3	28.4
Radio advertising	8.2	8.2	9.3	7.1	4.7
Cinema advertising	0.2	0.2	0.3	0.5	0.4
Outdoor advertising	2.9	5.8	5.5	6.3	5.6
Internet and mobile advertising	0.0	0.0	3.1	15.0	53.1

Data source: WARC.

Marx's Concepts for Critical Journalism, Communication, and Media Theory

put pressure on the news media's advertising revenues. For capitalist organised news media, profit-making has become more difficult with the rise of Google and Facebook. Robert McChesney (2013, 230–231, 195–215) argues that the best way to overcome the economic crisis of the news media is to eliminate the profit motive, to transform news media into non-profit and non-commercial enterprises.

7.3.2 Labour

Labour is a concept for Marx that represents the dialectical antithesis of capital. For Marx, capitalism is a class society based on the class contradiction between capital and labour. The value of commodities is produced by labour. Workers receive a wage, which is part of the value of commodities. But workers also produce surplus value, an unpaid part of the value from which capital's profit arises. For Marx, surplus-value production is the crucial aspect of capitalism. In order to survive, a capitalist enterprise must accumulate more and more capital, making more and more profit.

Marx distinguishes between concrete work and abstract labour. Concrete work produces the use-value of the commodity, abstract labour produces the commodity's value. Concrete work is "the creator of use-values" (Marx 1867, 133) that satisfy certain human needs. Abstract labour is a matter of "how much" (Marx 1867, 136), the temporal duration of labour. "Since the magnitude of the value of a commodity represents nothing but the quantity of labour embodied in it, it follows that all commodities, when taken in certain proportions, must be equal in value" (Marx 1867, 136). The surplus-value producing workers, who do not own the means of production, surplus-value, commodities and profit, are for Marx the decisive productive force of capitalism. In capitalism, the working class is "merely a machine for the production of surplus-value" and the capitalists class is "a machine for the transformation of this surplus-value into surplus capital" (Marx 1867, 742).

Capitalists have an economic interest in reducing labour costs and investment costs and increasing productivity in order to increase their profits. However, this is also associated with potential problems for workers such as unemployment through rationalisation and automation and precarisation. In the field of journalism, there is a tendency towards the expansion of precarious labour on the one hand, and on the other, discussions about whether artificial intelligence (AI)-based digitalisation and automation will lead to the de-skilling and increased unemployment of journalists (Diakopoulos 2019; Mosco and McKercher 2009).

A survey by the European Federation of Journalists (2015) found that 50 per cent of respondents were freelancers, self-employed, or bogus self-employed. Thirty-four per cent of respondents said they were dissatisfied or very dissatisfied with their work. Another survey (Koksal and Grégoire 2017) by the EFJ of its affiliates showed that 83.0 per cent of responding organisations said work overload was a problem for journalists, 76.6 per cent said stress was a problem and 59.6 per cent said lack of time was a problem. 80.9 per cent said journalists' salaries were unfair compared to their workload. One hundred per cent said that working conditions had worsened over the years.

A study by the National Council for the Training of Journalists (NCTJ) (2018), in which 885 British journalists took part, looked at working conditions, among other things. Seventy-five per cent of the participants in the study said they were satisfied with their work. The median annual income was relatively low at £27,500, the same level as in 2012, and with prices rising due to inflation, this means that British journalists have seen real wages fall in recent years. Fifty-six per cent felt that they were unfairly paid.

The overall picture is that journalists are characterised by what Boltanski and Chiapello (2005) call artistic labour: they identify themselves with their job, while at the same time many of them work relatively precariously, feel their salary is too low, and are confronted with a lot of stress and work overload.

Knowledge workers often work long hours and under time pressure. They are confronted with a combination of the two strategies of capital to increase surplus-value production, which Marx calls absolute and relative surplus value production (see Fuchs 2016, Chapters 7, 10, and 14). In absolute surplus-value production, the working day is extended in absolute terms, so that more commodities are produced by extending working time without wage compensation. In relative surplus-value production, productivity is increased so that more goods are produced in less time. Management methods such as control, supervision, work pressure play just as much a role as the mechanisation, and automation of production. Whether AI-based automation in journalism will increase productivity and lead to an increase in unemployment and de-skilling or whether journalism will prove to be more resistant to automation remains to be seen. The structural transformation of the media towards greater capitalisation, digitalisation, and monopolisation has led media capital to make greater use of the methods of absolute and relative surplus- value production to try to counteract the pressure on profits by intensifying and extensifying the exploitation of journalistic labour.

Marx's Concepts for Critical Journalism, Communication, and Media Theory

7.3.3 Ideology

In *The German Ideology*, Marx and Engels laid the foundations of the method of ideology critique (vgl. Fuchs 2020b, 2020c, Kapitel 9). Marx compares ideology there to a camera obscura, where "relations appear upside-down" (Marx and Engels 1845/46, 36). Ideology is a form of consciousness and practice whereby ideologues attempt to distort parts of reality and make certain people believe that these distortions are reality. The aim, according to Marx, is to legitimise domination and distract from the complex causes of social problems.

In *Capital*, Marx (1867, 163–177) analyses the connection between capitalism and ideology with the concept of the fetish character, through which things like the commodity, capital, and money appear as natural properties of society, although they are specific to capitalism. Georg Lukács (1923/1971) took up Marx's concept of the fetish to characterise ideology as reifying and reified consciousness, which Max Horkheimer (1947), based on Lukács, also refers to as instrumental reason.

In recent years, authoritarian capitalism has emerged in many parts of the world (Fuchs 2018, 2020d), in which predominantly very far-right and far-right politicians, groups and parties spread nationalism, racism, authoritarianism, and fake news. They propagate distrust of expert opinion and make people believe that what they agree with ideologically and that which appeals positively to their feelings and emotions is true. Post-truth politics declares lies to be true and facts to be false (Fuchs 2021a, 2021b, Chapter 6). Fake news is not new, but exists wherever there is ideology and tabloid media. Fake news is factually false. Fake news is predominantly spread on social media. Fake news production ignores journalistic professional norms. Fake news is ideological: its producers want to misinform and mislead people.

Donald Trump is a kind of fake news factory. He has produced false news and right-wing ideology that he spreads via social media such as Twitter (see Fuchs 2018, Fuchs 2021a, 2021b, Chapter 9). At the same time, he calls media, journalists who report factually on Trump and question his claims "fake news".

In the example shown in Figure 7.1, Trump suggests that illegal immigrants are to blame for unemployment, low wages, and the American welfare system's crisis. This ignores the fact that the commodity form dominates large parts of society and that the high level of exploitation of the working class has led to severe inequalities. Trump pretends to defend the interests of the American worker, even though as a multi-billionaire he is one of the richest Americans, and promises in a nationalist way to make America great again.

Donald J. Trump ✓
@realDonaldTrump

It is time for DC to protect the American worker, not grant amnesty to illegals. Let's Make America Great Again!

Together, we are rebuilding our nation

Donald J. Trump for President
Help continue our promise to Make America Great Again!
🔗 donaldjtrump.com

8:30 PM · Apr 23, 2015 · Twitter Web Client

231 Retweets   **277** Likes

FIGURE 7.1   An example of ideology on Twitter
Source: https://twitter.com/realDonaldTrump/status/591308288739962881.

With Marx, one can say that Trump spreads ideology that distracts from the class conflict between capital and labour and fetishises the US nation. Immigrants are presented as enemies of the US nation and the US working class. Neoliberalism and the unequal distribution of wealth between capital and labour are silenced. Marx (1870, 474) made it clear that nationalism in 19th century Britain was a strategy of capital to make the English worker "feel himself to be a member of the ruling nation" in relation to migrant workers. For Marx, nationalist ideology is the "secret of the maintenance of power by the capitalist class" and "is kept artificially alive and intensified by the press" (Marx 1870, 475). Marx's analysis of ideology is still relevant in the 21st century in the age of digital and authoritarian capitalism, with the role of the press often taken by social media.

7.4 Conclusion and Outlook

The Political Economy of Communication and the Media is an internationally established research approach within media and communication studies, as evidenced by institutions such as the Political Economy Section in the International Association of Media and Communication Research and journals such as *tripleC: Communication, Capitalism &*

Critique or *The Political Economy of Communication*. The critique of the political economy of communication and the media, based on Marx's work, is an essential component
of the approach of the Political Economy of Communication and the Media (Fuchs 2017,
Wasko 2014).

This chapter has shown that engagement with the works of Karl Marx provides concepts
that are relevant to the critical analysis of journalism, communication, media, and culture
in the 21st century and in the age of digital capitalism.

Notes

1 Translation from German: "Vorbilder des Journalismus".
2 Translated from German: "Gerade als Journalist legte er eine Untersuchungsweise an den
   Tag, die Wechselwirkungen analysierte und die unterschiedlichsten Faktoren zu berücksichti-
   gen versuchte".
3 Translation from German: "Erhaltung des Friedens und der Ruhe in Deutschland"[3] http://www.
   heinrich-heine-denkmal.de/dokumente/karlsbad2.shtml, accessed on 14 April 2021.
4 Ibid.
5 https://www.emarketer.com/content/facebook-google-duopoly-won-t-crack-this-year,
   https://www.emarketer.com/content/global-digital-ad-spending-2019.

References

Boltanski, Luc and Ève Chiapello. 2005. *The New Spirit of Capitalism*. London: Verso.
Diakopoulos, Nicholas. 2019. *Automating the News. How Algorithms Are Rewriting the Media*.
   Cambridge, MA: Harvard University Press.
European Federation of Journalists. 2015. *EFJ Survey Reveals Precarious Working Conditions of
   Journalists Working for Digital Media in Europe*. https://europeanjournalists.org/blog/2015/
   11/03/efj-survey-reveals-precarious-working-conditions-of-online-journalists-in-europe/
Fuchs, Christian. 2021a. *Social Media: A Critical Introduction*. London: Sage. Dritte Auflage.
Fuchs, Christian. 2021b. *Soziale Medien und kritische Theorie*. München: UVK/utb. Second edition.
Fuchs, Christian. 2020a. *Communication and Capitalism. A Critical Theory*. London: University of
   Westminster Press. DOI: https://doi.org/10.16997/book45
Fuchs, Christian. 2020b. *Marx heute. Eine Einführung in die kritische Theorie der Kommunikation,
   Kultur, digitalen Medien und des Internets*. München: UVK/utb.
Fuchs, Christian. 2020c. *Marxism: Karl Marx's Fifteen Key Concepts for Cultural & Communication
   Studies*. New York: Routledge.

Fuchs, Christian. 2020d. *Nationalism on the Internet: Critical Theory and Ideology in the Age of Social Media and Fake News*. New York: Routledge.

Fuchs, Christian. 2018. *Digitale Demagogue. Authoritarian Capitalism in the Age of Trump and Twitter.* London: Pluto Press.

Fuchs, Christian. 2017. Die Kritik der Politischen Ökonomie der Medien/Kommunikation: ein hochaktueller Ansatz. *Publizistik* 62 (3): 255–272.

Fuchs, Christian. 2016. *Reading Marx in the Information Age: A Media and Communication Studies Perspective on Capital Volume I.* New York: Routledge.

Habermas, Jürgen. 1991. *The Structural Transformation of the Public Sphere. An Inquiry into a Category of Bourgeois Society.* Cambridge, MA: MIT Press.

Habermas, Jürgen. 1987. *The Theory of Communicative Action. Volume 2.* Boston, MA: Beacon Press.

Hardt, Hanno. 2001. *Social Theories of the Press. Constituents of Communication Research, 1840s to 1920s.* Lanham, MD: Rowman & Littlefield. Second edition.

Herres, Jürgen. 2005. Karl Marx als politischer Journalist des 19. Jahrhundert. *Beiträge zur Marx-Engels-Forschung Neue Folge* 2005: 7–28.

Horkheimer, Max. 1947. *Eclipse of Reason*. New York: Continuum.

Horkheimer, Max and Theodor W. Adorno. 2002. *Dialectic of Enlightenment. Philosophical Fragments.* Stanford, CA: Stanford University Press.

Hunt, Tristam. 2009. *Marx's General. The Revolutionary Life of Friedrich Engels.* New York: Metropolitan Books.

Jakobs, Hans-Jürgen and Wolfgang R. Langenbucher, Hrsg. 2004. *Das Gewissen ihrer Zeit: Fünfzig Vorbilder des Journalismus.* Wien: Picus.

Jarren, Otfried and Werner A. Meier. 2002. Mediensysteme und Medienorganisationen als Rahmenbedingungen für den Journalismus. In *Journalismus – Medien – Öffentlichkeit*, edited by Otfried Jarren and Hartmut Weßler, 9–173. Wiesbaden: Westdeutscher Verlag.

Koksal, Mehmet and Denis Grégoire. 2017. Journalism, an Increasingly Precarious Profession. *HesaMag: The European Trade Union Institute's Health and Safety at Work Magazine* 15: 10–16.

Lenin, Vladimir I. 1917. Meeting of the All-Russia Central Executive Committee, November 4 (17), 1917. In *Lenin Collected Works*, Volume 26, 285–293. Moscow: Progress.

Lukács, Georg. 1923/1971. *History and Class Consciousness.* London: Merlin.

Luxemburg, Rosa. 1922. The Russian Revolution. In *The Russian Revolution and Leninism or Marxism?* 25–80. Ann Arbor: University of Michigan Press.

Marx, Karl. 1871. The Civil War in France. In *Marx & Engels Collected Works (MECW)*, Volume 22, 307–359. London: Lawrence & Wishart.

Marx, Karl. 1870. Letter of Marx to Sigfrid Meyer and August Vogt, 9 April 1870. In *Marx & Engels Collected Works (MECW)*, Volume 43, 471–476. London: Lawrence & Wishart.

Marx, Karl. 1867. *Capital*, Volume I. London: Penguin.

Marx, Karl. 1855. Napoleon and Barbès – The Newspaper Stamp. In *Marx & Engels Collected Works (MECW)*, Volume 14, 121–123. London: Lawrence & Wishart.

Marx, Karl. 1844. Economic and Philosophic Manuscripts of 1844. In *Marx & Engels Collected Works (MECW)*, Volume 3, 229–346. London: Lawrence & Wishart.

Marx, Karl. 1843. Comments on the Latest Prussian Censorship Instruction. In *Marx & Engels Collected Works (MECW)*, Volume 1, 109–131. London: Lawrence & Wishart.

Marx, Karl. 1842. Proceedings of the Sixth Rhine Province Assembly. First Article. Debates on Freedom of the Press and Publication of the Proceedings of the Assembly of the Estates. In *Marx & Engels Collected Works (MECW)*, Volume 1, 133–181. London: Lawrence & Wishart.

Marx, Karl and Friedrich Engels. 1845/46. The German Ideology. Critique of Modern German Philosophy According to its Representatives Feuerbach, B. Bauer and Stirner, and of German Socialism According to its Various Prophets. In *Marx & Engels Collected Works (MECW)*, Volume 5, 15–539. London: Lawrence & Wishart.

McChesney, Robert. 2013. *Digital Disconnect.* New York: New Press.

McLellan, David. 1973. *Karl Marx. His Life and Thought.* London: Macmillan.

Mosco, Vincent. 2012. Marx Is Back, but Which One? On Knowledge Labour and Media Practice. *tripleC: Communication, Capitalism & Critique* 10 (2): 570–576.

Mosco, Vincent and Catherine McKercher. 2009. *The Laboring of Communication.* Lanham, MD: Lexington.

National Council for the Training of Journalists (NCTJ). 2018. *Journalists at Work. Their Views on Training, Recruitment and Conditions.* Newport: NCTJ.

Sandoval, Marisol and Christian Fuchs. 2010. Towards a Critical Theory of Alternative Media. *Telematics and Informatics* 27 (2): 141–150.

Shaw, Padmaja. 2012. Marx as Journalist: Revisiting the Free Speech Debate. *tripleC: Communication, Capitalism & Critique* 10 (2): 618–632. DOI: https://doi.org/10.31269/triplec.v10i2.389

Stalin, Josef W. 1927. Interview with Foreign Workers' Delegations, November 5, 1927. In *Stalin Works*, Volume 10, 212–243. Berlin: Dietz.

Wasko, Janet. 2014. The Study of the Political Economy of the Media in the Twenty-First Century. *International Journal of Media & Cultural Politics* 10 (3): 259–271.

Williams, Raymond. 1976. *Communications.* Harmondsworth: Penguin.

Chapter Eight

Towards a Critical Theory of Communication as Renewal and Update of Marxist Humanism in the Age of Digital Capitalism

8.1 Introduction

This chapter's task is to outline some foundations of a critical, Marxist-Humanist theory of communication in the age of digital capitalism. Foundations of the approach of a radical Digital Humanism have been outlined in the book *Digital Humanism. A Philosophy for 21st Century Digital Society* (Fuchs 2022). This chapter is a kind of prolegomena to my *Digital Humanism* book. Is was written as a preparatory work.

Since the 1980s, Marxist theory has become unfashionable. In social philosophy and theory, postmodernism and poststructuralism challenged grand narratives, universalism and decentred the focus on the economy. Postmodernism became, as David Harvey (1990) points out, a legitimating ideology of capitalism's flexible regime of accumulation. Identity politics and cultural reductionism replaced class politics and political economy. In his last interview before his death, Stuart Hall, who championed poststructuralism and identity politics in Cultural Studies, remarked on contemporary theory that "in its attempt to move away from economic reductionism, it sort of forgot that there was an economy at all" (Jhally 2016, 337) and that it is a "real weakness" that there is a lack of engagement with the "Marxist tradition of critical thinking" (Jhally 2016, 338). The move away from Marx and the critical analysis of class and capitalism took place at the time of the expansion of neoliberalism, which had the paradoxical effect that Marxian analysis became

DOI: 10.4324/9781003331087-10

political ever more relevant as social inequalities increased and new forms of austerity and precarious labour emerged while the academic and intellectual mainstream denied its relevance. In their hatred of Marx and Marxism, postmodernism and neoliberalism have formed a strange ideological consensus.

In 2008, a new world economic crisis started as a result of the developing antagonisms of neoliberal capitalism (Foster and Magdoff 2009, Harvey 2010, Roberts 2016, Wallerstein et al. 2013). Ever since there has been a rising interest in Marx's works (Fuchs and Monticelli 2018). Today, it has become harder to deny that Marx can and should inform the analysis of 21st-century society. In the light of this development, this chapter's aim is to contribute to the renewal of Marxist theory. Given the importance of information and communication technologies and communication work in contemporary society, social theory needs to ask: What is communication? What is the role of communication in society? What is the role of communication in capitalism? What is the role of communication in digital capitalism? This chapter contributes to answering these questions by renewing the engagement with a particular tradition of Marxist theory, Marxist Humanism.

Section 8.1 outlines the importance of Marxist Humanism today. Section 8.3 analyses the role of communication in society. Section 8.4 deals with the connection of communication, alienation, and capitalism. It gives special attention to communication in digital capitalism. Digital capitalism is a dimension of contemporary society where the accumulation of capital, influence, and cultural hegemony is mediated by digital technologies such as the computer, the Internet, the mobile phone, tablets, robots, AI-driven ("smart") technologies, etc. Section 8.5 analyses the connection of struggles and communication with a special focus on examples from social struggles in digital capitalism. Section 8.6 draws some conclusions in the context of digital capitalism and struggles for digital Socialist Humanism.

8.2 Marxist Humanism Today

Marxist Humanism emerged in 20th-century social theory. Its theoretical foundations are Hegel's dialectical philosophical and Marx's *Economic and Philosophic Manuscripts of 1844*. Its axiological and political concern has been the establishment of democratic socialism as an alternative to capitalism, fascism, Stalinism, and other forms of authoritarian statism. It focuses its analyses on the human being, human essence, human practices, alienation, political praxis, class struggles, ideology critique, and the dialectics of subject/object, practices/structures, labour/capital, the economic/the non-economic, continuity/discontinuity, etc.

Representatives of Marxist Humanism have, among others, included Theodor W. Adorno, Günther Anders, Kevin Anderson, Simone de Beauvoir, Ernst Bloch, Angela Davis, Raya Dunayevskaya, Zillah Eisenstein, Barbara Epstein, Frantz Fanon, Erich Fromm, Lucien Goldmann, André Gorz, David Harvey, Max Horkheimer, C.L.R. James, Karl Korsch, Karel Kosík, Henri Lefebvre, Georg Lukács, Herbert Marcuse, Maurice Merleau-Ponty, Kwame Nkrumah, Julius Nyerere, Bertell Ollmann, the Praxis Group in Yugoslavia, Sheila Rowbotham, M.N. Roy, Edward Said, Jean-Paul Sartre, Adam Schaff, Kate Soper, E.Thompson, and Raymond Williams (see Alderson and Spencer 2017, Fromm 1965). Marxist Humanism's decline had to do with the general decline of Marxist theory under neoliberal conditions, the postmodern turn against Marxism, structuralism's attack on the human being that fostered the rise of post-Humanism, and the influence of Althusser and Foucault in social theory (Alderson and Spencer 2017).

There are *five reasons* why we need a renewal of Marxist Humanism today. The *first reason* is the emergence of authoritarian capitalism. In critical theory, the concept of authoritarianism goes back to Erich Fromm (1941/1969), who defines it as a social character who submits to those in power and enjoys dominating others. For Fromm, fascism is the most developed form of authoritarian society and authoritarian capitalism. Max Horkheimer (1939/1989, 78) sees authoritarian and therefore also fascist potentials immanent in capitalism itself. But not every form of capitalism fully develops its authoritarian potentials. Adorno et al.'s (1950) F-scale outlines a large number of characteristics of the authoritarian personality. The core of this approach are four features: authoritarianism combines the antidemocratic belief of the necessity of strong, top-down leaders, nationalism, the friend/enemy-scheme and ideological scapegoating, and the belief in law-and-order politics, violence, militancy, and war as the best political means (Fuchs 2018a). Authoritarian capitalism is a society that combines capitalism with these principles. New forms of nationalism and authoritarianism have emerged in recent years. They pose dangers to democracy and can result in a new world war, genocide, fascism, etc. Marxist Humanism stresses socialism and Humanism as opposition to fascism.

The *second reason* are the limits of postmodernism in contemporary capitalism. Althusser and Foucault have had a major influence on the emergence and development of postmodernism and poststructuralism that have attacked Marxist theory, class politics, the notions of the human being, truth, alienation, commonalities, universalism, etc. While there are postmodern theorists who made productive use of Marx, certain versions of postmodernism have contributed to the decline of Marxist theory in an age

Marxist Humanism Today

when class contradictions have been exploding. Marxist Humanism foregrounds praxis as class struggle and Marxist theory. It is a critique of postmodernism. Postmodernism has advanced a relativism and anti-universalism where there is no truth. In an age of fake news, post-truth, new nationalism/fascism, we need a political concept of truth. Marxist Humanism enables us to think critically about what is true and false. Postmodernism has fostered identity politics without class politics and as a consequence liberal reformism. Humanist Marxism advances democratic socialist politics. Postmodernism has advanced the hatred of Marx. In a time of major capitalist crisis, Marx is urgently needed. Post-colonial theory and thought has advanced forms of reverse orientalism (Chibber 2013, Warren 2017) where everything non-European and non-Western has been automatically considered as being progressive, which partly legitimates authoritarianism. Marxist Humanism stresses universalism and human beings' commonality.

The *third reason* is the need for dialectical analysis. Post-Humanism, the concept of the Anthropocene, Actor Network Theory, New Materialism, etc. are attacks on the human being that collapse the dialectic of unity and differences into structures that eliminate or reduce the importance of humans. Post-Humanism collapses the dialectic of human/non-humans and human/technology (robots) into the post-human cyborg. Bruno Latour's Actor Network Theory declares that things and instruments such as machines are just like humans social actors and together with the latter form actor networks. As a consequence, Latour collapses the differentiation between the human as the social being and the non-human into the actant as the social (see also Fuchs 2020a, 20–21). Deep Ecology and animal liberation theory collapse the dialectic of nature/society into an undifferentiated whole. Postmodernism collapses the dialectic of class/non-class into identity and the dialectic of culture/economy into the culture. The concept of the Anthropocene blames the human being and not capitalism for the environmental crisis. The result of these developments has been the proliferation of undialectical, reductionist thought. While postmodernism and its various currents have continuously claimed that Marxism is reductionist and economistic, they have themselves advanced new forms of reductionism. In contrast, Marxist Humanism is dialectical. It foregrounds the importance of humans in society and the dialectical relations that the human being is part of.

The problems of structuralism constitute *the fourth reason*. (Post-)Structuralism reduces humans to bearers of structures that resemble puppets on a string. It underestimates the importance of human practices, human thought, communication, production, and social struggles in society. In contrast, Marxist Humanism stresses practices, praxis and the dialectic of practices/structures in society. For example, Althusser sees humans not as active agents but bas earers and "the 'supports' (Träger) of [...] functions" (Althusser & Balibar 2009, 199) defined by society's articulated structures and the mode of production. In Lacanian theory, humans "interact like puppets" and are "tools in the hands of the big Other" (Žižek 2007, 8). Lucien Goldmann in a debate with Foucault and Lacan argued that a famous slogan in the May 1968 Paris protests read that "structures do not take to the streets", which means that "it is never structures that make history, but men, although the action of these always has a structured and significant character" (in: Foucault 1969, 816). Lacan commented that "if there is anything that the May events demonstrate, it is precisely the descent of structures into the street" (in: Foucault 1969, 820). Structuralist accounts of society fetishise structures that are interpreted as autonomous actors acting on and independently from humans. They disregard Marx's dialectical insight that humans "make their own history, but they do not make it as they please; they do not make it under circumstances chosen by themselves, but under circumstances directly encountered, given and transmitted from the past" (Marx 1852, 103).

The fetishism of difference is *the fifth reason*. Postmodernism's focus on difference has parallels to the ideology of the new right that demands the separation of cultures. The new forms of nationalism that have proliferated in the past ten years fetishise difference by ascertaining pride in the nation and the hatred of immigrants, refugees, people of colour, etc. Marxist Humanism stresses the universality of humanity, humans' common features, and the indivisibility of humanity.

Marxist Humanism is a counter-narrative, counter-theory, and counter-politics to these developments. A critical, dialectical theory of communication can draw on and start from this intellectual tradition. The methodological approach that the present author takes in this context is to make visible, engage with, draw on, start from, use, interpret, and further develop elements from often unknown, hidden, ignored, neglected, and forgotten Marxist-Humanist works (see Fuchs 2016a, 2016b, 2016c, 2017a, 2017b, 2017d, 2018b, 2019a, 2019b, 2019c, 2020a, 2020c).

The very basic questions from which the resulting approach starts is: What is communication? What is the role of communication in society? Section 8.3 deals with these questions.

8.3 Communication in Society

This section first analyses the relationship between work and communication (Subsection 8.3.1) and then broadens out the discussion to the analysis of communication's role in society in general (Subsection 8.3.2).

8.3.1 Work and Communication

When thinking about a critical theory of communication, most scholars will immediately think of Habermas' theory of communicative action, which is the most prominent and most widely read and cited critical approach to the analysis of communication in society.

The epistemological and methodological approach the present author takes is very different from the one that Habermas chose in the creation of his theory of communicative action. The German philosopher engaged primarily with non-Marxist mainstream theorists of language and communication, especially George Herbert Mead, Jean Piaget, and John Searle. Habermas implicitly has sustained the old, but incorrect prejudice that Marxism has nothing important to say on communication and culture. The approach that the present author has developed in contrast tries to invalidate this claim by showing that there is a rich, but ignored the tradition of thinking critically about language and communication in Marxist theory.

Starting from Hegel's Jena philosophy, Habermas in the 1968 essay "Work and Interaction" developed thoughts about work and interaction that in the 1980s formed one of the theoretical foundations of his opus magnum *Theory of Communicative Action* (Habermas 1985a, 1985b). In the Jena lectures, Hegel (1803/1804, 1805/1806) argues that work and interaction are two manifestations of the spirit. In his interpretation of Hegel's Jena philosophy of the spirit, Habermas (1968) argues that work and interaction are two aspects of society that are based on two different rationalities, namely strategic action (work) and understanding (interaction). In *Theory of Communicative Action*, Habermas formalises and further develops this distinction as the antagonism between system/lifeworld, steering media (money, power)/language, work/interaction, system integration/social integration, and instrumental action/communicative action. In a key formulation, Habermas (1985b, 281) characterises his own theory as "media dualism" that is based on "two contrary types of communication media". The German philosopher builds his theory on the assumption that work and communication form two independent substances of society that are radically different. "On the human level, the reproduction of life is determined culturally by work and interaction" (Habermas 1971, 196). In his latest book *Auch eine Geschichte der Philosophie* (*This Too a History of Philosophy*) published in 2019 in German, Habermas reproduces the dualistic assumption that society consists of two substances. He writes that "society's structures not only contribute to *social integration* by values, normatively binding expectations and communicative understanding, but also contribute to society's *system integration* by functional mechanisms such as relations of power and exchange" (Habermas 2019, 137, translation from German).

Habermas is influenced by Kant's dualism of subject and object and Weber's (2019) dualism of purposive action on the one hand and value-rational, affectual, and traditional action on the other hand. Habermas reproduces Weber's dualism of economy and society as the dualism of system and lifeworld. His theory of communication is a Kantian and Weberian Humanism that lacks the Hegelian and Marxian dialectical logic that conceives of two moments as being simultaneously identical and different. Marxist Humanism therefore promises to be a good foundation for a dialectical critical theory of communication.

Work and communication are not two separate human processes. They are identical and different. In his early philosophical works such as *Economic and Philosophical Manuscripts* (Marx 1844c) and *German Ideology* (Marx & Engels 1845/46), Marx asked himself what the human being is and how capitalism cripples the human being. He built his critical theory of capitalism on these foundations. A basic insight of these works is that the human being is a societal being. "The individual *is the social being*" (Marx 1844c, 299). Humans shape and are shaped by the social relations they enter in everyday life:

> Not only is the material of my activity given to me as a social product (as is even the language in which the thinker is active): my *own* existence *is* social activity, and therefore that which I make of myself, I make of myself for society and with the consciousness of myself as a social being.
>
> (Marx 1844c, 298)

Marx adds the insight that the social relations humans enter are relations of production. The "production of material life itself [...] in order to sustain human life" is "a fundamental condition of all history" (Marx and Engels 1845/46, 42).

The human being is a producing, social, societal being. By producing their conditions of life, humans socially produce and reproduce society. Social production, production in social relations, and the production of the social and society are the key features of the human being. Materiality of society means that humans produce sociality and socially produce. Production for the satisfaction of human needs is the key feature of society. This means that work is the key process constituting society. It is an economic process but extends from the economy into political and cultural life. Humans also produce political relations, where they take collective decisions, and cultural relations, where they make meaning of the world. Therefore, production not just creates "eating and drinking, housing, clothing" but also "various other things" (Marx and Engels 1845/46, 42), including social, societal, economic, political, and cultural relations. Marx's key sociological insight is that everything that exists in society is a social relation and is produced as social relation. Communication, i.e. "the production of ideas" and "the mental intercourse" of humans, is not immaterial but part of "material activity" (Marx and Engels 1845/46, 36). Communication is "the language of real life" (36). Humans are "producers of their conceptions, ideas, etc." (36).

Marx and Engels argue that communication is a production process. There is a dialectic of work and communication: humans *communicate productively* and *produce communicatively*. Communication aims at the production of a specific social use-value, namely that humans understand the world and understand each other. Therefore, *communication is productive*. The production of use-values that satisfy human needs cannot be achieved individually, but only in social relations. Communication is the process that organises social relations. Therefore, *humans produce communicatively*.

Already classical bourgeois economics assumed that the human being is by nature an entrepreneur of the self and a homo oeconomicus, a rational economic being that is egoistic, self-interested, competitive, and profit-maximising. Adam Smith argued that "the propensity to truck, barter, and exchange one thing for another" is "a certain propensity in human nature" and "the necessary consequence of the faculties of reason and speech" (Smith 1776, 18). Authors such as Brown (2015, Chapter 3) argue that with the rise of neoliberalism, the concept of the homo oeconomics has further proliferated. (Neo-)liberalism essentialises and fetishises the capitalist. The critique of neoliberalism is prone to deny that human beings are economic beings by claiming that they are primarily political or cultural animals. Such assumptions just replace one reductionism by another one. For Marx, humans are simultaneously economic and non-economic beings. As social production, the economic operates inside of the political and the cultural. But the political and the cultural have their own emergent dynamics and go beyond production. Power and meanings are produced and reproduced and at the same time constitute structures, organisations, and institutions that have particular logics.

In his *Politics*, Aristotle (2013, §1253a) characterises the human being as zōon logon echon (ζῷον λόγος ἔχων). Hannah Arendt (1958, 27) and Charles Taylor (2016, 338) point out that the translation of this term as "rational animal" is imprecise. Logos is Greek for both rationality and speech. The Greek language here points us towards the fact that rationality and language are intertwined and not two separate human substances. In contrast, the Cartesian dualism of mind and body separates two aspects of the human being that belong together. According to Alfred Sohn-Rethel (1978), this separation goes back to the invention of the division of labour in class societies that invented the division between mental and manual labour. It is a basic human propensity that there is a dialectic of the human as rational, producing animal and the human as languaging, communicating animal. Language and communication are rational and human and society's rationality is organised through communication. Marx (1867b, 346, translation from German) summarises this dialectic by writing that the human being is "by nature [...] a societal animal" ("gesellschaftliches Tier"), which includes that communication is production and communication organises production.

Aristotle (2009, §1139b) points out that human action is teleological: "everyone who makes makes for an end". Aristotle's teleology influenced Marx's assumption that human work is purposeful activity. Humans produce with means of production in order to achieve the goal of satisfying needs. For Marx (1867a, 284), the human being "also realizes [*verwirklicht*] his own purpose" in work. In his widely ignored book *Ontologie des gesellschaftlichen Seins* (*Ontology of Societal Being*), Georg Lukács (1986a, 1986b) argues that work as teleological positing is the model of human activity.

Teleological positing implies that humans are working beings. They set themselves goals that they want to achieve by utilising certain means. The teleological positing of work means the "intervention into concrete causal relations in order to bring about the realization of the goal" (Lukács 1978, 67), "the positing of a goal and its means" (22), that the human being as worker and producer is a "conscious creator" (5). Communication means that humans are "answering beings" (Lukács 1986b, 339, translation from German). Language makes possible the "distancing of the object from the subject" (Lukács 1978, 100). By communicating, humans can repeat production processes in a variety of spaces at a variety of times. Production becomes routinised and regularised so that society can reproduce itself. Society's reproduction is the repetition of social production.

Language is a "complex inside of the complex" of society (Lukács 1986b, 181, translation from German). It "mediates [...] both the metabolism of society with nature and the interactions between humans that takes place purely inside of society" (181, translation from German). As a particular form of teleological positing, communication has a work character and is a peculiar form of work that enables the mediation of humans' social relations.

8.3.2 Society as Sphere of Communicatively Organised Production

Communication is the process of the production of humans' sociality, social relations, groups, organisations, social systems, structures, and institutions. It is therefore also the

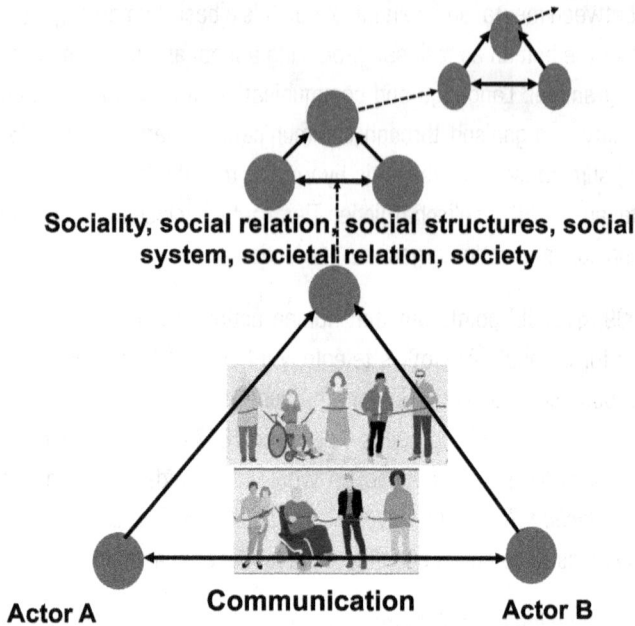

FIGURE 8.1 Communication as the mediation and production of human sociality and social relations in society

process that organises and mediates the production and reproduction of society in a dynamic manner. Figure 8.1 visualises the role of communication in society. Communication is the production process of human sociality and humans' social relations.

Society is the totality – a complex of complexes, as Lukács (1986a, 1986b) says –, in which humans produce and reproduce social relations that condition, enable, and constrain their practices. It is a dialectical process where human social practices and social relations condition each other mutually. Society consists of the three realms of the economy, politics, and culture. These realms are neither separate nor fully reduceable to one system nor equally foundational for society. They are all economic because all social systems are systems of production (Table 8.1). At the same time, all types of social systems have their particular, emergent qualities and features whereby their sum is more than the total of the production of their parts.

Raymond Williams (1977) outlines that the relationship of the economic and the non-economic (the "base" and the "superstructure") has in Marxist theory been characterised as one of determination, reflection, mediation, typification (representation, illustration), homology, and correspondence. Williams criticises that all of these approaches leave the economic and the non-economic separate and are therefore not "materialist enough" (92, 97). Williams argues that culture is material. The same is true of politics. This means that the

TABLE 8.1 Society's three realms of production

Realm of society	Teleological positing
Economy	Production of use-values
Politics	Production of collective decisions
Culture	Production of meanings

economy in the form of teleological positing operates inside culture and politics. Ideas, policies, laws, meanings, ideologies, etc. are just like cars and computers produced by humans in social relations. Williams (1980, 50) writes that "communication and its material means are intrinsic to all distinctively human forms of labour and social organization". Communication is intrinsic to and operates inside of social systems and organises the production of sociality. Because of the work character of communication, also work is intrinsic to communication. All social realms and systems are at the same time economic and non-economic.

Orthodox approaches have reduced society to an economic base. For example, Louis Althusser (1969, 135–136) argues that the advantage of

> the spatial metaphor of the edifice (base and superstructure) is simultaneously that it reveals that questions of determination (or of index of effectivity) are crucial; that it reveals that it is the base which in the last instance determines the whole edifice.

E. Thompson criticises Althusser's approach as "mechanical materialism" (Thompson 1978, 247) that disregards that society's instances and levels "are in fact human activities, institutions, and ideas" that humans experience (97).

The river is a much better metaphor for society than a house or a clockwork. Society is a dynamic and productive flow of human activities. Georg Lukács metaphorically describes society as "the river of everyday life" (Lukács 1963, 13, translation from German; see the visualisation in Figure 8.2). The river as society's dialectic foregrounds the role of networks, processes, and streams of social production. Rivers have various branches that dynamically flow in and out of the main current. The metaphor of the river envisions society as dialectical, creative, and contradictory flow of human production. The political and the cultural are productive currents that flow out of and back into the economy. Communication is the societal rivers' water that mediates and enables life inside and reproduction of the stream.

In a capitalist society, rivers are often not as blue and clean as the title of Johann Strauss's waltz "On the Beautiful Blue Danube" implies. Capitalist reality more looks like the polluted

Communication in Society

FIGURE 8.2   Society as dialectical river

FIGURE 8.3   The polluted river as metaphor for alienation in class and capitalist societies
Source: Wikimedia Commons, Jan Jörg [Public domain].

river shown in Figure 8.3. The polluted river is a metaphor for how structures of class and domination damage life, humans, society, and nature. A critical theory of communication needs to also look at communication's role in alienated society, i.e. class societies and capitalist society. The section of this chapter that follows discusses communication in capitalism.

8.4 Communication, Alienation and Digital Capitalism

This section first discusses what alienation is about (Subsection 8.4.1) and then analyses the connection of alienation and communication in capitalist society (Subsection 8.4.2) with a special focus on examples from digital capitalism.

8.4.1 What Is Alienation?

Humans are the "ensemble of the social relations" (Marx 1845, 4) in which they interact with other humans in everyday life. We are and are becoming in the course of our lives through the social relations we produce, reproduce, enter, and where we meet others as part of society. Social relations, organisations, institutions, and society can be organised in different manners. In co-operative social relations, humans act in manners that benefit all or at least the many. In competitive, instrumental social relations, humans try to take advantage of each other so that one or some benefit at the expense of others. There is a difference between co-operative and instrumental reason. Instrumental reason guides human action in manners so that some instrumentalise others, whereas co-operative reason shapes actions in ways that create advantages and a better life for all. Instrumental and co-operative actions are two forms of purposive action. Whereas the first is interested in creating benefits for the few, the second wants to create benefits for the many.

Alienation is the term that Marx uses for characterising dominative and unequal social relations where humans do not control the conditions under which they live. In alienated relations, humans do not control the relations, means, and results of social production. Marx characterises alienation as "*loss of self*" (Marx 1844a, 228), "*powerlessness*" (228), "the *loss* of the object" (Marx 1844c, 273), "the loss of his [the human's] reality" (279), "the product as a loss" (279). Alienation means a power gap and the loss and lack of control. On the one hand, Marx sees alienation as economic alienation, i.e. as class relations, relations where the worker's activity "belongs to another; it is the loss of his self" (Marx 1844c, 274). But on the other hand, he characterises religious ideology and the bourgeois state as alienation (Fuchs 2018c), which shows that besides and together with economic alienation there are also political and cultural forms of alienation. David Harvey (2018) therefore argues that alienation is a universal process that extends beyond economic production into the realisation of value, the consumption and distribution of commodities, politics, culture, and social life. He speaks of universal alienation.

Harvey (2003, 2005) defines the new imperialism and neoliberalism as the commodification of (almost) everything and accumulation by dispossession. Commodification and exploitation and therefore the attempt to universalise alienation are immanent features of capitalism. Neoliberalism has managed to break down welfare state barriers to the universalisation of economic alienation so that commodification was able to intensify and extend itself.

Erich Fromm draws a distinction between Humanism and authoritarianism. In authoritarian social forms, "an authority states what is good for man and lays down the laws and

Communication, Alienation and Digital Capitalism

norms of conduct" (Fromm 1965, 6). In Humanist social forms, the human being is "both the norm giver and the subject of the norms" (6). Authoritarianism is a type of character structure, ideology, social structure, and social system where humans are treated like things and instruments. Humanism is a type of character structure, ideology, social structure, and social system where humans are treated in a humane way so that they can realise their potentials and society can realise its possibilities so that many benefit. Georg Lukács (1971) uses the term reification for processes where humans are treated like things. Axel Honneth (2008) argues for the renewal of the concept of reification in critical theory and interprets it as processes that create and sustain disrespect. Reification (*Verdinglichung*) is closely related to alienation (*Entfremdung*). Whereas *reification* more foregrounds the *process* of reducing humans to the status of things, *alienation* has more stress on the *result* of this process, namely that humans aren't what they could, deserve and should be, but are out of control of the conditions that shape their lives.

Class and dominative societies are built on authoritarian, alienated, reifying, and disrespectful structures that turn humans into mere objects, instruments, and things. Human subjects thereby become the objects of control, domination, and exploitation. Table 8.2 shows what forms instrumental reason and co-operative reason take on in society. Alienation is the colonisation of society by instrumental reason so that instrumentality dominates over co-operation. In instrumental, alienated societies, there is an antagonism between instrumental, alienating forces and forces that struggle for advancing the logic of co-operation.

There is a basic antagonism between instrumental and co-operative reason. It takes place both at the level of practices and structures that mutually shape each other. In the economy, reification and alienation take on the form of class relations where private property owners exploit workers. In a socialist economy, there is in contrast to class societies common ownership of the means of production and workers collectively govern and control the organisations they work in. There is an economic democracy. In the political system, reification and alienation mean domination of one group over others

TABLE 8.2 Alienation as the antagonism between instrumental and co-operative reason in society

	Reification practices, alienated structures	Co-operative practices, Humanistic structures
Economy	Exploitation: private property	Self-management: commons
Politics	Domination: dictatorship	Participation: democracy
Culture	Disrespect: ideology, demagoguery	Love: friendship

and in the extreme case dictatorship. Co-operative political reason in contrast means a participatory democracy, where humans collectively control the conditions that shape their lives (Macpherson 1973, Pateman 1970). In alienated, reified culture, there are ideologies that try to legitimate dominative interests by misrepresenting and dissimulating reality and structures that give respect and fame to few and disrespect and disregard the many, who lack voice and visibility. Co-operative cultural reason in contrast means that everyone is treated in a respectful manner, is recognised, and has a voice in the public sphere.

Erich Fromm (1947, 1965, 1976) introduces the social character as a level that mediates between individual psychology and society. The social character is a dominant, typical psychological character structure that has a higher likelihood in a certain social group than in other groups. Authoritarianism and Humanism are the two basic social characters that Fromm identifies. Authoritarian individuals are destructive, exploitative, competitive, aggressive, and hateful. Humanists are creative, caring, loving, co-operative, and helpful. A human being's psyche and consciousness are shaped by the social relations they enter over the course of their life and are therefore influenced by the experiences they make and the micro-, meso-, and macro-levels of society, including the family, personal relations, the economy, political life, and cultural relations.

Capitalism is a mode of economic production, where humans are forced to sell their labour-power to capitalists who own the means of production as private property and to produce commodities that are sold on the market in order to yield monetary profit that is reinvested with the goal of accumulating ever more capital. According to Marx, in the capitalist economy, the working class is "a machine for the production of surplus-value" and the capitalist class "a machine for the transformation of this surplus-value into surplus capital" (Marx 1867a, 742) and an "extractor of surplus labour and an exploiter of surplus-labour" (425).

In feudal societies, the feudal economy was closely integrated with the monarchical political system. The political rulers were also members of the property-owning class. Religious power formed an important ideological, political, and economic force interacting and legitimating the monarchy. With the rise of capitalism, the economy became disembedded from the political system and a new political economy emerged consisting of the class relation between capital and labour as well as the modern nation-state. The authority of the monarch, the aristocracy, and religion started to decline and in their place, the authority of the capitalist class in the economy and a ruling political elite in the political system emerged. A division of labour between capitalist owners, managers, political

TABLE 8.3 Capitalist society

Sphere	Dominant structure	Dominant processes	Underlying antagonism
Economy	Capital/labour-class relation	Capital accumulation	Capitalists vs. workers
Politics	Nation-state	Accumulation of decision-power and influence	Bureaucrats vs. citizens
Culture	Ideologies	Accumulation of reputation, attention, respect	Ideologues/celebrities vs. everyday people

bureaucrats, and ideologues emerged. Bourgeois economy, state, and ideology are at the same time relatively autonomous, intersecting, interpenetrating, and interacting.

Given that economic production shapes and takes on particular forms in the political and the cultural system, the capitalist system is not just an economic mode of production but a type of society, a societal formation. Capitalism is a type of society where the logic of accumulation shapes the capitalist economic mode of production, the nation-state as a mode of governance and mode of political production, and ideologies such as individualism, racism, nationalism, etc. operate as a mode of legitimation and mode of cultural production.

Table 8.3 shows the dominant structures and processes in capitalist society's three spheres. Capitalism is a general societal realm shaped by the logic of accumulation. In the economy, accumulation implies and is based on the competition between actors on the market who have to strive for controlling and accumulating capital. In capitalism's political system, there is competition between political groups who strive to accumulate influence and decision-power. In capitalism's cultural system, there is competition between individuals who strive to become celebrities that accumulate reputation, attention, and respect. Structures of accumulation imply that there are winners and losers. A tiny minority of capitalists, managers, governors, and celebrities, and influencers accumulate power whereby workers, citizens, and everyday people are disempowered.

8.4.2 Communication in the Context of Alienation and Digital Capitalism

Instrumental reason and co-operative reason also shape communication (see Table 8.4). Alienation is the expression and manifestation of instrumental reason.

The class character of knowledge work and communication constitutes the *authoritarian and alienated economic type of information*. The property-owning class controls the

TABLE 8.4 Communication in the context of instrumental and co-operative reason

	Instrumental reason creating alienation	Instrumental reason and alienation in capitalism	Co-operative reason
Economic system	Knowledge and communication as private property commodities, exploitation of knowledge labour, means of communication as private property	Knowledge and communication as capital and commodities	Knowledge and communication as commons, co-ownership, and co-production in self-managed knowledge-creating companies
Political system	Dictatorial control of knowledge and communication processes	State control of knowledge and communication	Participatory knowledge and democratic communication, public service media
Cultural system	Ideological knowledge and communication	Communication of individualism and nationalism	Socialist-Humanist knowledge and communication, citizen media

means of communication. In a capitalist society, many communication technologies are organised as private property. There is a class relation between a dominant class and an exploited class of knowledge and communication workers who create knowledge and forms of communication that they do not own, govern, and control. In capitalism, communication and knowledge are organised in the form of cultural commodities that are sold on the market in order to accumulate capital. They are part of capitalism's cultural economy.

Let us have a look at an example of economic alienation in the context of digital capitalism: digital advertising. In *digital capitalism's economy*, we find monopoly corporations such as Google, Apple, Facebook, Amazon, or Microsoft that control digital services such as search engines, phones, social networks, online shopping, or operating systems. Figure 8.4 shows the development of global ad revenues.

The relevance of Internet advertising has continuously grown. Digital advertising today controls the largest share of global ad revenues. In 2018, Google and Facebook together accounted for 72.1 per cent of the world's digital ad revenues and 31.9 per cent of the total global ad revenues.[1] Google and Facebook are the world's largest advertising agencies.

A *Humanistic organisation of the information economy* implies the collective ownership of the means of communication and the organisation of communication and

Communication, Alienation and Digital Capitalism

Share of Media Types in World Ad Revenue (in %), data source: WARC

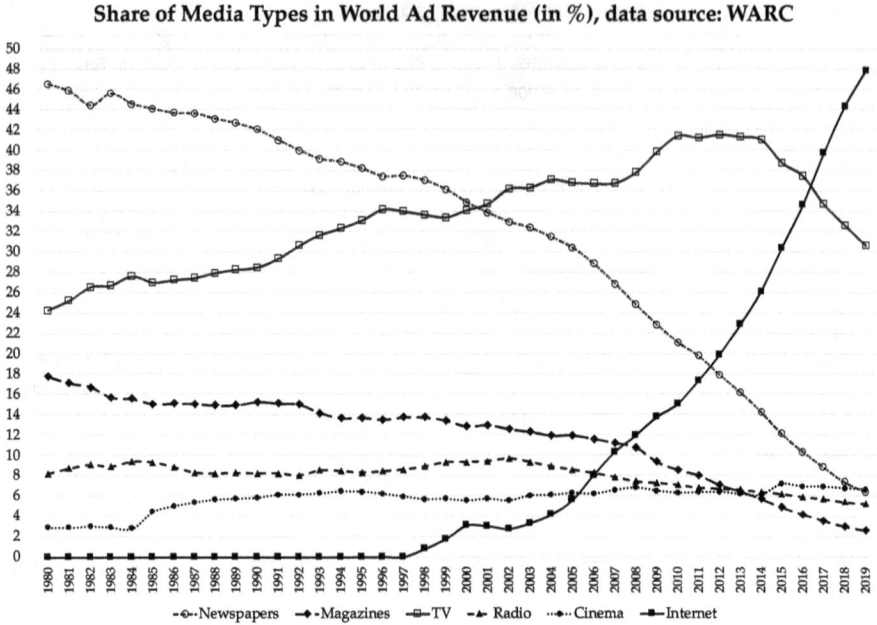

-○-Newspapers -◆-Magazines -□-TV -▲-Radio ····●···Cinema -■-Internet

FIGURE 8.4 The development of various types of advertising

culture as common goods and gifts. There are self-managed cultural companies (cultural co-operatives).

When *communication and knowledge* are organised in an *authoritarian and alienated manner at the political level*, there is a state monopoly of the means of communication that is used for disseminating ideological knowledge and political opposition and opponents' voices are stifled, repressed, or eliminated. For example, broadcasting and publishing in Nazi-Germany were strictly controlled by the state that ensured that nothing but the fascist ideology was broadcast and published. After Hitler came to power, a state-owned broadcasting company, the Reichs-Rundfunks-Gesellschaft (RRG, Reich Broadcasting Corporation), was created. It replaced regional broadcasting companies. The Reich Chamber of Broadcasting required all media workers to register so that their background and worldviews could be checked and monitored. *Gleichschaltung* meant that the Nazi-state made sure that the content broadcast and published by the media was aligned with fascist ideology, racism, anti-Semitism, etc. In the authoritarian organisation of political communication, there is mass propaganda that tries to make individuals to listen to the authoritarian leader. There are authoritarian elements not just in fascism, but in all forms of capitalism. Capitalist media want us to listen and admire the ruling class, the bureaucratic elite, celebrities, and influencers. "We listen to every voice and everybody but not to ourselves. We are constantly exposed to the noise of opinions and ideas hammering at us from everywhere: motion pictures, newspapers, radio, idle chatter" (Fromm 1947, 121). In authoritarian communication, humans are compelled and encouraged to give attention to a leader (an ideology, system, group, or individual).

Let us have a look at political alienation in the context of contemporary authoritarian digital capitalism. In the *political domain of digital capitalism*, we have seen the rise of new forms of nationalism and right-wing authoritarianism that constitute a new phase of capitalist development that can be termed authoritarian capitalism (Fuchs 2018a). Right-wing authoritarians make use of the Internet and social media for spreading their ideology (Fuchs 2020d). Donald Trump is the most well-known example. With 71.5 million Twitter followers in late January 2020, he is the individual with the tenth highest number of followers. He has more followers on Twitter than Justin Timberlake and Kim Kardashian. Figure 8.5 shows a typical example of how Trump uses Twitter for scapegoating immigrants as criminals and blaming them for social problems in order to distract attention from how these problems are grounded in capitalism's class and power structures.

Democratic governance of the means of communication and public knowledge is a key feature of the *Humanistic organisation of political communication.* Citizens and cultural workers participate in media organisations' decision-taking procedures.

There is no state or other monopoly of voice. Citizens are empowered by the media to speak and listen to each other. Media reports do not simply cover and glorify the elite, but give attention to the lives of everyday people. "To be able to listen to oneself is a prerequisite for the ability to listen to others" (Fromm 1947, 79). The *Humanistic organisation of political communication* enables humans to listen to each other. It also enables them to listen and give attention to themselves. In such a system, humans engage with each other. There are public service media that are independent, which means that such

BUILD A WALL & CRIME WILL FALL!

4:59 am - 23 Jan 2019

49,437 Retweets 211,118 Likes

♡ 76K   ↺ 49K   ♡ 211K

FIGURE 8.5 Donald Trump's use of Twitter
Source: https://twitter.com/realDonaldTrump/status/1088058726794387456.

Communication, Alienation and Digital Capitalism

media are independent of state and corporate power and provide engaging information, communication, education, and entertainment services. Public service media are enabled by laws but not controlled by the state.

In a *cultural system* that is organised in *authoritarian and alienated manner*, we find the constant public communication of ideology. Ideologies are forms of knowledge that legitimate domination and class society. By producing and disseminating ideology, particular individuals and social groups aim at convincing and winning over the individuals of the public so that they create hegemony that agrees with exploitation and domination and sees these phenomena as necessary, natural, and good. Ideologues use strategies such as acceleration, brevity, dissimulation, distortion, lies, manipulation, personalisation, scandalisation, scapegoating, superficiality, etc. Ideologues produce and spread false knowledge. They want to create and reproduce false consciousness.

Let us have a look at an example of alienated culture in the context of digital capitalism: the Cambridge Analytica scandal. In the *cultural realm of digital capitalism*, we have seen the emergence of the new forms of online communication of ideology. In this context, online fake news is of particular importance. Online fake news are fabricated news stories that are spread on the Internet and social media. The goal is to reify the consciousness of citizens through right-wing propaganda that appeals to emotions such as anger, fear, hatred, and sadness. Fake news is ideology communicated online in the form of manufactured news. Examples of alt-right websites are Breitbart, Drudge Report, InfoWars, Daily Caller, Daily Wire, and WorldNetDaily.

The combination of digital advertising, digital authoritarianism, and digital ideology has enabled the Cambridge Analytica scandal. Cambridge Analytica paid money to Global Science Research for conducting fake online personality tests in order to obtain the personal Facebook data of almost 90 million users. The data was used for targeting political ads and fake news to voters. Facebook benefited financially because big data flows are part of its capital accumulation model. It therefore allowed open interfaces that supported large-scale data gathering by external actors. The lack of political regulation of the Internet has enabled digital surveillance. Right-wing authoritarians use all means necessary, including data breaches and privacy violations, to spread their ideology. Cambridge Analytica was enabled by the combination of far-right ideology, Facebook's digital capitalist practices, and neoliberal politics.

Because of the convergence of production and consumption as prosumption, we have seen how particular questions concerning consumers have become questions of work and production. The users of Facebook and Google produce commodities, namely data and attention that enable targeted ads that are sold to ad clients. They are digital workers (Fuchs 2017c). Surveillance, privacy violations, and data breaches are not simply consumer issues but questions about digital labour that not just privacy advocates but also trade unions should deal with. The reason why Google and Facebook collect and never delete masses of personal data is that data is the digital oil that drives these giant corporations' profits. Internet use is not just a matter of consumers' rights but a matter of workers' rights. We need digital trade unions and branches of existing unions that deal with digital labour issues and campaign together with consumer protection organisations, human rights organisations, and privacy advocates. In digital capitalism, questions about privacy rights, human rights, and consumer rights are questions about the rights of digital workers.

A *culture that is organised in a Humanistic manner* does not require, produce, and disseminate ideology. It is unideological. It produces knowledge that encourages critical thinking, self-activity, and creativity.

Given the intensification of capitalism and alienation under neoliberalism, the question arises about how alternatives and struggles for alternatives can look like and what role communication plays in this context. The section that follows focuses on this topic.

8.5 Communication and the Struggle for Alternatives in the Age of Digital Capitalism

Social and class struggles are an important feature of Marxist Humanist approaches. Given that Marxist Humanism stresses the human being, socialism as Humanism, Humanism as socialism, and praxis, the logical implication is that it foregrounds the importance of class and social struggles as part of and for attaining Humanist Socialism.

There is an etymological connection between communication, community, and the commons. In a true communication society, the etymological origin of communication is realised. A communication society that lives up to its promises is a society of the commons. Communication then does not mean instrumentalisation, commodification, bureaucratisation, and ideologisation of knowledge sharing and making something common so that the many benefit. Commoning is a true communication society's fundamental principle. A communication society is a society where humans exert common control of the conditions that govern and shape their lives.

Communications are in such a society commons-based, i.e. communication systems whose "*primary freedom* [. . .] *lies in not being a trade*" (Marx 1842, 175). The basic economic antagonism that shapes communication, culture, and technology today is the one between commodification and commonification.

A society of the commons is a society that realises the creation of the economic commons (wealth and self-fulfilment for all), the political commons (participatory democracy), and the cultural commons (voice and recognition of all).

Raymond Williams envisions a communicative and cultural democracy. In such a democracy, there is the co-operation of public service media, local community media, and cultural co-operatives. Williams envisions "new kinds of communal, cooperative and collective institutions" (Williams 1983, 123). Democratic communications are using the logic and rationality of co-operation. In a democratic communication system, corporations, the state, and celebrities do not control voice and visibility. In such a system, we find true freedom of speech that enables humans to listen, speak, and engage. Democratic means of communication are "means of participation and of common discussion" (Williams 1976, 134). Williams argues that the key means of production should be publicly owned and given for use to self-managed organisations, which needs to make sure that there is a diversity of political opinion and that state control of opinions is avoided (Williams 1979, 370).

For Marx, human beings are practical because they transform society through practices. By praxis, Marx refers to a certain form of practice. Praxis means political practices that aim at or organise a human-centred society. Praxis is the practical struggle for the creation and sustainment of a commons-based society. The creation of a true and good communication society is in need of struggles that are informed by "the *categorical imperative to overthrow all relations* in which man is a debased, enslaved, forsaken, despicable being" (Marx 1844b, 182). Praxis includes class struggles that aim at abolishing exploitation, class, and domination. Praxis wants to establish an "absolute humanism" (Gramsci 1971, 417).

Social struggles need their own culture, which includes the creation and communication of stories that focus on how exploitation and domination damage humans and society and how resistance can be self-organised. The communication of injustices and resistance is an important aspect of the self-organisation of protest.

Praxis communication is a particular form of human communication that has an ethical and political character. It is oriented toward the struggle for Humanism and socialism. *Praxis communication* is always *communicative practice*. But only a subset of *communicative practices* is *praxis communication*. Communication is not automatically good. It is not automatically a means that questions exploitation and domination. Communication is a practice by and in which humans reproduce and produce social relations. Progressive activists use communication technologies such as the Internet for challenging exploitation and domination.

Let us have a brief look at how social struggles are changing in the age of digital capitalism.

Given the changes of the working class and the importance of the social worker, the social factory, digitalisation, globalisation, the rise of prosumption and freelancers in capitalism, new concepts, new strategies, and new methods of struggle are needed in the age of digital capitalism. A Marxist-Humanist theory of communication aims to inform struggles for a good, commons-based, public Internet in a good, commons-based society that has a vivid, democratic public sphere.

Neoliberalism's individualisation of labour, the emergence of digital labour, and the blurring of the boundaries between labour and leisure, the private and the public, production and consumption, the office/factory and the home, have created new challenges for trade unions and the organisation of the working class.

Given the globalisation, digitalisation, and informatisation of labour and the emergence of productive consumption (prosumption), we need new methods of strike. A strike of knowledge workers will not be effective if it isn't qualitatively different from traditional strikes organised in transportation or manufacturing. In general, strike as the refusal of labour needs digital and global means and levels of organisation.

A study of communication in the protests of Occupy movements showed that activists use multiple media for mobilisation-oriented communication (Fuchs 2014): classical interpersonal communication via phones, email, face-to-face, and private social media profiles as well as more public forms of communication such as Facebook groups, Twitter and email lists. Posting announcements on alternative social media is much more uncommon than doing the same on Twitter and Facebook. Correlation analysis showed that a higher level of protest activity tends to result in a higher level of media use for protest mobilisation. A higher level of engagement in protests has positive influences on the usage of media for political mobilisation. Mobilisation in face-to-face communication tends to positively influence other forms of mobilisation communication. Posting announcements on Facebook in order to mobilise others tend to positively impact other forms of mobilisation communication.

Communication and the Struggle for Alternatives in the Age of Digital Capitalism

In digital capitalism, class and social struggles have taken on new forms. Adbusters is a Canadian campaign and culture jamming group. It was very influential in the creation of the Occupy Wall Street movement. In September 2018, Adbusters organised #Occupy-SiliconValley, a one-day strike against Amazon, Apple, Facebook, and Google. Here is an excerpt from #OccupySiliconValley's call for action:

> How do we take on the largest and most corrupt corporate Goliaths to ever exist? […] 1 Google No Search Day: The ONLY thing we search is: does google do evil? We force the megabot to do some soul-searching. We see if it can tell us, the people, what's really going on behind that insidious techno-curtain.

#OccupySiliconValley was not simply a consumer boycott. It was a digital labour strike. It was an example of what dimensions strikes should take into account in the age of digital capitalism.

Digital Socialist Humanism is the alternative to digital capitalism (Fuchs 2020b). It is a democratic socialist society where digital technologies benefit the many and help creating wealth, participation, recognition, and voice for all. Social struggles on the Internet, utilising the Internet, and against digital capital are a key element of socialist praxis communication today. But we cannot wait until after the disappearance of digital capitalism to create alternatives. The creation of alternative Internet platforms is itself part of the struggle for digital socialism. Platform co-operatives and public service Internet platforms are two types of digital alternatives. They are both non-profit models of Internet organisation. Platform co-operatives are self-managed, collectively owned and controlled Internet platforms. Users and the platform's digital workers operate, own, and govern a platform co-operatives. Public service Internet platforms are Internet platforms that are controlled and operated by public service media such as the BBC.

A public service YouTube operated by a network of public service media such as BBC, ARD, France Télévisions, etc. is an alternative to Google's commercial YouTube. A public service YouTube should encourage the creation of videos on topics that are important for democracy. This can be done by creating challenges and campaigns where users are invited to create and upload videos that accompany certain radio and TV programmes. Collective production of such videos should be encouraged in institutions such as school classes, groups of pupils and students, council houses, adult learning groups, unions, religious and philosophical groups, civil society organisations, etc. Digital creativity can be fostered by offering public service media's archive material in digital format using a Creative Commons CC-BY-NC licence that allows adoption and change of the material for non-commercial purposes. Public service media shouldn't co-operate with capitalist media but with community and citizen media, platform co-operatives, and other public cultural institutions such as museums, universities, and libraries.

The following section summarises the basic findings of this chapter.

8.6 Conclusions: Humanist Socialism in the Age of Digital Capitalism

This chapter has argued for the renewal of Marxist Humanism and Humanist Socialism in 21st-century digital capitalism. Marxist-Humanist theory stresses the importance of humans in society. It is a practice- and praxis-oriented approach that stresses the transformative capacity of class and social struggles against alienation and ideologies and for a society that combines Humanism and socialism.

A Marxist-Humanist theory of communication stresses that communication is a form of human practice and the process that produces understanding, sociality, social relations, social systems, social structures, and society. There is a dialectic of work and communication. In alienated societies, we are confronted by alienated forms of communication that are governed by instrumental reason. Figure 8.6 summarises the antagonism between instrumental and co-operative reason in the realms of society in general and communication in particular.

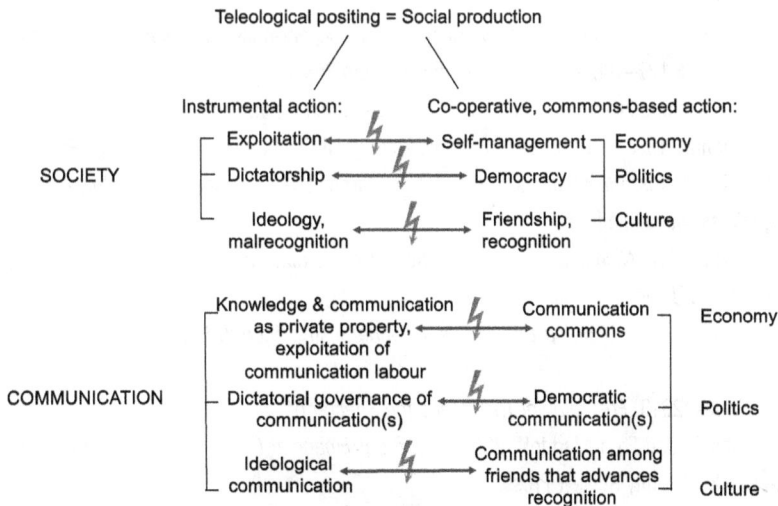

FIGURE 8.6   The antagonism between instrumental and co-operative in society in general and the realm of communication

Praxis is the social struggle for a Socialist-Humanist society. The establishment of democratic means of communication is a form of praxis communication. A democratic public sphere requires democratic means of communication that are operated not-for-profit; inform, educate and entertain in unbiased manners unbiased by ideology and economic and political power; and give everyday people public voices in society.

Digital socialism is the Humanist alternative to digital capitalism (for an overview, see the 15 contributions in Fuchs 2020b). Digital socialism is the struggle for an Internet and a digital media landscape, and a digital society that is not dominated by corporations but that is controlled by users, workers, and citizens in the form of a participatory digital democracy.

Note

1 Data sources: WARC, SEC-filings forms 10-K for Google/Alphabet and Facebook (financial year 2018).

References

Adorno, Theodor W., et al. 1950. *The Authoritarian Personality.* New York: Harper & Brothers.

Alderson, David and Robert Spencer. 2017. *For Humanism. Explorations in Theory and Politics.* London: Pluto.

Althusser, Louis. 1969. Ideology and Ideological State Apparatuses. In *Lenin and Philosophy and Other Essays*, 127–186. New York: Monthly Review Press.

Althusser, Louis and Étienne Balibar. 2009 [1968]. *Reading Capital.* London: Verso.

Arendt, Hannah. 1958. *The Human Condition.* Chicago, IL: The University of Chicago Press.

Aristotle. 2013. *Aristotle's Politics.* Translated by Carnes Lord. Chicago, IL: The University of Chicago Press. Second edition.

Aristotle. 2009. *The Nicomachean Ethics. Oxford World's Classics.* Translated by David Ross. Oxford: Oxford University Press.

Brown, Wendy. 2015. *Undoing the Demos. Neoliberalism's Stealth Revolution.* New York: Zone Books.

Chibber, Vivek. 2013. *Postcolonial Theory and the Specter of Capital.* London: Verso.

Foster, John B. and Fred Magdoff. 2009. *The Great Financial Crisis. Causes and consequences.* New York: Monthly Review Press.

Foucault, Michel. 1969. Qu'est-ce qu'un auteur? In *Dits et écrits I 1954–1969*, 789–821. Paris: Gallimard.

Fromm, Erich. 1976. *To Have or to Be?* London: Continuum.

Fromm, Erich, ed. 1965. *Socialist Humanism. An International Symposium.* Garden City, NY: Doubleday.

Fromm, Erich. 1947. *Man for Himself. An Inquiry into the Psychology of Ethics.* Abingdon: Routledge.

Fromm, Erich. 1941/1969. *Escape from Freedom.* New York: Avon.

Fuchs, Christian. 2022. *Digital Humanism. A Philosophy for 21st Century Digital Society.* Bingley: Emerald.

Fuchs, Christian. 2020a. *Communication and Capitalism. A Critical Theory.* London: University of Westminster Press. https://doi.org/10.16997/book45

Fuchs, Christian, ed. 2020b. Communicative Socialism/Digital Socialism. *tripleC: Communication, Capitalism & Critique* 18 (1): 1–285.

Fuchs, Christian. 2020c. Erich Fromm and the Critical Theory of Communication. *Humanity & Society* 44 (3): 298–325. DOI: http://dx.doi.org/10.1177/0160597620930157

Fuchs, Christian. 2020d. *Nationalism on the Internet: Critical Theory and Ideology in the Age of Social Media and Fake News.* New York: Routledge.

Fuchs, Christian. 2019a. Henri Lefebvre's Theory of the Production of Space and the Critical Theory of Communication. *Communication Theory* 29 (2): 129–150.

Fuchs, Christian. 2019b. M. N. Roy and the Frankfurt School: Socialist Humanism and the Critical Analysis of Communication, Culture, Technology, Fascism and Nationalism. *tripleC: Communication, Capitalism & Critique* 17 (2): 249–286. DOI: https://doi.org/10.31269/triplec.v17i2.1118

Fuchs, Christian. 2019c. Revisiting the Althusser/E. Thompson-Controversy: Towards a Marxist Theory of Communication. *Communication and the Public* 4 (1): 3–20.

Fuchs, Christian. 2018a. *Digital Demagogue: Authoritarian Capitalism in the Age of Trump and Twitter.* London: Pluto.

Fuchs, Christian. 2018b. Towards a Critical Theory of Communication with Georg Lukács and Lucien Goldmann. *Javnost – The Public* 25 (3): 265–281.

Fuchs, Christian. 2018c. Universal Alienation, Formal and Real Subsumption of Society Under Capital, Ongoing Primitive Accumulation by Dispossession: Reflections on the Marx@200-contributions by David Harvey and Michael Hardt/Toni Negri. *tripleC: Communication, Capitalism & Critique* 16 (2): 406–414. DOI: https://doi.org/10.31269/triplec.v16i2.1028

Fuchs, Christian. 2017a. Günther Anders' Undiscovered Critical Theory of Technology in the Age of Big Data Capitalism. *tripleC: Communication, Capitalism & Critique* 15 (2), 584–613. DOI: https://doi.org/10.31269/triplec.v15i2.898

Fuchs, Christian. 2017b. Raymond Williams' Communicative Materialism. *European Journal of Cultural Studies* 20 (6): 744–762.

Fuchs, Christian. 2017c. *Social Media: A Critical Introduction.* London: Sage. Second edition.

Fuchs, Christian. 2017d. The Praxis School's Marxist Humanism and Mihailo Marković's Theory of Communication. *Critique* 45 (1–2): 159–182.

Fuchs, Christian. 2016a. *Critical Theory of Communication: New Readings of Lukács, Adorno, Marcuse, Honneth and Habermas in the Age of the Internet.* London: University of Westminster Press. DOI: https://doi.org/10.16997/book1

Fuchs, Christian. 2016b. Georg Lukács as a Communications Scholar: Cultural and Digital labour in the context of Lukács' "Ontology of Social Being". *Media, Culture & Society* 38 (4): 506–524.

Fuchs, Christian. 2016c. Herbert Marcuse and Social Media. *Radical Philosophy Review* 10 (1): 113–143.

Fuchs, Christian. 2014. *OccupyMedia! The Occupy Movement and Social Media in Crisis Capitalism.* Winchester: Zero Books.

Fuchs, Christian and Lara Monticelli, eds. 2018. Marx@200: Debating Capitalism & Perspectives for the Future of Radical Theory. *tripleC: Communication, Capitalism & Critique* 16 (2): 406–741.

Gramsci, Antonio. 1971. *Selections from the Prison Notebooks.* New York: International Publishers.

Habermas, Jürgen. 2019. *Auch eine Geschichte der Philosophie. Band 1: Die okzidentale Konstellation von Glauben und Wissen.* Frankfurt am Main: Suhrkamp.

Habermas, Jürgen. 1985a. *The Theory of Communicative Action. Volume 1: Reason and the Rationalization of Society.* Boston, MA: Beacon Press.

Habermas, Jürgen. 1985b. *The Theory of Communicative Action. Volume 2: Lifeworld and System: A Critique of Functionalist Reason.* Boston, MA: Beacon Press.

Habermas, Jürgen. 1971. *Knowledge and Human Interests.* Boston, MA: Beacon Press.

Habermas, Jürgen. 1968. Arbeit und Interaktion. Bemerkungen zu Hegels Jensener "Philosophie des Geisters". In *Technik und Wissenschaft als "Ideologie"*, 9–47. Frankfurt am Main: Suhrkamp.

Harvey, David. 2018. Universal Alienation. *tripleC: Communication, Capitalism & Critique* 16 (2): 424–439. DOI: https://doi.org/10.31269/triplec.v16i2.1026

Harvey, David. 2010. *The Enigma of Capital and the Crises of Capitalism.* Oxford: Oxford University Press.

Harvey, David. 2005. *A Brief History of Neoliberalism.* Oxford: Oxford University Press.

Harvey, David. 2003. *The New Imperialism.* Oxford: Oxford University Press.

Harvey, David. 1990. *The Condition of Postmodernity. An Enquiry into the Origins of Cultural Change.* Cambridge, MA: Blackwell.

Hegel, Georg Wilhelm Friedrich. 1805/1806. *Jenaer Systementwürfe III.* Hamburg: Felix Meiner Verlag.

Hegel, Georg Wilhelm Friedrich. 1803/1804. *Jenaer Systementwürfe I.* Hamburg: Felix Meiner Verlag.

Honneth, Axel. 2008. *Reification. A New Look at an Old Idea. With Commentaries by Judith Butler, Raymond Geuss and Jonathan Lear.* Oxford: Oxford University Press.

Horkheimer, Max. 1939/1989. The Jews and Europe. In *Critical Theory and Society: A Reader*, ed. Stephen E. Bronner and Douglas Kellner, 77–94. New York: Routledge.

Jhally, Sut. 2016. Stuart Hall: The Last Interview. *Cultural Studies* 30 (2): 332–345.

Lukács, Georg. 1986a. *Zur Ontologie des gesellschaftlichen Seins. Erster Halbband Bände. Georg Lukács Werke, Band 13*. Darmstadt: Luchterhand.

Lukács, Georg. 1986b. *Zur Ontologie des gesellschaftlichen Seins. Zweiter Halbband Bände. Georg Lukács Werke, Band 14*. Darmstadt: Luchterhand.

Lukács, Georg. 1978. *The Ontology of Social Being. 3: Labour*. London: Merlin.

Lukács, Georg. 1971. *History and Class Consciousness*. London: Merlin.

Lukács, Georg. 1963. *Die Eigenart des Ästhetischen. 1. Halbband. Georg Lukács Werke Band 11*. Darmstadt: Luchterhand.

Macpherson, Crawford B. 1973. *Democratic Theory*. Oxford: Oxford University Press.

Marx, Karl. 1867a. *Capital. A Critique of Political Economy*, Volume 1. Translated by Ben Fowkes. London: Penguin.

Marx, Karl. 1867b. *Das Kapital. Kritik der politischen Ökonomie. Erster Band. MEW Band 23*. Berlin: Dietz.

Marx, Karl. 1852. The Eighteenth Brumaire of Louis Bonaparte. In *Marx & Engels collected Works*, 99–197. London: Lawrence & Wishart.

Marx, Karl. 1845. Theses on Feuerbach. In *Marx & Engels Collected Works (MECW)*, Volume 5, 3–5. London: Lawrence & Wishart.

Marx, Karl. 1844a. Comments on James Mill, Élémens d'economie politique. In *Marx & Engels Collected Works (MECW)*, Volume 3, 211–228. London: Lawrence & Wishart.

Marx, Karl. 1844b. Contribution to the Critique of Hegel's Philosophy of Law. In *Marx & Engels Collected Works (MECW)*, Volume 3, 175–187. London: Lawrence & Wishart.

Marx, Karl. 1844c. Economic and Philosophic Manuscripts of 1844. In *Marx & Engels Collected Works (MECW)*, Volume 3, 229–346. London: Lawrence & Wishart.

Marx, Karl. 1842. Debates on the Freedom of the Press. In *Marx & Engels Collected Works (MECW)*, Volume 1, 132–202. London: Lawrence & Wishart.

Marx, Karl and Friedrich Engels. 1845/46. *The German Ideology*. In *Marx & Engels Collected Works (MECW)*, Volume 5, 19–539. London: Lawrence & Wishart.

Pateman, Carole. 1970. *Participation and Democratic Theory*. Cambridge: Cambridge University Press.

Roberts, Michael. 2016. *The Long Depression. Marxism and the Global Crisis of Capitalism*. Chicago, IL: Haymarket Books.

Smith, Adam. 1776. *An Inquiry into the Nature and Causes of the Wealth of Nations*. London: Wordsworth.

Sohn-Rethel, Alfred. 1978. *Intellectual and Manual Labour: A Critique of Epistemology*. London: Macmillan.

Taylor, Charles. 2016. *The Language Animal. The Full Shape of the Human Linguistic Capacity*. Cambridge, MA: The Belknap Press.

Thompson, Edward P. 1978. *The Poverty of Theory & Other Essays*. London: Merlin.

Wallerstein, Immanuel et al. 2013. *Does Capitalism Have a Future?* Oxford: Oxford University Press.

Warren, Rosie, ed. 2017. *The Debate on "Postcolonial Theory and the Specter of Capital"*. London: Verso.

Weber, Max. 2019. *Economy and Society*. Cambridge, MA: Harvard University Press.

Williams, Raymond. 1983. *Towards 2000*. London: Chatto & Windus.

Williams, Raymond. 1980. *Culture and Materialism*. London: Verso.

Williams, Raymond. 1979. *Politics and Letters: Interviews with New Left Review*. London: Verso Books.

Williams, Raymond. 1977. *Marxism and Literature*. Oxford: Oxford University Press.

Williams, Raymond. 1976. *Communications*. Harmondsworth: Penguin Books.

Žižek, Slavoj. 2007. *How to Read Lacan*. New York: W. W. Norton & Company.

Chapter Nine
Digital Democracy, Public Service Media, and the Public Service Internet

---

9.1 Introduction

This chapter deals with a specific aspect of the democratic mandate of public service media. In doing so, it analyses the relationship between digital democracy and public service media. The main question is: What contributions can public service media make to digital democracy?

Some sub-questions are asked about this overall topic of public service media and digital democracy:

> Question 1: What are digital democracy and the digital public sphere?
>
> Question 2: What are the main trends in the development of digital media today, what are digital media's democratic possibilities and deficits, and what role can public service media play in strengthening digital democracy and digital public sphere?
>
> Question 3: What legal framework is needed so that public service media can strengthen digital democracy?

This chapter is divided into four parts besides the introduction: Sections 9.2 and 9.3 deal with research question 1, Section 9.4 deals with research question 2 and Section 9.5

DOI: 10.4324/9781003331087-11

with research question 3. Section 9.6 draws conclusions and formulates recommendations for action.

9.2 Democracy and the Public Sphere

The term "democracy" comes etymologically from the Greek word demokratia.
(δημοκρατία), which is formed from the two words demos (δῆμος) and kratos (κρατός,
Macht). Democracy therefore means power emanating from the people. Democracy models and theories of democracy differ according to who is considered part of the people
and what is understood by power. Therefore, there is not one understanding of democracy, but there are rather many different models of democracy.

David Held (2006), in his book *Models of Democracy*, which is one of the most widely read
introductions to democratic theory, distinguishes between two basic models of democracy, namely direct democracy and liberal representative democracy. Direct democracy is
understood to be "a system of decision-making about public affairs in which citizens are
directly involved" (Held 2006, 4). Liberal representative democracy is "a system of rule
embracing elected 'officers' who undertake to 'represent' the interests and/or views of
citizens within the framework of the 'rule of law'" (Held 2006, 4). In democratic theory, a
distinction is also made between parliamentary and presidential democracy, competitive
and consociational democracy, as well as between majority and consensus democracy
(Schmidt 1997, Waschkuhn 1998).

Held (2006) distinguishes nine models of democracy:
1) Classical Athenian democracy:
   direct citizen participation in the agora;
2) Liberal democracy:
   political freedom as liberal civil rights, election of representatives, the rule of law,
   the constitution, the separation of powers;
3) Direct democracy or plebiscitary democracy:
   direct participation of citizens in the political decision-making process through
   voting or through rotating councils that are elected by citizens and can be voted
   out at any time;
4) Competitive elitist democracy:
   parliamentary government with strong executive and extensive decision-making
   power of leaders, competition between rival political elites and parties for dominance in the state;

5) Pluralist democracy:

civil rights, separation of powers, the government mediates between a plurality of competing interests and tries to balance them, protection of minorities;

6) Legal democracy:

majority principle coupled with the constitutional state and the rule of law; minimisation of state intervention in the economy, civil society and private life; maximisation of the extension of market economy principles to society, the minimal state, emphasis on individual freedom;

7) Participatory democracy:

grassroots democracy, the extension of democracy from the political system to the workplace and local communities, creation of a resource base as well as space, time and educational opportunities as the basis of grassroots democracy, technological minimisation of socially necessary work coupled with the reduction of working hours as the material foundation of grassroots democracy;

8) Deliberative democracy:

the focus is on political debate and communication among citizens, debate on political issues and discussions between citizens and political representatives; citizens' forums, consultative assemblies, deliberative polls for opinion assessment;

9) Democratic autonomy:

constitutional guarantees of fundamental rights, parliamentary election of representatives combined with direct democratic elements, citizens' forums and other deliberative mechanisms, extension of democracy to municipal services and self-managed companies, transnational democratic institutions (cosmopolitan democracy).

Models 1, 2, and 3 are classical approaches to democracy, while models 4–9 are newer approaches. With regard to Held's two basic models of democracy, it can be said that models 2, 4, 5, and 6 are manifestations of liberal representative democracy, while models 1, 3, 7, and 8 are forms of direct democracy. Model 9 represents a combination of the two basic models.

Communication is an important and indispensable aspect of the political system in all models of democracy: In Athenian democracy, direct political communication of citizens took place face to face in the marketplace. In liberal democracy, party programmes must be communicated to citizens. In elite democracy, leaders communicate their programmes and decisions to the people. Similarly, competing positions are communicated to the people. In pluralist democracy, representatives of different interests communicate through the state in order to reach a balance or to negotiate. In legal democracy, the market is considered an important instrument of communication between consumers and citizens. In participatory democracy, there is enough space and time for grassroots political communication among citizens to bring about decisions. In deliberative democracy, consultative processes take place to organise ongoing communication on political issues. In democratic autonomy, grassroots and deliberative forms of communication (e.g. citizens' forums or assemblies) are combined with representative democratic forms of communication (e.g. canvassing or media coverage of the programmes of the parties campaigning for election).

On a general level, it can be said that the public sphere is a central mechanism of any political system. By "public" we generally mean goods and spaces that are "open to all" (Habermas 1991, 1). For example, one speaks of public education, public buildings, public parks, public squares, public meetings, public rallies, public opinion, public service media, etc. Public goods and institutions are not reserved for a clique or a club of the privileged, but are intended for the general public, i.e. all members of a community. Often, but not exclusively, public goods and institutions are organised and regulated by the state. There may be certain conditions of access, such as payment of the licence fee as a legal condition of access to public broadcasting. However, these access conditions should be affordable for the general public, i.e. they should not discriminate according to income, class status, gender, origin, abilities, level of education, etc. The political dimension of the public sphere was already present in ancient Greece, where the sphere of the polis was "common (koine) to the free citizens" (Habermas 1991, 3).

The public sphere is a sphere of public political communication that mediates between the other subsystems of society, i.e. the economy, politics, culture, and private life. In the ideal type of the public sphere, it is a sphere that organises "critical publicity" (Habermas 1991, 237) and "critical public debate" (Habermas 1991, 52). The public sphere mediatises political communication. It is a mediating space of political interaction in which citizens meet, inform themselves politically and communicate politically, and in which political opinions are formed.

Public communication is an important aspect of the existence of humans as social beings and society. In modern society, the media system is the most important organised form of public communication (Fuchs 2016). In the media system, media actors produce public information. News informs citizens about political events and is an occasion for political communication. In a complex society, there is a system differentiation as well as a differentiation of social roles. In a class society, such differentiations take the form of the division of labour and the division of power. Various organisations and interest groups in the economy, politics, culture, and civil society (companies, business associations, trade unions, workers' associations, clubs, citizens' initiatives, lobbyists, religious communities, parties, politicians, social movements, non-governmental organisations, etc.) try to influence the form and content of public political information. This is done, for example, through media presence, public relations, advertising, organisational interlocking and networks, etc. The media system interacts with the economy, politics, culture, and private life. Media organisations are not only cultural organisations that produce and publicly disseminate content, but also economic organisations that need resources to exist. Media organisations are also politically shaped by legal regulations on the one hand and by tax benefits (e.g. tax levies, public subsidies) on the other. Figure 9.1 presents a model of the role of the media system in the public sphere.

Media have (a) a political-economic and (b) a cultural dimension. On the one hand, they need resources such as money, legal frameworks, staff, and organisational structures in order to exist. In this respect, they are economic organisations. However, they are special economic organisations that are also cultural organisations, since they produce meanings of society that serve public information, public communication, and the formation of opinions. Since opinion formation and communication also include political opinion formation and political communication, media organisations have implications for democracy and the political system. As cultural organisations, all media organisations are public because they publish information. As economic organisations, on the other hand, only certain media

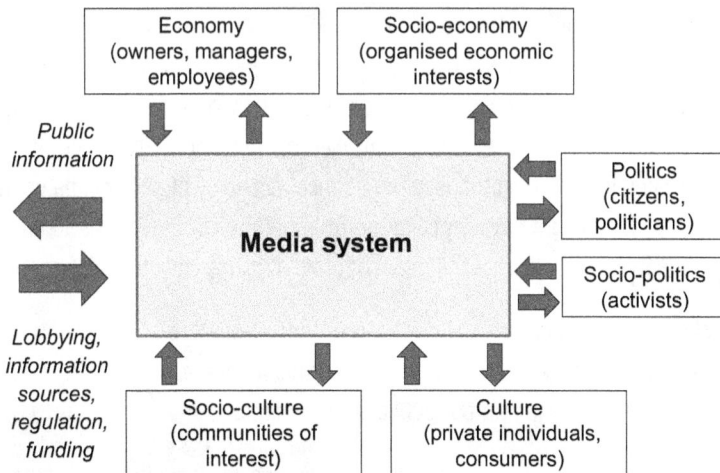

FIGURE 9.1   The media system as the public sphere's communication system

TABLE 9.1 Two levels and four types of media organisations

	Capitalist media	Public service media	Civil society media	Authoritarian state media
Political economy (relations of ownership and production, legal relations)	Media companies that are privately owned for-profit organisations	Media institutions that are enabled by the state, are not-for-profit organisations and have a defined public service remit that they follow and advance	Non-profit civil society media organisations that act	State-controlled, state-owned, state-censored media; such media are either state-owned or privately owned under state control or have mixed models where the state plays a key role; might be not-for-profit or for-profit
Culture (public circulation of meanings and ideas)	Production and distribution of information that support members of the public in the production of meanings, interpersonal communication and the formation of opinions	Production and distribution of information that support members of the public in the production of meanings, interpersonal communication, and the formation of opinions	Production and distribution of information that support members of the public in the production of meanings, interpersonal communication, and the formation of opinions	Production and distribution of information that aim at the member of the public's production of meanings in manners that adhere to state ideology and propaganda

organisations are public, while others take on a private sector character, i.e. are organisations that have private owners and operate for profit. Public service media and civil society media, on the other hand, are not profit-oriented and are collectively owned by the state or a community. Table 9.1 illustrates these distinctions. Public service media are public in the sense of the cultural public and the political-economic public. They publish information and are owned by the public. A special form are authoritarian state media. These are media where the publishing process is strictly controlled by an authoritarian state. Journalistic work is controlled by state institutions. The political economy of such media can take on different forms. They might have a not-for-profit imperative but serve yet another instrumental rationality, namely the advancement of state ideology and state propaganda.

Since public service media are public organisers and mediators of political information, communication, and opinion-forming, the democratic mandate is usually also enshrined as part of the public service remit of public service media.

The BBC Charter is the legal framework that governs the activities and organisation of the BBC for a certain period of time. The current BBC Charter came into force on

1 January 2017 and is valid until the end of 2027. It states that it is part of the public service remit for the BBC to "provide impartial news and information to help people understand and engage with the world around them [...] [so that they can] participate in the democratic process, at all levels, as active and informed citizens" (http://downloads.bbc.co.uk/bbctrust/assets/files/pdf/about/how_we_govern/2016/charter.pdf, aufgerufen am 20. Dezember 2017). In Austria, the ORF Act regulates the establishment, mission, principles, organisation and control of the Austrian Broadcasting Corporation. According to the ORF Act, the core public service mandate of the ORF includes, among other things "the promotion of understanding for all issues of democratic life"[1] (ORF-Gesetz, §4 [1]). Similar definitions of public service media's democratic remit can be found in many other countries that have an independent public service broadcaster.

Both legal texts just mentioned define a democratic remit for public service media: public service media must ensure that their services and offerings help to form active and informed citizens who can participate in the democratic process and have an understanding of democratic issues. The democratic remit is a special quality feature of public service media. Democracy is a public common good that is meant to protect the rights of all and that is produced and reproduced only through the collective political behaviour of all citizens. This collective political behaviour includes not only voting, but also the formation of public and individual political opinion as well as political communication. Public service media, as public communication systems with a public cultural and economic character, play a special communicative and informational role in democracy. The democratic remit should therefore guarantee that public service media contribute to democratic communication.

Digital media such as the Internet, social media, and the World Wide Web are relatively new type of media compared to print media and broadcasting. They became popular in the last fifth of the 20th century. Questions of democracy and the public sphere must therefore be rethought in the context of digital media.

9.3 Digital Democracy and the Digital Public Sphere

Kenneth L. Hacker and Jan van Dijk (2000) define digital democracy in the introduction to the anthology *Digital Democracy* as follows:

> Digital democracy is the use of information and communication technology (ICT) and computer-mediated communication (CMC) in all kinds of media (e.g.

the Internet, interactive broadcasting and digital telephony) for purposes of enhancing political democracy or the participation of citizens in democratic communication [...] We define digital democracy as *a collection of attempts to practise democracy without limits of time, space and other physical conditions, using ICT or CMC instead, as an addition, not a replacement for traditional 'analogue' political practices.*

(Hacker and van Dijk 2000, 1)

Several comments should be made on this definition:

- The term "digital democracy" is relatively widespread today. However, terms such as electronic democracy, teledemocracy, cyberdemocracy, Internet democracy, virtual democracy, or electronic participation are also used equivalently.

- Since 2000, when Hacker and van Dijk gave this definition, the media landscape has evolved. The term "digital telephony" is hardly used today. Rather, people usually speak of "mobile telephony" and the "mobile phone". Furthermore, social media should certainly be added to the example technologies (blogs, micro-blogs, social networks, wikis, etc.).

- The term "information and communication technologies" is often used synonymously with the terms computer technology and digital technology/media. However, information and communication technologies also include classical media such as the painting, the theatre, music, the concert, the book, the newspaper, the cinema, the telephone, and radio. Information and communication technologies are information and communication systems that are mediated by social and societal practices. The computer and the Internet are digital information and communication technologies.

- Digital democracy is not linked to a specific model of democracy. There are certainly different forms of digital democracy that are linked to certain models of democracy (such as direct democracy, liberal and representative democracy, or participatory democracy). Digital democracy is therefore not about specific technological applications, but about technically mediated practices in which certain democratic models and ideas are realised. Digital democracy is based on a dialectic of technology and politics.

Jan van Dijk (2000, 40) distinguishes four democratic information processes: information distribution and allocation, information registration, consultation, and conversation. Based on these information processes, he distinguishes three models of digital

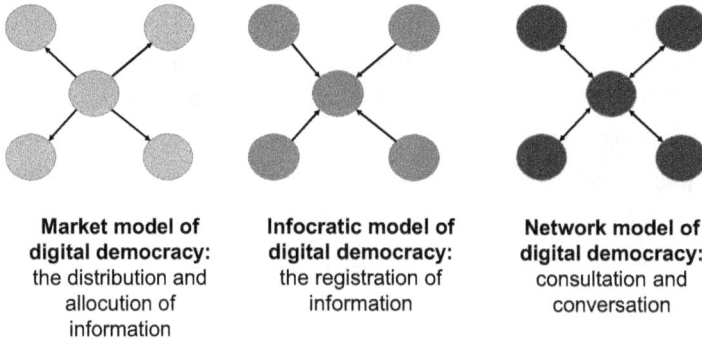

Market model of digital democracy: the distribution and allocution of information	**Infocratic model of digital democracy:** the registration of information	**Network model of digital democracy:** consultation and conversation

FIGURE 9.2   Three models of digital democracy (based on van Dijk 2000, 49)

democracy that manifest themselves in certain forms of communication and communication technologies. Figure 9.2 illustrates these three models.

In the market model of digital democracy, political information is distributed by central actors such as governments, ministries, parties, parliaments, offices, etc. via computer networks. The model is an expression of liberal and elite democracy when the emphasis is on political institutions and leaders, and legal democracy when the private sector character of digital media organisations is emphasised. The infocratic model of digital democracy is about the registration of information via computer networks. This includes, for example, filling out online forms, submitting applications online, online services provided by public authorities (e.g. online tax returns), online surveys, online voting, or expressing consent by pressing "like" or follow buttons on social media. van Dijk (2000, 51) argues that this model is an expression of the plebiscitary and legal models of democracy. In the network model, political issues are discussed by citizens via computer networks and there is the possibility for online consultations of political institutions with citizens. For van Dijk, this model is an expression of the plebiscitary, legal, pluralist, and participatory models of democracy.

In linking forms of communication and democracy, van Dijk refers to David Held's (2006) distinction between different models of democracy. However, he does not take into account all the models discussed by Held. For example, participatory democracy and deliberative democracy are not distinguished but equated. van Dijk reduces participatory democracy to deliberation and communication. van Dijk (2000, 44) regards "electronic discussion" as the epitome of participatory digital democracy. While deliberative democracy is predominantly based on communication between citizens who have different interests and lifeworlds, participatory democracy, however, is mainly about the extension

Digital Democracy and the Digital Public Sphere

of grassroots democracy beyond politics in the narrow sense to different areas of society as well as the collective control of economic, political, and cultural power (Fuchs 2017, 67–68, 95–96). Grassroots democracy also has to do with new social protest movements, which often have a grassroots form of organisation, struggle for aspects of participatory democracy as societal formation (Fuchs 2008, Chapter 8). Jan van Dijk fails to take into account that the use of computer technologies by grassroots democratic social movements for political mobilisation and the organisation of protest ("cyber-protest") is an aspect of participatory digital democracy (Fuchs 2014, 2018).

Power is a complex theoretical concept (Fuchs 2008, 225–247): In objective concepts of power, power is located in institutions. In subjective concepts of power, it emanates from individuals and their human and social skills and practices. Dialectical concepts of power speak of a dialectic of political practices of individual and social subjects and objective power structures. Based on these concepts of power, four general models of democracy can be distinguished: Representative democratic models emphasise that institutions and institutionalised roles (parliamentarians, chancellors, presidents, ministers, etc.) represent the power of the electorate and the people. In direct democracy/plebiscitary models, it is emphasised that power emanates from the electorate as political subjects and that collective political decisions should be made through referendums and popular consultations rather than through representative institutions. In deliberative democracy, the focus is on political subjects communicating and discussing political issues comprehensively. In the grassroots democracy model (also referred to as participatory democracy), the focus is on creating political and economic structures that provide people with space, time, development, and educational opportunities that promote democratic practices and political communication, so that social institutions are controlled, organised, and managed in a grassroots democratic manner and political participation is encouraged.

The models of liberal democracy, elite democracy, and pluralist democracy are primarily forms of representative democracy. Athenian democracy and plebiscitary democracy are primarily forms of direct democracy. Grassroots democracy corresponds to the model of participatory democracy. Deliberative democracy represents a distinct form of democracy based on communicative consultation processes between citizens, politicians, and politicians/citizens. Participatory democracy is based on deliberation, but above all, it emphasises the need for institutions and resources that make democracy possible, the lack or weakness of which creates democratic deficits. The "success of deliberative politics" depends on "the institutionalization of the corresponding procedures and conditions of communication" (Habermas 1994, 7). The model of deliberation can be combined with representative democracy, direct democracy, and participatory democracy. Deliberative democracy is communicative democracy, as it considers political communication as the central democratic process. Legal democracy combines forms of direct democracy and representative democracy. Democratic autonomy combines representative democracy, direct democracy, and grassroots democracy.

Information processes can be understood as coupled processes of cognition, communication, and co-operation (Hofkirchner 2002): In societal relations, people constantly inform themselves about their environment and process sensory impressions and experiences cognitively. Cognition is the basis of the communication process, in which parts of an individual's human experiences are shared with other people through symbolic interaction, leading to feedback processes that involve the symbolic sharing of experiences. In communication, experiences are symbolically communicated so that the respective lifeworld of the other individual(s) become(s) signified and new meanings emerge. Some communication processes lead to co-operation, i.e. the joint production of new social systems and social structures. Figure 9.3 illustrates the role of information processes in digital democracy.

Political information processes take place within the public sphere, which is an interface of economy, politics, and culture and interacts with these subsystems of society. Digital democracy is a form of the public sphere in which digital media are used to practice democracy. This happens through democratic information, communication, and

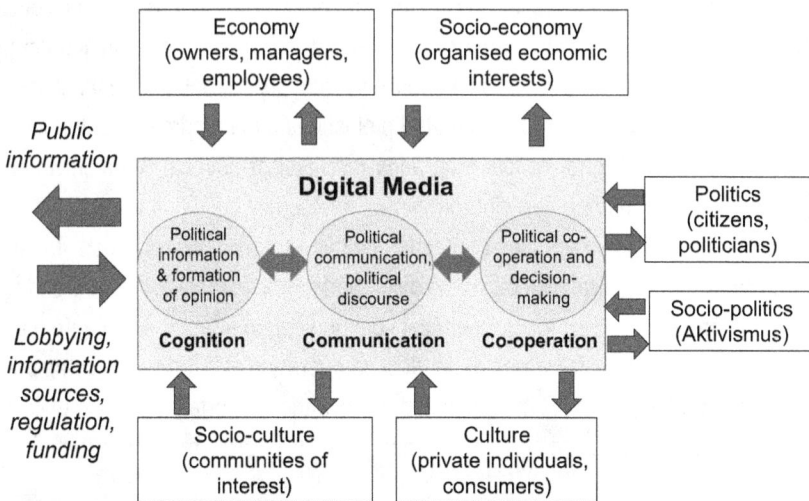

FIGURE 9.3 Digital democracy's information processes

co-operation. Representative democratic models of digital democracy emphasise how political institutions use digital media to inform citizens politically. They operate primarily at the level of political information. Plebiscitary models of digital democracy are primarily concerned with how citizens can use digital media to register information and opinions with the state. Like digital representative democracy, they operate primarily at the level of political information, but in the opposite direction: while the flow of information in digital representative democracy runs more strongly from the institutions to the citizens, in plebiscitary digital democracy it takes place more strongly in the opposite direction. Deliberative digital democracy emphasises above all the level of political communication, which takes place via digital media. Participatory digital democracy is predominantly about political co-operation, in which social structures and social systems are jointly produced, reproduced, and organised via digital media. Participatory democracy involves providing resources, making space and time available and supporting the development of skills that allow people to critically influence social processes. The democratic theorist Crawford Macpherson (1973) speaks of participatory democracy as aiming to maximise the development opportunities of people and society and minimise the extractive power whereby humans are exploited people and society is destroyed. Participatory digital democracy is about, among other things, providing time, digital resources, and digital spaces that allow people to develop and realise their skills. It also involves people using digital media to organise social movements using digital media as macro-publics that advocate for the creation of participatory democracy.

The political information processes and models of digital democracy can thus be consistently coupled and are not necessarily mutually exclusive. Political communication presupposes political cognition. Political co-operation presupposes political communication. Representative digital democracy and digital plebiscites remain primarily at the level of political information. Digital deliberation adds the level of political communication to that of political information. Participatory digital democracy builds on political information and communication processes to practice political forms of co-operation. Table 9.2 gives an overview of typical aspects of the discussed digital democracy models and their information processes. Processes of political communication affect the way information processes are organised. Processes of political co-operation affect the way communication and information processes are organised. Thus, although certain elements of certain digital democracy models can be used at other levels, they often take other forms.

The methods of representative digital democracy are the most widespread and most practised form of digital democracy. Almost every politician, almost every party, and

TABLE 9.2 Forms of digital democracy

Model of democracy	Example applications
Political information/cognition in the model of digital representative democracy	Websites of parties, politicians, parliaments, ministries, and government agencies; online government information campaigns, state bureaucracy's and public authority's online applications, online forms, online channels; use of Facebook, Twitter, YouTube, and blogs by politicians and parties in election campaigns and everyday political life
Political information/cognition in the model of plebiscitary digital democracy	Online voting, electronic elections, electronic referendums, online opinion polls, registering as a follower of a politician or party on social media, registering a political preference by clicking approval buttons on social media
Political communication in the model of deliberative digital democracy	Online discussion forums, political e-mail discussion lists, political teleconferencing, electronic town halls, electronic meetings
Political co-operation in the model of participatory digital democracy	Cyber-protest, online petitions, computer-mediated participatory budgeting; application of computer-mediated decision-making systems in political, economic, and cultural contexts; wiki politics: participatory development of political information as well as political principles, demands, programmes, and laws with the help of wikis and other computer-based collaboration systems

almost every political institution today has a web presence, an e-mail address through which they can be publicly reached, a social media presence, etc. Table 9.3 gives an overview of the prevalence of certain political information processes in the EU in 2016 and 2020.

In 2016, 42 per cent of EU citizens viewed information on government websites, according to EU statistics. In 2020, this share had increased to 47 per cent. The share was particularly high in Denmark, Finland, Sweden, the Netherlands, Latvia, and Estonia. It was particularly low in Romania, Bulgaria, Italy, and Poland. According to these statistics, 28 per cent of EU citizens submitted forms online in 2016. In 2020, this share had increased to 38 per cent. The use of online forms (e.g. online tax returns) is particularly widespread in Denmark, Estonia, Finland, and the Netherlands, Sweden, while it is particularly low in Romania, Bulgaria, the Czech Republic, Italy, and Slovakia. It can be seen that when mechanisms of digital representative democracy are used, there is a digital divide between Northern and Central Europe on the one hand and Eastern and Southern Europe on the other. This certainly has to do with Europe's unequal social and economic development. Overall, however, digital information processes are already relatively established in Europe. At the level of political information and representation, therefore, major democratic innovations are not necessarily to be expected in the future. Table 9.4 shows the spread of digital plebiscites and deliberation mechanisms in Europe.

Digital Democracy and the Digital Public Sphere

TABLE 9.3 Practices of digital representative democracy in the EU in 2016 and 2020

Country	Proportion of people aged 16 to 74 who have used the Internet for obtaining information from public authorities within the last 12 months	Share of people aged 16 to 74 who submitted completed forms online within the last 12 months
EU 27	2016: 42%, 2020 (EU 27): 47%	2016: 28%, 2020: 38%
Belgium	2016: 46%, 2020: 46%	2016: 35%, 2020: 41%
Bulgaria	2016: 15%, 2020: 19%	2016: 7%, 2020: 15%
Czech Republic	2016: 33%, 2020: 53%	2016: 12%, 2020: 29%
Denmark	2016: 85%, 2020: 89%	2016: 71%, 2020: 68%
Germany	2016: 53%, 2020: 65%	2016: 17%, 2020: 26%
Estonia	2016: 66%, 2020: 67%	2016: 68%, 2020: 75%
Ireland	2016: 40%, 2020: 37%	2016: 48%, 2020: 54%
Greece	2016: 44%, 2020: 52%	2016: 26%, 2020: 27%
Spain	2016: 47%, 2020: 54%	2016: 32%, 2020: 49%
France	2016: 47%, 2020: 48%	2016: 49%, 2020: 64%
Croatia	2016: 34%, 2020: 36%	2016: 17%, 2020: 25%
Italy	2016: 19%, 2020: 19%	2016: 12%, 2020: 14%
Cyprus	2016: 36%, 2020: 48%	2016: 22%, 2020: 40%
Latvia	2016: 67%, 2020: 68%	2016: 31%, 2020: 63%
Lithuania	2016: 43%, 2020: 54%	2016: 33%, 2020: 45%
Luxembourg	2016: 55%, 2020: 30%	2016: 35%, 2020: 36%
Hungary	2016: 46%, 2020: 60%	2016: 24%, 2020: 37%
Malta	2016: 40%, 2020: 46%	2016: 19%, 2020: 35%
Netherlands	2016: 72%, 2020: 81%	2016: 55%, 2020: 73%
Austria	2016: 53%, 2020: 62%	2016: 33%, 2020: 50%
Poland	2016: 23%, 2020: 27%	2016: 19%, 2020: 34%
Portugal	2016: 42%, 2020: 39%	2016: 29%, 2020: 34%
Romania	2016: 8%, 2020: 10%	2016: 4%, 2020: 7%
Slovenia	2016: 41%, 2020: 56%	2016: 17%, 2020: 32%
Slovakia	2016: 44%, 2020: 51%	2016: 15%, 2020: 19%
Finland	2016: 78%, 2020: 85%	2016: 60%, 2020: 74%
Sweden	2016: 74%, 2020: 79%	2016: 48%, 2020: 74%
United Kingdom	2016: 42%, 2020: N/A	2016: 34%, 2020: 39%

Data source: Eurostat.

TABLE 9.4 Digital plebiscites and digital deliberation in the EU in 2015 and 2019

Country	Percentage of individuals aged 16–74 who participated in online consultations or online voting in the last three months
EU 27	2015: 7%, 2019: 10%
Belgium	2015: 5%, 2019: 5%
Bulgaria	2015: 3%, 2019: 4%
Czech Republic	2015: 5%, 2019: 6%
Denmark	2015: 13%, 2019: 15%
Germany	2015: 13%, 2019: 17%
Estonia	2015: 11%, 2019: 26%
Ireland	2015: 3%, 2019: 7%
Greece	2015: 5%, 2019: 3%
Spain	2015: 10%, 2019: 11%
France	2015: 6%, 2019: 9%
Croatia	2015: 9%, 2019: 10%
Italy	2015: 6%, 2019: 7%
Cyprus	2015: 2%, 2019: 4%
Latvia	2015: 3%, 2019: 6%
Lithuania	2015: 5%, 2019: 10%
Luxembourg	2015: 18%, 2019: 16%
Hungary	2015: 2%, 2019: 5%
Malta	2015: 12%, 2019: 16%
Netherlands	2015: 7%, 2019: 9%
Austria	2015: 7%, 2019: 9%
Poland	2015: 2%, 2019: 6%
Portugal	2015: 10%, 2019: 12%
Romania	2015: 2%, 2019: 3%
Slovenia	2015: 5%, 2019: 5%
Slovakia	2015: 2%, 2019: 5%
Finland	2015: 15%, 2019: 15%
Sweden	2015: 12%, 2019: 13%
United Kingdom	2015: 9%, 2019: 15%

Data source: Eurostat.

Digital Democracy and the Digital Public Sphere

With 8 per cent of the EU population who participated in online consultations or online voting in 2015 and 10 per cent in 2019, the use of digital elections and digital consultations in Europe is relatively low. Mechanisms of plebiscitary and deliberative politics are thus not widespread.

Plebiscites face the risk of charismatic, populist leaders defining the issues being voted on and of fundamental rights being violated or restricted. The way questions are asked in referendums and plebiscites often influences the outcome. Plebiscites are therefore subject to a certain risk of manipulation. If the majority is in favour of restricting or abolishing the fundamental rights of certain groups, it can be difficult to argue against this, as plebiscitary populists then often argue that the people have spoken, that the will of the people applies in democracy and that all objections are undemocratic. However, direct majority decisions are considered the essence of politics only in plebiscitary systems. General democratic fundamental rights, as enshrined in constitutions, serve to protect the dignity and liberties of all people regardless of the outcome of plebiscites.

How problematic plebiscites can be has recently been demonstrated in Hungary. Viktor Orbán's government held a plebiscite in 2017 asking (Bakos 2017): "What should Hungary do if Brussels wants to force the country to allow illegal immigrants into the country — despite the recent series of terrorist attacks in Europe?". There were two answer options: 1. "We should allow illegal immigrants to move freely in the country"; 2. "Illegal immigrants must be monitored until the authorities decide on their case". Later that year, the Fidesz government sent out questionnaires about George Soros to Hungarian voters, consisting of seven yes/no questions:

> Seven questions are put to the eligible voters: Whether they support Soros in 'convincing Brussels to relocate at least one million migrants per year from Africa and the Middle East to the territory of the European Union'? Whether they think that EU member states, including Hungary, should dismantle their border fences and open their borders to migrants? How they feel about Brussels' plan to introduce a mandatory quota for the resettlement of migrants? Whether they support the idea of funding migrants for the first years of their stay with the equivalent of 29,000 Euros a year? Whether migrants should be punished more leniently for criminal offences? Whether European languages and cultures should be diluted to facilitate the integration of illegal migrants? And whether voters are in favour of countries being politically attacked and financially punished for opposing immigration?
>
> (Löwenstein 2017)

The state theorist Carl Schmitt (1933), who was a member of the Nazi party from 1933 onwards, argued that the political system of Nazi fascism was based on the "primary importance of the political leadership" (8–9). Schmitt regarded the state, the party, and the people as the three pillars of Nazi-fascist society. In the political system of Nazi fascism, there was the legal possibility of the government enacting laws or holding a referendum on their introduction. "The Reich Government acknowledges the authority of the people's will which it has called upon, and as a consequence, considers it binding" (Schmitt 1933, 10). On 14 July 1933, the Referendum Act was introduced in Nazi Germany, which stated: "The Reich government may ask the people whether they agree or disagree with a measure intended by the Reich government".[2] The political leadership was responsible for deciding whether, when and on which question a referendum was to be held and how the questions and answers were to be formulated. Four referendums were held in the German Reich, namely on withdrawal from the League of Nations in 1933, the merging of the functions of president and chancellor in 1934, the occupation of the Rhineland in 1936, and the annexation of Austria to Nazi Germany in 1938. The approval rate was 95.1 per cent, 88.1 per cent, 98.8 per cent, and 98.5 per cent (99.7 per cent in Austria).[3] The example shows that plebiscites do not automatically have a democratic character, but are also compatible with fascist systems where they serve to legitimise the will of the leader.

The principle of accumulation of consent and likes dominant on social media today is an application of the plebiscite to digital technology and online culture. Social media lives by constantly organising micro-plebiscites. Today's dominant social media are constant plebiscites. They elevate the plebiscite to a lifestyle of digital culture. Every user-generated content on Twitter, Facebook, YouTube, and similar platforms demands acclamation through the click of a consent or emotional button. In the age of social media, we experience the plebiscite by mouse click and mobile phone. Since we live in times of new nationalisms and a shift of the political spectrum to the right, it cannot be ruled out that there will be society-wide digital plebiscites on populist and nationalist issues in the future. These can be organised particularly quickly via the Internet. If, for example, a refugee is suspected of murder, an immediately scheduled online referendum can lead to a majority in favour of the deportation or internment of all refugees. Are you in favour of introducing the death penalty for serious criminals? Should human rights be suspended for Muslims in the face of Islamist terror? Should the police be allowed to use torture in order to be able to act quickly and effectively in case of imminent danger? Should warships be deployed at the sea border and tanks at the land border to protect the homeland against the influx of refugees? If such questions are put to a referendum, plebiscites by mouse click combined with political fear-mongering and scapegoating by the tabloid media and

Digital Democracy and the Digital Public Sphere

politicians can lead to the enforcement of legislative initiatives that achieve a majority among the electorate and violate basic Humanistic principles and human rights. The dangers of digital plebiscites should therefore be taken very seriously in today's times.

9.4 Digital Media's Democratic Deficits and Democratic Capacities

For Jürgen Habermas (1991), the public sphere is a concept of critique that allows us to examine how power relations limit the possibilities of democratic communication. In feudalistic societies, the political and economic systems were identical. The ruling emperors, kings, and aristocrats were also the owners of the land, which they leased to peasants, thereby receiving rent. The public sphere was a non-democratic, representative public sphere in which the aristocracy and the church publicly represented and displayed their power before the people. With the emergence of capitalism, society was differentiated into the three relatively autonomous spheres of the economy, politics, and private life. The modern public sphere emerged as a mediatising sphere that creates an interface between the economy, politics, and private life and establishes links between these three spheres (see Figure 9.1). Capitalism realised liberation from the feudal yoke of serfdom and promised the realisation of new freedoms such as freedom of expression, freedom of the press, and the democratic election of representatives.

Habermas shows how the logics of capital and bureaucracy have undermined these promises and turned them into new unfreedoms. The bourgeois public sphere "contradicted its own principle of universal accessibility" (Habermas 1991, 124). Money and power structure access to and communication of the public sphere in complex ways. Freedom of expression and the ability to freely form opinions are limited by the fact that not everyone has the level of education and material resources needed to participate effectively in the public sphere. The freedom of assembly and association is restricted by the fact that large economic and bureaucratic organisations have "an oligopoly of the publicistically effective and politically relevant formation of assemblies and associations" (Habermas 1991, 228). The consequence, according to Habermas, is that there is a refeudalisation of the public sphere: corporations, political parties, and profit-oriented media organisations, which often exercise financial power through advertising orientation and journalistic power through their monopoly or oligopoly position in the market, become modern feudal lords who control the power of opinion and thus the public sphere.

In his *Theory of Communicative Action*, Habermas (1987) further developed the concept of the refeudalisation of the public sphere into the concept of the colonisation of the lifeworld. If the steering media of money and power assert influence, the result is the monetarisation or bureaucratisation of communication and the social relations based on it. "The communicative practice of everyday life is one-sidedly rationalized into a utilitarian life-style" so that "consumerism and possessive individualism, motives of performance, and competition gain the force to shape behavior" (Habermas 1987, 325). "The bureaucratic disempowering and desiccation of spontaneous processes of opinion- and will-formation expands the scope for engineering mass loyalty and makes it easier to uncouple political decision-making from concrete, identity-forming contexts of life" and establishes "a legalistic reference to legitimation through procedure" (Habermas 1987, 325).

The colonisation and refeudalisation of the public sphere have led to market, advertising, and PR logic dominating politics, so that politics becomes an apolitical market in which people and ideology are marketed. Citizens are seen and treated as "political consumers" (Habermas 1991, 216). The public sphere is thus transformed from a debating to a culture-consuming public (159–175). It becomes a pseudo-public sphere (150). "The public sphere assumes advertising functions" (175). The striving for profit maximisation of the media goes hand in hand with a flattening, tabloidisation, and "depoliticization of the content" (169).

The digital public sphere today is a colonised and feudalised public sphere dominated and shaped by the logic of accumulation and acceleration. Almost all of the dominant social media platforms are commercially oriented (see https://www.alexa.com/topsites). Wikipedia is the only dominant web platform that is non-profit and non-commercial. Two of the nine for-profit platforms sell goods through their platforms, seven use personalised advertising in combination with free services to make a profit.

In the World Wide Web, public, semi-public, and private communication takes place at the same time. The boundary between the public and the private sphere is thus blurred in the online world. At the same time, the private online plays a role not only in the form of private communication, but also as private property: the vast majority of Internet companies are privately owned and act in a profit-oriented way by selling attention, data, or digital content as a commodity. The colonisation and feudalisation of the digital public sphere takes, for example, the following forms (cf. Fuchs 2017, 2018, Chapter 7):

Digital Media's Democratic Deficits and Democratic Capacities

- Digital labour: The capital accumulation model of personalised advertising combines the surveillance of all online activity with the exploitation of user activity that produces data that is sold as a commodity to enable and personalise online advertising;
- Digital surveillance: In the surveillance-industrial Internet complex, surveillance by Internet corporations is combined with political surveillance of citizens. The governmental thinking that has proliferated since 9/11 that online surveillance can stop terrorism has proven to be inaccurate. The danger of the surveillance-industrial complex is that the presumption of innocence is abolished and a culture of constant suspicion is created.
- Digital monopolies: Google has a monopoly in search engines, Facebook in social networking, YouTube in video platforms, Amazon in online shopping. Facebook and Google together form an oligopoly of online advertising.
- Digital attention economy: Although anyone can easily produce and provide user-generated content on the Internet, online attention is unevenly distributed: Corporations, large political organisations, and celebrities achieve very high levels of attention, which manifests itself in the form of "likes", "follows", "retweets", etc.
- Digital commercial culture: Social media is dominated by shallow entertainment and advertising, while political and educational content is in the minority.
- Digital acceleration: Information flows and communication on social media have a very high speed. Therefore, there is usually no time for complex and in-depth analysis and discussions. Due to the high speed of online information flows, the attention span is usually very short.
- Lack of space and time: Information is presented in the form of very short snippets of information on Twitter and other social media. The limited information space (e.g. a maximum of 280 characters on Twitter) does not provide an opportunity for discussion and to present the complexity and contradictions of society. Politics on social media therefore often takes very one-dimensional, superficial, truncated, polarising, spectacular and personalised forms.
- Unsocial social media and individualism: Many social media are about accumulating attention and approval for individual profiles. An online culture of individualism is the result. Social media is primarily about the ego ("I") and not the common ("we"). Twitter, Facebook, and YouTube are not really "social" media at all, but individualistic media.

- Post-factual online politics and fake news: In the age of new nationalisms and the rise of authoritarian capitalism, a political culture has spread on the Internet that is dominated by right-wing ideology and false news that spreads quickly.

- Automated algorithmic politics: To a certain extent, algorithms determine online visibility and automated computer programs ("bots") replace human activities. As a result, it becomes more difficult to distinguish which online information and consent are produced by humans and which by machines.

- Fragmented publics: Micro-publics are formed on the Internet, causing society to fragment into smaller and smaller communities that are often self-contained, have no contact with each other, and no possibility to deal constructively with political conflicts and clashes of interest. The result is filter bubbles, online hatred, and cyber-bullying.

These eleven tendencies together lead to a digital public sphere that is marked and divided by economic, political, and cultural asymmetries of power. The digital public sphere takes the form of the colonised and feudalised public sphere through the logic of accumulation, advertising, monopolisation, commercialisation, commodification, acceleration, individualism, fragmentation, automation of human activity, surveillance, and ideologisation. The Internet and social media are dominated by commercial culture. Platforms are largely owned by large profit-oriented corporations. Public service media operate on the basis of a different logic. However, the idea of a public service Internet has not yet been able to gain acceptance and sounds alien to most ears, as there are hardly any alternatives to the commercial Internet today.

The communication scholar Slavko Splichal (2007, 255) gives a precise definition of public service media:

> In normative terms, public service media must be a service *of* the public, *by* the public, and *for* the public. It is a service *of* the public because it is financed by it and should be owned by it. It ought to be a service *by* the public – not only financed and controlled, but also produced by it. It must be a service *for* the public – but also for the government and other powers acting in the public sphere. In sum, public service media ought to become 'a cornerstone of democracy'.

The means of production of public service media are publicly owned. The production and circulation of content are based on a non-profit logic. Access is universal, as all citizens are given easy access to the content and technologies of public service media. In political terms, public service media offer diverse and inclusive content that promotes political understanding and discourse. In cultural terms, they offer educational content that contributes to the cultural development of individuals and society.

Due to the special qualities of public service media, they can also make a particularly valuable democratic and educational contribution to a democratic online public sphere and digital democracy if they are given the necessary material and legal opportunities to do so. Three ideas to expand digital democracy are the public service YouTube, Club 2.0, and the online advertising tax.

9.4.1 Public Service YouTube

Digital media change the traditional relationship between media production and media consumption. While in classical broadcasting these two aspects are separated, on the Internet consumers can become producers of information (so-called prosumers, i.e. producing consumers). User-generated content offers the possibility for the audience to become a producing audience. In this way, the educational and democratic mandate of public service broadcasting can be extended in the form of a participatory mandate. In this context, participation means offering an online platform with the help of which citizens can make user-generated audio-visual content publicly available.

YouTube holds a de facto monopoly in the realm of user-generated video distribution platforms. Public service media have the necessary experience and resources to develop, offer and operate online video and online audio platforms. This could create real competition for YouTube's dominance. YouTube is often criticised for distributing fake news, hateful, terrorist, and far-right content. Relatively little is done about these problems because video content is not vetted by humans when it is uploaded. YouTube works according to the logic "The more user-generated content, the better, as this creates more advertising opportunities and more profit". YouTube's advertising- and profit-orientation lead to blindness to the quality of the content. A public YouTube, on the other hand, could fulfil public service media's democratic remit by not simply allowing videos on all topics ("anything goes") to be uploaded, but by opening up certain politically and democratically relevant topics (e.g. as accompaniment to certain TV or radio programmes) to users for uploading content at certain times and for a limited period of time.

The principle should be followed that all submitted contributions are published and archived and thus made accessible to the public without time limit, thus creating a user-generated democratic online public sphere. However, the videos submitted should be checked by trained moderators before release to see if they contain racist, fascist, sexist, or otherwise discriminatory content. Such content should not be released.

The individualism of today's social media could be broken by deliberately addressing and encouraging social, cultural, and civic contexts such as school classes, university seminars, adult education courses, workplace communities, civil society organisations, etc. to submit collectively produced videos.

Public service media have large archives with vast amounts of content. These contents could be digitised and made available on a public service video and audio platform. The Creative Commons (CC) licence is a licence that allows content to be reused. The CC-BY-NC licence allows content to be reproduced, redistributed, remixed, modified, processed, and used for *non-commercial* purposes as long as the original source is acknowledged.[4] The CC-BY-NC licence is very suitable for digitised content from the archives of public service media that is made publicly available. In this way, the creativity of the users of a public service audio and video platform can be promoted, as they are allowed to generate and distribute new content with the help of archive material. In this way, public service media's educational remit could take on the form of a digital creativity remit. There is also the possibility that at certain points in time, topics are specified and users are given the opportunity to edit and remix certain archive material and upload their new creations with the help of this material. A selection of the content submitted in this way could be broadcast on television or radio on a regular basis or specific occasions. All submitted contributions could be made available on the platform.

Public service video and audio platforms can be offered in individual countries (as ORFTube, BBCTube, ARDTube, ZDFTube, SRGTube, etc.). However, it also makes sense for public media broadcasters to co-operate and jointly offer such platforms or to technically standardise their individual platforms and network them with each other. The fact that in the field of television there are cooperations, for example, between ORF, ZDF, and SRG for 3sat or between ARD, ZDF, and France Télévisions for Arte, makes it clear that it makes sense to create similar forms of co-operation in the field of online platforms. A pan-European public YouTube could rival the commercial YouTube in terms of popularity and interest and could create real competition for the Californian Internet giant Google/

Alphabet that owns YouTube. However, the argument that one is too small oneself and that one has to start at the European level is often used to postpone concrete projects or not start at all. If the legal conditions are in place nationally, it may be easier to start at the national level in order to then set an international example and, in a further step, advance European co-operation.

Dörr, Holznagel, and Picot (2016) prepared a report for ZDF on the role of public service media in the context of the Internet, social media, big data, and cloud computing. The authors state that a strictly limited time period for which public service media content remains available online time is not up to date and is unpopular with fee payers:

> The current framework conditions for broadcast-related telemedia must be adapted to current user expectations. The requirements for the length of time spent on the net must therefore be made more flexible. [...] With regard to the presence of linear content on its own platform, the time span during which the audiovisual offer is available should no longer be rigidly defined. Such a regulation is not required by European law and is no longer in keeping with the times in view of the increased importance of online services. [...] It is impossible to explain to the payers of the licence fee why the programmes produced with these fees should not be available to the public irrespective of the broadcasting date and why the ÖRR does not make its archives publicly accessible and usable – similar to public libraries.
>
> (Dörr, Holznagel and Picot 2016, 91 [translated from German])

In the context of the concept of a "Public Open Space", Dörr, Holznagel, and Picot (2016) advocate that public service media network with other public institutions to make politically and culturally relevant content available online:

> It is repeatedly argued that the offerings of public service media should be merged with other services that are important for political and cultural discourse, such as those of museums or scientific and cultural institutions. The keyword for this debate is the desire to create a national public communication space, a Public Open Space. [...] The cultural responsibility of public service media [...] certainly suggests something like this in the changed media world. Moreover, valuable integration effects can be achieved with such an approach. [...] Within this framework, it is also possible to intensify the integration of the content of public service media with that of other cultural and scientific

institutions. [...] In addition, it should be pointed out that such an approach would also significantly strengthen the cultural archive function and the open access of public content.

(Dörr, Holznagel und Picot 2016, 95–96 [translated from German])

The initiative Public Open Space argues for a

public interest-oriented digital platform (#PublicOpenSpace) that enables intensive cooperation between the world of media, education, culture and society. [...] The initiative 'PUBLIC OPEN SPACE' develops the perspective of a new digital, non-commercial platform (#PublicOpenSpace), which makes content and offers accessible while taking social diversity into account, as well as offering a public discourse space for the entire population. However, this requires a transformation process that necessitates new cooperations and alliances between media with a public service mandate and public institutions from the fields of science and education, civil society, art and culture. This includes, in particular, non-profit media committed to a comparable mission as well as civil society knowledge and education initiatives. The aim is to create an attractive, comprehensive and quality-oriented digital communication space #PublicOpenSpace, which, on the basis of the protection of private data and personal privacy and with a guarantee of content quality and diversity on all playout paths, allows users to communicate in a network oriented towards democratic values and thus represents a contribution to the success of a digital democracy. Such a #PublicOpenSpace should make the knowledge and material that has come about with public funding permanently digitally accessible and usable to a broad public. Suitable versions of open, Wikipedia-compatible licences such as Creative Commons (CC-BY-SA) offer new possibilities for this. It is therefore particularly important that, in addition to all public providers, archives and museums, public educational and cultural institutions, universities and civil society organisations are represented and involved. In particular, it must be ensured that citizens can express themselves publicly and thus help shape the democratic discourse.[5]

Forty-five representatives from science, civil society, and politics have signed a thesis paper on the future of public service broadcasting. One of their demands is that public service broadcasters should become platforms.

In the interest of the general public, there must be strong platforms that offer the public an easily recognisable contact point for public service offerings [...] A common, open and non-commercial platform of all public service providers as 'Public Open Space' would be conceivable. On this platform, not only content produced by public service broadcasters should be available, but also, for example, content from museums, the Federal Agency for Civic Education, Wikipedia, etc.[6]

(translated from German)

Volker Grassmuck (2017, translated from German) argues for the Public Open Space to be understood as a non-commercial platform of public knowledge, which is a "strong public service platform of its own", which is designed "together with other public and civil-society knowledge and cultural institutions, together with the users" and which is "deally pan-European" (213). The Public Open Space is a co-operation of public service media, a "co-operation with public scientific institutions" (215), a "co-operation with civil society initiatives" such as Wikipedia (216), a "co-operation with users" (217), and a "space of deliberative democracy" (218).

The concept of Public Open Space advocates an online platform on which various public service media, other public, and civil society institutions and users make content available as common property and public knowledge. A public YouTube is a specific expression and aspect of Public Open Space and could be part of a comprehensive open public platform. While the public service YouTube refers to publicly produced and user-generated video content, the Public Open Space is about all possible forms of open, commons-based content, i.e. not exclusively about videos published on a platform. Public service media could collaborate with non-profit civil society and cultural institutions by inviting such institutions to run special projects on the public service YouTube.

The public service YouTube is a concrete utopia of participatory democracy. A concrete utopia is a realistic and realisable project that goes beyond the current state of society and realises democratic innovations. A public service YouTube that aims at user-generated production of democratic content promotes political participation and co-operation of citizens as well as concrete, active, and creative engagement with democratic content through digital production and cooperative production. Participatory democracy means infrastructure, space, and time for democratic processes. The public service YouTube offers a material possibility and infrastructure for the practice of digital democracy.

9.4.2 Club 2.0

The dominant media are high-speed spectacles that are superficial and characterised by a lack of time. They erode the public sphere and the culture of political debate. They leave no time or space to grasp the complexity of society and develop arguments. We need the de-commodification and deceleration of the media today. We need slow media.

Slow media and slow political communication are not new. Club 2 in Austria and After Dark in the UK are prototypical examples. The journalists Kuno Knöbl and Franz Kreuzer created the concept of Club 2 for the Austrian Broadcasting Corporation (ORF). It was a discussion programme that was usually broadcast on Tuesday and Thursday. The first episode was screened on 5 October 1976, the last on 28 February 1995. About 1,400 episodes were broadcast on ORF (Der Standard 2001). Club 2 had a new edition on ORF from 2007 to 2012. However, a slightly different concept was used that did not respect the original concept.

In the United Kingdom, the media production company Open Media created a similar format based on Club 2 under the name After Dark. After Dark was broadcast once a week on Channel 4 between 1987 and 1991 and occasionally thereafter. In 2003, After Dark was shown on BBC for a short time.

The producer of After Dark Sebastian Cody describes the Club 2/After Dark concept as follows:

> the number of participants in these intimate debates (always conducted in agreeable surroundings and without an audience) was never less than four, never more than eight (like, as it happens, group therapy); the discussion should be hosted by a non-expert, whose job rotates, thus eliminating the cult of personality otherwise attaching to presenters; the participants should be a diverse assortment, all directly involved in the subject under discussion that week; and, most importantly, the programme was to be transmitted live and be open-ended. The conversation finishes when the guests decide, not when TV people make them stop.
>
> (Cody 2008)

The concept of Club 2 sounds rather unusual to many people today, as we are so used to short duration, high-speed formats, and the lack of time in the media and our everyday lives. Open, uncensored, controversial live discussions that engage the viewer differ from accelerated media in terms of space and time: Club 2 was a public space where guests

Digital Media's Democratic Deficits and Democratic Capacities met and discussed with each other in an atmosphere that offered unlimited time, that was experienced publicly and during which a socially important topic was discussed. Club 2 was a democratic public sphere organised by public service broadcasting.

Space and time are two important dimensions of the political economy of the public sphere. However, a social space that provides enough discussion time does not guarantee an engaged, critical, and dialectical discussion that transcends one-dimensionality, delves into the depth of an issue, and clarifies the commonalities and differences of worldviews and positions. Public space and time must be intelligently organised and managed so that appropriate people participate, the atmosphere is appropriate, the right discussion questions are asked and it is ensured that all guests have their say, listen to each other and that the discussion can proceed undisturbed, etc. Unrestricted space, a dialectically controversial and intellectually challenging space, and intelligent organisation are three important aspects of publicity. These are preconditions of slow media, non-commercial media, decolonised media, and public interest media.

We need slow media. Offline and online. A deceleration of the media. And slow media 2.0. Is a new version of Club 2 possible today? How could a Club 2.0 look and be designed? If one speaks of a second version ("2.0"), this means on the one hand that Club 2 should be revitalised in a new form in order to strengthen the public sphere in times of authoritarian capitalism. On the other hand, it also means that one has to take into account that society does not stand still, has developed dynamically, and therefore new public communication realities such as the Internet have emerged. A Club 2.0 therefore also needs a somewhat updated concept of Club 2 that leaves the basic rules unchanged but expands the concept. Whether Club 2.0 is transformed from a possibility into a reality is not simply a technical question, but also one of political economy. It is a political question because its implementation requires the decision to break with the logic of commercial, entertainment-oriented television dominated by reality TV. Club 2.0 is therefore also a political decision for public service media formats. Its implementation is also an economic issue, as it requires a break with the principles of colonised media, such as high speed, superficiality, scarcity of time, algorithmisation and automation of human communication, post-truth, spectacle, etc. The implementation of Club 2.0 is a question of resources and changing power relations in the media system.

Figure 9.4 illustrates a possible concept for Club 2.0. It is a basic idea that can certainly be varied. The essential aspects are the following:

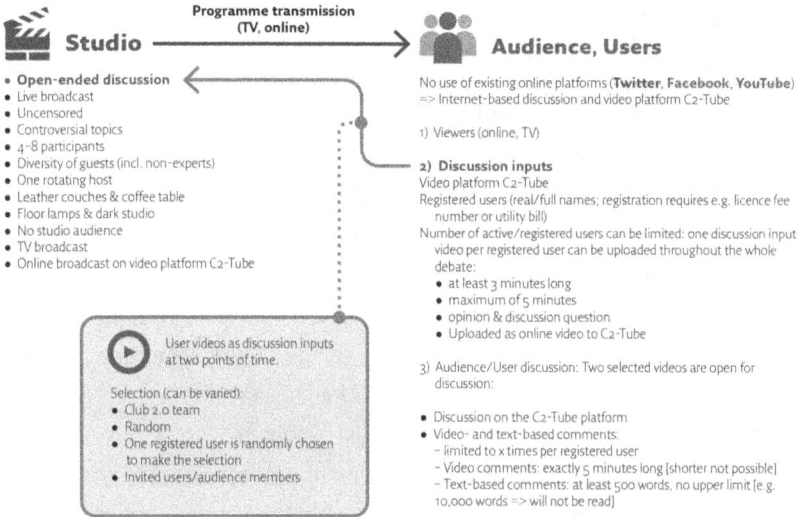

FIGURE 9.4 Concept of Club 2.0

Digital Media's Democratic Deficits and Democratic Capacities

- **Club 2's ground rules:**

  Club 2.0 uses and extends the traditional principles of Club 2. The television broadcast is based on the tried and tested Club 2 rules, which are crucial to the quality of the format. Club 2.0 broadcasts are open-ended, live, and uncensored.

- **Cross-medium:**

  Club 2.0 is a cross-medium that combines live television and the Internet, thereby transcending the boundary between these two means of communication.

- **Online video:**

  Club 2.0 is broadcast live online via a video platform.

- **Autonomous social media, no traditional social media:**

  Existing commercial social media (YouTube, Twitter, Facebook, etc.) are not suitable as they are not based on the principles of slow media and public interest media. The use of YouTube is likely to result in advertising breaks that would interrupt and destroy the discussion.

- **Autonomous video platform C2-Tube:**

  Club 2.0 needs its own online video platform (C2-Tube). C2-Tube allows viewers to watch the debate online and via a range of technical devices.

- **Interactivity:**

  C2-Tube also has interactive possibilities that can be used to a certain degree.

- **User-generated discussion inputs:**

  It is possible for users to generate discussion inputs and for these to be actively included in the programme. This characteristic is linked to a non-anonymous registration of users on the platform. Anonymity encourages Godwin's Law, which states: "As the length of an anonymous online discussion increases, the probability of a comparison to Hitler or the Nazis being made approaches one". The number of registered and active users can be limited. For example, the selection of active users can be done randomly. Alternatively, all registered users can be allowed to participate in the discussion. User-generated discussion inputs should preferably have a video format. The number of user-generated discussion inputs that can be uploaded to the platform should be limited (ideally to one upload per active user). Since information overload makes discussion difficult, it makes sense to set certain limits in order to facilitate a decelerated debate culture. Active users can make contributions to the discussion on the platform.

- **Interface between the studio discussion and the video platform:**

  At certain times during the live broadcast, a user-generated video is selected and shown as input for the studio discussion. In such videos, users formulate their opinion on the topic and can also introduce a discussion question. In a two- to three-hour discussion, about two to three such user-generated inputs could be used. It is inevitable that a selection mechanism will be used to decide which user-generated videos will be shown in the live broadcast. There are several ways to do this, such as random selection, selection by the production team, selection by a registered user determined at random, selection by a special guest, etc.

- **Discussion among users:**

  Club 2.0 allows users to discuss the programme topic with each other. The discussion can take place during and/or after the live broadcast. The selected videos that function as discussion inputs can be released for discussion on C2-Tube. Comments should be possible in video form and written form. There should be a minimum length for written comments and possibly a maximum length for video comments. In order to implement the slow media principles and avoid the Twitter effect of accelerated stagnation, the number of comments possible per user per discussion should be limited.

- **The forgetting of data:**

  Video data is very storage-intensive. Therefore, the question arises of what should happen to all those videos that are uploaded to the platform but are not broadcast and not opened for discussion. Since they are practically of less importance for public discussion, they could be deleted after a certain time. To do this, users need to be made aware that uploading a video in many cases involves forgetting the data. Contemporary social media store all data and meta-data forever. Forgetting data is therefore also a counter-principle. The online discussions consisting of written and video comments can either be archived and kept or deleted after a certain period of time.

- **Data protection and privacy friendliness:**

  Most social media platforms monitor users for economic and political purposes to achieve monetary profits through the sale of personalised advertising and to establish a surveillance society that promises more security but undermines privacy and installs a regime of categorical suspicion of all citizens. Club 2.0 should be very privacy-friendly and only store a minimum of data and meta-data necessary to run the platform. This includes not selling user data and using exemplary data protection routines. Data protection and privacy friendliness should therefore be design principles of Club 2.0. However, this does not mean that privacy protection should take the form of anonymous discussion, as anonymity can encourage online hooliganism, especially on politically controversial issues. Data protection is therefore much more about the storage and use of data.

- **Social production:**

  Today's dominant social media are highly individualistic. In contrast, the production of user-generated videos for Club 2.0 could take the form of cooperative, social production that transcends individualism and creates truly social media, so that Club 2.0 is integrated into educational institutions where people learn and create knowledge together by elaborating discussion inputs and collective positions and producing them in video form. This requires that the topics of certain Club 2.0 programmes are known somewhat in advance. This can be achieved by publishing a programme of topics. Groups of users can prepare videos together, which they can upload to the platform on the evening of the relevant Club 2.0 programme as soon as the upload option is activated.

Digital Media's Democratic Deficits and Democratic Capacities

Club 2.0 is an expression of the democratic digital public sphere. It manifests a combination of elements of deliberative and participatory democracy. Club 2.0 offers space and time for controversial political communication and enables citizens to participate collectively and individually in the discussion through videos and comments. The communicative aspect of deliberative democracy and the participatory idea of grassroots democracy are combined in the Club 2.0 model.

9.4.3 The Online Advertising Tax

The public sphere is not only a cultural space of political information and communication, but also has a political economy. Democratic innovations like Club 2.0 and a public YouTube need to be financed. One possibility is to finance these services fully or partially through the licence fee. The introduction of an online advertising tax and a digital services tax that taxes big digital capital is a good possibility to finance public service Internet services.

Google and Facebook form a duopoly in the field of online advertising. Advertising today is increasingly shifting from print to online, i.e. predominantly to Google and Facebook. However, both companies are masters of tax avoidance, which means that they pay very little tax in Europe, which in turn has led to sharp public criticism. The problem of how to effectively tax such online companies, however, has so far remained unsolved.

The sale of personalised online advertising enabled by Google and Facebook as a commodity takes place at the time of viewing or clicking on the advertisement. The advertiser pays for the personalised attention of the user, which is only possible through the collection and analysis of personal data. In other words, the users' attention given to the advertisement is sold. The users' online behaviour generates the data and meta-data necessary to enable and personalise online advertising. Facebook and Google users are not only prosumers (producing consumers who create data and meta-data), but also digital workers who create value (Fuchs 2017). The digital labour of paying attention to or clicking on online ads ultimately leads to a monetary transaction between the advertising platform (Google, Facebook, Twitter, etc.) and advertisers.

Assuming that monetary transactions should be taxed at the place where their value is produced, this means that online advertising should be taxed in the country where it is presented, viewed, and clicked on. The IP addresses of Facebook and Google users tell us which country they are in at certain times of use. Each country that Google and Facebook offer as a personalisation option for online advertising constitutes a digital permanent establishment. If these companies are legally obliged to evaluate and publish the annual advertising impressions per country, a revenue and profit share for a specific country can be calculated from this. If this country introduces a tax on online advertising, this can be used to determine an assessment basis for the online advertising tax. If online companies refuse to co-operate, the tax authorities can alternatively estimate the national share of the company's global total and profit share and possibly add a penalty for non-co-operation to the assessment basis.

Participatory democratic theory emphasises that democracy is not only a matter of communication and decision-making, but also requires resources that enable democratic institutions. The taxation of online advertising provides a basis for financing democratic innovations in the field of public service media.

9.5 Legal Aspects of Digital Democracy in the Realm of Public Service Media

Many public service broadcasters face legal limits. One legal limit that public service media encounter frequently is that they have to delete the offered content after some days. This deletion is called the retention period of public service media content.

The public service YouTube can provide past news, documentaries, and educational content on the basis of a CC-BY-NC Creative Commons licence in order to promote the public's engagement with politically and democratically relevant content. By enabling the reuse of content, the public service remit can take on particularly active and creative forms, whereby the educational and democratic mandate of public service media takes on new forms.

If democratic education, information, and communication are to be strengthened through creative and active engagement of citizens in the sense of public service media's democratic mandate, this regulation is counterproductive and prevents the potentials of digital media for the democratic mandate from being exploited. The educational and democratic mandate of public audio-visual media is severely restricted by legally established temporal and geographical restrictions (retention period of audio-visual public online content => deletion after a certain number of days; geoblocking) on online access to material relevant to democracy and education, which contributes to democratic information, education, and communication. The possibilities of digital media for storing and creatively changing and reusing audio-visual content are thus limited and not fully realised. Such legal limits should be abolished because they severely damage the digital potentials of public service media. The 2009 Communication from the European Commission on the Application of State Aid Rules to Public Service Broadcasting states, among other things, that an exception to the prohibition of state aid in the introduction of new services of public service media is only permissible under certain criteria. These include that these services serve the democratic, social and cultural needs of the population and that there is no disproportionate market impact. The Communication says:

> In order to guarantee the fundamental role of public service broadcasters in the new digital environment, public service broadcasters may use State aid to provide audiovisual services over new distribution platforms, catering for the general public as well as for special interests, provided that they are addressing the same democratic, social and cultural needs of the society in question, and do not entail disproportionate effects on the market, which are not necessary for the fulfilment of the public service remit.[7]

(§81)

The introduction of Public Value Tests and their market test resulted from this regulation.

In 2000, the EU formulated the Lisbon Strategy, as part of which it wanted to become "the most competitive and dynamic knowledge-based economy in the world" (European Council 2000). In terms of the Internet economy, this goal was not achieved: American corporations, primarily from California, dominate the Internet. It was misjudged that simply imitating and adapting the Californian model in Europe does not work, because the European media landscape has a different structure than the North American one. Public service media and alternative media (such as free radios) are important in Europe. In terms of public service media, this means that there is a very large, as yet underutilised potential to create public service Internet platforms to push back the dominance of Google, Facebook, and similar companies on the Internet in Europe.

Market and competition tests within the framework of Public Value Tests, as legally defined for example in Austria in Section 6 of the ORF Act or Great Britain as a "public interest test" in the BBC Agreement, are intended to prevent public service media from damaging competing services of commercial, profit-oriented providers. In the field of online media, however, there is no real European competition to Google, YouTube, Facebook, and Twitter. Public service Internet platforms are one way of practically challenging the monopoly position of these Californian companies. The competition regulations for public service media in the EU, which take the form of the market test in the course of Public Value Tests, have the effect of legally legitimising, securing, and deepening

Internet monopolies. Public Internet platforms such as a public YouTube have great democratic potential and could also advance a European Internet offer. This requires a rethink and changes at the legislative level. The competition and market test of Public Value Tests support the profit interests of the large American Internet corporations that dominate the market. It is time to abolish market tests and regulations that damage and limit the capacity of public service media to offer public service Internet platforms and other digital services.

9.6 Summary and Recommendations for Action

This chapter looked at the relationship between digital democracy and public service media. It addressed three questions:

Question 1: What are digital democracy and the digital public sphere?

Question 2: What are the main trends in the development of digital media today, what are digital media's democratic possibilities and deficits, and what role can public service media play in strengthening digital democracy and digital public sphere?

Question 3: What legal framework is needed so that public service media can strengthen digital democracy?

The findings can be summarised as follows:

Question 1: What are digital democracy and the digital public sphere?

- Communication is an important aspect of all models of democracy. One can distinguish between liberal-representative democratic, plebiscitary-direct democratic, deliberative, and participatory types of democracy.

- The public sphere is a sphere of public political communication that mediates between the other subsystems of society, i.e. the economy, politics, culture, and private life. The public sphere mediates political communication.

- Public service media as public communication systems with a public cultural and economic character play a special communicative and informational role in democracy. The democratic mandate should therefore guarantee that public service media contribute to democratic communication.

- Digital democracy means that democratic practices are based on digital media. Political information, communication, and co-operation processes of democracy are thereby supported by computer mediation. A distinction can be made

between liberal-representative democratic, plebiscitary, deliberative, and par-
ticipatory/grassroots democratic elements of digital democracy.

- Methods of representative digital democracy are the most widely practised
  form of digital democracy.

- Plebiscitary models of politics face the danger of accompanying the formation of an authoritarian state with charismatic leadership in which populist
  measures are legitimised by the people at the click of a mouse. The role of
  plebiscites in Nazi fascism illustrates the dangers of plebiscites. The dangers
  of plebiscites remain topical in the age of digital media.

- Democratic innovations are most likely to come from the participatory (digital)
  democracy model and the deliberative (digital) democracy model.

Question 2: What are the main trends in the development of digital media today, what
are digital media's democratic possibilities and deficits, and what role can public
service media play in strengthening digital democracy and digital public sphere?

- The logic of commerce and power limit the democratic character of the public
  sphere. The Internet and social media today are not an expression of a democratic public sphere and digital democracy, but are dominated by transnational
  corporations such as Google, Facebook, Baidu, Yahoo, Tencent, Amazon, and
  the Alibaba Group.

- The processes that Jürgen Habermas calls the feudalisation of the public sphere
  and the colonisation of the lifeworld and criticises as anti-democratic tendencies manifest themselves on the Internet as digital labour, digital surveillance,
  digital monopolies, a digital attention economy characterised by asymmetric
  power, digital commercial culture, digital acceleration, lack of space and time
  for discussion and complexity, anti-social social media, post-factual online politics, fake news, automated algorithmic politics, and fragmented publics.

- Overall, these tendencies lead to a digital public sphere characterised by economic, political, and cultural asymmetries of power. They are antithetical to
  digital democracy.

- A public service YouTube would expand the democratic and educational remit
  of public service media in the form of a participatory mandate and update the
  democratic and education remit for the digital age. The public service YouTube
  is an independent, non-profit video platform that offers archive material of public media on the basis of a Creative Commons CC-BY-NC licence and allows
  users to reuse and remix this content. Participation can take place by inviting

users to upload user-generated videos to accompany TV and radio programmes on specific topics.

- The Europe-wide co-operation of public service media as well as the co-operation between public service media and non-profit civil society and cultural organisations lends itself in the context of a public service YouTube.

- The public service YouTube is a specific audio-visual manifestation of the concept of Public Open Space and an expression of elements of participatory democracy.

- Club 2.0 is an update of the ORF concept of Club 2 in the age of digital media. Club 2.0 combines uncensored studio discussion, which is broadcast on television without a time limit and on its own video platform, with online user discussions and user-generated videos on the discussion topic. Individual user-generated videos are used as user-generated discussion inputs at certain points in the live broadcast and are aired on television as part of the live broadcast.

- The communicative aspect of deliberative democracy and the participatory idea of grassroots democracy are combined in the model of Club 2.0. Club 2 and its digital democratic update in the form of Club 2.0 are mediatised practices of deliberative and participatory democratic public sphere.

- Advertising today is increasingly shifting from print to online, and predominantly to personalised advertising by Google and Facebook that form a duopoly of online advertising, but at the same time are masters of tax avoidance, harming the public. The introduction of an online advertising tax pushes back monopolising tendencies and creates a financial basis for public digital democracy projects.

Question 3: What legal framework is needed so that public service media can strengthen digital democracy?

- The Broadcasting Communication issued by the EU Commission in 2009 has made it more difficult for public service media to develop and provide online public services that strengthen digital democracy. One expression of this trend is the market and competition test in Public Value Tests.

- As the Internet is dominated by transnational capitalist monopoly corporations, legal limitations and bans of public Internet platforms strengthen the monopoly power of these predominantly Californian companies.

Summary and Recommendations for Action

- Geoblocking, limited retention time, and legal deletion requirements of public service online content undermine the possibilities of the Internet and harm the realisation of the democratic mandate of public service media.

Based on this analysis, the following recommendations for action are formulated:

- It is recommended that public service media develop digital democracy innovations based on the models of deliberative and participatory democracy.
- It is recommended that public service media take active steps to build public service Internet platforms to counteract the lack of digital democracy on the Internet today.
- It is recommended that public service media revive Club 2 in the form of Club 2.0, realising Club 2 in its original format and combining it with an online video platform (C2-Tube). Club 2.0 would make it possible to adapt the democratic remit of public service media to the age of digital media, using elements of deliberative and participatory models of democracy.
- It is recommended that public service media prepare a detailed concept of Club 2.0 and commission accompanying studies on the introduction of Club 2.0 and the impacts on society.
- It is recommended that public service media seek to establish a public service YouTube in order to actualise the democratic remit of public service media in the age of digital media and contribute to the expansion of digital democracy and the democratic digital public sphere.
- It is recommended that public service media speak out in support of the requirement that a digital capital tax and an online advertising tax be introduced and that the revenues generated thereby be used to fund public service digital democracy projects.
- It is recommended that as a basic measure to strengthen digital democracy and to adapt the democratic mandate of public service media to the age of digital media, the national and EU legal foundations be changed in such a way that competition tests and market tests within the framework of Public Value Tests are omitted in the future.
- It is recommended that as a basic measure to strengthen digital democracy and to adapt the democratic remit of public service media to the age of digital media, the national and EU legal foundations be changed in such a way that geoblocking and the time-limited retention period of public service audio-visual content are

abolished and public service media content is made accessible globally and without time restrictions.

- It is recommended that, in order to strengthen the democratic remit of public service media, laws be amended in such a way that public service media can offer content without legal restrictions and prohibitions and without a limited retention time, provided the content advances public service media's remit in the digital age.

Notes

1 "die Förderung des Verständnisses für alle Fragen des demokratischen Zusammenlebens". Source https://www.ris.bka.gv.at/GeltendeFassung.wxe?Abfrage=Bundesnormen&Gesetzesnummer=10000785, accessed on 27 March 2021.

2 http://www.verfassungen.de/de/de33-45/volksabstimmung33.htm, accessed on 27 March 2021, translated from German: "Die Reichsregierung kann das Volk befragen, ob es einer von der Reichsregierung beabsichtigten Maßnahme zustimmt oder nicht".

3 https://de.wikipedia.org/wiki/Liste_der_Plebiszite_in_Deutschland, accessed on 27 March 2021.

4 https://creativecommons.org/licenses/by-nc/2.0/, accessed on 27 March 2021.

5 Translated from German, https://public-open-space.eu/, accessed on 27 March 2021.

6 Zur Zukunft öffentlich-rechtlicher Medien. Offener Brief, accessed on 27 March 2021: https://zukunft-öffentlich-rechtliche.de/wp-content/uploads/2017/08/Zehn-Thesen-zur-Zukunft-oeffentlich-rechtlicher-Medien_170914.pdf.

7 http://eur-lex.europa.eu/legal-content/DE/TXT/HTML/?uri=OJ:C:2009:257:FULL&from=EN, accessed on 27 March 2021.

References

Bakos, Prioska. 2017. Ein Fragebogen als neue Anti-Soros-Kampagne. *MDR Online*, 9. Oktober 2017, https://www.mdr.de/heute-im-osten/ostblogger/ungarn-volksbefragung-soros-100.html

Cody, Sebastian. 2008. *After Kelly.* After Dark, David Kelly and Lessons Learned. *Lobster* 55.

Der Standard. 2001. Der "Club 2" ging vor 25 Jahren erstmals auf Sendung. *Der Standard Online*, 5. Oktober 2001.

Dörr, Dieter, Bernd Holznagel and Arnold Picot. 2016. Legitimation und Auftrag des öffentlich-rechtlichen Fernsehens in Zeiten der Cloud. https://www.zdf.de/assets/161007-gutachten-doerr-holznagel-picot-100~original

European Council. 2000. *Lisbon European Council 23 and 24 March 2000: Presidency Conclusions.* https://www.europarl.europa.eu/summits/lis1_en.htm

Fuchs, Christian. 2018. *Digital Demagogue: Authoritarian Capitalism in the Age of Trump and Twitter.* London: Pluto.

Fuchs, Christian. 2017. *Social Media: A Critical Introduction.* London: Sage. 2. Auflage.

Fuchs, Christian. 2016. Social Media and the Public Sphere. *tripleC: Communication, Capitalism & Critique* 12 (1): 57–101.

Fuchs, Christian. 2014. *OccupyMedia! The Occupy Movement and Social Media in Crisis Capitalism.* Winchester: Zero Books.

Fuchs, Christian. 2008. *Internet and Society: Social Theory in the Information Age.* New York: Routledge.

Grassmuck, Volker. 2017. Der Bildungsauftrag öffentlich-rechtlicher Medien. In *ORF Public Value Jahresstudie 2016/17: Der Auftrag: Bildung im digitalen Zeitalter,* 91–220. Wien: ORF. http://zukunft.orf.at/rte/upload/texte/qualitaetssicherung/2017/orf_public_value_studie_web.pdf

Habermas, Jürgen. 1994. Three Normative Models of Democracy. *Constellations* 1 (1): 1–10.

Habermas, Jürgen. 1991. *The Structural Transformation of the Public Sphere. An Inquiry into a Category of Bourgeois Society.* Cambridge, MA: MIT Press.

Habermas, Jürgen. 1987. *The Theory of Communicative Action. Volume 2: Lifeworld and System: A Critique of Functionalist Reason.* Boston, MA: Beacon Press.

Hacker, Kenneth L. and Jan van Dijk. 2000. What Is Digital Democracy? In *Digital Democracy,* ed. Kenneth L. Hacker and Jan van Dijk, 1–9. London: Sage.

Held, David. 2006. *Models of Democracy.* Cambridge: Polity.

Hofkirchner, Wolfgang. 2002. *Projekt Eine Welt. Oder Kognition, Kommunikation, Kooperation. Versuch über die Selbstorganisation der Informationsgesellschaft.* Münster: LIT.

Löwenstein, Stephan. 2017. Ein Fragebogen als politisches Werkzeug. FAZ Online, 5. Oktober 2017. http://www.faz.net/aktuell/politik/volksbefragung-in-ungarn-was-ist-der-soros-plan-15229535.html

Macpherson, Crawford Brough. 1973. *Democratic Theory.* Oxford: Oxford University Press.

Schmidt, Manfred G. 1997. *Demokratietheorien.* Opladen: Leske + Budrich. 2. Auflage.

Schmitt, Carl. 1933. State, Movement, People. The Triadic Structure of the Political Unity. In *Carl Schmitt: State, Movement, People. The Triadic Structure of the Political Unity. The Question of Legality,* ed. Simona Draghici, 1–52. Corvallis, OR: Plutarch Press.

Splichal, Slavko. 2007. Does History Matter? Grasping the Idea of Public Service at its Roots. In *From Public Service Broadcasting to Public Service Media. RIPE@2007,* ed. Gregory Ferrell Lowe and Jo Bardoel, 237–256. Gothenburg: Nordicom.

van Dijk, Jan. 2000. Models of Democracy and Concepts of Communication. In *Digital Democracy,* ed. Kenneth L. Hacker and Jan van Dijk, 30–53. London: Sage.

Waschkuhn, Arno. 1998. *Demokratietheorien: Politiktheoretische und ideengeschichtliche Grundzüge.* München: Oldenbourg.

Part III

Conclusion

Chapter Ten

The Structural Transformation of the Public Sphere and Alienation

Challenges and Opportunities for the Advancement of Digital Democracy

---

10.1 Introduction

Over the last 15 years, the term "social media" has become established. As a rule, this category is used as a collective term for social networks such as Facebook and LinkedIn, video platforms such as YouTube, photo-sharing platforms such as Instagram, blogs, and microblogs such as Twitter and Weibo, messenger apps such as WhatsApp, livestreaming platforms, video apps, and wikis such as Wikipedia. It is not always clear what exactly is considered "social" about "social media" and why older information and communication media such as email, the telephone, television, and books should not also be considered social. The problem here is that in sociology there is not one, but many understandings of the social (Fuchs 2017, Chapter 2, 2021, Chapter 2).

Internet platforms like Facebook and Google, which dominate the social media sector, are among the largest corporations in the world. At the same time, social media have become an integral part of politics and public communication. Some right-wing politicians have lots of followers on various Internet platforms and spread propaganda and false news via these media. The Arab Spring and the various Occupy movements have shown that social media such as Facebook, Twitter, and YouTube are important in social movements. Today, no politician, no party, no NGO, and no social movement can do without

DOI: 10.4324/9781003331087-13

profiles on social media. Therefore, the question of the connection between social media and the public sphere arises. This chapter sheds light on this question.

Section 10.2 introduces a concept of the public sphere as a concept of critique. Section 10.3 uses the concept of public sphere to critique capitalist Internet platforms. Section 10.4 is about the potentials of a public service Internet.

10.2 The Public Sphere as a Concept of Critique

The public sphere forms an important aspect of any political and social system. Habermas understands "public" to mean spaces and resources that are "open to all" (Habermas 1991, 1). That is why we speak, for example, of public service media, public opinion, public education, public parks, etc. The concept of the public sphere has to do with the common good, with the idea that there are institutions that are not only used and owned by a privileged few, but from which everyone benefits.

Public institutions and goods are often, but not necessarily, regulated and organised by the state. There may be certain access requirements. For example, public service media in many countries are financed by a legally regulated licence fee. Such access conditions should be affordable for everyone and there should be no discrimination by class, income, origin, gender, etc. in access to public resources. Accordingly, a park to which only people with white skin colour had access at the time of segregation in the United States or South Africa was not a public good.

The public sphere also has to do with public debate about society, interests and decisions that are taken collectively and bindingly for all. It therefore has an inherently political character. The public sphere mediates between other spheres of society as a kind of interface between economy, culture, politics, and private life. An ideal-typical public sphere is a sphere that organises "critical publicity" (Habermas 1991, 237) and "critical public debate" (Habermas 1991, 52). If criticism is silenced or suppressed, there is no public sphere.

The public sphere is a sphere of public political communication that mediates between the other subsystems of society, i.e. the economy, politics, culture, and private life. The public sphere is a medium of political communication. Through the public sphere, it is possible for people to learn about, discuss and participate in politics.

The media system is part of the public sphere in modern society. Figure 10.1 illustrates a model of the role of the media in the modern public sphere (see Fuchs 2016). Media

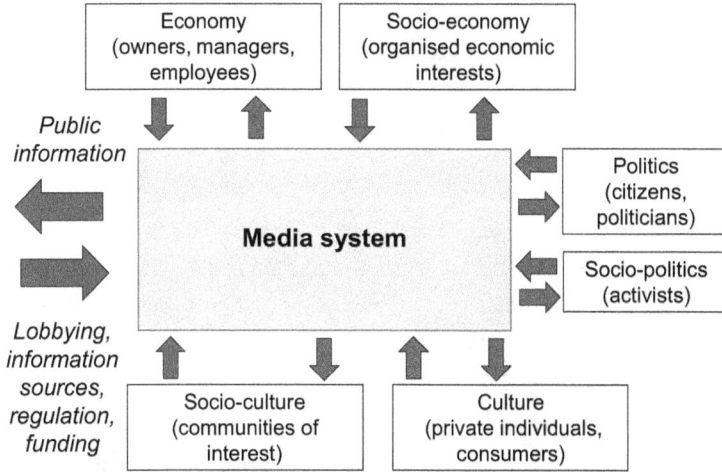

FIGURE 10.1 The media system as part of the public sphere. Further development on the basis of Habermas (2008), Diagram 1 and 2

organisations produce publicly accessible information in the media system. Such information usually serves to inform about news, to educate, and to entertain. Through public news, members of the political system inform themselves about important events in society and politics. News is a trigger of political communication. People talk about what is based in politics and ideally participate in the decision-making process themselves. In capitalist society, different interest organisations such as employers' associations, workers' associations such as trade unions, lobby organisations, political parties, NGOs, private individuals, social movements, etc. try to influence the media companies' reporting. This happens, among other things, through interviews, press releases, lobbying, advertising, public relations, the interweaving of organisations, etc. The media system interacts with the economy, politics, and culture. Citizens (purchase, broadcasting fee, subscriptions, etc.), the state (e.g. media funding) as well as business organisations (advertising) enable an economic resource base for the media to operate with. Politics regulates the framework conditions under which the media operate. Culture is a context of worldviews and ideologies that shape the climate of society and thus also have an influence on the media system and its organisations.

Following Jürgen Habermas, Friedhelm Neidhardt, and Jürgen Gerhards, we conceive of the **public sphere as a communication system** that is in principle universally accessible and open for participation by everyone, provides public access to information and enables public voice, visibility, attention, communication, and debate about topics that matter for and in society. The "public can be perceived as a knowledge-producing system that follows its own rules of establishing attention and, sometimes, consent" (Neidhardt 1993, 347).

Neidhardt and Gerhards argue that the public sphere includes speakers, media of communication, and audiences.

> There must exist: speakers. who say something; an audience, that listens; and mediators who relate speakers and the audience if they are not in immediate contact with one another-that is, journalists and the mass media. [...] The speakers try to win the attention and the consent of a larger collectivity of fellow citizens, and out of this collectivity a subsample becomes interested and engaged in those topics and opinions the speakers offer them. This subsample is the audience. It is defined by a minimum of activity in the form of observing, listening, reading. attending a meeting, or sometimes becoming speakers themselves. The audience is thus constituted by participation. [...] Speakers are conceived as all those behind the mass media who raise their voices in order to reach the public and to constitute audiences. Regularly these are 'prolocuters' of societal institutions, of interest organizations and civic groups; often, too, some are experts and intellectuals.
>
> (Neidhardt 1993, 340, 342)

> We define the public sphere (1) as a specific communication system that is distinct from other social systems. The system is constituted on the basis of the exchange of information and opinions. Individuals, groups and institutions raise certain issues and express opinions on the issues. If one does not necessarily think of the term discussion as academic events – because public communication includes demagogic communication of persuasion as well as a rational weighing of arguments – one can describe the public sphere as a system of discussion. [...] The peculiarity of the communication system of the public arises (2) from the fact that all members of a society may participate, the audience is fundamentally 'unclosed', the boundary of the system is open.[1]
>
> (Gerhards and Neidhardt 1990, 15)

There are **different types of publics** organised at different levels of society: Micropublics are small publics where humans directly encounter each speech to each other, mainly face-to-face, in everyday situations and spaces such as "cafés, coffee houses, and salons"[2] (Gerhards and Neidhardt 1990, 20). Meso-publics are medium-sized publics that take on the form of public events. An example is a rock concert or an evening-filling book presentation with accompanying audience discussion. Macro-publics are large-scale publics at the level of society where many humans access information or communicate. Mass media often play an important role in macro-publics. The public sphere is an interface of society that interacts with the economic system, the political system, and the cultural system. Based on these assumptions, Figure 10.2 presents a model of the public sphere.

We distinguish between micro-, meso-, and macro-publics as three types of public that together constitute the public sphere. Economic, political, and cultural actors interact with the public sphere in that they are the subject of news, information, and entertainment. Furthermore, economic, political, and cultural groups often try to lobby in the public sphere to gain visibility and support for their views and positions. Financial resources from the economy provide funding for media organisations operating in the public sphere (e.g. in the form of ad revenue, subscription fees, licence fees, etc.). Policies and governments' laws regulate the media. Norms, moral values, worldviews, and ideologies

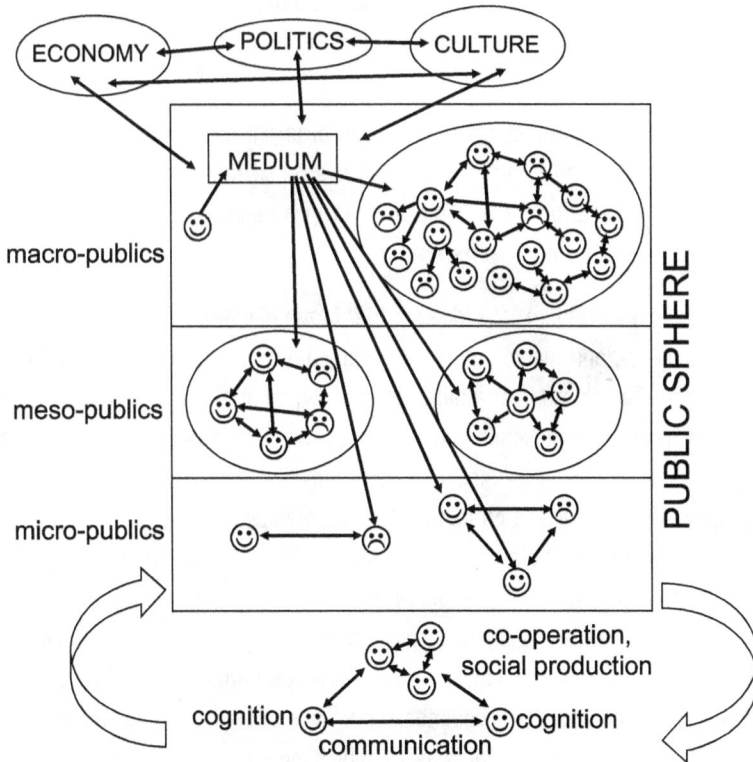

FIGURE 10.2   A model of the public sphere

as cultural structures influence public opinion, public debates, and the public sphere at large. At the level of human practices, human beings cognise, which means that they perceive, experience, and interpret the world; they communicate with each other about what is happening in their social environment and society; and they co-operate and socially produce new realities and social relations. Processes of cognition, communication, and co-operation are the practices that form the foundation of the public sphere where opinions, content, and knowledge are produced. Opinions, content, and knowledge produced in the public sphere influence the way humans think, communicate, and produce.

The traditional public sphere in modern society has been shaped by mass communication and mass media, where there is a small group of information producers using mass media for spreading information that is received and interpreted by audience members in various ways. Figure 10.3 visualises the digital transformation of the public sphere that has two main features (see Fuchs 2021):

- Prosumption:

  On the Internet, consumers of information become potential producers of information, so-called prosumers (productive consumers);

- Convergence:

  On the Internet, the boundaries between different social practices, social roles, social systems, and different publics converge so that humans on Internet platforms with the help of single profiles act in a variety of roles with a variety of practices and a variety of different publics.

The patterned boxes in Figure 10.3 indicate that in the digital public sphere, human practices, micro-, meso-, and macro-publics, economy, politics, and culture are mediated by digital platforms. The dotted lines indicate that on digital platforms, individuals' practices, cognition processes, communication processes, co-operation processes, their activities in various publics, and their social roles in the economy (e.g. as worker or manager), politics (e.g. as citizen or politicians), and culture (e.g. as member of a certain religion or community), converge on digital platforms' user profiles. The information and communication processes organised with the help of digital platforms are different from traditional mass media in that all users are enabled to produce content and communicate with others through the platforms. A digital platform is an online software environment that organises human information, activities, and communication via mobile phone apps, the Internet, and the WWW. Platforms are also social systems, which means they have a political-economic organisation and specific cultures. In the platform economy, we find organisational models

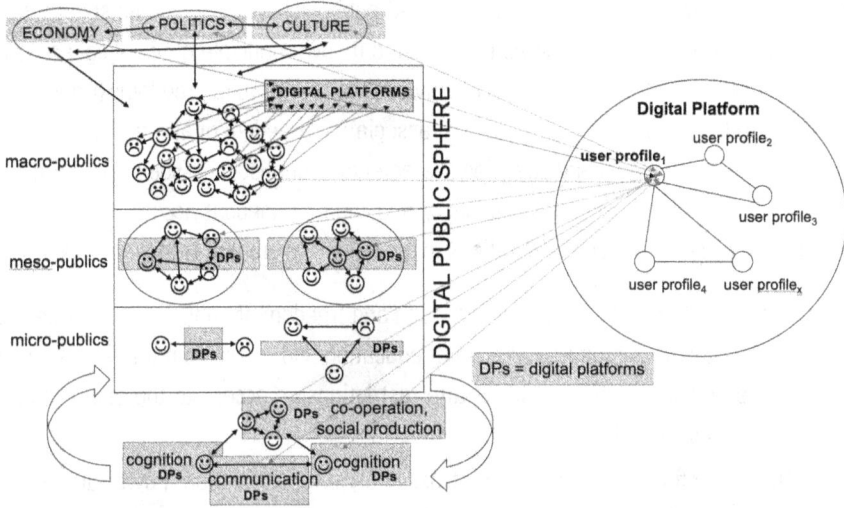

FIGURE 10.3 The digital transformation of the public sphere

that determine specific forms of ownership, work, economic activities, and relations of production. Platform governance involves laws and policies that determine what the actors involved in platforms are allowed to do, not to do, and are expected to do.

For Habermas, the public sphere is autonomous from capital and state power, that is, from economic and political power. In the public sphere, the "[I]Laws of the market [...] [are] suspended as were laws of the state" (Habermas 1991, 36). State censorship of political opinion and private ownership of the means of production of public opinion contradict the democratic character of the public sphere. For Marx, socialism is an alternative to the capitalist economy and the bourgeois state. Marx describes the Paris Commune, which existed from March to May 1871, as a socialist form of public sphere. It was an attempt to organise politics and the economy democratically.

> The Commune was formed of the municipal councillors, chosen by universal suffrage in the various wards of the town, responsible and revocable at short terms. The majority of its members were naturally working men, of acknowledged representatives of the working class. The Commune was to be a working, not a parliamentary, body, executive and legislative at the same time. [...] Public functions ceased to be the private property of the tools of the Central Government. Not only municipal administration, but the whole initiative hitherto exercised by the State was laid into the hands of the Commune.
>
> (Marx 1871, 331)

The Public Sphere as a Concept of Critique

Marx was a critic of the capitalism's restricted public sphere. "The public sphere with which Marx saw himself confronted contradicted its own principle of universal accessibility" (Habermas 1991, 122). Liberal ideology postulates individual freedoms (freedom of speech, freedom of expression, freedom of association, freedom of assembly) as universal rights. The particularist and stratified character of capitalist class society undermines these universal rights. It creates inequality and thereby unequal access to the public sphere. There are two inherent limitations to the public sphere that Habermas discusses:

- The restriction of the freedom of speech and freedom of public opinion: If people do not have the same formal level of education and the same material resources at their disposal, this may constitute restrictions on access to the public sphere (Habermas 1991, 227).
- The restriction of the freedoms of assembly and association: Powerful political and economic organisation possess "an oligopoly of the publicistically effective and politically relevant formation of assemblies and associations" (Habermas 1991, 228).

Habermas argues that the bourgeois public sphere is colonised and feudalised as a result of these restrictions. Such a public sphere is not a true public sphere, but a class-structured political space. The public sphere is a concept of immanent critique that lends itself to the critique of the deficits and problems of modern society. Habermas does not say that the public sphere exists everywhere, but that it should exist. Immanent critique compares proclaimed ideals with actuality. If it finds that reality contradicts its own ideals, it becomes clear that there is a fundamental contradiction and that reality must be changed to overcome this incongruity. The bourgeois public sphere creates its own limits and thus its own immanent critique.

Public spaces and public spheres do not exist only in the West. The claim that the public sphere is a Western-centric or Eurocentric concept is misguided. Such a critique also risks justifying undemocratic regimes that are anti-Western and promote authoritarianism under the guise of opposition to Western-centrism and Eurocentrism. The public teahouse is an ancient cultural practice and space that can be found in many parts of the world. Di Wang compares the Chinese teahouse of the early 20th century to British public houses (Wang 2008). It is a public space that people from all walks of life and classes frequent for different reasons. The Chinese word for the teahouse is 茶馆 (cháguǎn). Chengdu is the capital of the south-western Chinese province of Sichuan. "Teahouses in Chengdu, however, were renowned for their multiclass orientation. One of the 'virtues' of Chengdu teahouses was their 'relative equality'" (Wang 2008, 420). Women were excluded at first, but had full access from around 1930. These teahouses were not only cultural spaces but also political meeting places where political debates took place and where political plays were performed, attracting the interest not only of citizens but also of government informers. Wang discusses the importance of teahouses in the 1911 railway protests in Chengdu. Public meeting places are spheres of citizen engagement that can become spheres of political communication and protest.

The various Occupy movements that emerged after the global economic crisis that began in 2008 were movements in which protest and the occupation of spaces converged. Self-managed public spheres were created for political communication. The creation of these public spheres took place not only in the West, but in many parts of the world in times of global capitalist and social crisis. A common aspect of these protests was that in many of them the tactic of transforming spaces into public spheres and political spaces was used and that these protests took place in a general social crisis. Resistance is as old as class society. Public spheres have been produced as resistant publics throughout the history of class societies. So public spheres exist wherever people gather to organise collectively and express their anger and resentment at exploitation and domination.

One of the connections between Habermas' *Structural Transformation of the Public Sphere* (Habermas 1991) and his *Theory of Communicative Action* (Habermas 1984, 1987) is the elucidation of how stratification processes work in modern society. While Habermas speaks of the "refeudalisation" of the public sphere in his early work (Habermas 1991, 142, 158, 195, 200, 231), later the term colonisation of the lifeworld comes to the fore, encompassing "monetarization and bureaucratization" (Habermas 1987, 321, 323, 325, 386, 403). According to Habermas (1987, 323), these two processes "instrumentalise" the lifeworld and thus the public sphere. In my own approach, I assume that it is not two but three processes of exercising power that colonise and refeudalise the public sphere (Fuchs 2008, 2011, 2014, 2015, 2020a):

- Through *commodification* and *class structuration*, the logic of money, capital, and the commodity form penetrates people's everyday lives and lifeworlds.
- Through *domination*, society is organised in such a way that particular interests prevail and some people or groups or individuals gain advantages at the expense of others.
- *Ideologisation* presents partial interests, exploitation, and domination as natural and necessary by presenting reality in a distorted or manipulated way.

The commodity form, domination, and ideology are the three main forms of stratification in capitalist society. The critical theory of the public sphere is a critique of the commodity form, a critique of domination, and a critique of ideology. A critical theory of the public sphere is therefore a critique of alienation. What Horkheimer (1947) called instrumental reason, Marcuse (1941) called technological rationality[3] and Lukács (1923/1971) called reification, takes on three forms in capitalism:

- Class structuration and the commodity form instrumentalise people's labour power and people's needs in capitalist consumption.
- Political rule instrumentalises people's ability to act politically in such a way that they do not make decisions themselves but leave them to dominant groups.
- Ideology tries to bend and instrumentalise people's consciousness and their subjective interests.

Karl Marx (1867) emphasised that the logic of accumulation shapes capitalism. This logic has its origin in the capitalist economy. But it also shapes modern politics and modern culture, which are about the accumulation of political and cultural power. The accumulation of power takes the form of the accumulation of capital, decision-making power, and defining power. Accumulation results in asymmetries of power, namely class structures, structures of domination, and ideology (see Table 10.1).

Alienation means that people are confronted with structures and conditions that they cannot control and influence themselves. Individuals do not control the economic, political, and cultural products that influence their lives and everyday life. Alienation means the "*loss* of the object, his product" (Marx 1844, 273). Alienation means "vitality as a sacrifice of life, production of the object as loss of the object to an alien power, to an *alien* person" (Marx 1844, 281). Use-values, collectively binding decisions, and collective meanings are social products resulting from human practices. In

TABLE 10.1 Antagonisms in three types of alienation

Type of alienation	Alienating subjects	Alienated subjects
Economic alienation: exploitation	Ruling class, exploiters	Exploited class
Political alienation: domination	Dictator, dictatorial groups	Excluded individuals and groups
Cultural alienation: ideology that results in disrespect	Ideologues	Disrespected individuals and groups

TABLE 10.2 The main actors in alienated society and in Humanist society. Based on Fuchs (2020a, 103: Table 4.4)

	Alienated society	Humanism
Economy	The exploited	The socialist/commoner
Politics	The dictator	The democrat
Culture	The ideologue/demagogue	The friend

capitalist society, however, they are controlled by only a few, resulting in objectively alienated conditions.

Table 10.2 illustrates the antagonism between alienated and Humanist society along the three social dimensions of economy, politics, and culture. In an alienated society, the main actors are the exploiter in the economy, the dictator in politics, and the ideologue/demagogue in culture. Humanism is the alternative to the alienated society. In a Humanist society, the main actors are the socialist and the commoner in the economy, the democrat in politics, and the solidary friend in culture.

10.3 The Capitalist Colonisation of the Digital Public Sphere

In discussions about the Internet and social media, it is relatively often heard that through the possibilities of prosumption (consuming producers on the Internet: Media consumers become producers of content) and user-generated content, an electronic democracy, a digital/virtual public sphere, and a participatory culture are emerging. These arguments are also widespread in the academic debate.[4] A far-reaching democratisation of society, including the capitalist economy, is inferred from a technical change, although class antagonisms, political antagonisms, and ideological lines of conflict continue to exist and have even deepened. Is today's Internet and social media a new public sphere that expands democracy, or a new form of colonisation of the public sphere?

Jürgen Habermas has been sceptical in respect to the question of whether or not, how, and to what degree the Internet and social media advance a public sphere. He argues that the Internet is democratic only in that it "can undermine the censorship of authoritarian regimes" but that it also fragments the public into "a huge number of issue publics" (Habermas 2006, 423). In a recent essay, Habermas (2021) interprets studies of the public sphere as confirmation of his view that the Internet and social media have resulted in "semi-public, fragmented and self-circulating discussion" and deform the public sphere (Habermas 2021, 471, translation from German). In his most recent monograph, Habermas (2019, volume 2: 799, translated from German) argues that containing the "dangers of the oligopolistically dominated and for the time being destructively rampant Internet communication" requires transnational political regulation, which shows the importance of policies in the context of the (digital) public sphere.

Users of today's Internet and social media face ten problems (see Fuchs 2016, 2017, 2019b, 2021):

1) **Digital capitalism/digital class relations:**

   Digital capital exploits digital labour. It results in capitalist digital monopolies and contributes to the precarisation of life.

2) **Digital individualism**:

   Digital individualism consists of users accumulating attention with and approval of individual profiles and postings on social media. Its logic treats people as mere competitors, undermining interpersonal solidarity.

3) **Digital surveillance**:

   State institutions and capitalist companies carry out digital surveillance of people as part of the digital-industrial and surveillance-industrial complex.

4) **Anti-social social media**:

   Social media are anti-social social media. Edward Snowden's revelations and the Cambridge Analytica scandal have shown that capitalist social media are a danger to democracy. Right-wing ideologues and demagogues spread digital authoritarianism on social media and attack the public service media, independently acting media and quality media as "metropolitan elite media".

5) **Algorithmic politics**:

   Social media are characterised by automated, algorithmic politics. Automated computer programmes ("bots") replace human activity, post information, and generate "likes". This has made it more difficult to distinguish which information and which approval comes from a human or a machine.

6) **Filter bubbles**:

   Fragmented online publics are organised as filter bubbles in which opinions are homogeneous and disagreements either do not exist or are avoided.

7) **Digital tabloids**:

   The digital culture industry has organised social media as digital tabloids controlled by digital corporations. Online advertising and tabloid entertainment dominate the Internet, displacing engagement with political and educational content.

8) **Influencer capitalism**:

On social media, so-called "influencers" shape public opinion, creating power asymmetries in terms of online attention and visibility, and living a commodified online culture that presents the world as an endless shopping mile and a huge shopping mall.

9) **Digital acceleration**:

Due to digital acceleration, our attention capacity is strained by superficial information that hits us at very high speed. There is too little time and too little space for conversations and debates on social media.

10) **Fake news**:

Post-truth politics and fake news are spreading globally through social media. In the age of new nationalisms and new authoritarianism, a culture has emerged in which false online news is spread, many people distrust facts and experts, and there is an emotionalisation of politics through which people do not rationally examine what is real and what is fiction, but assume something is true if it suits their state of mind and ideology (see Fuchs 2018, 2020a).

These ten tendencies have led to a digital public sphere colonised and feudalised by capital, state power, and ideology, characterised by economic, political, and cultural asymmetries of power. The Internet certainly has potentials to socialise human activities in the form of communication, cooperative work, community building, and the creation of digital commons. However, class relations and structures of domination colonise the Humanistic potentials of the Internet and society. In contemporary capitalism, people are confronted with an antagonism between precarity and austerity. The Internet and social media are shaped by class structures and inequalities.

Social media today are insufficiently social. They are dominated by capitalist corporations, demagogues, and ideologues, although they carry germinal forms and potentials for a world and forms of communication beyond capitalism. Digital alternatives like Wikipedia, digital workers' cooperatives,[5] alternative online media like Democracy Now! digital commons like Creative Commons or free software are the manifestation of a truly social and socialised Internet. Within capitalism, however, such projects often remain precarious and can only challenge the power of the dominant corporations and actors (Google, Facebook, Apple, Microsoft, Amazon, etc.) in a very limited way. The history of alternative projects within capitalism is a history of resource scarcity and precarious, often unpaid and self-exploitative labour.

The Capitalist Colonisation of the Digital Public Sphere

TABLE 10.3 Three forms of digital alienation

Form of digital alienation	Manifestations of digital alienation
Economic digital alienation:digital exploitation	(1) Digital capital/digital labour (digital class relations), digital monopolies; (2) digital accumulation/individualism/competition
Political digital alienation:digital domination	(3) digital surveillance, (4) anti-social social media/digital authoritarianism, (5) algorithmic politics, (6) fragmented online publics and online filter bubbles
Cultural digital alienation:digital ideology	(7) digital culture industry/digital tabloids, (8) influencer capitalism, (9) digital acceleration, (10) false news/algorithmic politics

TABLE 10.4 Antagonisms in three forms of digital alienation

Form of alienation	Alienating subjects	Alienated subjects
Economic alienation: exploitation	Digital capital	Digital labour
Political alienation: domination	Digital dictators	Digital citizens
Cultural alienation: ideology, disrespect	Digital ideologues	Digital humans

In Table 10.3, the ten problems of social media and the Internet in digital capitalism already elaborated are related to the three forms of alienation. There are thus economic, political, and cultural forms of digital alienation.

In Table 10.4, digital alienation is presented in the form of three antagonisms: class antagonism, in which digital capital exploits digital labour; political antagonism between digital dictators and digital citizens; and cultural antagonism between digital ideologues and digital people. Alienation is the instrumentalisation of human beings. In digital alienation, people are instrumentalised with the help of digital technologies such as the Internet, mobile phones, social media, apps, Big Data, Industry 4.0, artificial intelligence, cloud computing, etc. Digital alienation is the instrumentalisation of humans online.

For a detailed analysis of the digital antagonisms through which the public sphere is colonised and feudalised in digital capitalism, we must refer the reader to further literature (Fuchs 2016, 2017, 2018, 2019b, 2019c, 2020a, 2020b, 2020c, 2021). However, we can cite individual examples here.

In the year 2020, the world's largest Internet corporations were Apple, Microsoft, Alphabet/Google, Amazon, Alibaba, and Facebook. In the Forbes list of the 2,000 largest corporations in the world, they ranked ninth (Apple), 13th (Microsoft, Alphabet/Google), 22nd

(Amazon), 31st (Alibaba), and 39th (Facebook) in the same year.[6] Digital commodities sold by these corporations include hardware (Apple), software (Microsoft), online advertising (Google, Facebook), and digital services such as online shopping (Amazon, Alibaba). The turnover of these six groups amounted to 857.5 billion US dollars in 2019. The turnover of these six groups is roughly equal to the GDP of the 22 least developed countries in the world, whose combined GDP in 2018 was 858.3 billion US dollars. These countries are Sudan, Haiti, Afghanistan, Djibouti, Malawi, Ethiopia, Gambia, Guinea, Liberia, Yemen, Guinea-Bissau, Congo, Mozambique, Sierra Leone, Burkina Faso, Eritrea, Mali, Burundi, South Sudan, Chad, the Central African Republic, and Niger (United Nations 2019). Five digital corporations are together economically more powerful than 22 states. And these corporations constitute monopolies in operating systems (Microsoft), search engines (Google), online shopping (Amazon and Alibaba), and social networks (Facebook). The Internet economy is dominated by a few global corporations. Therefore, one cannot speak of digital capitalism having led to an end of monopoly power or a plural economy. Capital concentration is an inherent tendency of capitalism.

Table 10.5 shows data on the ten most viewed YouTube videos. YouTube is the world's most used Internet platform after Google.[7] In discussions about the digital public sphere,

TABLE 10.5 The most watched YouTube videos of all times

Position	Title	Video Type	Owner	Number of Views
1	Pinkfong Kids' Songs & Stories – Baby Shark Dance	Children's music	SmartStudy (Samsung Publishing)	8.3 billion
2	Luis Fonsi – Despacito	Music	Universal Music (Vivendi)	7.3 billion
3	Ed Sheeran – Shape of You	Music	Warner Music	5.3 billion
4	LooLoo Kids – Johny Johny Yes Papa	Children's music	Mora TV	5.1 billion
5	Wiz Khalifa – See You Again	Music	Warner Music	5.1 billion
6	Masha and the Bear – Recipe for Disaster	Children's entertainment	Animaccord Animation Studio	4.4 billion
7	Mark Ronson – Uptown Funk	Music	Sony Music	4.1 billion
8	Psy – Gangnam Style	Music	YG Entertainment (distributed by Universal)	4.0 billion
9	Miroshka TV – Learning Colours – Colourful Eggs on a Farm	Children's music	Miroshka TV	3.9 billion
10	Cocomelon Nursery Rhymes – Bath Song	Children's music	Moonbug Entertainment	3.9 billion

Source: https://en.wikipedia.org/wiki/List_of_most-viewed_YouTube_videos, accessed on 14 April 2021.

The Capitalist Colonisation of the Digital Public Sphere

it is often heard that user-generated content means that everyone has a voice on social media and that the public sphere has become pluralistic and participatory. On the
Internet, it is true that anyone can easily produce and publish digital content. But there
are asymmetries of visibility and attention. Entertainment dominates over education and
politics. At the content level, social media is primarily digital tabloid media. Multimedia
corporations and celebrities dominate online visibility and online attention. All of the ten
most viewed YouTube videos are music videos. Copyright is controlled by profit-oriented
corporations. The example shows that Internet platforms have not created a participatory culture, but that media corporations and celebrities control online attention and the
online public sphere.

The Cambridge Analytica scandal dominated the world news in the first half of 2018.
Cambridge Analytica was a consulting firm founded in 2013 that was active in the use of
Big Data, among other things. Donald Trump's former far-right adviser Steve Bannon was
the vice president of this company. Cambridge Analytica bought access to the personal
data of 90 million people collected on Facebook via a personality test. Personal data
was collected from participants' Facebook profiles. Cambridge Analytica used this data
in Donald Trump's election campaign to spread personalised fake news. This scandal is
remarkable in several respects:

- The Cambridge Analytica scandal shows that right-wing extremists will resort to
  any means at their disposal to spread their ideology. This also includes fake news
  and surveillance.
- The Cambridge Analytica scandal shows that Facebook accepts dangers for democracy in order to make money from data. Facebook operates on the logic that
  ever-larger amounts of data processed and collected on the Internet are good for
  the profits of the corporation, which uses them to personalise advertising, i.e. to
  tailor it to individual user behaviour, and to sell it.
- The Cambridge Analytica scandal shows that the neoliberal deregulation of the
  economy has led to Internet corporations being able to act as they wish.
- The Cambridge Analytica scandal shows the connection between digital fascism,
  digital capitalism, and digital neoliberalism, which poses a threat to democracy.

The three examples (Internet corporations' economic power, YouTube's attention economy, Cambridge Analytica) exemplify individual dimensions of the ten forms of colonisation of the digital public sphere discussed in this section. The first example shows the
power of Internet corporations, which illustrated aspects of digital monopolies (aspect

one of the ten problems of today's Internet). The second example was about the digital attention economy on YouTube. This is an expression of digital tabloidisation and the digital culture industry (Problem 7), where celebrities dominate attention and visibility (Problem 8). The Cambridge Analytica scandal illustrates a combination of several of the ten problems, namely digital capitalism (Problem 1), digital surveillance (Problem 3), digital authoritarianism (Problem 5), and online fake news (Problem 10).

The three examples illustrate that the assumption that the Internet and social media are a democratic, digital public sphere is a myth and an ideology that trivialises the real power of Internet corporations and phenomena such as online fake news and online fascism. But the question is whether a democratic Internet is possible. The next section deals with this question in the context of public service media.

10.4 For a Public Service Internet

The digital public sphere has the form of the colonised and feudalised public sphere through the logic of accumulation, advertising, monopolisation, commercialisation, commodification, acceleration, individualism, fragmentation, the automation of human activity, surveillance, and ideologisation. The Internet and social media are dominated by commercial culture. Platforms are largely owned by large profit-oriented corporations. Public service media operate on the basis of a different logic. However, the idea of a public service Internet has not yet been able to gain acceptance and sounds alien to most ears, as there are hardly any alternatives to the capitalist Internet today.

Media have (a) a political-economic and (b) a cultural dimension. On the one hand, they need resources such as money, legal frameworks, staff, and organisational structures in order to exist. In this respect, they are economic organisations. However, they are special economic organisations that are also cultural organisations, since they produce meanings of society that serve public information, communication, and opinion-forming. Since opinion formation and communication also include political opinion formation and political communication, media organisations have implications for democracy and the political system. As cultural organisations, all media organisations are public because they publish information. As economic organisations, on the other hand, only certain media organisations are public, while others take on a private sector character, i.e. are organisations that have private owners and operate for profit. Public service media and civil society media, on the other hand, are not profit-oriented and are collectively owned by the state or a community. Table 10.1 illustrates these distinctions. Public service media are public in the sense of the cultural public and the political-economic public. They publish information and are owned by the public.

The communication studies scholar Slavko Splichal (2007, 255) gives a precise definition of public service media:

> In normative terms, public service media must be a service *of* the public, *by* the public, and *for* the public. It is a service *of* the public because it is financed by it and should be owned by it. It ought to be a service *by* the public — not only financed and controlled, but also produced by it. It must be a service *for* the public — but also for the government and other powers acting in the public sphere. In sum, public service media ought to become 'a cornerstone of democracy.'
>
> (Splichal 2007, 255)

The means of production of public service media are publicly owned. The production and circulation of content are based on a non-profit logic. Access is universal, as all citizens are given easy access to the content and technologies of public service media. In political terms, public service media offer diverse and inclusive content that promotes political understanding and discourse. In cultural terms, they offer educational content that contributes to the cultural development of individuals and society.

Due to the special qualities of public service media, they can also make a particularly valuable democratic and educational contribution to a democratic online public sphere and digital democracy if they are given the necessary material and legal opportunities to do so.

Signed by more than 1,000 individuals, the public service media and public service Internet Manifesto calls for the defence of the existence, funding, and independence of public service media and the creation of a public service Internet (Fuchs and Unterberger 2021). Among those who have signed the Manifesto, which was initiated by Christian Fuchs and Klaus Unterberger, are Jürgen Habermas, Noam Chomsky, the International Federation of Journalists, the European Federation of Journalists, the International Association for Media and Communication Research (IAMCR), and the European Communication and Research Education Association (ECREA).

Two ideas for the expansion of digital democracy and the creation of public service Internet platforms are the *public service YouTube* and *Club 2.0*.

10.4.1 Public Service YouTube

Digital media change the traditional relationship between media production and media consumption. While in classical broadcasting these two aspects are separated, on the Internet consumers can become producers of information (so-called prosumers, i.e. producing consumers). User-generated content offers the possibility for the audience to become a producing audience. In this way, the educational and democratic mandate of public service broadcasting can be extended in the form of a participatory mandate. In this context, participation means offering an online platform with the help of which citizens can make user-generated audio-visual content publicly available.

YouTube holds a de facto monopoly in the realm of user-generated video distribution platforms. Public service media have the necessary experience and resources to develop, offer and operate online video and online audio platforms. This could create real competition for YouTube's dominance. YouTube is often criticised for distributing fake news, hateful, terrorist, and far-right content. Relatively little is done about these problems because video content is not vetted by humans when it is uploaded. YouTube works according to the logic "The more user-generated content, the better, as this creates more advertising opportunities and more profit". YouTube's advertising- and profit-orientation leads to blindness to the quality of the content. A public YouTube, on the other hand, could fulfil public service media's democratic remit by not simply allowing videos on all topics ("anything goes") to be uploaded, but by opening up certain politically and democratically relevant topics (e.g. as accompaniment to certain TV or radio programmes) to users for uploading content at certain times and for a limited period of time.

The principle should be followed that all submitted contributions are published and archived and thus made accessible to the public without time limit, thus creating a user-generated democratic online public sphere. However, the videos submitted should be checked by trained moderators before release to see if they contain racist, fascist, sexist or otherwise discriminatory content. Such content should not be released.

The individualism of today's social media could be broken by deliberately addressing and encouraging social, cultural, and civic contexts such as school classes, university seminars, adult education courses, workplace communities, civil society organisations, etc. to submit collectively produced videos.

Public service media have large archives with vast amounts of content. These contents could be digitised and made available on a public service video and audio platform. The Creative Commons (CC) licence is a licence that allows content to be reused. The

CC-BY-NC licence allows content to be reproduced, redistributed, remixed, modified, processed, and used for *non-commercial* purposes as long as the original source is acknowledged.[8] The CC-BY-NC licence is very suitable for digitised content from the archives of public service media that is made publicly available. In this way, the creativity of the users of a public service audio and video platform can be promoted, as they are allowed to generate and distribute new content with the help of archive material. In this way, public service media's educational remit could take on the form of a digital creativity remit. There is also the possibility that at certain points in time, topics are specified and users are given the opportunity to edit and remix certain archive material and upload their new creations with the help of this material. A selection of the content submitted in this way could be broadcast on television or radio on a regular basis or specific occasions. All submitted contributions could be made available on the platform.

Public service video and audio platforms can be offered in individual countries (as ORFTube, BBCTube, ARDTube, ZDFTube, SRGTube, etc.). However, it also makes sense for public media broadcasters to co-operate and jointly offer such platforms or to technically standardise their individual platforms and network them with each other. The fact that in the field of television there are cooperations, for example, between ORF, ZDF, and SRG for 3sat or between ARD, ZDF, and France Télévisions for Arte, makes it clear that it makes sense to create similar forms of co-operation in the field of online platforms. A pan-European public YouTube could rival the commercial YouTube in terms of popularity and interest and could create real competition for the Californian Internet giant Google/Alphabet that owns YouTube. However, the argument that one is too small oneself and that one has to start at the European level is often used to postpone concrete projects or not start at all. If the legal conditions are in place nationally, it may be easier to start at the national level in order to then set an international example and, in a further step, advance European co-operation.

The public service YouTube is a concrete utopia of participatory democracy. A concrete utopia is a realistic and realisable project that goes beyond the current state of society and realises democratic innovations. A public service YouTube that aims at user-generated production of democratic content promotes political participation and co-operation of citizens as well as concrete, active and creative engagement with democratic content through digital production and cooperative production. Participatory democracy means infrastructure, space, and time for democratic processes. The public service YouTube offers a material possibility and infrastructure for the practice of digital democracy.

10.4.2 Club 2.0

The journalists Kuno Knöbl and Franz Kreuzer created the concept of Club 2 for the Austrian Broadcasting Corporation (ORF). It was a discussion programme that was usually broadcast on Tuesday and Thursday. The first episode was screened on 5 October 1976, the last on 28 February 1995. About 1,400 episodes were broadcast on ORF.

The concept of Club 2 sounds rather unusual to many people today, as we are so used to short duration, high-speed formats, and the lack of time in the media and our everyday lives. Open, uncensored, controversial live discussions that engage the viewer differ from accelerated media in terms of space and time: Club 2 was a public space where guests met and discussed with each other in an atmosphere that offered unlimited time, that was experienced publicly and during which a socially important topic was discussed. Club 2 was a democratic public sphere organised by public service broadcasting.

Space and time are two important dimensions of the political economy of the public sphere. However, a social space that provides enough discussion time does not guarantee an engaged, critical, and dialectical discussion that transcends one-dimensionality, delves into the depth of an issue, and clarifies the commonalities and differences of worldviews and positions. Public space and time must be intelligently organised and managed so that appropriate people participate, the atmosphere is appropriate, the right discussion questions are asked and it is ensured that all guests have their say, listen to each other and that the discussion can proceed undisturbed, etc. Unrestricted space, a dialectically controversial and intellectually challenging space and intelligent organisation are three important aspects of publicity. These are preconditions of slow media, non-commercial media, decolonised media, and public interest media.

Is a new version of Club 2 possible today? How could a Club 2.0 look and be designed? If one speaks of a second version ("2.0"), this means on the one hand that Club 2 should be revitalised in a new form in order to strengthen the public sphere in times of authoritarian capitalism. On the other hand, it also means that one has to take into account that society does not stand still, has developed dynamically, and therefore new public communication realities such as the Internet have emerged. A Club 2.0 therefore also needs a somewhat updated concept of Club 2 that leaves the basic rules unchanged but expands the concept. Whether Club 2.0 is transformed from a possibility into a reality is not simply a technical question, but also one of political

For a Public Service Internet

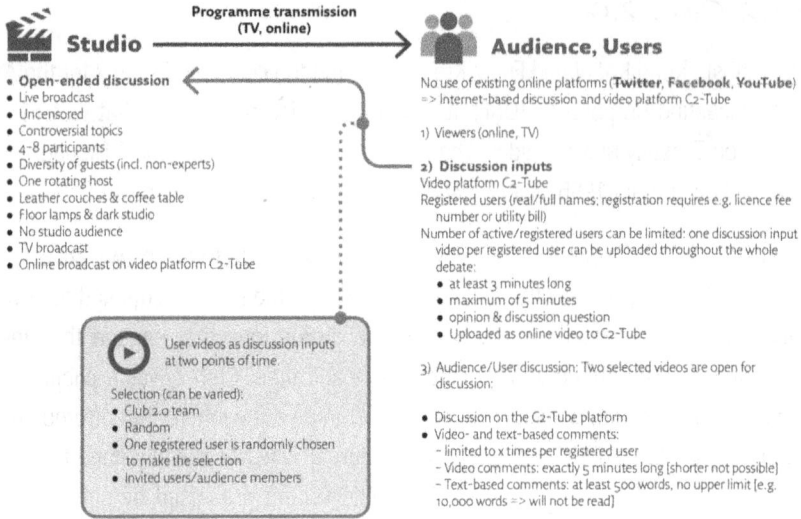

FIGURE 10.4 Concept of Club 2.0

economy. It is a political question because its implementation requires the decision to break with the logic of commercial, entertainment-oriented television dominated by reality TV. Club 2.0 is therefore also a political decision for public service media formats. Its implementation is also an economic issue, as it requires a break with the principles of colonised media, such as high speed, superficiality, scarcity of time, algorithmisation and automation of human communication, post-truth, spectacle, etc. The implementation of Club 2.0 is a question of resources and changing power relations in the media system.

Figure 10.4 illustrates a possible concept for Club 2.0. It is a basic idea that can certainly be varied. The essential aspects are the following:

- **Club 2's ground rules:**

  Club 2.0 uses and extends the traditional principles of Club 2. The television broadcast is based on the tried and tested Club 2 rules, which are crucial to the quality of the format. Club 2.0 broadcasts are open-ended, live, and uncensored.

- **Cross-medium:**

  Club 2.0 is a cross-medium that combines live television and the Internet, thereby transcending the boundary between these two means of communication.

- **Online video:**

  Club 2.0 is broadcast live online via a video platform.

- **Autonomous social media, no traditional social media:**

  Existing commercial social media (YouTube, Twitter, Facebook, etc.) are not suitable as they are not based on the principles of slow media and public interest media. The use of YouTube is likely to result in advertising breaks that would interrupt and destroy the discussion.

- **Autonomous video platform C2-Tube:**

  Club 2.0 needs its own online video platform (C2-Tube). C2-Tube allows viewers to watch the debate online and via a range of technical devices.

- **Interactivity:**

  C2-Tube also has interactive possibilities that can be used to a certain degree.

- **User-generated discussion inputs:**

  It is possible for users to generate discussion inputs and for these to be actively included in the programme. This characteristic is linked to a non-anonymous registration of users on the platform. Anonymity encourages Godwin's Law, which states: "As the length of an anonymous online discussion increases, the probability of a comparison to Hitler or the Nazis being made approaches one". The number of registered and active users can be limited. For example, the selection of active users can be done randomly. Alternatively, all registered users can be allowed to participate in the discussion. User-generated discussion inputs should preferably have a video format. The number of user-generated discussion inputs that can be uploaded to the platform should be limited (ideally to one upload per active user). Since information overload makes discussion difficult, it makes sense to set certain limits in order to facilitate a decelerated debate culture. Active users can make contributions to the discussion on the platform.

- **Interface between the studio discussion and the video platform:**

  At certain times during the live broadcast, a user-generated video is selected and shown as input for the studio discussion. In such videos, users formulate their opinion on the topic and can also introduce a discussion question. In a two- to three-hour discussion, about two to three such user-generated inputs could be used. It is inevitable that a selection mechanism will be used to decide which user-generated videos will be shown in the live broadcast. There are several ways to do this, such as random selection, selection by the production team, selection by a registered user determined at random, selection by a special guest, etc.

- **Discussion among users:**

  Club 2.0 allows users to discuss the programme topic with each other. The discussion can take place during and/or after the live broadcast. The selected videos that function as discussion inputs can be released for discussion on C2-Tube. Comments should be possible in video form and written form. There should be a minimum length for written comments and possibly a maximum length for video comments. In order to implement the slow media principles and avoid the Twitter effect of accelerated stagnation, the number of comments possible per user per discussion should be limited.

- **The forgetting of data:**

  Video data is very storage-intensive. Therefore, the question arises of what should happen to all those videos that are uploaded to the platform but are not broadcast and not opened for discussion. Since they are practically of less importance for public discussion, they could be deleted after a certain time. To do this, users need to be made aware that uploading a video in many cases involves forgetting the data. Contemporary social media store all data and meta-data forever. Forgetting data is therefore also a counter-principle. The online discussions consisting of written and video comments can either be archived and kept or deleted after a certain period of time.

- **Data protection and privacy friendliness:**

  Most social media platforms monitor users for economic and political purposes, to achieve monetary profits through the sale of personalised advertising, and to establish a surveillance society that promises more security but undermines privacy and installs a regime of categorical suspicion of all citizens. Club 2.0 should be very privacy-friendly and only store a minimum of data and meta-data necessary to run the platform. This includes not selling user data and using exemplary data protection routines. Data protection and privacy friendliness should therefore be design principles of Club 2.0. However, this does not mean that privacy protection should take the form of anonymous discussion, as anonymity can encourage online hooliganism, especially on politically controversial issues. Data protection is therefore much more about the storage and use of data.

- **Social production:**

  Today's dominant social media are highly individualistic. In contrast, the production of user-generated videos for Club 2.0 could take the form of cooperative, social production that transcends individualism and creates truly social media, so that Club 2.0 is integrated into educational institutions where people learn and create knowledge together by elaborating discussion inputs and collective positions and producing them in video form. This requires that the topics of certain Club 2.0 programmes are known somewhat in advance. This can be achieved by publishing a programme of topics. Groups of users can prepare videos together, which they can upload to the platform on the evening of the relevant Club 2.0 programme as soon as the upload option is activated.

Club 2.0 is an expression of the democratic digital public sphere. It manifests a combination of elements of deliberative and participatory democracy. Club 2.0 offers space and time for controversial political communication and enables citizens to participate collectively and individually in the discussion through videos and comments. The communicative aspect of deliberative democracy and the participatory idea of grassroots democracy are combined in the Club 2.0 model.

10.5 Conclusions

Jürgen Habermas' concept of the public sphere in his book *The Structural Transformation of the Public Sphere* is often portrayed by critics as idealistic, idealising, Eurocentric, and anti-pluralistic. Such critiques fail to recognise that Habermas' concept of the public sphere is above all an immanent concept of critique that makes it possible to compare the real state of society with democratic possibilities.

I have argued in this chapter and other works for an interpretation of Habermas based on Marx and Marx's theory of alienation. I distinguish three forms of alienation that colonise and feudalise the public sphere: economic alienation (commodification and class structuration), political alienation (domination), and cultural alienation (ideologisation).

The critical theory of the public sphere is suitable as one of the foundations of a critical theory of the Internet and social media, i.e. of communicative action in the age of digital capitalism. A critical theory of the digital public sphere makes it clear that the Internet and social media do not constitute a democratic public sphere in digital capitalism. In digital capitalism, humans are confronted with problems such as digital class relations, digital individualism, digital surveillance, digital authoritarianism, algorithmic politics, online filter bubbles, the digital culture industry, digital tabloids, influencer capitalism, digital acceleration, and online fake news.

Conclusions

A critical theory of the digital public sphere should avoid digital defeatism and digital Luddism. Digital technologies interact with society. The contradictions of society are expressed in them. A digital public sphere is not simply a democratisation of the Internet, but must go hand in hand with a strengthening of democracy in the economy, politics, and culture. There are already non-capitalist forms of the economy today. In the field of the media, public service media play an important role alongside alternative media. This chapter has pointed out that the development of a public service Internet is a democratic alternative to the capitalist Internet and digital capitalism.

Right-wing and far-right forces have frequently attacked public broadcasting in recent years. In Switzerland, a referendum on the abolition of broadcasting fees was held in 2018 as a result of an initiative by the neoliberal Jungfreisinnigen. In Austria, the Freedom Party (FPÖ), when it was part of a coalition government (2017–2019), wanted to replace the licence fee with tax funding for the Austrian Broadcasting Corporation (ORF), which would have caused the public service broadcaster to lose its independence. In Britain, the right-wing government of Boris Johnson wants to decriminalise the non-payment of licence fees, which could lead to the end of the BBC. Johnson and his supporters have repeatedly criticised the BBC as being far removed from the interests of the people and a manifestation of an urban liberal elite in London that has disregarded the majority will of the people after a Brexit. The Alternative for Germany (AfD)'s media spokesperson Martin E. Renner formulates the criticism of Germany's public service broadcasters ARD and ZDF as follows:

> The availability of information, broadcasts and programmes is in principle almost unlimited due to digitalisation. Conversely, everyone has the opportunity to freely disseminate information and opinions via social media or their own platforms. [...] Through the state-guaranteed compulsory contributions, which add up to the unbelievable amount of around 8 billion euros per year, the state organises a market power in the media sector and thus intervenes in competition and indirectly in the freedom of information. [...] Therefore, in order to adapt the offer of the existing public broadcasters to the wishes and needs of their users, all that is needed is the complete abolition of the compulsory fees. [...] It is thus to be casually re-educated in the sense of the 'political correctness' defined by them. At present, it is all about propagating 'diversity' and conjuring up the beautiful, ideal world of multi-culturalism.[9]

The AfD wants a purely private, profit-oriented media system. Public service media's democratic and educational remit is dismissed as "political correctness". The AfD wants a private sector, *völkisch* broadcasting system and a capitalist-*völkisch* Internet.

These right-wing attacks on public service broadcasting have not yet been successful. In the Coronavirus crisis, public service media have reached a new heyday, as the population considers the public service combination of information, education, and entertainment to be immeasurable, especially in times of crisis. While before the start of the coronavirus crisis on 25 February 2020, the RTL soap opera *Gute Zeiten, schlechte Zeiten* was the most watched German TV programme among 14–49 year-olds with 1.5 million viewers and a market share of 20.2 per cent,[10] among the same group of viewers on 29 March, the ARD news programme Tagesschau had the highest reach with an audience share of 28.2 per cent and 3.2 million viewers.[11] Among the total audience aged 3 and over, the Tagesschau even achieved 11 million viewers and an audience share of 29.2 per cent.[12] Special programmes on the crisis on ARD and ZDF were also particularly popular. On 25 February, by comparison, just under 4.9 million people watched the Tagesschau.[13]

Independent, critical, non-commercial public service media are an expression of the democratic public sphere. A public service Internet is a dimension of the democratisation of digitalisation.

Notes

1 Translated from German:

> Wir fassen Öffentlichkeit (1) als ein spezifisches Kommunikationssystem, das sich gegenüber anderen Sozialsystemen abgrenzt. Das System konstituiert sich auf der Basis des Austauschs von Informationen und Meinungen. Personen, Gruppen und Institutionen bringen bestimmte Themen auf und äußern Meinungen zu den Themen. Denkt man bei dem Begriff Diskussion nicht unbedingt an akademische Veranstaltun gen – denn öffentliche Kommunikation schließt demagogische Überzeugungskom munikation ebenso ein wie ein rationales Abwägen von Argumenten – kann man Öf fentlichkeit als ein Diskussionsystems bezeichnen. [...] Die Besonderheit des Kommunikationssystems Öffentlichkeit ergibt sich (2) daraus, daß alle Mitglieder einer Gesellschaft teilnehmen dürfen, das Publikum ist grundsätzlich ,unabgeschlossen', die Grenze des Systems ist offen.

2 Translated from German: "Kneipen, Kaffeeehäuser und Salons".
3 On the topicality of Marcuse's concept of technological rationality in digital capitalism, see Fuchs (2019a).

4 See for example, Jenkins (2008). A critique of Jenkins' works and similar approaches can be found in Fuchs (2017, 2019b, Chapters 3, 5, 8).

5 Siehe https://platform.coop/, https://ioo.coop/directory/, http://cultural.coop/.

6 Data source: https://www.forbes.com/global2000/list, accessed on 14 April 2021.

7 Data source: https://www.alexa.com/topsites, accessed on 14 April 2021.

8 https://creativecommons.org/licenses/by-nc/2.0/, accessed on 27 March 2021.

9 Data source: https://www.dwdl.de/magazin/68116/afd_ohne_den_rundfunkbeitrag_waere_alles_besser/page_1.html, accessed on 14 April 2021. Translated from German:

> Die Verfügbarkeit von Informationen, Sendungen und Programmen ist durch die Digitalisierung prinzipiell nahezu unbegrenzt. Umgekehrt besteht die Möglichkeit für jedermann über socialmedia oder eigene Plattformen Informationen und Meinungen frei zu verbreiten. […] durch die staatlich garantierten Zwangsbeiträge, die sich auf die unglaubliche Höhe von rund 8 Milliarden Euro pro Jahr aufsummieren, organisiert der Staat eine Marktmacht im Mediensektor und greift so in den Wettbewerb und indirekt in die Informationsfreiheit ein. […] Um das Angebot der bestehenden öffentlich-rechtlichen Sender den Wünschen und Bedürfnissen ihrer Nutzer anzupassen, bedarf es daher nur der vollständigen Abschaffung der Zwangsgebühren. […] Es soll so beiläufig umerzogen werden im Sinne der von ihnen definierten 'political correctness'. Aktuell geht es darum, 'Diversität' zu propagieren und die schöne heile Welt des Multi-Kulturalismus zu beschwören.

10 Data source: https://web.archive.org/web/20200226090231/https://www.dwdl.de/zahlenzentrale/, accessed on 18 April 2020.

11 Data source: https://web.archive.org/web/20200330171813/https://www.dwdl.de/zahlenzentrale/, accessed on 18 April 2020.

12 Data source: https://web.archive.org/web/20200330171813/https://www.dwdl.de/zahlenzentrale/, accessed on 18 April 2020.

13 Data source: https://web.archive.org/web/20200226090231/https://www.dwdl.de/zahlenzentrale/, accessed on 18 April 2020.

References

Fuchs, Christian. 2021. *Social Media: A Critical Introduction*. London: Sage. Third edition.

Fuchs, Christian. 2020a. *Communication and Capitalism. A Critical Theory*. London: University of Westminster Press. DOI: https://doi.org/10.16997/book45

Fuchs, Christian. 2020b. *Nationalism on the Internet: Critical Theory and Ideology in the Age of Social Media and Fake News*. New York: Routledge.

Fuchs, Christian. 2020c. *Marxism: Karl Marx's Fifteen Key Concepts for Cultural & Communication Studies*. New York: Routledge.

Fuchs, Christian. 2019a. Herbert Marcuse: Einige gesellschaftliche Folgen moderner Technologie. *Zeitschrift für Didaktik der Philosophie und Ethik* 41 (1): 70–74.

Fuchs, Christian. 2019b. *Soziale Medien und Kritische Theorie. Eine Einführung.* München: UVK/utb.

Fuchs, Christian. 2019c. *Rereading Marx in the Age of Digital Capitalism.* London: Pluto.

Fuchs, Christian. 2018. *Digitale Demagogue. Authoritarian Capitalism in the Age of Trump and Twitter.* London: Pluto Press.

Fuchs, Christian. 2017. *Social Media: A Critical Introduction.* London: Sage. Second edition.

Fuchs, Christian. 2016. Social Media and the Public Sphere. *tripleC: Communication, Capitalism & Critique* 12 (1): 57–101. DOI: https://doi.org/10.31269/triplec.v12i1.552

Fuchs, Christian. 2015. *Culture and Economy in the Age of Social Media.* New York: Routledge.

Fuchs, Christian. 2014. *Digital Labour and Karl Marx.* New York: Routledge.

Fuchs, Christian. 2011. *Foundations of Critical Media and Information Studies.* London: Routledge.

Fuchs, Christian. 2008. *Internet and Society: Social Theory in the Information Age.* New York: Routledge.

Fuchs, Christian and Klaus Unterberger. 2021. *The Public Service Media and Public Service Internet Manifesto.* London: University of Westminster Press. DOI: https://doi.org/10.16997/book60

Gerhards, Jürgen and Friedhelm Neidhardt. 1990. *Strukturen und Funktionen moderner Öffentlichkeit: Fragestellungen und Ansätze.* WZB Discussion Paper, No. FS III 90–101. Berlin: Wissenschaftszentrum Berlin für Sozialforschung (WZB).

Habermas, Jürgen. 2021. Überlegungen und Hypothesen zu einem erneuten Strukturwandel der politischen Öffentlichkeit. In *Ein neuer Strukturwandel der Öffentlichkeit? Sonderband Leviathan 37*, ed. Martin Seeliger and Sebastian Sevignani, 470–500. Baden-Baden: Nomos.

Habermas, Jürgen. 2019. *Auch eine Geschichte der Philosophie.* Two volumes. Frankfurt am Main: Suhrkamp.

Habermas, Jürgen. 2008. Hat die Demokratie noch eine epistemische Dimension? Empirische Forschung und normative Theorie. In *Ach, Europa,* 138–191. Frankfurt am Main: Suhrkamp.

Habermas, Jürgen. 2006. Political Communication in Media Society: Does Democracy Still Enjoy an Epistemic Dimension? The Impact of Normative Theory on Empirical Research. *Communication Theory* 16 (4): 411–426.

Habermas, Jürgen. 1991. *The Structural Transformation of the Public Sphere. An Inquiry into a Category of Bourgeois Society.* Cambridge, MA: The MIT Press.

Habermas, Jürgen. 1987. *The Theory of Communicative Action,* Volume 2. Boston, MA: Beacon Press.

Habermas, Jürgen. 1984. *The Theory of Communicative Action,* Volume 1. Boston, MA: Beacon Press.

Horkheimer, Max. 1947. *Eclipse of Reason.* New York: Continuum.

Jenkins, Henry. 2008. *Convergence Culture.* New York: New York University Press.

Lukács, Georg. 1923/1971. *History and Class Consciousness.* London: Merlin.

Marcuse, Herbert. 1941. Some Social Implications of Modern Technology. In *Collected Papers of Herbert Marcuse, Volume One: Technology, War and Fascism*, 41–65. New York: Routledge.

Marx, Karl. 1871. The Civil War in France. In *Marx & Engels Collected Works (MECW)*, Volume 22, 307–359. London: Lawrence & Wishart.

Marx, Karl. 1867. *Capital*, Volume I. London: Penguin.

Marx, Karl. 1844. Economic and Philosophic Manuscripts of 1844. In *Marx & Engels Collected Works (MECW)*, Volume 3, 229–346. London: Lawrence & Wishart.

Neidhardt, Friedhelm. 1993. The Public as a Communication System. *Public Understanding of Science* 2 (4): 339–350.

Splichal, Slavko. 2007. Does History Matter? Grasping the Idea of Public Service at Its Roots. In *From Public Service Broadcasting to Public Service Media. RIPE@2007*, ed. Gregory Ferrell Lowe and Jo Bardoel, 237–256. Göteborg: Nordicom.

United Nations. 2019. *Human Development Report 2019*. New York: United Nations Development Programme.

Wang, Di. 2008. The Idle and the Busy. Teahouses and Public Life in Early Twentieth-Century Chengdu. *Journal of Urban History* 26 (4): 411–437.

Index

Note: **Bold** page numbers refer to tables; *italic* page numbers refer to figures and page numbers followed by "n" denote endnotes.

For Product Safety Concerns and Information please contact our EU
representative GPSR@taylorandfrancis.com
Taylor & Francis Verlag GmbH, Kaufingerstraße 24, 80331 München, Germany